SWAHILI POETRY

Specimen page from the manuscript by Muhammad Kijuma of his version of the
Utendi wa Liyongo

SWAHILI POETRY

BY

LYNDON HARRIES, M.A., Ph.D.

LECTURER IN SWAHILI AT THE
SCHOOL OF ORIENTAL AND AFRICAN STUDIES
UNIVERSITY OF LONDON

OXFORD
AT THE CLARENDON PRESS
1962

Oxford University Press, Amen House, London E.C.4

GLASGOW NEW YORK TORONTO MELBOURNE WELLINGTON
BOMBAY CALCUTTA MADRAS KARACHI LAHORE DACCA
CAPE TOWN SALISBURY NAIROBI IBADAN ACCRA
KUALA LUMPUR HONG KONG

PRINTED IN GREAT BRITAIN

PREFACE

THE purpose of this book is to provide a wide selection of Swahili texts illustrating the prosodic forms and the themes of Swahili poetry. The basis of the work has been the texts written in the Swahili-Arabic script in the Library of the School of Oriental and African Studies, the University of London. These include manuscripts collected by Taylor, Hamilton, Hichens, Werner, and the present writer. European scholars have published articles on Swahili poetry in journals concerned with African studies, but for the general student the material is not easily accessible.

Unless stated otherwise the texts are transliterated from the Swahili-Arabic script. We are not concerned primarily with the work of transliteration, but with the provision of texts in roman script that can be related to modern standard Swahili. Although the orthography employed is an approximation to standard orthography, it is not identical with it, for in many instances dialectical variants have been left unchanged and certain conventions foreign to standard Swahili have been kept, as, for example, in preserving the rhyming sequences.

It will be seen that there is a very strong Arabic influence in Swahili poetry. The question arises as to what is the proper method for transcribing words, and especially proper names, which the Arabist may recognize as truly Arabic forms. Within the Swahili context the words are written according to Swahili, and not Arabic, convention. For example, the Arabist should not be surprised to find us writing 'Swahili *takhmis*' instead of 'Swahili *takhmīs*', or ''Isa na Abdallah' instead of ''Īsā na 'Abdallāh'. In this connexion it is important to note that in Swahili words derived from Arabic, the vowels *a*, *u*, and *i* may often be permissible alternatives. Usually the forms occurring in the poetry are nearer to the Arabic original, but this is not invariably so. The whole question of vowel alternances in Swahili in relation to corresponding vowel qualities in the Arabic equivalents demands much further investigation. As a general guide it may be sufficient to suggest that in identifying words related to Arabic, the student should seek first to identify the consonants while bearing in mind that alternative forms occur in Swahili with different vowels.

In standard Swahili orthography no diacritical marks are used in words of Arabic derivation. This poses a serious problem for anyone concerned with transliterating either from Swahili-Arabic script or from the Arabic script. Even amongst Swahili speakers and writers there is a considerable measure of uncertainty as to the pronunciation and orthography of Arabic loan-words. On the other hand, any partial use of diacritics results in confusion and infringes the usually recognized conventions even in the spelling of familiar names, e.g. Sa'īd, Sa'id, Said, Saiyid, or Sayyid; Muḥammād, Muḥammad, Muhammād, or Muhamadi. As this book is intended primarily for students of Swahili, it has seemed preferable to conform to Swahili orthography and so to omit diacritical marks except in the textual notes in the trans-literation of Arabic words.

Few people have done more to promote the study of Swahili poetry than the late Sir Mbarak Ali Hinawy of Mombasa, who died in December 1959. I am especially grateful for his help in the initial work of collecting some of the manuscripts used for this book, for his gift to the Library of the School of Oriental and African Studies of manuscripts that belonged to him in the Hichens Collection, and for allowing me to make photostat copies of manuscripts in his private library at his home in Mombasa in 1956. My thanks are also due to the Editors of *Africa*, *African Studies*, *Afrika und Übersee*, and of the *Bulletin of the School of Oriental and African Studies* for permission to use separate poems edited by me in their publications, and to the Swahili poet, Shaaban Robert, and the East Africa Swahili Committee for the inclusion of Shaaban's Swahili lecture on Swahili poetry. Shaaban Robert is the most outstanding Swahili author at the present time, and his lecture, delivered originally in Tanga as one of a series of lectures sponsored by the Jumuiya ya Taaluma ya Kiswahili, provides the student with a suitable text which is highly relevant to the preceding chapters of this book. I am grateful also to my colleagues, Professor R. B. Serjeant and Mr. D. Cowan, for their help in relation to the Arabian content of the poetry. I am also grateful to my friend, Cecil Hutchinson, for his generous help in preparing the Index.

No attempt has been made to reproduce the Swahili measures and rhyme schemes in the English translation of the poetry, for this would have been too great a task. The translation is set out in such a way as to correspond with the order of words in the Swahili version as far as possible, and the caesurae have been shown clearly. Occasionally the sentence is carried over from one *kipande* (hemistich) to another, so that punctuation marks in the English translation have been used sparingly. Where a *kipande* begins a sentence within the verse, capital letters are not employed at the beginning of such sentences. The method adopted is intended to convey a true translation while preserving something of the format of the original Swahili verses.

The texts provided in this book include some of the best of the earlier poems, but it is only a selection. The comparative richness of the Swahili literate tradition is a matter of the greatest interest, not least to the Swahili people themselves today. So to my Swahili readers I offer this book in acknowledgement of their love for versification, reminding them of a phrase from the poem *Waji-waji*: *Aonao kosa akitoa hana lawama*. Who finds a mistake and removes it is not to be blamed.

L. H.

CONTENTS

I

THE TECHNIQUE OF COMPOSITION

THE Swahili people of the East African coast are unique amongst the Bantu-speaking peoples of East Africa in possessing a long tradition of versification in literary form. Poems are still written in the traditional manner. A typical example that has recently come to our attention is the poem of Ali Yusuf Abubakar of Lamu. Written in 1957 in the Swahili-Arabic script, the poem of sixty-two verses rhyming *aaab xxxb*, &c. is addressed to the poet's nephew who has won a scholarship to an Indian college and who, during his absence from home, has given up the practice of his religion. The poem is homiletic and resembles very closely similar poems written 200 years ago, not only in its prosodic form but in its general homiletic appeal.

It is difficult to estimate the output of poems written at the present time in the traditional manner, not least because they are private property meant for private use and are, of course, hand-written. There is, however, a considerable output of Swahili rhymed verses appearing regularly in roman script in the vernacular press. In papers like *Mambo Leo, Baragumu*, &c., the omission of this regular feature would arouse strong protests from many readers who are not themselves Swahilis. Even though the demand for space for Swahili articles on contemporary subjects is a very pressing one, Swahili poetry continues to hold an entrenched position in the popular press, especially in Tanganyika.

The verse appearing in roman script in the vernacular press is not usually of such a high standard as poems written in the Swahili-Arabic script, but at least it shows a strong desire to retain the tradition of verse composition which the Swahilis have practised for at least 300 years. Basically, the tradition is Arabian. It is well known that the Swahili people have incorporated into their way of life much that is of Arabian origin. The very first attempts to paraphrase an Arabic poem into Swahili were made for reasons not exclusively literary. The Arabian, and therefore the Islamic content of Swahili life, has always been for the

Swahilis a matter of prestige. The true Swahilis of the coast prefer, in fact, to be known as Arabs. Verse composition after the
Arabian pattern involved the question of pride in Swahili origins;
it revealed knowledge of Arabian life and of Islam, a sure guaran-
tee for the highest prestige among the Swahili people.

It is true that versification in Swahili is practised today in
roman script by many who cannot claim Swahili blood, but
usually they are Muslims. Religion is the bond that gives them
the right to share a medium of expression that has its origin in the
Muslim religion. It is not religious verse that they write for the
popular press, but the medium employed indicates familiarity
with the Swahili way of life, which is fundamentally Islamic.

This wider modern practice of Swahili versification has led to
a departure from its earlier intention—to express the spirit and
the practice of Islam. Today the medium is employed for more
secular ends. Any news item may be the subject of a few verses,
but this is in the tradition established during the nineteenth century by writers like Muyaka bin Haji of Mombasa, who brought
poetry out of the mosque and into the market-place.

In the present work we shall consider the kind of poetry
that was written up to the end of the nineteenth century.
Modern Swahili poetry needs separate presentation. It may be
asked how the earlier poetry compares with classical Arabic poetry
or with the poetry of any other people. What is its intrinsic
merit?

In answering, it is essential first to emphasize the difficulty any
Westerner must have in estimating the worth of poetry written in
a foreign language often concerning local situations and happenings. It would be wrong to attempt an assessment only from a
study of the texts as provided in this book. Many of the poems
were meant to be sung or intoned and have a social and a religious value which the bare texts may not reveal. Poems of the
nineteenth century were often written to suit an immediate
historical situation. It may be that even after the most diligent
investigation we cannot recapture the exact implication of a verse
because we may not be able to reconstruct the exact situation.
There are hundreds of short Swahili poems in the Library of the
School of Oriental and African Studies in London which still
defy interpretation partly because no one is able to provide the
context in which the poem was written.

The early poems were written as much for the eye as for the ear. To appreciate them fully they must be read by a Swahili who can himself appreciate the manner in which they have been written in the Swahili-Arabic script. Quite often a play on words can be understood only from an examination of the script.

Although Swahili poetry derives from Arabic poetry, in many respects there are fundamental differences. It cannot properly be compared with Arabic poetry, for it is *sui generis*. The Arabist may recognize the obvious connexion between Swahili poetry and Arabic poetry, especially in much of its subject-matter, but Swahili poetry cannot be considered as an extension of Arabic poetry or even as a modification of it. Swahili poetry exists in its own right and therefore must be estimated, as to its merit, for what it is in itself. At the same time, those Arabists who have had some experience of Swahili poetry do not fail to show the deepest interest and recognize that without a knowledge of its Arabian background even Swahili-speaking Africans may fail to understand that in their poetry the Swahilis have a possession of which they may well be proud.

Similarly, without some experience of the African background of Swahili poetry the Arabist may not appreciate all that the poetry has to offer. From the amalgam of two traditions we find in Swahili poetry a positive contribution to literature. In the early literature the epic poetry is of particular interest, not least because in this medium the Swahili poet was able to move freely away from the imitation of Arabian models. Then in the nineteenth century the quatrain was used in an original manner. The poems of Muyaka bin Haji particularly show a delicacy and skill of treatment, together with a right choice of subject-matter, that are altogether worthy of praise. Although it was, and still is, possible for Swahili versification to degenerate into a clever trick of easy rhyming, at its best it has qualities that are truly poetic. The moving scene of the death of Liyongo in the *Hadithi ya Liyongo* is an example of Swahili poetry at its best, and many other examples can be found in the shorter poems of Muyaka bin Haji.

Few modern poems in Swahili reveal the technique of the earlier work. This may be because the authors have had no easy access to the full range of prosodic forms. Some of the earlier verse has itself given rise to an oral tradition, as in Pemba,[1] and it

[1] W. H. Whiteley, *The Dialects and Verse of Pemba*, Kampala, 1958.

is interesting to find that though the subject-matter is original and very often topical, the prosodic forms retain the earlier techniques.

Along the Swahili coast there was from very early times contact with Arab seamen and traders. The more spontaneous religious verse was brought to the Swahili coast by these Arabs of the Yemen and Hadramawt, especially the latter. An important influence in establishing the tradition of Swahili versification was also that of the educated religious leaders, nearly all Saiyids, in whose hands most of the secular and religious education lay.

It sometimes happened that the advent of a Saiyid family was the direct result of a plea for aid against the Portuguese invaders by individual Muslim rulers of the Swahili coastal citadels. Perhaps the best example of this is the request made, according to the Swahili chronicler, Bwana Kitini, by the Sultan of Pate (probably Muhammad V) to Sheikh Abu Bakr b. Salim (died A.D. 1584) that he should 'pray to Allah on our behalf that he may deliver us from our enemies'. The Sheikh (Ar. Shaikh) sent his two sons, Ali and Husein, to Pate with a contingent. They settled in Pate where the names of districts, like Sarambi and Inati, derive from the names given by members of the family to their homes there.

Some measure of confirmation regarding this tradition is given in Shamsu Dhahira al-Dhahiya, by Saiyid Abd al-Rahman b. Muhammad b. Husein al-Mashhur (Deccan, Haiderabad, A.D. 1911), though according to this account it was the descendants of Ali and Husein who settled in East Africa, not Ali and Husein themselves. In any case, there is no doubt whatsoever that members of this distinguished Hadrami family came to live on the Swahili coast and amongst them were some of the most outstanding poets. We may mention now Saiyid Abdallah b. Ali b. Nasir (A.D. 1720–1820), author of the poem *al-Inkishafi*, and Saiyid Abu Bakr b. Abd al-Rahman (known to the Swahili as Saiyid Mansab), author of many Swahili religious poems.

The Saiyids were Arabs, but because they wrote in Swahili it is customary to include them in the category of Swahili poets. The later descendants of the Saiyids were, of course, born of African mothers. The Saiyids brought with them didactic and homiletic verse in Arabic, and these were paraphrased in Swahili, the poems often including the interlinear Arabic version which did not necessarily correspond in meaning with the Swahili version. This type of verse was supplemented by even freer renderings of popular tales of Islam, some with reference to actual events in the life of the Prophet Muhammad or to historical happenings in early Islam, but usually with an indistinguishable border-line between fact and fiction. These we may refer to as romantic epics; they do not appear to be later than the homiletic shorter poems, but rather contemporaneous with them.

The earliest extant Swahili manuscript poem known to scholars is *Utendi Wa Tambuka*, an epic or heroic poem written in Pate for Fumo (Sultan) Laiti Nabhani, and is dated A.D. 1728 (in the Library of the Seminar für Afrikanischen Sprachen, Hamburg, No. 3554 H. 119). Another early poem, dated A.D. 1749, is *al-Hamziyah* by Saiyid Aidarus, the interlinear Swahili version of the Arabic poem, *Umm al-Qura* ('Mother of Cities'), by Muhammad ibn Said al-Busiri (manuscript in Library of SOAS, No. 53823).

In the nineteenth century the use of the Swahili-Arabic script was extended to include ritual songs of Bantu origin, especially *mavugo* or wedding songs, together with original compositions unrelated to any Arabic original.

THE WORK OF THE COPYIST

The number of original manuscripts in the Swahili-Arabic script is difficult to gauge because the poet almost invariably employed a copyist or a narrator who memorized the poem and later wrote it down. He did not copy the poem in the sense of making an exact reproduction of what the poet had already written. In the case of the long heroic poems or epics the narrator who has seen the story he wishes to relate in some Arabian source is a distinct person from the copyist. The narrator here is the poet who employs the copyist to write as he dictates, though one may sometimes doubt whether in fact there are two people involved. It became a convention for any heroic poem to include a section at the beginning of the poem in which the narrator gives instructions to his scribe and mentions his writing-materials.

Certainly one does not expect to find, in Swahili, poems in the poet's own hand, though when the narrator and the copyist can be shown to be the same person, then the narrator *is* the poet.

In the case of the shorter homiletic and religious verses, like *al-Inkishafi*, copies were made because of the intrinsic merit of the verses, and not because of any instruction from the poet. These were, indeed, faithful copies of as much as could be rendered of the original, bearing in mind that once again the *original* poem was probably written by a copyist from dictation. Such copies became the common property of relatives who circulated them in the kinship group for recitation on social occasions, or else they were the property of the mosques for use in public recitals. In both cases the manuscripts were subject to the depradations of careless handling, of the white ant and of the damp.

Our dependence upon copies brings certain obvious disadvantages. There may not be enough copies of an early poem for us to ensure by comparative study the identity of obscure words. The copyists frequently omit the date of the original composition and even the name of the composer, while including the name of the copyist and the date of his own work. The narrator of epic poems seldom gives his name or the date of composition. This absence of precise dating makes it very difficult to establish an historical survey of Swahili verse. There are a number of short poems associated with the traditional Swahili hero, Liyongo, and these are certainly of early origin, but there is no certain way of ascertaining the exact period of their composition.

The conventional description of the copyists' writing-materials survived in the prelude to some of the poems long after the copyists had adopted more modern materials for writing. It seems plain that the copyists lined their paper by the use of a board around which was wrapped a silken cord so that parallel ridges could be impressed on the paper. Mica-sand was sprinkled on the writing to dry it. Black ink was made from rice, burned, and then ground to powder, mixed in water with a little gum, lemon-juice, and sometimes lamp-black. Red ink was made from cinnabar or native mercuric oxide and was prepared locally from the *mzingufuri* or *mzinjifuri* plant (Ar. *zinjafr*), *Bixa orellana*. Coloured title-pieces adorned some of the manuscripts, but generally of rather inferior design and execution. The sections of a line or rhyme-endings were usually divided or marked by stops (Sw. *kituo/zituo*, or *kikomo/zikomo*), though in some manuscripts there is no division at the medial rhyme and a space takes the place of the marked stops, which were shaped like inverted hearts and often rubricated. As with Arabic, of course, the Swahili-Arabic script is written, and the manuscripts paginated, from right to left.

The following description is typical of the conventional directions to the copyist from the narrator and is taken from the long epic poem called in Swahili *Utendi wa Ras il-Ghuli*, a Yemenite legend, the Swahili version of which is discussed and illustrated in Chapter 3 :

Ewe mwanangu Hamisi   nipatie karatasi   uniletee upesi   pasiwe 1
kutaahari.

Karatasi iwe Shamu   iliyo njema na emu   na ambapo ni adimu   twaa hiyo ya hariri.

Wendapo ukinunuwa   jitahidi kuteuwa   nawe ni mtu mwelewa
si mchache wa nadhari.

Ogopa kwenda dukani   usihusiri ndiani   ufike kwa Selemani   au kwa Isa mzuri.

Nipatie na mapesa   uyachukue kabisa   ukiwasili kwa Isa   un- 5
unue zingufuri.

Zingufuri uteuwe   zaibaki uitowe   u safi hata ujuwe   itiwapo
yanawiri.

Utafute na kibawo   kizuri kisicho tawo   na uzi na uje nawo   ulio
mwema hiari.

Na uzi iwe wa tasi   na pote zaingie kasi   hipiga iwe nafasi   itulie
masitari.

Mbwene hadithi ajabu   yali ndani ya kitabu   kwa lugha ya
kiArabu   ina maneno hiari.

Hadithi hii jueni   naliona chuoni   ya zita zali Yemeni   zamani 10
zake Bashiri.

Haona kunipendeza   hifikiri nikiwaza   moyoni nikelekeza   maneno kuyafasiri.

Hapenda kuyabadili   kwa lugha ya kiSwahili   kiArabu ni
halili   wajuao kutafsiri.

Ndipo mi kujikalifu   kiArabu kuakifu   maneno kuyasanifu
niwape zote habari.

Hachelea ni mjinga   sijui sana kutunga   na maneno kuya-
panga   yataka mtu mahiri.

Wasije kiza kuona   kesho kishika maana   wakiwamo kuni- 15
nena   wakuu hata swariri.

Wakanandika aibu   wala pasipo sababu   kunirudi ni thawabu   wala nami sikasiri

Roho yangu hairudi   nikaona sina budi   papo hamwita wa-
ladi   nikawa kumdabiri.

Nikamwambia Hamisi   shika hima karatasi   na kalamu kwa
upesi   usiwe kutaahari.

Ogopa kutaharabu   nikwambie mathulubu   nikupalo ukutu-
bu   pasiwe kutaahari.
20 Ni kuandika kwa upesi   suturi ziwe nafasi   kila neno kwa
kiasi   usandike mshadhari.
Na hati iwe hasiha   maneno yawe wadhiha   penye dhumma na
fataha   na jazimu na kasiri.
Irabu uzifanidi   kwa madha na tashididi   ziwe baidibaidi   zisiwe
mtaghayari.
Uzipangie na harufu   zifuatane sufufu   zisiwe fupi na ndefu   itulie misitari.
Na ladha ya ukatibu   ni kutulizia irabu   na kuandika taratibu   ndipo watu wakukiri.
25 Irabu ukizihimu   zikawa zote timamu   asomaye hufahamu   hupendeza wamukiri. . . .

Hamisi my son get me some paper bring it to me quickly without delay.
Let it be Syrian paper   which is good and well chosen   but if
it be scarce   then take silk-paper.
When you go to buy it   try hard to select it well   for you are
an intelligent person   not without discretion.
Take care (lit. fear) going to the shop   don't tarry on the
way   go to Selemani's   or to Isa he is all right.
5 Get me also some money take it all when you get to Isa's buy
some red ink.
Choose the red-ink well   remove the mercury   let it be clean so
that you know   when applied it glows.
Look also for a scriving-board a nice one without a curve and
bring a cord as well   a good choice one.
And let the cord be well-combed   and the twisted threads
taut   when I mark it for spacing   that the ridges stay
impressed.
I have seen a wonderful story   it was in a book   in the Arabic
language   it has choice words.
10 Know that this story   I saw it in a book   is about the Yemeni
wars   in the days of the Prophet.
I found that it pleased me   thinking and considering it   I set
my heart   to translating the words.
I wanted to change it   into the Swahili language   Arabic is
lawful   for those who know how to translate.

And so I exercised myself   by changing the Arabic   composing the words   so that I might give them the whole story.

I feared for I am a fool   I don't know much how to compose   or how to set out the words in order   it needs a skilful person.

Lest finding it obscure   and tomorrow getting the meaning   they 15 should speak against me   the elders and even the children.

And should write me off as a disgrace   but without reason   To correct me is a gift (easy)   nor am I angry.

So I took heart   and saw that I must   and straightway I called a lad   and turned towards him.

And I said to him, Hamisi   take up the paper at once   and the pen quickly   without delay.

Take care not to spoil it   let me tell you readily   write what I give you   without any delay.

Writing quickly   let the lines be well spaced   each word in proper measure   don't write in the margin.

And let the writing be elegant   so that the words are clear   on the signs dammah and fathah   the sukūn and the ending.

Select the vowel-signs   with the signs for doubling   so that they are separate   and that there be no ambiguity.

Set out the letters   that they follow in ordered rows   don't let them be short and long   let the lines be well disposed.

The style of writing   is in the disposition of the vowel-signs   and in orderly writing   then people proclaim you.

If you do the vowel-signs quickly   so that they are all com- 25 plete   whoever reads understands   they are pleased and proclaim him (i.e. the copyist). . . .

SWAHILI PROSODIC FORMS

Swahili prosody has not hitherto been the subject of separate investigation, and so its principles have to be deduced at first hand from a study of the poetry. Swahili terms do not exist in every instance to describe features of the prosody, and Arabic words, if they are used, should be given the definition appropriate to their Swahili use.

In Swahili a verse, *baiti* (Ar. *bait*), is often written as a single line, but there are many examples in which the verse is written in two lines with a medial caesura in each line. It is the rhyming system that provides the clue to the verse-form in Swahili poetry.

As in Arabic, the end of a verse is marked by a rhyme which is the same for all verses throughout the poem. Internal rhymes mark the ending of each section (Sw. *kipande*) of a verse.

In translating the poems into English it is customary to divide the poem into lines which, in fact, are not written as separate lines in the Swahili-Arabic script. This is done most often with verses rhyming *abababbc*, giving in the translation four lines, as follows *ab ab ab bc* when in the script the whole verse is written as a single line or as two lines with medial caesurae (Sw. *kituo/zituo*). Classification of Swahili poetry should be by the number of sections (Sw. *vipande*) in a verse and this is determined by the rhyming system. Although in the majority of instances Swahili poets endeavoured to enclose the whole verse in a single line, failure to do so was not important so long as the rhyming system was adequately shown.

Swahili metres are the measure of a section (Sw. *kipande*) in terms of the number of vocalized syllables (Sw. *herufi*, Ar. pl. *ḥarūf*) to the *kipande*. Vowel length is not significant, so that it is not possible, as in Arabic, to arrive at any system whereby the measure of syllables can take into account the metrical feet within a measure. In measures of Swahili verse there may be major (usually penultimate) and minor stresses, but there is no metric system of stress, nor can this be related to the subject of vowel-length or of metrical feet.

The term applied to the number of vocalized syllables in a *kipande* is *mizani* (cf. Ar. *al-mīzān*). Verse of eight *mizani*, for example, has eight vocalized syllables to each *kipande* in the verse.

The importance of syllabic division in Swahili prosody cannot be overestimated, and yet it might be overlooked since the script may obscure the syllabic measure in the pronunciation, e.g. a syllabic nasal may not be written, but must be pronounced, a nasal that in everyday pronunciation would not be syllabic must be given the value of a syllable, or a vowel written as a long vowel may have to be pronounced short, all for the sake of preserving the syllabic measure. To ensure the syllabic measure, the pronunciation takes precedence over the writing.

A rhyme (Sw. *kina*, pl. *vina*) is monosyllabic in Swahili poetry and consists of consonant plus vowel. Verses defective in rhyme or in syllabic measure are called *guni*. Verses with defective rhyme are also called *mashairi ya kutupa vina*, i.e. verses discarding rhyme.

Swahili poets termed all verse written for public performance *mashairi*, including *nyimbo*, songs. Except in the case of *takhmis* (Ar. *takhmīs*, lit. quintain), a name and a prosodic form borrowed from Arabian poetry, no classification by Swahili names of prosodic types of Swahili verse can be effected. In the *takhmis*, a verse or stanza consists of five lines, whether or not in the Swahili-Arabic script the copyist actually uses only five lines to complete the stanza. In our presentation of verses with eight *vipande*, we may consider these as quatrains, though there is no separate term for a quatrain in Swahili. It has become a European convention to write them in translation in quatrain form and there is no special reason for dispensing with this convention provided that it is understood that the Swahili copyist did not in his manuscript employ four lines, one beneath the other, but rather either a single line or two lines.

The epics called *utendi/tendi* or, in southern Swahili, *utenzi/tenzi* were so called probably because of their heroic content, for *tendi* or *tenzi* means acts or deeds.

The term *uimbo/nyimbo* song/s, is never applied to the earlier homiletic verse, though it is likely that even this type of earlier work was meant to be sung or intoned. Occasionally in the epics a song is incorporated into the narrative, but in a different prosodic form from the regular narrative itself, e.g. the song of Saada in the *Hadithi ya Liyongo*. This can be said to correspond to the inclusion of songs in the Arabian narrative verse to which the Swahili epics are related (see p. 28).

The term *hadithi*, a story or tale, is sometimes employed for the shorter epic, though this may be an alternative use for *utendi*.

Swahili poems are still sung to tunes of which the names correspond to the old Arabian or Persian modes *maqamat*, patterns of melody based with a certain freedom on one or other of the modal scales and characterized by stereotyped turns, by mood, and by pitch. The following ten *maqamat* are said, by Swahili informants, to be known in places like Mombasa, Malindi, and Lamu:

Rasit[1]	Jirka[2]	Rasidi[3]	Bayat[4]	Sika[5]
Hijaz[6]	Nawandi[7]	Hijaz Kar[8]	Duka[9]	Swaba[10]

[1] Curt Sachs, *The Rise of Music in the Ancient World*, W. W. Norton & Co. Inc., New York, 1943, p. 284: 'Ar. Rast, starting from the tonic, dignified in tempo and carriage and avoiding grace notes'; id., p. 283, quoting from A. Z. Idelsohn: 'though generally known in musical circles, yet lives as a Persian art maqam only; the Arabian people just do not sing it'. *[For footnotes 2–10 see page 12.]*

All these, except the last, can be tentatively identified with a corresponding oriental scale. The tendency is for the Arab mode to be employed without words on musical instruments, e.g. on the gramophone records Gallotone GB. 1245 T, 'Sika for small orchestra', and Gallotone GB. 1239 T. 'Nahawand (Nawandi) Violin solo'. No doubt the modern popularity of these Arabian tunes is partly due to modern Egyptian influence and is found only among the Swahili *élite*, but it is generally held that poems with Arabian influence, especially the epics, have always been sung to Arabian tunes. There is no manuscript evidence for this, though there are many passages within the narrative to remind the reader that the poems are meant to be sung.

[2] H. G. Farmer, *Arab Music and Musical Instruments*, London, 1914, p. 99, quoting Salvador-Daniel: 'Ar. jorka, the jorka mode, cf. Aeolian mode of the Greeks (some authors call it the Grave Lydian), and the "seventh tone" of plain-song, having G for its base: grave and serious'.

[3] Curt Sachs, op. cit., p. 253: 'Of Rasd, there is no trace of the scale, says Rouanet, yet he mentions a Nuba Rasd and says the Touchiat Mezmoun is played with it, there being no Touchiat Rasd. From this it would appear that Rasd and Mezmoun had something like a common scale . . . There is a mode Rasd in the old Eastern Arabian and Persian systems, the first tetrachord of which resembles Mezmoun. Its scale is A.A. sharp, C.D.E.F. sharp, G.A.'

[4] Ibid., p. 214: 'Two of the most popular Oriental scales, Bayat and Isfahan, are composed of a syntonon tetrachord and a ditoniaion pentachord'; ibid., p. 284: '(Bayat) stresses the fourth'.

[5] Ibid., p. 284: 'Sikah, the third below tonic'; and p. 305: 'the tritonic maqam Sikah, which uses a B-scale without signature is more and more frequently given a perfect fifth by sharpening the note'.

[6] Ibid., p. 214: 'Ar. Hijaz, the most oriental scale of all, consists of a chromatic tetrachord and a diatonic pentachord.'

[7] Alfred Berner, *Studien zur arabischen Musik*, Leipzig, 1937, p. 15: 'Outstanding Egyptian virtuosos have been put to the test of measuring devices with the first pentachord of a melody in the maqam Nahawand'; and Curt Sachs, op. cit., p. 282: 'Ar. Nahawand, a true hypodorian on G.'

[8] Lavignac, in the article 'Musique Arabe' in the *Encyclopédie de la Musique*, gives *hijaz* as 'one of the sub-divisions of the fourth note of the Basic scale', and *qarar-hijaz* as 'the corresponding interval in the upper tetrachord' (communicated by Dr. A. A. Bake).

[9] Lavignac, op. cit., gives *dukahan* 'the second note of the Basic scale which could be the starting-point of a new maqam; the word is composed of the Persian *du* (two) plus the ending -kah common to all the original names of the notes of the Basic scale, e.g. yakah, sikah, etc.' (communicated by Dr. A. A. Bake).

[10] Not identified.

2

THE LINGUISTIC MEDIUM

THERE can be no doubt that the Swahili literate tradition had its centre in the coastal belt from Mombasa northwards, and especially in Lamu. Even today poems well known in Lamu are comparatively unknown in Zanzibar or Dar es Salaam. The tradition of verse-making had a very slender hold in Zanzibar, and it is significant that when Sheikh Muhyi 'l-Din, the Kadhi (Ar. Qāḍī) of Zanzibar (b. A.D. 1789, died A.D. 1869), wrote poetry in the traditional manner, he adopted the literary conventions belonging to the poets of the north.

Texts emanating from places where in speech there may be some variance of dialect do not usually show *in the script* any such variants. The earlier religious poetry established the convention of employing uses from the Amu dialect, i.e. the dialect spoken in Lamu, but in the nineteenth century poetry written in Mombasa reveals many usages that are identified with the Mvita dialect spoken in Mombasa. The general tendency, however, was to employ Amu forms because these had become conventions of Swahili poetry in the traditional manner. While many dialect variants could be shown in the script if the copyist wished, some variants are not shown because of the nature of the script itself. For example, the Tikuu dialect spoken to the north of Lamu along the coastal belt differs in important respects from the Amu dialect, the predominant medium for Swahili verse. The Tikuu version of the *Dream Song* taken down in roman script by Werner[1] in 1913 from the dictation of the blind poet of Witu, Mzee b. Bisharo al-Ausiy, shows the Tikuu use of dental consonants represented by *dh* and *th*, variants of *z* in the Amu dialect, but the same Arabic symbol, viz. ﮐ, represents any one of the three sounds in unrelated words when used in the Swahili-Arabic script. In the latter script this poem is indistinguishable from a version written by a poet of Lamu.

---

[1] Alice Werner, *Bulletin of School of Oriental and African Studies*, vol. iv, pp. 248–9.

There are many difficult words in the poetry. Even those words that cannot be found in standard Arabic dictionaries may yet have a distinctly Arabic flavour about them. Some are dialect forms from southern Arabia, Hadramawt, and Oman, but they may not be recorded in any dictionary. Words not known to Swahili scholars and occurring in the earlier texts, if they could not be found in Arabic dictionaries, were usually relegated to a convenient limbo called Kingozi or Kingovi, the dialect said to belong either to the Malindi district (according to Krapf) or to the nobility of Pate (according to Hichens). Sacleux is probably right in rejecting such statements. In his dictionary under the entry *kiNgozi* he writes :[1]

Contrairement à l'opinion de qqs indigènes qui supposent l'existence d'une ancienne ville ou localité Ngozi ou d'un clan de waNgozi, du côté de Malindi disent les uns, dans l'archipel des Comores pensent les autres, le Kingozi n'a jamais été un langage parlé . . . Le Kingozi n'est même pas une variété dialectale . . . C'est en réalité une forme libre, qui vise au purisme et à l'archaïsme, puisant pour cela dans les dialectes du Nord, réputés les plus fidèles a l'état primitif de la langue, le kiGunya surtout.

Intermediate between Kingozi and modern Swahili is said to be the dialect known as Kikae. This term is probably an invention, for -*kae* is a contraction of -*kale*, long ago, and the prefix of Cl. 7 is the one employed in Swahili nominals denoting a language or dialect.

The names Kingozi and Kikae do not denote any observable Swahili dialects and as such they may never have existed. Before a Swahili word in the earlier poetry can be described as 'obsolete' it would have to be established that it does not exist in a contemporary coastal dialect. No comprehensive investigation of these dialects has been made, so that whether or not a word is in fact obsolete remains an open question.

In relation to the grammar of modern standard Swahili, there are three factors to be borne in mind in studying the grammar of Swahili poetry from the Swahili-Arabic script. Firstly, the peculiarities inherent in the use of the Swahili-Arabic script; secondly, the exigencies of the poetical measure whereby grammatical accuracy is sacrificed for the sake of the syllabic measure and of the rhyme; and, thirdly, the basically northern dialect employed, the Amu dialect.

[1] Ch. Sacleux, C.S.Sp., *Dictionnaire Swahili-Français*, Paris, 1939, tome I, p. 386.

For transliterating, the first of these factors presents the greatest difficulties, but for grammatical analysis it is the second which renders interpretation difficult. Even when the poems have been transliterated and the dialectical features understood, the grammar remains often as a kind of portmanteau speech in which the grammatical items have either been discarded or squeezed together in order that the essentials should be included within the space allowed by the syllabic measure.

THE SWAHILI-ARABIC SCRIPT

The Swahili-Arabic script is still used by many Swahilis on the East African coast, and for a few it is the only script they know. Its use in the writing of Swahili has been discussed at length by European scholars.[1] Velten and Büttner stress the unsuitability of the script for writing a Bantu language, though it should be added that with extra symbols and with sufficient care the script can be an adequate medium for this purpose, at least in relation to Swahili.

The majority of copyists, however, have followed the practice of the earliest writers who made no special effort to adapt or extend the range of Arabic symbols. A reformed Swahili-Arabic orthography was a late innovation, as late as the 1930's, and not a very successful effort at that.

The orthographic conventions established in the poetry were founded upon the attempt to make the unmodified Arabic script serve for the writing of Swahili. Deficiencies that are obvious to the foreign reader may not have caused any special difficulty for the Swahili reader familiar, not only with Arabic and Swahili, but also with the general sense of the subject-matter. There has always been a tendency for European scholars to emphasize the unsuitability of the script, just as Swahili readers find the roman script unsuitable in many respects. Swahilis do not share the European point of view here, and their disinclination to accept a reformed Swahili-Arabic orthography promoted by a Swahili may be interpreted as an indication of their satisfaction with the script as it is. Sheikh al-Amin b. Ali's attempt at reform in a

[1] J. W. T. Allen, *Maandiko ya Kizungu*, London, 1938: 'Arabic Script for students of Swahili', *Tanganyika Notes and Records*, Nov. 1945. M. W. H. Beech, *Aids to the Study of Ki-Swahili*, London, n.d. C. G. Büttner, *Suaheli-Schriftstücke in arabischer Schrift*, Stuttgart, 1892. A. Seidel, *Suaheli-K. Grammatik*, Heidelberg, 1900. E. Velten, *Erlernung der Schrift der Suaheli*, Göttingen, 1901. J. Williamson, 'The Use of the Arabic Script in Swahili', *African Studies*, vol. vi, No. 4, 1947.

newspaper published in the 1930's in Mombasa gained very little support.

Even so, the deficiencies of the script must be noted. The Arabic script has no symbols to represent the common Swahili sounds represented in roman script as *p*, *v*, *ch*, *ny*, *ng'*, and *g*. Two Arabic vowel-signs have to do duty for four vowel-sounds in Swahili, *kasrah* representing either *i* or *e*, and *dammah* either *u* or *o*. The distinction between the sounds in either of these pairs is not always maintained in unaccented positions, but the distinction may be important in verbal radicals and in accented positions in nominals, e.g. *-tu-* 'alight', 'come to rest', and *-to-* 'take out', 'give out'; *-li-* 'cry', and *-le-* 'nurture', 'bring up'. This distinction is very frequent in verbals, e.g. *nina* 'I have', and *nena* 'speak' (imp.), *-liwa* 'be eaten', and *-lewa* 'be drunk'. Generally it is true that the context provides the clue as to which vowel is intended, but ambiguity does arise.

The aspirated consonants *t'*, *p'*, *k'*, and *ch'* are not represented in the Arabic script. These sounds are not indicated even in roman script by Swahili scribes transliterating from the Arabic script and are not shown in standard Swahili. Taylor, working in Mombasa, observed the occurrence of aspiration in spoken Swahili and he invented symbols based on corresponding Arabic symbols to represent them, viz. ث for *t'*, پ for *p'*, ک for *k'*, and چ for *ch'*. These were never adopted by the Swahili scribes. For any phonetic rendering the aspirated consonants would have to be shown in the roman script, but it is not always possible to know, at least in the older manuscripts, whether these consonants in unidentified words were aspirated or not. Continental scholars like Dammann usually mark aspiration, but in view of the uncertainty in this respect and because of the absence of any indication of aspiration in standard Swahili, it has been decided in what follows to omit any signs of aspiration in the Swahili transliteration.

It has to be borne in mind that not all Swahili copyists were experts in the use of the Arabic script. In most scripts Arabic literary conventions are retained, but not consistently, in contexts where in Swahili they may no longer be applicable. Other Arabic conventions are retained but with a different purpose which in turn may not be properly applied. For instance, in Arabic the letters ya ﺱ and wau ﻭ take *sukun* when they form diphthongs, but not when they lengthen vowels. In Swahili the same symbols may denote long vowels, but are frequently employed where the vowel is in fact a short one, and these uses with *sukun* do not in Swahili denote a diphthong. Similarly, the same Arabic letters may take *sukun* to indicate the absence of a long vowel and are then transliterated as *u* or *w* and *i* or *y* respectively. In Swahili the consistent adoption of this method of denoting vowels *u* and *i* would have been an advantage, but in fact *sukun* is very seldom employed in this manner above ya and wau. Even so, while Swahili scribes preferred to treat ya and wau as consonants in the Arabian sense, vocalizing them with a vowel-sign, in transliteration the consonantal value is arbitrarily either observed or ignored.

More than half of the characters in the Arabic alphabet may each represent more than one sound in Swahili. To give some idea of the difficulty of transliterating and interpreting the older texts we give below the Swahili names of some Arabic characters with their possible equivalents in roman letters:

Arabic character	*Swahili roman*
bei	b, p, mb, mp, bw, pw, mbw, mpw
tei	t, nt
jimu	j, nj, ng, ng', ny
khe	kh, h
dali	d, nd
rei	r, d, nd
zei	z, nz
shini	sh, ch
twei	t, tw, chw
thwei	z, th, dh, dhw
ghaini	gh, g, ng, ng'
fei	f, fy, v, vy, mv, p
kafu	k, g, ng, ch, sh, ny
kyafu	k, g, ng, ch, sh, ny
ya	y, ny

With so many alternative sounds represented by single symbols it is not surprising that Steere should have written of the Swahili-Arabic script that 'it is absolutely necessary to have a good idea of what you are to read before you can read it at all'. Swahili readers familiar with the alternatives usually have no special difficulty in reading the script.

Conversely, there are distinctions of sound in Arabic which are lost in the speech of some of the Swahili people. These distinctions are maintained by Swahilis who know Arabic, but are not consistently observed in texts by Swahili copyists. They are lost in texts in roman script for which there is no Swahili-Arabic equivalent and also in standard Swahili. German scholars of Swahili usually try to observe the distinctions in their transliteration, but where speech reference is not contemporaneous with the text this leads to obvious difficulties. The distinction may be lost between the following Arabic characters:

ح and ه, in roman appear as *h*

ذ, ض, ظ, appear as *dh*

س and ص , appear as *s*

ط and ت, appear as *t* or *tw*

There is no letter in roman script to represent Arabic 'ain ع ; it is either omitted or the adjacent vowel is doubled, but an inverted comma is very seldom used to indicate its presence. In relation to syllabic measure, however, it may have the force of a consonant and yet may be omitted in the transliteration.

In the early scripts the writers were quite uninfluenced by usage in roman script. Culturally their background was Arabian and there was no standardized system of representing in Arabic script even the essential features of a Bantu language. Only in recent years, when literate Swahilis have become familiar, not least through the vernacular press, with the generally accepted method of writing Swahili in roman script, has there been any attempt to introduce a form of Arabic-Swahili writing which gives the proper values to Swahili syllables.

Certain extra symbols had been used by a few writers, especially the Perso-Arabic letters for *p* and *ch* (پ and چ), but no attempt had been made to fill all the gaps in a recognized system. Sheikh al-Amin of Mombasa introduced a reformed orthography to the Swahili reading public in the 1930's, both in a newspaper and in a book of worship and prayers published at Tanga.[1] But it is significant that he had to publish his books on *Worship, Marriage and Divorce, Some European Appreciations of Islam,* and his graded

---

[1] *Muslim Prayers and Worship*, Tanga, n.d.

lessons on Muslim doctrine, in roman characters. The extra letters adopted by Sheikh al-Amin are as follows:

پ for *p* چ for *ch* غ for *g* ڤ for *v*

He added two vowel-signs, viz. ١ and ٱ for *e* and *o* respectively.

He gave fixed values to a number of commonly used, but differently spelt, combinations, as follows:

مٛب for *mb* ند for *nd* کو for *kw* نج for *nj*

نز for *nz* مٛوٛ for *mbw* نٛ for *ny*

This attempt to introduce a standard system had little influence, and the general picture today is what it has been from the beginning; a script commonly acknowledged to be inadequate continues to be preferred. It has sometimes been assumed that Swahili copyists were all experts, but this is not really so. Taylor of Mombasa knew from experience that Muhammad Abubakar b. Umar al-Bakari (Muhammad Kijuma) was a very good copyist and that Rashidi Abdallah was quite the opposite. One has only to glance at the published specimens to see the enormous differences in standard of knowledge of Arabic, in skill of execution, in spelling, and in legibility.

THE GRAMMAR OF THE POETRY

For a proper phonetic interpretation of Swahili texts in the Swahili-Arabic script speech reference is essential. The relevance of speech reference has sometimes been forgotten by students of the language. Variant readings of a manuscript have mistakenly been identified with the actual symbols employed in the manuscript itself. For instance, scholars have discussed the geographical occurrence of the *-ele* and *-ile* verbal endings by reference to the manuscripts, apparently overlooking the fact that in the Swahili-Arabic script there is only one way of representing either ending. The alternative forms belong to the speech reference, that is, to the Swahili reader who dictated the transliteration, and not to the manuscript.

Hichens observed[1] that 'all words written by the Swahili scribes are disposable into syllables, each of which consists of one consonant and one vowel'. But this is not suitable for maintaining

[1] W. Hichens, in manuscript notes in the Library of the SOAS.

grammatical distinctions since in Swahili, unlike Arabic, vowels occur with no supporting consonant. In some instances the difference between a simple vowel and a vowel preceded by its supporting consonant is in Swahili a grammatical distinction, e.g. *-o-*, concord of Cl. 2, and *-yo-*, concord of Cl. 6 or Cl. 9. Adjacent vowels can be shown in the following ways:

(i) When alif, wau, or ya is used after a consonant and without a vowel-sign or with *sukun*, a long or double vowel is indicated, e.g.

kaa كَا   kii كِي   kuu كُو

(ii) If a vowel-sign is used on one of these letters, then it retains its consonantal value. Hamza is also used on alif, e.g.:

kaa كَ   jua جُأ

kia كِ   kaya كَيَ   juwa جُوَ

Wau and ya are frequently employed in the scripts where in fact no semi-vowel is heard in speech or written in standard Swahili. To maintain a measure of grammatical accuracy in the transliteration, the Arabic consonant wau or ya has often to be omitted in roman script.

The consonantal value of rhymed terminal syllables, however, should be regularly observed in transliteration because its retention is often essential to the rhyme-pattern, e.g.:

> Hawawezi kukimbiya   kutembea ni mamoya
> They cannot run   nor can they walk . . .

The rhyme here is in *-ya* (*ya* with *fathah* are the symbols) and to present accurately the rhyming sequence the *-ya* must be retained, though only in *mamoya* is the *-y-* a functioning consonant. It is not necessary to show the same consonant in *kutembea* (as *kutembeya*); the consonant is there in the Swahili-Arabic script, but in non-rhyming positions it may be omitted in the transliteration.

Similarly, *-w-* should be retained in rhyming sequences, e.g.:

> Kajifunga kwa sitawa   silaha za kuteuwa   pandu tatu kachukuwa
> He girded himself with vigour   with chosen weapons   and
>   carried three catapults . . .

Here *-w-* is a functioning consonant in *sitawa*, in the passive *kuteuwa* (which does not need to be transliterated *kutewuwa*), but it is an essential complement to the rhyme in *kachukuwa*.

In this connexion the Amu equivalent for standard Swahili reflexive infix *-ji-* is written in the Swahili-Arabic script with its supporting consonant *ya*. Hichens gives the Amu equivalent as *-i-*, which in fact is an Amu alternative also for *-yi-*, but the form *-i-* would not be observable from the script. In comparison with standard Swahili other Amu variants may well be observable from the Swahili-Arabic script, since the Amu equivalents for standard Swahili consonantal values may not be represented by the same Arabic symbol, i.e. it may be an altogether different consonant. In the Amu dialect the distinction between the following consonants and their equivalents in standard Swahili is made evident by the symbols employed in the Swahili-Arabic script, viz.:

Amu	Standard Swahili
y	j *and* l
d	j *and* z
s	f *and* h
t	ch
z	v
nd	ng
ny	ng

The distinction *y/j* or *y/l*, *d/j*, &c., indicates dialect variance. No confusion can arise here because different symbols are needed for all of these variants except the last, i.e. in relation to the symbol employed for the Amu equivalent. Where different symbols are needed it would be possible to show some dialect differences as between, say, the Amu and the Pemba dialects. This does happen in texts recorded from oral tradition, but wherever original composition was primarily a literary work, the Amu dialect was the one employed.

Whereas the semi-vowel *-w-* is often written in the script where it is excluded from the grammar, the same semi-vowel is often omitted in the script where it belongs to the grammar. Nasal consonants, especially in nasal combinations, are also often omitted in the script. In speech the nasal of a nasal combination, like *nd* or *mb*, has syllabic value only rarely, but in reading from the Swahili-Arabic script it may be necessary to give syllabic value to the nasal consonant of a nasal combination for the sake of the syllabic measure, *even though it may not be written in the script*.

Both syllabic measure and the rhyme may affect the shape of words. Omission of the subjectival concord, whatever the person or class, is very common. For this reason it cannot be presumed that the written word is in every instance the same as in speech. For instance, the *-ile* endings occur in verbals as a recognizable suffix of a tense-sign, but an *-ile* suffix may not in some contexts be what it seems. Note the following:

> . . . fikiri uzingatile   ujingani usingile   tusumbukalo milele . . .
> . . . Think and remember   don't be foolish   what annoys us for ever . . .

In these three abstracted *vipande* the terminal rhyme is in *-le*, but in the last word of the first two *vipande* the consonant *-l-* is introduced for the sake of the rhyme in the third *kipande*. In current speech the words are subjunctives to be read as *uzingatie* and *usiingie*. From the Swahili-Arabic script they could be transliterated (among other ways) also as *uzingatele* and *usingele*, but, of course, they are not examples of the *-ile* or *-ele* perfect ending.

Conversely, while the transliteration of a subjunctive ending may properly be *-iye* (more freely *-ie*), this may, according to the meaning, alternatively be a dialectic variant of the perfect ending *-ile*.

The important thing here is to emphasize the danger of presuming that because words occur with a certain shape in the poetry, they had the same shape in the current Amu dialect. The grammar of Amu cannot be safely deduced from the grammar of the poetry, but only vice versa. If it be considered that we identify the literary medium too closely with the Amu dialect, we do so only in the sense that the Amu dialect may be regarded as typical of the northern dialects in general. The literary medium is northern, but, as we have already noted, the script itself does not show dialect variants except of the more general kind distinguishing northern Swahili from southern Swahili.

No comprehensive study of the northern dialects in general or of the Amu dialect in particular has yet been made. There is therefore no absolute criterion to which our texts may be referred. Stigand, Sacleux, and others have provided notes of certain features characteristic of northern dialects, and these we may easily recognize, but the extension of this work does not belong to the interpretation of the scripts, but to the investigation of speech-forms.

In Appendix B to his edition of the Swahili poem *al-Inkishafi*,[1] Hichens attempted to provide the chief differences between Kiamu and southern Swahili as *evidenced in the poem*. All that these amounted to were the consonantal differences, some endings in *-ile* (perfect), participles in *-e*, and the historical past tense with infixed tense-sign *-liki-*. It is significant that his criterion for comparison of the text with current speech was the southern dialects of Swahili (though a more intimate knowledge of even some of these would have established identity of form in some instances, and his criterion or standard of comparison was more truly standard Swahili). The comparison should have been made with reference to current speech in the Amu dialect.

Hichens did what was possible in the absence of further information about the Amu dialect or about the northern dialects in general, and we can do no more. Our standard of comparison in the notes will be standard Swahili. We prefer not to outline any tentative grammar of the poetry since, as we have shown, the literary medium may at times obscure the true character, phonological, and lexical, of the material. The most we can do is to provide an analysis, wherever possible or necessary, of separate items in the texts on a basis of comparison with what are likely to be the equivalents in standard Swahili. It is not considered necessary to note every occurrence of any single feature once it has been observed in a single item.

[1] W. Hichens, *al-Inkishafi*, London, Sheldon Press, 1939.

3

UTENDI VERSES

THE *utendi* verse-form consists of four *vipande* of which the first three rhyme together and the fourth carries a rhyme which is repeated as the terminal rhyme throughout the poem. This important verse-form is employed for writing epics or heroic poems and for much shorter homiletic and didactic poems. The shorter epics are also called *hadithi*.

Originally the long *utendi* (pl. *tendi*; known in the south as *utenzi/tenzi*) was intended to be sung or intoned by one or more to a musical accompaniment and before an audience. Steere, who compared the musical setting of such works to Gregorian chants, stated that a musical score was sometimes prepared, but none has found its way into the hands of European scholars. Occasionally it is still possible to find a *utendi* being intoned in public on the veranda of a house. Public recital ensured that at least the gist of the story would reach the ears of the ordinary man. Much of the shorter homiletic verse, however, was of a more private nature, intended either for the Swahili aristocracy or for a didactic purpose. A number of these were meant as instruction for the younger members of the community on social behaviour and religious practice. In the present century the *utendi* verse-form has been used for writing poems embodying oral tradition, e.g. the Swahili legend of Liyongo, or for circumstantial accounts of historical events, especially of wars and battles, e.g. the Maji-Maji rebellion of 1905.

The nearest parallel in English literature to the earlier long *utendi* is perhaps the *Morte D'Arthur* of Malory, and the spirit of these early Swahili epics is expressed in the words of one of our own poets who himself wrote one of the earliest epic poems in the English language:

> O goodly usage of those antique times,
> In which the sword was servant unto right;
> When not for malice and contentious crimes,

But all for praise, and proof of manly might,
The martiall brood accustoméd to fight.
(Spenser, *Faerie Queene*, III. i. 13)

Werner compared *tendi* poems to the 'loose rhymes' of the Welsh bards, used by them for fluent narrative of a less elevated kind.[1] For true comparison, however, we must refer to the Arabian narratives, mostly in rhymed prose, called Maghazi literature (Ar. *maghāzī* 'raids'), consisting of legendary accounts based on a modicum of historical facts dealing with the wars of the Prophet Muhammad after the Hijra. Some of the shorter *tendi* can be related to Arabian Maulid literature, dealing with the birth and early life of the Prophet, and, indeed, in Swahili these poems are called Maulidi. In the Maghazi poems the history of Muhammad's childhood and his first years after his call are postulated as known; these poems are limited to later times in which the Prophet by force of arms strove for Islam. A third category of Arabian legendary narratives is called in Arabic *futūḥ* 'conquests' and these are concerned with the later conquests of Islam under the first Caliphs. No Swahili *utendi* is known to relate to this category of Futuh literature, though the possibility of finding such a Swahili poem is not ruled out.

Of the Maghazi narratives examined by Paret,[2] the following have a Swahili counterpart in *utendi* form: Tabuk (Sw. *Chuo cha Herkal*), Hunain (Sw. *Utendi wa Hunaini*), Abdarrahman (Sw. *Utendi wa Abdarahamani*), Miqdad (Sw. *Hadithi ya Mikidadi na Mayasa*), and Ras (Sw. *Utendi wa Ras al-Ghuli*). Paret's list is not exhaustive and it may well be that other Swahili *tendi*, like *Utendi wa Fatuma*, *Utendi wa Huseini*, &c., can be related to other Maghazi narratives not listed by him. Enough is known of both types of literature to show that the long Swahili *tendi* resemble in many respects the Maghazi narratives. There can be no doubt that the Swahili *tendi* derived from the Maghazi legendary literature.

This does not mean that even where a direct relationship is obvious the story is the same in both the Arabian and the Swahili versions. Werner wrote of the Swahili poem in *utendi* form about Miqdad:

There are various romantic legends connected with Miqdad, extant both in poetry and prose. Paret has made an extensive examination of

[1] Alice Werner, *The Story of Miqdad and Mayasa*, Azania Press, 1932, p. 10.
[2] Rudi Paret, *Die legendäre Maghāzī-Literatur*, Tübingen, 1930.

the (Arabian) manuscripts. . . . Not one corresponds with the Swahili poem. It may therefore be accepted as an original composition based on traditional matter which has no doubt undergone considerable modification in the transit between the Hijaz and the Swahili coast.[1]

Werner also noted that some Swahili epics have been taken from the Arabian prose romances, of which a great many have been catalogued and summarized by Ahlwardt, but in no case can the matter of any one Swahili poem of this type be identified with that of a particular prose romance. Of the Swahili *Utendi wa Ayubu,* Werner wrote: 'Of the prose romances catalogued by Ahlwardt, there are several dealing with the history of Job which may have been utilized in the Swahili poem, Utendi wa Ayub...[2]

Of another Swahili poem of the same type Werner wrote: 'Ahlwardt's catalogue mentions four prose romances on the life of Mary on any or all of which the Swahili poem with the title, Kisat Sayyid na Isa, may be founded'.[3]

Reference is sometimes made in the Swahili texts to the Arabian traditionalist from whom the Swahili author claims to have taken the general theme of his poem, but seldom can the matter of the Swahili epic be traced to a specific Arabian source. In the *Utendi wa Abdarahamani*, for instance,[4] the author claims to have seen the story in a collection by the Arabian traditionalist, Anas ibn Malik Abu Hamzah, but from which collection the Swahili poem received its theme there is no indication in the text. Reference to the collections of this prolific traditionalist, which include the Musnad of Ahmad ibn Hanbal, is indeed vague, and although the reference may be accepted, it is unlikely that the author followed his source closely.

Traditions of the Sunni school of Islam have had the most influence amongst the Swahili people. The Swahili epic, *Utendi wa Miraj*,[5] is based upon a well-known book of Sunni tradition, Mishkatu 'l-Masabih,[6] much used by Indian Muslims, but once

---

[1] Alice Werner, op. cit., p. 7.

[2] Alice Werner, in *The Moslem World*, vol. x (1920), p. 26.

[3] Ibid., p. 27.

[4] E. Dammann, *Dichtungen in der Lamu-Mundart des Suaheli*, Hamburg, 1940, pp. 141–214; other versions of this utendi in Swahili are not the same as the one in Dammann.

[5] In Dammann, op. cit., pp. 1–73; other Swahili versions exist which are not the same, e.g. in the manuscripts of the Library of the SOAS.

[6] Originally compiled by Imam Husain al-Baghawi, and called *Masabihu*

again the Swahili poet has introduced into his work a freedom of
treatment that makes any exact comparison of the two works
difficult.

The Swahili writers of the popular epic limited their borrowing
to the general matter of Arabian legend and romantic tradition
relating to the Prophet, and upon this basis were free to write as
they wished. Paret observed that in the Maghazi narratives one
never finds exactly the same account occurring a second time
even within the same context. The same applies to Swahili *tendi*.
They are independent stories intended for entertainment. Each
deals with an episode or with a phase during the first Muslim
campaigns and each *utendi* is rounded off as a complete story.
Such a cycle of independent stories tends to be dissociated from
fact, though some factual references are employed. Paret noted
of the Maghazi literature that the independent nature of these
narratives is evidenced by the fact that several of them have
appeared in Arabic, separate from the others, in print. Com-
ponents of a factual, chronological history could not lead such
an independent life, whereas complete stories forming a cycle
may well do so.

What Paret has written[1] of the general purpose and character
of the Maghazi literature is true of the earlier Swahili epics. They
were meant to amuse and elevate the uneducated masses who liked
to see their religious, social, and political ideals realized in the
history of former times. He mentions the frequent occurrence of
the formula 'The narrator says', a formula typical of folk literature. The same formula occurs in Swahili epics. In the *Utendi wa
Ras al-Ghuli* the end of one section of the narrative and the
beginning of another is shown by the use of this formula (*kala
rawil*) in rubricated verses. Both in the Maghazi poems and in
Swahili *tendi* there are direct indications that the poems were
publicly read or intoned by narrators. There are direct addresses
to the audience and invitations to join in the recital of a blessing
or of a verse from the Quran.

Another distinct feature of the Maghazi poems is that the Imam
Ali regularly plays a leading part in the narrative. The same is true
of the early Swahili *tendi*. The Imam Ali enjoys a special position

's-Sunnah, or 'The Lamps of Tradition', and revised in A.H. 737 by Sheikh Waliyu
'l-Din.
    [1] Paret, op. cit., p. 154.

of trust with the Prophet and on all dangerous occasions he is the last refuge of the oppressed Muslims.

The rhyming prose in the Maghazi poems consists of non-metrical passages provided with end-rhymes. Fitted into this prose narrative are song insertions (Paret calls them *Leidenlagen* and he examined about a thousand of them) and these are composed according to the Arabic system of metric feet. The stylistic difference between the rhymed prose and the song insertions is that the former express the epic character of the narrative, while the latter express the emotional crises of the characters and are more subjective.

The most popular measure for Swahili epic poems is in eight *mizani*, though the poet often varies the measure to seven *mizani*. In his edition of the *Utendi wa Herkal*,[1] Knappert has given a fairly comprehensive list of Swahili *tendi*. Included in the list is the *Utendi wa Ras al-Ghuli*, concerning which Knappert states that Sacleux was the only European with a copy of this poem. In 1944 the present writer had the opportunity to study a manuscript copy of this poem in Mikindani after being present at a public recital of the poem. Helped by a local Swahili, Musa Husein, a transliteration of 125 pages of this very long poem of over 5,000 verses was made, including many long and complete passages. The copy was the property of one Mzee Saidi and lacked thirty-three pages, but the main body of the work survived. The poem is a very good example of the early Swahili epic.

There are many printed editions in Arabic of the story of Ras al-ghul,[2] though the story is not the same in the separate versions. Editions in Arabic can be bought in Indian shops even in East

---

Utendi wa Ras al-Ghuli (selected passages)

Twaa mwanzo wa kalamu siku moya twafahamu ondokele muungamu tume wetu il-bashiri.

Kondoka kwake amini achenda msikitini mle katika nyumb-ani wakati wa alfajiri.

Baada alipofika Bilali akatamuka keta adhini haraka na wakati umejiri.

[1] Jan Knappert, *Het Epos Van Heraklion*, Druk, Alkmaar, 1958.
[2] Paret, op. cit., p. 131.

Africa in places like Mombasa and Zanzibar, but they do not correspond with the Swahili treatment of the story. The Swahili poem deals with the adventures of the Companions of the Prophet in avenging a Muslim woman whose children have been slain by an unbelieving king in the Yemen.

The poem opens in the manner proper to all Swahili epics by the setting forth of the chief attributes of God, and this is followed by the description of the writing-materials and of the method of writing. The poet often repeats in a different form an idea expressed already in the previous verse; this metaphrastic verse is typical of the longer poems. Certain phrases tend to turn up again and again. In some parts of the poem the narrative, normally in the third person, shifts to the first person. The end of one section of the narrative and the beginning of another is shown by such rubricated verses as the following:

Kala rawil kitabu maneno tuyabawibu tuyapange kulla babu msome mkifikiri.
Haya niliyosanifu ya Ali maarufu tuyaweke muakafu turejee kwa Zuberi . . .

The narrator says (of) the book let us arrange the words let us arrange them of every kind that you may read and ponder.
These that I have composed about the famous Ali let us bring them to an end and then let us return to Zuberi . . .

In setting out the following extracts from the *Utendi wa Ras al-Ghuli*, the verses are numbered for the convenience of the reader of this book and not according to the order of verses in the manuscript.

The Epic of Ras al-Ghuli

Take down the beginning of the story One day, we understand, there appeared the Beloved Our Prophet the Bringer of News.
At his coming forth, the Trusted One went to the mosque there inside the building at the time of dawn.
After he had arrived He called for Bilali He called for him to call the people to prayer quickly for the time had come.

Akaadhini Bilali sauti akiratili wakapulika rijali wakuu hata swariri.

5 Sahaba wakakutana kwa wote ajemaina na Ali na Athmana wa kadha Shekhe Umari.

Mashiyukhu ansari kwa wote wakadhihiri pasi mti kuhusiri wa kadha Abu Bakari.

Kwa wote wakiwasili akaajili Rasuli kuwasalisha rijali kwa sauti tajihiri.

Walipokwisha kusali wakishukuru Jalali sahaba na Shekhe Ali na jamii ya ansari.

Wali ndani msikiti na zuo wakitafiti pasi kupita wakati wakibaini ghubari.

10 Sahaba wachangaliya wawene watu wakiya wote wapanda ngamiya jumla ya watu ashari.

Wakija zao haraka msikitini kifika wakaajili kushuka wakinawihi bairi.

Na mkuu wa kaumu mtu mke mahashumu akibaliri salamu na kumuuza habari.

Papo aketa kauli kama i wapi Rasuli kipendo chake Jalali nionyeni tahisiri.

Keta i wapi Sayyidi kipendo chake Wadudi tume wetu Muhammadi adhiliye makufari.

15 Nionyeni maadhamu tume wa Mola karimu nimekuja madhulumu nimpe zangu habari.

Akapulika Amini na watu msikitini Shekhe Abu 'l-Hasani achondoka tahisiri.

Awela hima kondoka achenenda kwa haraka langoni alipofika akema akibusuri.

Kifika akitazama akimwona harima langoni amesimama akimuuza habari.

Harima keta naamu ndimimi mtakadamu namtaka muungamu nimpe zangu habari.

20 Ali akamjibu akamwambia karibu nikuonyeshe Habibu Tume wa Mola Jabari.

Ali katanguliya mtu mke kandamiya wakenenda kwa pamoya hata kwa tume Bushiri.

Mtu mke yukheini kisogea kwa Amini akimtunza usoni atoa anga na nuri.

And Bilali called them to prayer   sending out the cry   and the people heard   from the elders to the children.

And the Companions met together   all of them together   both 5 Ali and Othman   as well as Shaikh Umar.

The leading Helpers   they were all present   with no one absent   and so Abu Bakr was there also.

When all had arrived   the Prophet came forward   to lead the people in prayer   with a high voice.

After they had prayed   giving thanks to the Glorious God   the the Companions with Shaikh Ali   and the congregation of the Helpers.

They were inside the mosque   studying the holy books   when almost at once   they discerned a cloud of dust.

The Companions watched   and saw people coming   all riding 10 camels   the number of them being ten.

They were coming in a hurry   and on arriving at the mosque   they proceeded to dismount   watering the camels.

And the leader of the party   a woman of distinction   giving greeting   and asking for the Prophet.

She spoke straightway   saying, Where is the Prophet   the Beloved of the Glorious God?   Show me without delay.

She said, Where is the Prophet   the beloved of the Beloved   our Prophet Muhammad   who sets at nought the infidels?

Show me the Exalted One   the Prophet of the Bountiful God 15 I have come an oppressed person   that I may give him my news.

And the Trusted One heard   and the people in the mosque   Shaikh Ali (lit. father of Hasan)   was leaving the mosque without delay.

He began quickly to leave   going in a hurry   and when he reached the doorway   he stood to look.

Arriving there and looking   he saw a woman   standing at the door   and he asked her her news.

The woman said, Yes   I am the one who spoke   I want the blessed Lord   that I may give him my news.

Ali answered her   and said Come near   let me show you the 20 beloved   the Prophet of the Great God.

Then Ali led the way   and the woman followed behind   the two of them went together   into the presence of the Prophet.

The woman went humbly   as she approached the Trusted One   looking at his face   as it gave out brightness and light.

Mtu mke achanguka mwili kitetemeka akiwa kupapatika kana
kinda la tuyuri.

Kitulia pale iti ukapita na wakati wakidhani ni mauti ajali
imedhihiri.

²⁵ Baadaye achondoka shela akayifunika akitoa mashtaka kwa
Tume kustajiri.

Papo aketa kalamu kumweleza Muungamu nimekuja madhulumu akitoa ushairi.

Ndiwe Mtume mursali kipendo chake Jalali kushushiwa
Jiburili takupa zote habari.

Kipendo chake Muweza mambo yote kakueneza dalili na
miujiza ya dhahiri na siri.

Akakupa na wakati wa kuombea umati siku za zilzilati
ndiwe Bashiri nadhiri.

³⁰ Ushairi ukikoma kumsifu Muungamu kwa fasihi ya kalamu kama lulu manthuri.

Na Tume akimuuza ulilo nalo neleza pasi neno kulisaza unipe
zote habari.

Nipe uliyokujiya nami yapate neleya uneleze yote piya ya
mwanzo hata aheri.

Mtu mke akanena nisikize Maulana nitakupa yote maana habari zilizojiri.

Twaa mwanzo wa kalamu takupa yangu isimu Wafari binti
Salamu ndilo jina madhukuri.

³⁵ Na baba yangu fahamu ali mtu mahashumu ni mkuu wa
kaumu ana askari kafiri.

Nisikize Mtume wetu huku janibu ya kwetu kuna jeshi ya
watu sulutani wa kufari.

Takupa tena Habibu jina la huyu kilabu jinale itwa Shihabu ali
mtu mashuhuri.

Wala hajui halaki na mwanawe mnafiki isimuye Muhariki ali anidi jabari.

Kukufuru akashika ajali ikamfika akifa wakamzika kwa mila
ya ukufari.

⁴⁰ Akiyadhuku mauti pasi muda na wakati likinenda iti ati kwenda
pambana na nari.

Akitawala mwanawe akinga kuzi na mwewe ya Mola asiya-
juwe akazidi kukufuri.

The woman fell down   her body trembling   she fluttered   like
a chick from the brood.

And resting there below   a little while passed   and they
thought she was dead   that disaster had befallen.

But then she arose   and covered herself with a black shawl   and 25
brought her complaint   seeking help from the Prophet.

Then she raised her voice   to explain to the Blessed One   I
have come as one oppressed   and she told her tale.

You are the Prophet, God's messenger   the Beloved of the
Glorious One   upon whom the Angel descended   and
so she told her tale.

Beloved of the Almighty   you judge all things at His will   signs
and wonders   what is open and what is secret.

God gave you also the opportunity   to pray for the community
on the Day of Judgment   you are the Bringer of Warnings.

Her prayer being ended   in praise of the Blessed One   with 30
elegance of speech   like precious pearls.

The Prophet asked her   Tell me what you have to say   leaving
nothing out   give me all your news.

Tell me why you have come   so that I may understand   explain everything to me   from the beginning to the end.

And the woman spoke   Listen to me O Lord   I will tell you
everything and the meaning   of all that took place.

Beginning at the beginning   I will first give you my name   it
is Wafari daughter of Salamu   it is indeed a well-known name.

And my father, understand   was a very famous man   a leader 35
of the people   with pagan warriors.

Listen to me O Prophet   in the district where I live   there is
a great company of people   with an infidel Sultan.

I will tell you more O beloved one   the name of this infidel   it
was Shihabu   he was a notorious person.

But he knew not his creator   and his son is a deceiver   whose
name is Muhariki   a proud and violent man.

In a state of unbelief   disaster came to him (Shihabu)   so on
his death they buried him   according to infidel custom.

Tasting death   and before much time had passed   his body 40
journeyed beneath the earth   going to meet with the flames
of hell.

And his son ruled in his place   and was just like a bird of prey
knowing nothing of God   but blaspheming more and more.

Akitawala kilabu asijue wa kirabu akashika kughudhubu kwa jeuri kukifiri.

Na kwetu kukakhutufu kadha ya Mola latifu na baba akata-wafu kwenda mwitika Jabari.

Tukakutana kuzika na tanga tukatandika siku tatu ziki-fika kondoa tusihusiri.

45 Baada tanga kondowa na mali nikaigawa kwa kila zake hitowa tukashukuru Jabari.

Wakikutana rijali wakema wake ni wali kuhukumu kila hali watu wote wakakiri.

Nikazaa auladi wakiwa kana usudi takuambia na idadi watoto edashara.

Nikazaa na binati aroba amrati walikuwa baidhati mshabaha wa kamari . . .

(The woman then goes on to explain that she herself is a Muslim. Her defence of Islam at the expense of her own personal safety is typical of the religious spirit of the poem. In the section that follows Ras al-Ghuli is referred to as Laini (Ar. *la'in*, lit. 'accursed').)

Na mimi ni muislamu pame na yangu kaumu kumwabudu Mkarimu ni laili wa nahari.

50 Tumtiile Latifu na Tumewe Msharafu kesho tupate woko-fu tuepukane na sairi.

Na adhabu ya kaburi Munkari wanakiri katika yetu dha-miri ibada tumeikiri.

Laini akasikiya kikusanya jeshiya tuliko wakatujiya wasiwe kutaahari.

Wakatujia lukuki kwa siyufu na mikuki wakitukusa hilaki tu-kaona yao shari.

Wakikamata wangu wakiwafunga kwa pingu wakiwakusa machungu na mwenyewe hibusuri.

55 Laini akanambiya ewe Wafari sikiya nakuona wapoteya umo katika hatari.

Nawe nini kufuata dini yetu ukaata hapa nilipokupata taku-toa kwa jeuri.

So the heathen dog ruled   he couldn't even read   but set
  himself to cheat   and behave with contempt.
And sorrow befell our home   by the decree of the Benignant
  God   for my father died   having been called by the
  Almighty.
Then we met for the burying   and went into mourning   and
  when the three days were ended   we finished mourning
  without delay.
And when the mourning was finished   and I had divided up the 45
  property   having made all my pious offerings   we thanked
  God.
Then the men met together   and the women and their daugh-
  ters stood   to judge the position   and all gave assent.
And I gave birth to boys   who were like lions   I will tell you
  how many   there were eleven of them.
I gave birth also to daughters   four girls   they were beautiful
  (lit. white)   as lovely as the moon . . .

And I am a Muslim   together with my people   we worship
  the Beneficent One   by night and by day.
Let us obey the Beloved   and His Prophet the Great Lord   so 50
  that tomorrow we may be saved   and keep away from hell.
And as to the punishment of the grave   Muslims accept the
  decree of Munkari   according to our conscience   we in our
  worship confess   it.
Laini heard my confession   and collecting his army   they
  came to where we were   without any delay.
They came in number innumerable   with swords and
  spears   bringing destruction upon us   and we beheld their
  wickedness.
Seizing my own children   they fastened them in chains   and
  involved them in bitter suffering   while I myself looked on.
Laini spoke to me   O Wafari listen to me   I see that you are 55
  lost   and that you are in the midst of danger.
Why do you follow (Islam)   and have given up our religion?
  Here where I have come upon you   I will deal violently
  with you.

Na uendapo ukirudi kwa dini ya Muhammadi takufungua kuyudi nikutoe na mavari.

Hamwambia huyapati haihati haihati sitatuluku salati nika-abudu shari.

Nilivyojua Jalali na haramu na halali na kushahidi Rasuli hayo muhali kujiri.

60 Akasikia kilabu maluuni wa ajabu kaingiwa na ghadhabu na mato akidawiri.

Kwa papo akitamuka kana yangu hukushika nitakukusa mashaka na adhabu kukifiri.

Akema kunijalidi akitwaa ailadi kiwatinda kwa hadidi kana kutinda bakari.

Na maneno akinena akiwa kunitukana kana leo utaona na mauti shamari.

Nami papo hamjibu laiti yuko Habibu Sayyidi wa Arabu Muhammadi il-Bashiri.

65 Hayo unayonitenda kunipiga kana punda kwa Mungu akipenda Mtume asingekiri.

Akasikia kilabu yale niliyomjibu akangiwa na ghadhabu maneno akakifiri . . .

(The narrative completes the woman's story and the group of Muslims join with her in a lament for what has taken place.)

Kilia mno ajuza kilio kikendeleza na tume akanyamaza kulia asifikiri.

Mambo uliyonambiya kwa yote nimesikiya jamiya yatato keya kwa weza wake Jabali.

Baada kwisha habari mtu mke na Bashiri mtume asikasiri akiweta asikari.

70 Wale katika baraza mtume akiwauza nina neno taweleza munijibu tahisiri.

Nawauza waarabu na jamiya sahabu iti ya huyu kilabu iliko munihubiri.

Nambieni niijuwe mseme nami nelewe mneleze upandewe huko aliko kufari.

And if it be that you should return   from the Muslim religion   I
will untie your bonds for you   and remove you from this
foolishness.

And I told him, That you will never do   by no means at all   I
will not change my prayers   and worship evil.

The way I know the Glorious One   and what is forbidden and
lawful   and witness to the Prophet   what you suggest is
impossible.

And the infidel dog heard   the amazing accursed one   and he 60
became full of wrath   his eyes going round and round.

And thereupon he spoke   If you do not hold to what I want   I
will bring great trouble to you   and inflict dire punishment.

And standing there to scourge me   he took my boys   and
slaughtered them cruelly   just like killing a goat.

With a spate of words   he was abusing me   like saying, Today
you will see   and it will be bloody death.

And then I answered him   O if only the Beloved were here
the Lord of Arabia   the Prophet Muhammad.

These things that you do to me   beating me like a donkey   lov- 65
ing God as he does   the Prophet would not acquiesce in them.

And the infidel dog heard   what I replied to him   and he was
full of wrath   blaspheming in speech. . . .

She made known her great lament   and the cry of lament went
up   but the Prophet kept silence   not thinking to wail.

The things you have told me   I have heard them all   A
company will go out   in the power of the Almighty.

When the tale had ended   between the woman and the Prophet   the Prophet without showing any anger   called his
soldiery.

And those who were with him in conclave   the Prophet asked 70
them   I have something to say   so answer me straight
away.

I ask you men of Araby and the group of my Companions   the
country of this infidel dog   tell me where it lies.

Tell me so that I may know   speak with me so that I may
understand   explain to me where exactly   this infidel is to be
found.

Umari bin Umeya   akamjibu Nabiya   iti yake yaneleya
magereza na kusuli.

Iti ya huyu johali   najua kila mahali   wala sitaki dalili   usiku
wala na hari.

75 Akatamuka Amini   Umari nipe yakini   walikwenda tenda
nini   iti yao makufari . . .

(Then follows Umari's account of his adventures in the country of Ras
al-Ghuli, in which he tells how the latter murdered his own father. The
emphasis is upon the pagan environment and the presence of Umari, the only
Muslim, in their midst, the extreme dangers he encounters and eventually
his escape. At the end of his account Umari offers to go again to the same
pagan country to avenge the woman Wafari, but the Prophet forbids him on
the grounds that he is known to Ras and his people. Zuberi fears that the
Prophet may forbid him also to go, and he leaves the company secretly and
goes on a camel intending to be the first to avenge the Muslim woman's
suffering. The next section given here is where the Prophet is told of Zuberi's
departure by the Angel Gabriel.)

Zuberi kwisha kondoka   Jibrili akashuka   kwa Rasuli akafika
ya kuja mpa habari.

Akasema Jibrili   akamwambia Rasuli   akusalimu Jalali
salamu nyingi kathiri.

Baadaye ya salamu   amenituma Karimu   ya kuja kupa
kalamu   na habari za Zuberi.

Asema Mola Rabuka   kana Zuberi katoka   kumwendea
mshirika   sultani wa kufari.

80 Nawe huko usimame   Shekhe Ali umutume   kwa upesi
amwandame   asiwe kutaahari.

Akasikia Rasuli   alosema Jibrili   papale akaajili   ya mtu
kumdabiri.

Akatumuka Amini   kumwambia Selemani   ni kuondoka
alheni   ukamwite Haidari.

Selemani il-Farisi   asifanye majilisi   akitoka kwa upesi   kwa
Ali akadhihiri.

Baada ya kuwasili   kamwambia Shekhe Ali   nimetumwa na
Rasuli   akutaka tahisiri.

85 Shekhe Ali i yuheni   kimjibu Selemani   aketa ewe mwandani   sikiza zangu habari.

Haidari akasema   leo nilele na homa   siwezi hata simama   kwa
homa kunikithiri.

Kipulika Selemani   karejea kwa Amini   kwa papo mahadha-
rani   akema kumhubiri.

Umari son of Umeya   then answered the Prophet   I know
    where his country lies   its prisons and its forts.
The country of this cruel man   I know every place in it   nor
    do I need signs   (to find the way) by night or day.
And the Prophet then spoke   Umari tell me the truth   What 75
    went you to do   in the country of these infidels? . . .

When Zuberi had left   the Angel came down   and came to
    the Prophet   to give him the news.
And the Angel said   speaking to the Prophet   The Almighty
    greets you   with countless greetings.
And after the greetings   the Generous One has sent me   that
    I may come to announce   and tell you about Zuberi.
The Lord God says   that Zuberi has left   he has gone to the
    unbeliever   to the infidel sultan.
And there where you stand   send Sheikh Ali   to follow him 80
    quickly   without any delay.
And the Prophet heard   what the Angel said   and thereupon
    ordered   that someone should look for him.
And the Trusted One spoke   and told Selemani   Go straight-
    way   and call Haidari (i.e. Sheikh Ali).
Selemani the horseman   without stopping to talk   left
    quickly   and came into the presence of Ali.
On his arrival   he told Sheikh Ali   I have been sent by
    the Prophet   he wants you at once.
Sheikh Ali immediately   answered Selemani   and said O my 85
    friend   listen to my news.
Haidari (Ali) said   Today I am in bed with fever   I can't
    even stand up   for the fever gets worse.
Selemani listened   and went back to the Trusted One   and
    there in the presence   he stood to speak to him.

Selemani akasema   kumwambia Muungamu   Shekhe Ali ana homa   kusimama hakadiri.

Tume aliposikiya   sahaba akawaambiya   na twenende kwa Aliya   twende tukambusuri.

90 Achondoka tahakiki   sahabaze na rafiki   Abu Bakari Sadiki   Athmani na Umari.

Nyumbani wakiwasili   akitamuka Rasuli   kumuuza Shekhe Ali   homa imekukithiri.

Sheikh Ali i yuhena   akamjibu Amina   najiona ahawana   kwa wezo wake Jabari.

Mtume akatamuka   aketa Ali kupulika   vua kanzu kwa haraka   kondoka asikadiri.

Selemani kimwondowa   na kanzu akamvuwa   na nde akamtowa   akisogea Bashiri.

95 Kitwaa maji baridi   kamtia asirudi   tangu rasi na jasadi   homa mara ikatiri . . .

(This miracle is typical of the acts attributed to the Prophet in this type of verse. Sheikh Ali goes in search of Zuberi and is soon in conflict himself with Ras al-Ghuli. Each of the Four Companions is brought into the picture either as a single opponent of the pagan forces or as joining together against the power of the unbelievers. There are miraculous interventions by the Prophet when his followers are in special danger. The sections of the narrative are complete in themselves, like parts of a serial story. The scene of most that takes place is either Mecca or Medina, but the Arabian desert is always near. In one section Ali destroys a temple of idols, and in another there is a fight with a nameless pagan prince and his slave. Our last selected passage from this epic poem gives a description of this prince and the fight with the slave.)

Ali akapulika   farasi akatandika   walipotoka kondoka   wakabaini ghubari.

Ghubari ili adhimu   katika wangwa fahamu   pakangia na dhalamu   kana kunako matari.

Baada kwisha dhalamu   wawene kuja ghulamu   aja akitaranamu   naye kijana khiari.

Akitokea kwa kasi   kana upepo wa kusi   kivumicho cha farasi   kana mwamba wa bahari.

100 Naye mwana wa Arabu   tena kijana shibabu   kajilabisi thiabu   afkhari za hariri.

Naye kijana tuwili   yukinga simba mkali   na sura yake jamali   na wajihi mdawari.

And Selemani spoke   telling the Blessed One   Sheikh Ali
    is sick   he cannot even stand up.

When the Prophet heard   he told his Companions   Let us
    go then to Ali   let us go and see him.

He set out there and then   with his Companions and 90
    friends   Abu Bakr, Sadiki   Othman and Umar.

Having arrived at the house   the Prophet spoke   and asked
    Sheikh Ali   Has the fever strong hold on you?

Sheikh Ali straightway   answered the Trusted One   I find
    myself rather better   by the power of the Almighty.

The Prophet then spoke   and said, Ali listen   Take off your
    robe   (intending that) he should not fail to get up.

Selemani got him up   and took off his (Ali's) robe   then he
    took him outside   near to the Prophet.

Taking cold water   the Prophet sprinkled it over him   from 95
    head to foot   and at once the fever left him. . . .

Ali listened   and then saddled his charger   and when they
    were about to leave   they espied a cloud of dust.

The dust-cloud was very big   in the desert you understand   and
    a great darkness fell   as though rain were about to fall.

And after the darkness   they saw a young man coming   he
    was coming at great speed   and he was a very choice young
    man.

He appeared in haste   like the south-wind   and the sound of
    the horses   was like a wave of the sea.

He was a young Arab   and a most endearing youth   he wore 100
    fine clothes   garments of silk.

And he was a tall young man   like a fierce lion   with a
    beautiful face   and a well-rounded presence.

Ana upanga jadidi   na ngaoye hadidi   na durui ya daudi   na farasi shamari.

Nyumani kuna abidi   naye mtwana sawidi   yukinga kana asadi   mato kama zingufuri.

Ana upanga begani   na mkuki mkononi   na durui mwilini   nyumani kuna bairi.

105 Mle katika ngamiya   kapanda mtu jariya   imrati baidhiya   mweupe kama kamari.

Mshabaha wa tausi   mzuri hana kiasi   amejipamba libasi   nguo njema za hariri.

Ngamiani kajengewa   chema mno chandaruwa   kinameta kana juwa   wakiona kunawiri.

Kimejengwa kwa ajabu   kwa mbaoze za dhahabu   na ndani muna hijabu   ya dhahabu shamari.

Sahaba wachangaliya   wakitaka kumwendeya   wakitazama Aliya   akasema tusubiri.

110 Nawaona na ajili   ya kuwania kitali   tuuzeni kwanza dalili   mambo yataka shauri.

Nami hitunza naona   nguvu zake mbayana   ahimili na kuwana   ushujaa u dhahiri.

Mwate akae kitako   tumuuze atokako   atuambie aendako   atupe zake habari.

Mle katika kalamu   awele pita ghulamu   asipotoa salamu   na watu wakibusuri.

Achenda hata mtini   akishuka farasini   na mkewe ngamiani   awele kutaahari.

115 Katika safari yawo   wametukua kondowo   akitoa bwana wawo   kutinda asikasiri.

Akamtinda kwa hima   pale aliposimama   papale akitazama   awene pana shajari.

Asiwe kutama kani   kautia mkononi   kawezua pale tini   sahaba wakibusuri.

Awenepo twana lake   feeli ya bwana wake   kitako kisimweke   kondoka asikasiri.

Akitwaa ule mti   akiupiga na iti   usisalie katiti   wote ukadahathari.

120 Sahaba walipoona   mambo ya yule kijana   pame na yule mtwana   kwa papo wakakabiri.

He wore a new sword   and his shield was of iron   and (he
wore) Dravidian mail   and had a well-accoutred steed.

Behind him followed a servant   and he was a black slave   he
was like a lion   his eyes (red) as cinnabar.

He had a sword on his shoulder   and a spear in his hand   with
a coat of mail on his body   and behind him there was a camel.

Upon the camel   there rode a noble person   a beautiful 105
lady   white like the moon.

She was like a proud peacock   her beauty was without excess   she wore fair raiment   lovely robes of silk.

On the camel was built   an exceeding fine canopy   it shone
like the sun   and they saw it glisten.

It was set up in wonderful fashion   with rods of gold   and
inside there was filigree-work   of dressed gold.

The Companions watched   wanting to go to the stranger   and
they looked at Ali   who said, Let us be patient.

I think they intend   to engage in a conflict   let us ask first 110
for a sign   for this calls for deliberation.

As for me as I see it   his strength is evident   he is equal to
a fight   his bravery is plain to see.

Leave him to rest awhile   then we can ask from whence he
comes   and he can tell us whither he goes   and give us
his news.

As he spoke   the young man came passing by   without
deigning to give greeting   and the people looked on.

He went as far as a tree   and got down from his horse   and
his wife on her camel   remained behind.

In their equipage   they had carried a sheep   which their lord 115
took out   not thinking it ill to slaughter it.

And he slaughtered it quickly   there where he stood   and
looking there   he saw there was a tree.

Without exhausting himself   he put his hand to it   and
stripped it at the base   while the Companions looked on.

When his slave saw this   the action of his lord   he remained
no longer seated   but rose up at once.

He took that tree   and hit it on the ground   so that none
of it remained (whole)   it was all in pieces.

When the Companions saw   what the young man had 120
done   together with the slave   they faced there
bravely.

Akaajili mtwana　kondoo akamtuna　na kuni akakusanya　akiamiri na nari.

Na moto ulipowaka　kondoo akamweka　akiwiva akiweka si-
niani ya sufuri.

Akakeleti ghulamu　pame na wake harimu　wakajipiga lahamu　na mikate ya shairi.

Baada walipokuta　mikono wakikung'uta　mtwana aki-
yvuta　kondoa asikasiri.

125 Na ghulamu baadaye　mtumwawe amwambiye　pipa langu
nileteye　hilo linalo khamri.

Mtwana akasikiya　yale aliyomwambiya　awele kumleteya asiwe kutaahari.

Pipa lilipofika　mkononi kalishika　miomoni kalandika asi-
lisaze katiri.

Ukasikia kooni　inavyoshuka tumboni　kana jiwe la twaani　mtama au shairi.

Mikate iliyosa'a　mtwana akaitwa'a　hemani achenda
ka'a　kasidi kujistiri.

130 Baada ya kukeleti　akiwamo kula kuti　sisazie hata katiti　mikate wala tamri.

Akatamuka ghulamu　akamwambia hudamu　enda kwa
wale kaumu　hima asifanye usiri.

Ni kuondoka alheni　kawauze wale nani　wanatoka iti
gani　hima ulete habari.

Mtwana akasikiya　yale aliyomwambiya　achondoka
dhalhiya　asiwe kutaahari.

Akema kujilabisi　upangawe na turusi　na kurekebu
farasi　akitoka tahisiri.

135 Naye mtwana tuwili　yukinga kama jabali　achenda akaajili　kwa sahaba kidhihiri.

Akafika iyuheni　kiwauze ndinyi nani　mnatoka iti gani　na
muliko kudhamiri.

Nuumani kaajili　achondoka tasihili　akema akiratili akamjibu kufari.

Aketa ewe mtwana　nasema sikia sana　ndisi watu waungwana　mashujaa mashuhuri.

Ndisi watu maarufu　mashujaa mausufu　ndisi wavunda
sufufu　wajapokuwa kathiri.

So it came about that the slave   skinned the sheep   and
  collected firewood   setting it alight.
When the fire was lit   he placed the sheep thereon   and
  when it was cooked he put it   on the lid-tray of the cook-
  ing-pot.
The young man sat down   together with his lady   and they
  ate plentifully of the meat   with the barley-loaves.
When they had had enough   and were shaking out their
  hands   the slave made his way   to take away the dish.
And afterwards the young man   said to his servant   Bring 125
  me my cask   the one with the fermented wine.
The slave heard   what his master said to him   and he made
  to bring it to him   without delay.
When the cask was brought   the young man held it   and
  placed it to his lips   leaving nothing at all behind.
The noise in his throat   as the wine went down to his
  belly   was like that of the grinding-stone   for maize or
  barley.
The bread that was left   the slave took it   and to his tent
  made his way   to stay in privacy.
After sitting down   and while he was still eating food   of 130
  which nothing would remain   of bread and dates.
The young man spoke   and said to his servant   Go to those
  men   make haste and do not loiter.
I want you to go straightway   and ask them who they are   from
  what country they are   come quickly and bring the news.
The slave heard   what he was told   and set out at
  once   without tarrying.
He stood up to dress himself   with his sword and buck-
  ler   and mounting his horse   he left without delay.
And he was a tall slave   he was like a rock   he went and 135
  presented himself   to the Companions.
He arrived quickly   and asked them, Who are you?   From
  what country do you come   and what is your intention?
Nuumani appeared   and stood out immediately   he stood
  and proclaimed   giving answer to the infidel.
He called out, O slave   I speak, so listen well   we are free
  men   renowned for bravery.
We are famous men   warriors bold   we are the breakers of
  the ranks   even though they be many.

140 Sahaba zake Amini   tufungao Ramadhani   na kusoma Korani   kwa sala ni takibiri.

Akasikia kilabu   yale aliyomjibu   akangiwa na ghadhabu   kwa bwanawe kadhihiri.

Yule mtwana anidi   baada aliporudi   maneno akiradidi   awele toa habari.

Keta ewe hababu   watu hawa waarabu   wajizumuo sahabu   za Muhammadi Bashiri.

Na bwanawe akajibu   kwa hasira na ghadhabu   aketa ewe kilabu   nakuona huna kheri.

145 Ewe mwana mauluuni   hayo ulipobaini   walikosaje kuwana   wakaona yako shari.

Usingie kulumeni   kitokee kushotoni   kwa dharuba na tuani   kuwazinga mdawari.

Ukawakusa hilaki   kwa upanga na mkuki   pasi mtu mdiriki   ya kuvuta mashauri.

Baada ya kwisha sema   kaokota jiwe hima   na mtwana kasimama   kusikiliza amri.

Akalitupa kwa kuwa   iti ati likatuwa   pana jiwe likazuwa   pakiwaka kama nari.

150 Kamwambia rudi hima   ukawagame kauma   na mimi hikutazama   unavyo kuwahasiri.

Na mtwana akirudi   yukinga kana asadi   akifika akinadi   kwa sauti tajihiri.

Papo aketa kalamu   kunadia waislamu   ni yupi mtakadamu   utamboni adhihiri.

Na ajaye kubarizi   asiwe mtu ajizi   kwani harubu ni kazi   yataka mtu sabiri.

Aje mtu mfulana   ahimilio kuwana   kwa dharuba na tuana   tena nawapa hadhari.

155 Nawaambia msikiye   kula ambaye ajaye   na hayo afahamiye   asikae na ghururi.

Baada kwisha kauli   kibarizi Nuufeli   yukinga simba mkali   utamboni kadhihiri.

Baada ya kuonana   wakashtadi kuwana   kwa dharuba na tuana   na watu wakibusuri.

We are the friends of the Trusted One   who keep the Fast 140
   of Ramadan   and who read the Quran   with prayers and
   the formula.
And the infidel heard   what they answered him   and he
   became very angry   and entered his master's presence.
The strong slave   when he had returned   reported to his
   master   all that had been said.
And he cried out, O beloved master   these persons are
   Arabs   who claim to be friends   of the Prophet Muhammad.
And his master replied   with anger and wrath   saying, O
   infidel   I see that you are a fool.
O foolish son   when you observed these things   why did 145
   you fail to fight   that they might see your challenge?
Why did you not go in at the right   and come out at the
   left   with blows and feints   encircling them?
Why did you not bring destruction upon them   with sword
   and spear   without (leaving) anyone   capable of receiving
   counsel?
After speaking thus   he picked up a stone quickly   while
   the slave stood   to listen to the command.
And he threw the stone with strength   and it fell to the
   earth   it perforated another stone   and shone like the light.
And he told him, Go back quickly   and set upon this group 150
   of men   and I will look on   to see how you destroy
   them.
So the slave went back   he was like a lion   and on arrival
   he challenged   with a loud voice.
Straightway he called out   challenging the Muslims   Who
   is the first to fight?   Let him appear on the field of battle.
And whoever comes to the fray   let him not be a feeble person   for the conflict is hard   and needs a man of determination.
Let whosoever comes   be able to endure the fight   with
   blows and feints   I hereby give you warning.
I tell you and you must listen   whoever comes   let him 155
   understand these things   and not be foolish.
After he had spoken   Nuufeli answered the challenge   he was
   like a lion   and he appeared on the scene of battle.
After confronting one another   they set themselves to
   fight   with blows and feints   and the people looked on.

Ikashtadi kitali   mtwana na Nuufeli   kwa dharuba kali-
kali   pakizuka na ghubari.

Nuufeli yuna mkuki   kuinua asidiriki   mtwana amem-
dhiki   asipate tadibiri.

160 Nafasi asikupata   mtwana akamkamata   asiweze kutu-
kuta   kana kijana sairi.

Baada kumkamata   achenda kimkokota   kwa bwanawe
akipata   na watu wakibusuri.

Bwana wake kimuenga   akiwa kumsimanga   akisha akim-
songa   kumdhirisha umri.

Yule mtwana anidi   baadaye akirudi   akifika akinadi   aki-
barizi Jabiri.

Baada ya kuwasili   wakashtadi kitali   mtwana akaajili   Jabiri kumhasiri.

165 Akija tena Khalija   mtwana naye akija   wakiwana mara
moja   kwa upanga na hanjali.

Mtwana akaajili   kupiga dharuba kali   kamwawanya
mbalimbali   ukisha wake umuri.

Akashtadi anidi   sahaba kuwafisidi   watu saba kwa
idadi   aliokuwa hasiri. . . .

(While this reverse to the fortunes of the Prophet's friends is going on,
Sheikh Ali is watching. He eventually comes forward to fight both the slave
and his master and kills them in fierce battle. And so the narrative proceeds,
with the Prophet and his Companions ultimately victorious against the forces
of the idolatrous pagans.)

In contrast to heroic poems like *Utendi wa Ras al-Ghuli* dealing
with events in Arabia, heroic poems have been written in Swahili
to describe both legendary and factual events in Africa. These
show the natural development from Maghazi-type poems to more
indigenous compositions. Oral tradition found literary form, as,
for example, the tradition about the legendary Swahili hero,
Liyongo.

THE STORY OF LIYONGO

The main fabric of the Liyongo tradition is preserved in the
utendi by Muhammad bin Abubakar bin Umar al-Bakari (also
known as Muhammad Kijuma) written in A.D. 1913. Although the

The fight ensued   between Nuufeli and the slave   with
fierce blows   and the dust of battle flew.

Nuufeli had a spear   but he was not able to lift it   for the
slave overpowered him   and he could not right himself.

Not getting a chance   he was seized by the slave   so that 160
he could not move   as the attacking slave could move.

After the slave had seized him   he went dragging him
along   until he reached his master   and the people
watched.

His master looked at him   and triumphed mockingly over
him   and the slave throttled him   and cut short his life.

The strong slave   after he had gone back   came challenging again   and Jabiri accepted the challenge.

Reaching the field of battle   they entered into fierce conflict   and the slave succeeded   in bringing Jabari to
destruction.

Next came Khalija   and the slave came forward   and they 165
began at once to fight   with sword and scimitar.

The slave managed   to inflict a tremendous blow   and split
him apart   so ending his life.

The young slave fought   and destroyed the friends of the
Prophet   seven in number   whom he destroyed . . .

---

poem is fairly modern the tradition is certainly a very old one
amongst the Swahili people. He has been referred to as an African
Balder,[1] and the tradition concerning him has been compared with
the Arthurian legend[2] and with the Siegfried saga.[3] No mention
of Liyongo is found in Swahili historical chronicles, but the
poems concerning him are not the only literary evidence of the
oral tradition.[4]

[1] Sir J. G. Frazer, *The Golden Bough*, vol. xi, p. 314 (edn. 1913).
[2] W. H. Ingrams, *Zanzibar*, London, 1918, p. 184.
[3] Carl Meinhof, 'Das Lied des Liongo', *Zeitschrift für Eingeborenen-Sprachen*, vol. xv
(1924–5), p. 241.
[4] See the prose stories by Juma b. Mbwana, taken down by Taylor at Mombasa
in 1882; by Khamisi b. Kayi, taken down by Steere and published in his *Swahili*

The case for establishing the factual background of the tradition rests largely upon Liyongo's association with the citadel of
Shagga. This citadel is mentioned more than once in the poems
concerning Liyongo, though any other evidence for its former
existence is only slight. Shagga, also transcribed in the texts as
Shagha, Shaga, Xanga, Shanga, or Shaunga, is marked upon an
old Arab chart of Pate, east-south-east of Siu, south-east of Faza,
and almost due north-east of Pate citadel.[1] A possible reference
to Shagga is also made in the Kitab as-Sulwa fi-Akhbar Kulwa.[2]
This anonymous historical chronicle, written in A.D. 1498,
records the history of the sultans of Kilwa from the time of Ali I,
son of Hasan bin Ali, who migrated from Shiraz to the African
coast and founded the sultanate of Kilwa about A.D. 1160. In the
second chapter, which is concerned with the invasion of Kilwa
during the reign of Ali III, mention is made of Shagha, but there
is no absolute proof that this is the Shagga on Pate Island. De
Barros, the Portuguese chronicler, stated[3] that Sultan Daud I was
driven out of Kilwa by the 'rey de Xanga'.

Explicit reference is made to 'Shanga' on Pate Island in the
Swahili history of Pate as being a citadel of some importance at
the beginning of the thirteenth century, but this Swahili chronicle
is itself based upon oral tradition and cannot therefore provide
indisputable evidence of the early existence of Shagga. Archaeo-
logical investigations on Pate Island by Kirkman[4] have produced
no evidence for the former existence of Shagga there. Yet in view
of the strong oral tradition it is possible that the early existence
of Shagga has some factual basis, and this is perhaps the most that
can be said at present on the historical side.

Shagga may be identical, if not in the site of its citadel yet in
the name of its sultanate, with Shangaya or Shungwaya, a settle-
ment said to have been established by Arabs of the Zaidiyah sect
about A.D. 689 and which by tradition is held to be the point of
dispersal of subsequent Swahili tribes or clans.

Tales, London, 1870; by Muhammad b. Abubakar b. Umar al-Bakari in letters to
Hichens in 1936 and in notes taken for Hichens by Dammann at Lamu; by Mshamu
b. Kombo in Werner's, 'The Swahili Saga of Liongo Fumo', *BSOS*, vol. iv, pp. 247
et seq.; and a Pokomo version in *Pokomo Grammatik mit Übungsstücken*, Neukirchen,
1908, pp. 136 et seq.
  [1] Reproduced in a 'Swahili History of Pate', *J. Roy. African Society*, vol. xiv
(Apr. 1915), pp. 280 et seq.   [2] *J. Roy. Asiatic Society*, 1895, pp. 385–430.
  [3] De Barros, *Asia*, *Decada*, i. liv. viii, cap. vi (Lisbon and Madrid, 1563/1615).
  [4] Communicated to me by Mr. Kirkman.

From the records mentioned it seems clear that no indisputable evidence establishes the previous existence of Shagga, but that if the tradition preserved in the Swahili history of Pate be accepted, then any association that Liyongo may have had with the citadel was before the second quarter of the thirteenth century. This is the interpretation commonly accepted, but it is important to emphasize that this is based on tradition and not on historical evidence.

No single reference in the poems suffices to establish the historicity of Liyongo, but the cumulative effect of many references is to support the probability of his having been a real person. The conflict between Liyongo and his cousin, Daud Mringwari, Fumo (Chief) of Shagga, concerning the accession to the Shaggan rulership is the central theme of the tradition. The cause of the feud is one which can be observed throughout the course of Swahili history, viz. the conflicting claims of the two systems of inheritance, the Arabian matrilineal and the African matrilineal systems. Daud stood in relation to Liyongo as *mwuna wa shangazi*, i.e. the son of his paternal aunt. By the African matrilineal line of succession Daud was the rightful heir. Liyongo, as the eldest son, would have succeeded his father, Mringwari I, according to the Arabian law of succession.

In more than one of the poems associated with Liyongo his clan is referred to as being that of the Bauri. Descendants of this clan live today at Lamu, in Zanzibar, and also as a community at Bura, a village on the Ozi River where, according to tradition, Liyongo lived and ruled over the principality of Shaka, not to be confused with Shagga on Pate Island. These present-day members of the Bauri claim that their ancestral home was Baur or Bor, a village to the north-east of Saiwun in Hadramawt. Their long association with the Ozi River, the traditional site of Liyongo's principality, is perhaps not merely coincidental.

The following selected passages from Muhammad Kijuma's *Utendi wa Liyongo Fumo*, numbered according to the order of verses in the manuscript, include the *Song of Saada*, found also in other manuscripts as a separate poem, and the *gungu* songs. These are poems within a poem and have a different measure and rhyming pattern from the verses with four hemistichs. The end-line rhyme is in -*ya*, but occasionally the poet fails to maintain the rhyme and -*wa* appears as a permissible rhyme with -*ya*.

In the poem the Sultan of Pate is to be identified with Daud Mringwari, Sultan of Shagga. Liyongo is presented as a fearless warrior whom the Sultan wishes to dispose of as a likely usurper to his sultanate. He arranges a marriage between Liyongo and a Galla woman, hoping that Liyongo will stay in the Galla country. When Liyongo's son reaches manhood, the Sultan still has reason to fear Liyongo, so he offers a reward to Sanye (or Boni) and Dahalo tribesmen of the Tana valley for the head of Liyongo. Back in their forest-home they pretend to make Liyongo their overlord and comrade. There is a food shortage, and they share a *kikoa*, a contributory meal for which each guest, turn and turn about, provides the food. The plan is for each man in his day's turn to climb the dum-palm and pluck down the fruit; when Liyongo's turn comes they would shoot him with arrows in the tree-top. But Liyongo, according to this text, with great skill shoots down the ripest, topmost cluster of fruit. Another tradition (as in the *Song of Shagga*, p. 176) is that he seized the bole of the palm and shook down the fruit.

The Sanye and Dahalo tribesmen report to the Sultan who

Utendi wa Liyongo (selected passages)

6 Liyongo kitakamali   akabalehe rijali   akawa mtu wa kweli,   na haiba kaongeya.

Kimo kawa mtukufu   mpana sana mrefu   majimbo kawa maarufu   watu huja kwangaliya.

Walicnenda waGalla   kwa jumbe wa Pate dola   kwa kununua chakula   pamoja kumwangaliya.

WaGalla hawo juani   ni wakuu wa mwituni   kabila yao sultani   mashujaa wote piya.

10 Sulutani Pate bwana   papo naye akanena   waGalla mumemuona   Liyongo kiwatokeya.

WaGalla wakabaini   huyo Liyongo ni nani   kwetu hajajulikani wala hatujasikiya.

Mfalume kawambiya   waGalla kiwasifiya   humwegema watu miya   hawawezi hukimbiya.

advises them to encourage Liyongo to return to Pate where secret plans are made to capture him at a *gungu* dance-tourney (see Chapter 4, on the *gungu* songs). He is thrown into a prison cell. The Sultan allows him a last wish before he is killed and Liyongo asks that another dance-tourney be arranged. In the present text the *gungu*-songs included belong properly to the first tourney, not the second. Liyongo's mother sends him a file hidden in some bread; this is brought by the slave-girl Saada. He breaks his chains and appears unexpectedly at the dance-tourney.

Liyongo's son is feted by the Sultan of Pate who offers the young man his daughter's hand provided that he can discover from his father what weapon can deal him a mortal blow. The son betrays his father and kills him with a copper dagger, the only weapon, according to Liyongo, that could destroy him. Steere wrote: 'The poem of Liyongo used often to be sung at feasts and then all would get very much excited and cry like children when his death was related, and particularly at the point where his mother finds him dead.'[1]

The Epic of Liyongo

As Liyongo grew in perfection   he became a mature man   he 6
was a true man   and his beauty of appearance increased.
He was of glorious stature   very broad and tall   he became
famous in the provinces   and people came to behold him.
Some Galla went   to the court of Pate   to buy food   as well
as to look at him.
These Galla know ye   were chieftains in the forest   they were
of the ruling clan   and all of them brave men as well.
The Sultan, lord of Pate   straightway spoke   Men of the Galla 10
tribe have you seen   Liyongo appear to you?
The men of Galla declared plainly   This Liyongo, who is
he?   He is unknown as yet in our homeland   nor have
we heard of him.
The Sultan said to them   praising him to these men of
Galla   Even though a hundred men press upon him   they
cannot overcome him and they flee away.

[1] E. Steere, *Swahili Tales*, Preface, p. vi.

Ni mwanamume sahihi   kama simba una zihi   usiku na
asubuhi   kutembea ni mamoya.

Ghafula kikutokeya   mkojo hukupoteya   tapo likakuiliya   ukatapa na kuliya.

15 Mato kikukodoleya   ghafula utazimiya   kufa kutakuru-
biya   kwa khaufu kukungiya.

WaGalla wakipulika   kwa dhihaka wakateka   wakanena
twamtaka   na sisi kumwangaliya.

Na yeye alikiketi   kwao ni Ozi si katiti   i huku yake
baiti   kwa wangwana wa Mashaha . . .

(Liyongo's arrival in Pate at the Sultan's request is described in the next
passage.)

23 Liyongo siku ya pili   ndiya akakabili   kaenenda tasihili   ndiya akaemeya.

Kayifunga kwa sitawa   silaha za kuteuwa   panda tatu
katukuwa   kaziwagaa pamoya.

25 Na mtu kitoka Shaka   hata Pate ukafika   siku nne kwa
haraka   alo hodari sikiya.

Liyongo kenda muyini   akipata mlangoni   panda katiya
kanwani   kivuzia kapasuwa.

Liyongo akikabili   ndiya kenda rijali   alikwenda siku
mbili   na ya pili ni kungiya.

Kiivuzia hakika   muyini wakashutuka   panda ika-
pasuka   waGalla wakasikiya.

Wakauliza ni nini   yowe melipija nani   akajibu sulutani   ni
Liyongo amekuya.

30 Liyongo asimuhuli   akayipija ya pili   panda isihimili   na
ya pili kapasuwa.

Kayishika na ya tatu   wakajujumkana watu   wakazengeya
mapito   waGalla kukimbiliya . . .

(The Sultan's fears and the incident of the kikoa feast are described in the
verses that follow.)

49 Fitina zikamngiya   mfalume miya miya   kwa hila kaku-
sudiya   kumuua fahamiya.

He is a proper man   and like a lion he has a noble mien   (and
   for him) the night and day   are the same as he goes about.

If suddenly he should appear to you   you would urinate (from
   fear)   trembling would overwhelm you   and you would
   quake and cry.

If he should stare at you   you would faint right off   death 15
   would be near   because of the fear that has entered into you.

As the men of Galla listened   they laughed and jested   and
   they said, And we also want   to take a look at him.

Now (Liyongo) was living   at Ozi, no small way off   and
   there is his house   at the noblemens' (town) of Mashaha . . .

Liyongo on the next day   set his face to the trail   and 23
   journeyed swiftly   pressing along the road apace.

He girt himself well   with chosen weapons   and he carried
   three war-horns   and fastened them together temporarily.

And if a person leaves Shaka   and goes as far as Pate   (it 25
   takes) four days by hurrying   (for) whoever is a good walker,
   you understand.

Liyongo went to the town (Pate)   and when he reached the
   gate (of the town)   he put the horn to his mouth   and
   blowing it he rent it asunder.

Setting his face towards the town   Liyongo went like a
   man   he went for two days   and on the second day
   made his entry there.

Blowing the horn truly   the townspeople were startled   and
   the horn was split apart   and the men of Galla heard.

And they asked, What is it?   Who has made this fearful
   noise?   And the Sultan replied   It is Liyongo, he has
   come.

Liyongo brooking no delay   blew a second (war-horn)   but 30
   the horn was not equal to it   and the second one was split
   apart.

And he took up the third   and the people were in confusion   seeking some way of escape   and the men of Galla
   fled away . . .

Rumours came   to the Sultan a thousand of them   and he 49
   determined with guile   to kill him (Liyongo), understand.

50 Na sulutani niseme   alikucha mwanamume   tampoka
ufalume   kwa dhana alimdhaniya.

Liyongo akatambuwa   huzengeya kuuawa   pale Pate kaye-
puwa   barani akitembeya.

Mfalume changaliya   mwituni mekimbiliya   waSanye aliwa-
zengeya   na waDahalo pamoya . . .

57 Siku moya wakanena   na tuleni waungwana   kikoa ni tamu
sana   karamu isotindikiya.

Kikoa tule makoma   kukuta hatutokoma   kula tukii-
terema   kulla mtu siku moya.

Likisha shauri lawo   wakenenda kwa kikawo   mkoma
waupatawo   hupanda mtu mmoya.

60 Nao maana yawo   siku yeye apandawo   wamfume wote
hawo   zembe kwa uwo umoya.

Wakalipa wote piya   Liyongo akasiliya   ni wewe wakamwambiya   tumetaka fahamiya.

Liyongo kanena hima   uzengeeni mkoma   muyapendayo
makoma   nipate kuwanguliya.

Wakitembeya kwa safu   kuuzengeya mrefu   hata wakau-
shufu   ni huno wakamwambiya.

Liyongo akiuona   ni mrefu mno sana   yakamwelea maana   yale alowadhaniya.

65 Na yeye una hadhari   kilala huwa tayari   awajua wana
shari   wote pia kwa umoya.

Akawambiya ngojani   akatoa mkobani   chembe katia
ngweni   makoma kiwanguliya.

Achangusha ngaa ndima   ngaa ni mengi makoma   kwa
wote wakaatama   ajabu zikawangiya.

Wakanena kwa moyoni   amuwezao ni nani   huyu hawezekani   ni kutaka kwangamiya . . .

(The next passage includes the *Song of Saada* and the *gungu* songs at the dance-tourney.)

And the Sultan, let me say   feared this man   that he would rob 50 him of his kingdom   and he thought of him with suspicion.

Liyongo understood   that they looked for a way to kill him   and so he withdrew himself from Pate   and journeyed on the mainland.

And when the Sultan perceived   that he (Liyongo) had fled to the forest   he made contact with the Sanye tribesmen   and with the Dahalo as well . . .

One day they said   Now let us eat like gentlefolk   the 57 *kikoa* feast is very delicious   a feast that does not fail.

And for the *kikoa* let us eat the dum-palm fruit   we will not come to the end of being satisfied with it   those who eat the dum-palm fruit   one man shall climb each day.

When their plan was finished   they went their way   for those who get the fruit   one man climbs up (alone).

And their idea was   that on the day when he (Liyongo) would 60 climb up   they would all shoot him   with one swift volley.

They all made their contribution   and only Liyongo remained   it is you now, they told him   we want (the fruit), understand.

Liyongo spoke quickly   Choose a dum-palm   the fruits that you like   so that I may pluck them down for you.

Walking in single file   to choose a tall tree   until they saw it   they said to him, It is this one.

When Liyongo saw it   (that) it was a very tall tree   he understood the meaning   of those (things) that he had thought about them.

For he was always cautious   (even) while he slept he was on 65 guard   he knew that they purposed evil   all of them together.

And he said to them, Wait   and he took from a shaft   arrows and put (one) in the bow-string   and brought down the fruit for them.

He brought down the ripe topmost cluster   a cluster with many fruits   and they were all agape   and wonder filled their hearts.

And they murmured in their hearts   Who can get the better of him?   This man is undefeatable   and (to try to best him) is to want to be destroyed . . .

80 Liyongo nikwambiayo   shaha wa gungu na mwawo   tena
ni mkuu wawo   huwashinda wote piya.

Sulutani kabaini   mashaha walo muyini   kawambia kwa
sirini   pija gungu huwambiya.

Kwa wanaume na wake   na Liyongo mumwalike   naazimu
nimshike   ni siri nimewambiya.

Na habari kisikiya   Liyongo akikimbiya   nani mumezomwambiya   tawaua kwa umoya.

Naye huyu sulutani   kuua hawezekani   akinena kwa yakini   hutimiza mara moya.

85 Mashaha wakaalika   Liyongo wakatamuka   mwao tutaan-
dika   sote tuwe kwa umoya.

Mwao wakaandika   kulla ada wakaweka   sulutani
akapeka   majuma wapata miya.

Wakenenda kwa utungo   mafumo zembe zigongo   wakamshika Liyongo   gerezani akatiwa.

Akatiwa gerezani   kafungiwa kijumbani   asikari mlangoni   kwa zamu wachangaliya.

Kukifanywa mashauri   auwawe madhukuri   tulepuwe lake
shari   Liyongo namcheleya.

90 Wanginewe wakanena   kumuua siyo sana   huyu nda mui
zana   ni mwenye kututeya.

Na tumfanye amiri   zikiya zita ni kheri   atakufa kwa
uzuri   maana hatakimbiya.

Kiuawa ndiyo sana   kitouawa ni zana   hayo wote wakanena   sulutani kaambiwa.

Sulutani kafikiri   kumuua ndiyo kheri   kumuata ni
hatari   kwa hila tanizengeya.

Anipoke ufalume   kisa chanda nikiume   heri yangu mwanamume   kumuua mara moya.

Liyongo, what I tell you now   was Shaha of the *gungu* tour- 80
   neys and of the *mwao* dance   he was their leader   he
   excelled them all.

The Sultan explained   to the leaders of the town   and said
   to them in private   Proclaim a *gungu* tourney, he told
   them.

(A dance) for men and women   and invite Liyongo   I intend to seize him   and this is a secret that I have told you.

And if he gets wind of this   and he Liyongo runs away   (if)
   you have told him of this   I will slay you all.

And this Sultan   (if he sought) to slay, (no man) could gain-
   say him   for when he spake it was with certainty   he
   would fulfil his word at once.

The leaders sent out the invitation   to Liyongo they pro- 85
   claimed   we will prepare a *mwao* dance   so that we may
   all be together.

And they prepared the *mwao* dance   with every customary
   due   the Sultan sent   his men-at-arms about a hundred in
   number.

They marched in column   with spears and bows and battle-
   staves   and they seized Liyongo   and he was put in jail.

He was put in jail   and was shut up in a cell   with soldiers
   at the door   taking turn to watch.

Then there was debate   whether he should be killed   (they
   said) Let us keep away from this evil of his   I am afraid of
   Liyongo.

Others said   To kill him is not right   for he is the town's 90
   defence   he it is who strives for us.

So let us make him Commander-in-Chief   and then if war
   comes it would be better   he would die honourably   for
   he would not run away.

If he were killed that would be right   but if he were not killed
   he would be our defence   thus they all spoke   and the
   Sultan was told.

The Sultan thought   It is better to kill him   for if he is
   spared there would be danger   for he would embroil me in
   some scheme.

Let him deprive me of my kingdom   and I would gnaw the
   finger of repentance   it is better for me that this fellow   be
   killed at once.

95 Jamaa kawamkuwa   kwa shauri la kuuwa   wakajibu ndiyo
dawa   shauri letu ni moya.

Wakamtuma kitwana   kwa Liyongo akanena   kufa shaka
hapana   menituma kukwambiya.

Watamani jambo gani   menituma sulutani   utapowa kwa
yakini   ili uage duniya.

Mekwambiya bwana wetu   menituma mimi mtu   muhulla
wa siku tatu   fahamu utauawa.

Akajibu usikhini   kamwambie sulutani   mwao nimeta-
mani   na gungu liwe pamoya.

100 Na tume wa sulutani   akitoka kijumbani   kaja tume wa
nyumbani   chakula akamweteya.

Na mamake kwa hakika   kuti kizuri kipeka   asikari hum-
poka   chakula wakailiya.

Chakula wakimweteya   asikari huikiya   siku hiyo kamwam-
biya   mama unisalimiya.

Kanena kwa ushairi   enenda kamhubiri   mama afanye
tayari   haya nimezokwambiya.

> Ewe kijakazi nakutuma hujatumika   kamwambie mama
> ni muyinga hajalimuka.
> Afanye mukate pale kati tupa kaweka   nikeeze pingu na
> minyoo ikinyemuka.
> Nitatage kuta na madari yakiyekuka   niue rijali nao waki-
> wana hiteka.
> Ningie ondoni ninyepee ja mwana nyoka   ningie mwi-
> tuni ningurume ja simba buka.
> Nali mti pweke nimeziye katika nyika   si nduu si mbasi
> nimeziye kukupuka.
> Nduu ali mame awasiwe kinda kwitika.

104 Saada kabaleghesha   nyaka make kamuwasha   akaufanya wa
wisha   mukate kampekeya.

His kinsmen then he called   to plan with them the slay- 95
ing   and they agreed, Indeed, that is the thing to do   we
are of the same opinion.

They sent a slave-messenger   to Liyongo and said   Death is
certain   they have sent me to tell you.

What is there that you wish?   The Sultan has sent me   you
will receive it most certainly   so that you may make your
farewells to the world.

He has told you, our Lord   and he has sent me as messenger   that in the space of three days   understand you will
be killed.

And he replied, Do not be sure   tell the Sultan   that I wish
for a *mwao* dance   and for a *gungu* tourney as well.

And when the Sultan's messenger   had left the cell   there 100
entered a servant-maid   and she brought him food.

And when his (Liyongo's) mother for certain   sent good
food   the soldiers would deprive him of it   and would
eat the food.

Whenever they brought food to him   the soldiers confiscated
it   but on this day he said (to the slave-girl)   Greet my
mother for me.

And he spoke (in secret) rhyme   Go and tell her   let my
mother prepare   these things that I have told you of (i.e. in
the following poem).

> O maiden, I send you, for you have not yet been sent, Tell
> my mother, who is innocent and guileless.
>
> Let her make a loaf for me and put inside a file   So that
> I can cut through these handcuffs and break my chains.
>
> Let me cross these walls and the roof shall be broken
> through,   Let me kill men and as they fight I will laugh.
>
> Let me go into the reeds and creep like a fierce snake,   Let
> me enter the forest and roar like a fierce lion.
>
> I am like a lone tree alone in the treeless wilderness   With-
> out kinsfolk or friends, alone I am left an orphan.
>
> Only my mother is left, to whose whelp's cry her answering
> will be lent.

Saada perceived his plan   and his mother set the fires   to 104
make a loaf of bran   and sent him the bread.

105 Mukate huo sikiya   kata mbili hutimiya   kati tupa aka-
tiya   Liyongo kampokeya.

Asikari wakiona   ni wishwa wakatukana   wa wishwa hula
watwana   mpekee haya ngiya.

Ule Liyongo chumbani   kauvunda kwa sirini   tupa akaona
ndani   furaha zikamngiya.

Mama tupa akitiya   kitambaa metatiya   kafurahi mno
ghaya   sana kawafurahiya.

Hata usiku kufika   matezo wakayandika   kama ada wakaweka   tasa pembe siwa piya.

110 Na ngoma na nyingi kusi   kusisalie unasi   ikawa kama
harusi   watu wakiangaliya.

Wote wakakutanika   mahala pakatandika   na uzuri wakaweka   deuli na subahiya.

Wakatandika za zari   na nzuri za hariri   wakaimba mashairi   ngoma kusi kwa umoya.

Na mashairi ni haya   walokwimba kwa umoya   na watu
walipokeya   na Liyongo u pamoya.

 i Mringwari na taikha fuwanye ndooni hwitwa na Fumo Liyongo
        ndooni hwitwa na Liyongo Fumo na nduguye Shaha
        Bwana Mwengo.

 ii Mukaketi juu la uliliye wakusanye watenzi wa ringo   waku-
        sanye watenzi khiari wajuao kutunga zifungo.

iii Wayuao kufuasa zina na kuteza kwa kuumia shingo   huitwa
        hima inukani mwende watukufu wana wa zitengo.

iv Kuna gungu nyemi za harusi humuoza umbule Liyongo   pindi
        sizo watu wasiyakaa ukumbini kukawa kisongo.

 v Na muchenda vaani libasi mujifushe na ungi wa mengo   muji-
        pake na tibu khiari yalotuwa kwa zema ziungo.

vi Choche ni maambari na udi fukizani nguo ziso ongo   fukizani
        nguo za hariri na zisutu zisizo zitango.

This bread, understand   was of about eight pounds weight   and she   105
   placed the file inside   and Liyongo received her (the slave-girl).

When the soldiers saw   that it was made of bran they
   cursed   Only slaves eat loaves of bran   take it to him, go
   on, get in.

But Liyongo in his cell   broke the loaf in secret   and he saw
   the file inside   and was filled with joy.

His mother having sent the file   he tore his cloth   with joy
   on his bed (lit. resting-place)   and rejoiced over them (his
   mother and Saada) greatly.

And when night was come   and they made ready for the
   dances   and according to custom prepared   the gongs,
   horns, and trumpets.

With the drums and much hand-clapping   and no one being   110
   absent   it was just like a wedding   and the people watched.

They were all met together   the dancing-floor was spread   and
   bedecked   with silken cushions and wraps.

They spread out (rugs) of thread of gold   with silken (fabrics)
   of great beauty   and they sang poems   midst handclaps
   and drumming.

And the poems are these   which they sang together   the
   people sang the chorus   and Liyongo sang the air.

"Mringwari, drummers and chorus, come, you are called by the   i
   Lord Liyongo   come, Lord Liyongo calls you and his kinsman Shaha Mwengo.

Sit on the ceremonial divan, let them gather the dancers of the   ii
   pirouette   let them gather the graceful dancers skilled in
   composing enigmas.

Who know how to rhyme and to dance with the straining of the neck   iii
      you are called, hurry, arise and go, you nobles of high place.

There is a *gungu* ceremony, a nuptial dance, Liyongo's sister is   iv
   being wed   what time people cannot pause in the hall because of the crowd.

And when you go don your fine robes and sprinkle yourselves   v
   with perfume   perfume yourselves with choice *tibu*, fine-
   ground with admixtures of perfuming powders.

And with incense of ambergris and of aloe-wood, cense your spot-   vi
   less garments   cense your silken garments and cloths for
   your loins free from all blemish.

vii Patouri na zafarani na zabadi tahara ya fungo   na zito za kara-
fuu tuliani musitiwe kungo.

viii Na ambari na kafuri haya ndiyo mwisho wa tangu kiungo   mji-
pake mkajifukize muende kwenu mukita mwengo.

ix Watwaeni wari na upambo wapokee sabuka kwa mwango   na
wapija wakusi na yio watwaeni wari kwa miyongo.

x Hima hima inukani mwitwa limekuwa yeo wazi lango   na zakupa tuzo zimewekwa tumbi tumbi miyongo miyongo.

xi Fedhati na kowa za barhindi na mikufu ya kwawiya shingo   na
makapu makapu ya nguo ukumbini kwa Fumo Liyongo.

xii Pindi sizo watu wakafika ukumbini kukawa kisongo   wenye
zimo zimo zikakuwa wa wafupi wakinyoa shingo.

xiii Kulla mtu kuamba ni nyemi wenda wima na wenda zijongo   kwa
kupata pato la tijara lisoshiba na mtangotango.

xiv Pindo sizo Liyongo akima akatuza moyo usi shingo   akatuza
kimba wasichana na waume wakangia ringo.

xv Wale watu wote wakanena ndiyo mtendi Fumo si muongo   ni
mtendi Fumo ni mtendi ulijile mgunya na tango.

xvi Upijile mfupa na tanu wenye kula wakiramba bungo   wenye
kula wakashiba mno wakashiba ya mtengotengo.

xvii Baitize arobaini pazidiye nami ni miyongo   pazidiye na nne
nambao sahi sambe ni uwongo.

xviii Salaamu aleikum twaani hii twaani Shaha mekuya mwaoni   Shaha mekuya mwaoni hii mwaoni yote inukani niteze.

114 Kulla nyimbo zizidipo   na ngoma zitakatapo   alikizitinda
hapo   pingu na minyoo piya.

115 Zalipo kikaza kusi   alikikata upesi   hata zikikoma basi   inukani kawambiya.

Patchouli and saffron and musk newly cut from the glands of the vii
  spotted civet   and buds of clove mingle them in so that you
  lack nothing.

And ambergris and camphor, these are the last things of my viii
  philtre of perfume   perfume and cense yourselves and go to
  your place calling out for a minstrel.

Take the young girls with great show and receive the young men ix
  with united chorus   and the hand-clappers and singers, take
  the young girls in groups.

Haste, haste, rise up, you are called, today the door is wide   there x
  are baskets and baskets of presents and gifts by the hundred.

Of silver and Indian crystal and chains for adorning the xi
  neck   and baskets and baskets of garments in the great hall
  of the Lord Liyongo.

No sooner the people arrive in the hall than there is a great xii
  throng   with the tall folk on tip-toe and the short ones
  straining their necks.

And everyone says, This is joyful; both those who walk upright xiii
  and those who are bent   for gaining the best of the matter
  without surfeit of strolling about.

At that moment Liyongo arose and calmed his heart and sup- xiv
  pressed his rage   and he calmed himself as he sang while the
  maidens and youths danced around.

And those people cried out all together, It is Liyongo the poet, xv
  of that there is no mistake   it is the poet chieftain, the poet
  who came to the coastland with battle.

When he beat with a bone on the platter, those with food licked xvi
  china bowls   and those who had food feasted greatly, sitting
  at leisure.

His verses of song were forty, perhaps more   they exceeded four xvii
  tens and that is correct, for let me not state what is wrong.

By the grace of Allah, take these, take these, for the Shah has xviii
  come to the dancing   The Shah has come to the dance; arise
  everyone and let me play."

When the songs' refrain increased   and the drumming loudly 114
  swelled   he was cutting away there   at his handcuffs and chains.

While the clapping increased   he was cutting away quickly   until 115
  when the clapping stopped   he said to them, Lift up your
  eyes.

Wakainuka kuteza   Liyongo akatokeza   khaufu zaliwaka-
za   mbiyo zikawapoteya.

Kwa wote wakakimbiya   hapana alosaliya   Liyongo kayi-
tokeya   mabarani karejeya . . .
(The last selected passage from this poem recounts the death of Liyongo.)

165 Hwenda kiwaza ndiyani   na khaufu za moyoni   siku ya pili
jioni   hata Shaka akangiya.

Kwa babake akangiya   baba kamfurahiya   kwa mno kamshashiya   akimnyoa na ziya.

Kimkanda maguuni   pamoya na muilini   kwa utofuwe ndiyani   maanaye kumtuya.

Kijana kapumzika   kisa ndiyani katoka   kwa kunena na
kuteka   na wendi akitembeya.

Na sindano kipindoni   ameisita nguoni   kamwe mtu
haioni   akizengea ndiya.

170 Kulla siku humwendeya   Liyongo ameilaliya   kamwe hai-
pata ndiya   kijana kishawiriya.

Akimuona babake   hulipija yowe lake   ili baba ashu-
tuke   hashutuki kumuuya.

Kimwamkua ghafula   huinuka kwa ajila   hujibu nipa chakula   nina ndaa humwambiya.

Kijana kishawiriya   kwa khaufu kumngiya   illa yeye una
niya   siku zikateketeya.

Siku zalipokithiri   bwana akamukhubiri   huku sisi ni
tayari   kutengeza mambo piya.

175 Siku kupata waraka   na babake amechoka   kwa usindizi
menyoka   fahamu amepoteya.

Nyono zake huzivuwa   kama gurumo za vuwa   kijana
akaelewa   kwa kweli ameilaliya.

Kajua hana fahamu   kijana aliazimu   kwa ile yake hamamu   mke enda kuzengeya.

Kamtia kitovuni   naye ulele kwa tani   achamka hamu-
oni   kijana amekimbiya.

And pausing in their dance   Liyongo appeared   and fear fell
    upon them   and they were lost in fright as they ran away.
For they all ran away   there was no one left   Liyongo came
    forth   and returned once again to the mainland . . .

And thus upon his way he thought   with fear in his heart   and 165
    on the second day in the evening   he came as far as Shaka
    and entered the city.
He went into his father's house   and his father was glad for
    him   and welcomed him with joy   giving him a place to
    rest his limbs.
Massaging his limbs   together with his whole body   because
    of the weariness of the journey   with the idea of soothing
    him.
The youth took rest   and then came out into the street   talking
    and laughing   with his friends as he walked about.
Yet in the folds of his attire   he had hidden the dagger   but
    no man saw it   as he sought a way of killing his father.
Each day as he went to him   Liyongo was asleep   he could by 170
    no means find a way   and the youth was worried.
Then when he saw his father asleep   he would call him
    loudly   so that his father would be startled   and if not so
    then he would kill him.
But he would always quickly wake   and rise up for whatever
    reason   (and the youth) would say, Give me food   for I am
    hungry, he would say.
The youth was worried   and overwhelmed with terror   but
    he kept his purpose   and the days were consumed up as with
    fire.
As the days sped by   the Lord (of Pate) sent him news   (say-
    ing) Here we are ready   to prepare (for your wedding-day).
On the day that he received the letter   his father was tired   and 175
    lay stretched out in sleep   understand, he was flat out.
His breathing sounded loudly   like thunder in the rain   the
    youth understood   that indeed he was wrapt in sleep.
He knew that his father was unconscious   the youth intended
    (evil)   for the yearning that he had   to go and seek out a
    wife.
He pierced him in the navel   as he lay flat on his back   when
    he (Liyongo) awoke he did not see him   for the youth had fled.

Babake akishutuka   chembe uta akishika   kwa haraka
akatoka   nde muyi kaendeya.

180 Akapija ondo lake   kapatika chembe chake   kama hayi ada
yake   chembe utani katiya.

Na hapo nami tasema   ni karibu ya kisima   watu hawakusi-
mama   kwa wote walikimbiya.

Watu maji wasiteke   waume na wanawake   kwa pote habari
yake   majimbo yakaeneya.

Kuwa Liyongo mekwima   uko nde ya kisima   sasa watu
wamekoma   maji hawapati ndiya.

Hapana ayapatawo   mtu maji atekawo   kulla mtu uko kwawo   hapana wa kutokeya.

185 Wale watu muyini   maji ya msikitini   huyateka birikani   ndiyo hayo kutimiya.

Yamekwisha yote mayi   birikani mwa si mayi   na Liyongo
hanyamayi   chembe ngeni metiya.

Kwa ndaa wakazika   wote wakasikitika   ukumbi wakau-
weka   kufanya shauri moya.

Shauri likawa moya   kheri mama kumwendeya   mamake kisi-
kiliya   atamsikitiya.

Mamake wakamwendeya   naye mama karidhiya   wakatoka
kwa umoya   nde wakasikiliya.

190 Mamake akamwombowa   mashairi akitowa, kwa kasidi kum-
wongowa   Liyongo hayasikiya.

Na make kumuegema   alikicha tematema   kwa mbali kimte-
zama   na nasaha miya miya.

Nao hayakueleya   Liyongo ameifiya   kwa khaufu kuwan-
giya   hawakumkurubiya.

Kulla siku kimwendeya   mama wake akiliya   hainuki saa
moya   ni hasira hudaniya.

Warudipo nasahani   mama wake hubaini   siisi amedharani   ghadhabu zimemngiya.

195 Mwanangu meghadhibika   si ada kutopulika   ameiza kuinuka   siisi yetu khatiya.

His father waking up,   and seizing arrows and bow   he
    went outside   going into the town.

And he sank on one knee   and drew an arrow to its aim   as 180
    was his custom during life   he put an arrow in the bow-string.

And that place, I will say   was near to a well   but people did
    not stand about   for all had fled.

No one drew water there   man or woman   the news through
    all the land   had spread.

That Liyongo is standing   he is there by the well   now
    people have stopped (drawing water)   they have no way to
    get water.

There is no one to get it   no person to draw water   every-
    one stays at home   there is no one who appears.

The people of the town   for water for the mosque   draw it 185
    (i.e. take it) in a jug   until it is all finished up.

Soon all the water came to an end   and none in the jugs re-
    mained   but Liyongo does not leave off   for he has placed
    the arrow in the bow-string.

From hunger they buried people   and all were distressed   they
    arranged a council-meeting   to arrive at a decision.

The decision was unanimous   We had better go to his
    mother   if his mother comes   she will calm him with her
    sympathy.

They went to his mother   and his mother agreed   and they
    all left together   and came outside (the city wall).

And his mother besought him   singing songs (of lament)   on 190
    purpose to lead him   but Liyongo did not hear.

And his mother to approach him   feared in trembling   from
    afar she regarded him   with countless beseechings.

And they did not understand   that Liyongo (even then) had
    already died   for the fear that overcame them   they did not
    go near him.

So each day, going to him   his mother cried   but he did not
    get up even for a single hour   and it was thought he was
    angry.

When she returned from her pleading   his mother explained   I
    do not know what he blames   but anger has taken hold of
    him.

My son is angered   it is not his custom not to hear   he has 195
    refused to get up   and I do not know what is our misdeed.

Siyo yake mazoeya   kwa nasaha kimwendeya   husikia mara
    moya   sasa udhiya metiya.

Mamake kumkurubiya   khatari aicheleya   ghadhabu zikam-
    ngiya   yo yote huioleya.

Kuua hawezekani   kighadhibika haneni   huwa zitono za
    ndani   na kuingurumiya.

Mamake kitaajabu   akinena ni aibu   mara hini mehari-
    bu   ameiza kusikiya.

200 Kipata siku katiti   kaanguka ni maiti   wakatambua umati   Li-
    yongo ameifiya.

Wote wakakurubiya   mamake na watu piya   sana wakimw-
    angaliya   ni sindano ametiwa.

Ametiwa kitovuni   shaba sindano juani   wakamtiya muyi-
    ni   akazika kwa umoya.

Khabari ikaeneya   Pate ikasikiliya   mfalume kiayiwa   furaha
    zikamweneya . . .

(The poem ends with a description of Liyongo's son ostracized and full of
remorse, and he flees to the Galla country, his mother's original home.)

DIDACTIC TENDI

Didactic or homiletic verse was usually written by the Saiyids
in measure of eleven *mizani*. The longer the measure, the shorter
the poem. Some well-known writers preferred the shorter measure
of eight *mizani* for the same purpose and some didactic poems in
this measure are by unknown poets. Usually the writer brings his
own name into one of the verses towards the end of the poem.

Poems of this type give simple instruction both in Muslim
doctrine and practice and in social behaviour. Some were ob-
viously meant for the younger members of the community, like
the *Utendi wa Kiongozi Cha Banati*, by Sheikh Muhammad Jambein
al-Bakari of Lamu. The anonymous work, *Utendi wa Ahmad bin
Abd il-Kadir*, is another example. These poems tell no story.
Muhammad Kijuma wrote his *Utendi wa Siraj* expressly to instruct
adults, and Saiyid Mansab's *Utendi wa Akida Tu 'l-Awami* was
intended for young people. Similar poems were, and still are,
written for individual members of the family. Perhaps the best

This is not his usual way   for if I go to him with a request   he
  listens at once   but now he is gravely vexed.
His mother nearer to him crept   laying aside her danger   and
  anger swept over her   at all she then (so clearly) saw.
It is not possible (now for him) to slay   if he is angry he does not
  speak   it is the throes of death   and the groaning.
His mother marvelled   saying, It is cruel shame   all in this
  hour (my son) has died   he has refused to hear (my voice).
And so within the span of day   to earth he fell a corpse   and 200
  the throng of people realised   Liyongo has passed away.
They all drew near   his mother and the people as well   they
  all looked at him intently   It is a dagger, he has been stabbed.
He has been stabbed in the navel   a copper dagger, know
  ye   they bore him to the town   and he was buried
  without delay.
The news spread   (until) it reached Pate   and when the Sultan
  was told   he was filled with joy . . .

poem of this type is the *Utendi wa Mwana Kupona*, which was
edited by Werner and Hichens in 1934.[1]

Utendi wa Mwana Kupona

Mwana Kupona lived during the first half of the nineteenth
century, dying in or about 1860. Her husband was a well-known
character in Swahili history, Bwana Mataka, Sheikh of Siu, who
for over twenty years carried on a kind of guerrilla warfare
against Saiyid Said, the Sultan of Zanzibar. Mwana Kupona had
two children by Mataka, a son, Muhammad bin Sheikh, and a
daughter, Mwana Hashima binti Sheikh, to whom the poem is
addressed.

The poem was composed by Mwana Kupona some two years
before she died and in expectation of death. Manuscript copies of
this poem still exist in Lamu. Werner made her translation and
transliteration from six copies and notably from a copy made by

[1] The *Advice of Mwana Kupona upon the Wifely Duty*, Azania Press, 1932.

Muhammad Kijuma in 1912. With minor modifications we adopt
the Werner version; the published work already mentioned was
in a very limited edition of 300 copies and is now out of print.

Werner confirmed that many Swahili women in the Lamu area
are adept at composing verse and are fond of reading and hearing
poetry. Girls are taught to read and write and receive religious
instruction at schools usually kept by the wives and widows of
Muslim teachers, or a woman teacher may attend the girl's home.

The poem opens with an affectionate address to the daughter;
religious duties are dealt with at some length (vv. 22 et seq.) and
the popular misconception is removed that Swahili women are
indifferent to their religion and ill-versed in matters of the Faith.
Woman's obligatory and optional religious duties are specifically
mentioned in verses 11–14. As regards conduct, truthfulness,
discretion, and courtesy are specially insisted upon (vv. 13, 14),
as is the fivefold duty to God, to His Prophet, to father, mother,
and husband (vv. 22–23).

Directions for household management, social intercourse, and
kindness to the poor follow the main argument of the poem, viz.
the duties of a wife. The poet dwells on the happiness of her own
married life and on the grief of her irreparable loss. Then, turning
to the contemplation of her approaching separation from this
world, she commends to the care of the Eternal Goodness her

Utendi wa Mwana Kupona

Negema wangi binti   mchachefu hasanati   upulike wasi-
ati   asaa ukazingatiya.

Maradhi yamenishika   hata yametimu mwaka   sijapata kuta-
muka   neno lema kukwambiya.

Ndoo mbee ujilisi   na wino na karatasi   moyoni nina
hadisi   nimependa kukwambiya.

Kisake kutakarabu   bisumillahi kutubu   umtaje na Habibu   na sahabaze pamoya.

5 Ukisa kulitangaza   ina la Mola Muweza   basi tuombe majaza   Mngu tatuwafikiya.

younger brother, her sisters, and their children and her own. In verse 57 she directs her daughter to look after her brothers. The poem concludes with the very touching confession of faith of a devout Muslim woman.

The poem throws some interesting sidelights on the life of a well-to-do Swahili household. The warning against undue familiarity with servants (v. 20) suggests that relations between mistresses and slaves, apart from individual cases of hardship and cruelty, were easy rather than otherwise. This is borne out in prose texts collected by Velten which indicate that the lot of slaves in the Swahili community was usually a happy one.

The more personal attentions bestowed by a Swahili wife upon her husband are described in verses 30–35. These include acts of care that in Hadramawt and southern Arabia are still practised, like the gentle massage of the muscles to relieve fatigue; anointing with perfumes and aromatic substances, such as sandalwood; shaving from the nape of the neck, upward and forward, and then from the forehead backwards; ablutions and shower-baths, and fumigation with frankincense, aromatic aloewood, and fragrant resins. The toilet of the Swahili wife is described in verses 38–41 and includes bathing and cold showers, the care of the hair, hands, and feet, the uses of cosmetics, scents, and jessamine blossoms.

Mwana Kupona's Poem

Attend to me my daughter   unworthy as I am of God's award   Heed my last instructions   for it may be that you will apply yourself to them.

Sickness has seized upon me   and has now lasted a whole year   I have not had a chance to utter   a word of good advice to you.

Come forward and seat yourself   with ink and paper   I have matters at heart   that I have longed to tell you.

Now that you are near   Write, In the Name of God   name Him and the Beloved   together with his Companions.

When you have thus acknowledged   the Name of God the 5 Mighty   then let us pray for His bounty   as God shall deem fit for us.

Mwana adamu si kitu na ulimwengu si wetu walau hakuna mtu ambao atasaliya.

Mwanangu twaa waadhi pamoja na yangu radhi Mngu ata-kuhifadhi akepuane na ba'a.

Twaa nikupe hirizi uifungeto kwa uzi uipe na taazizi upate kuiangaliya.

Nikutungie kidani cha lulu na marijani nikuvike mke shani shingoni kikizaga'a.

10 Penda nikupe kifungo kizuri kisicho ongo uvae katika shingo utaona manufa'a.

Yangu utakaposhika mwanangu hutosumbuka duniani uta-vuka na akhera utakiya.

La kwanda kamata dini faradhi usiikhini na sunna ikim-kini ni wajibu kuitiya.

Pili uwa na adabu na ulimi wa thawabu uwe kitu maha-bubu kulla utakapongiya.

La tatu uwa sadiki ushikalo ulithiki mtu asoshika haki sandamane naye ndiya.

15 Tena mwanangu idhili mbee za makabaili uwaonapo mahali angusa kuwainukiya.

Wangiapo wenukiye na moyo ufurahiye kisa uwapeke mbeye watakapokwenda ndiya.

Ifanye mteshiteshi kwa maneno yaso ghashi wala sifanye ubishi watu wakayatukiya.

Nena nao kwa mzaha yawatiayo furaha yawapo ya ikira-ha kheri kuinyamaliya.

Wala situkue dhana kwa mambo usoyaona na kwamba na kunong'ona tahadhari nakwambiya.

20 Sitangane na watuma illa mwida wa khuduma watakuvutia tama labuda nimekwambiya.

A son of Adam is nought   and the world is not ours   nor is
there any man   who shall endure for ever.

My child, accept my advice   together with my blessing   God
will protect you   that He may avert you from evil.

Take this amulet that I give you   fasten it carefully upon a
cord   regard it as a precious thing   that you may cherish
it with care.

Let me string for you a necklace   of pearls and red coral   let
me adorn you as a beautiful woman   when it shines upon
your neck.

For love let me give you a clasp   a beautiful one without 10
flaw   wear it upon your neck   and you shall perceive benefits.

While you shall hold to my counsel   my child, you shall escape
trouble   you shall pass through this world   and cross over
to the next.

In the first place, hold fast to the Faith   do not neglect to fulfil
the *faradh*   and the *sunnah* when they are possible   and
the *wajibu*, to perform them.

Secondly, be of good behaviour   with a discreet tongue   that
you be as one beloved   wherever you shall enter.

Thirdly, be truthful   what you undertake take pains to do   a
person who holds not to justice   do not follow in his path.

Further, my child, learn how to behave   before people of 15
rank   when you see them at any place   hasten to pay them
respect.

When they enter do you rise up   and let your heart rejoice   afterwards conduct them forth   when they wish to
go their way.

Make yourself entertaining   by words without guile   but
do not make impertinent jokes   which people dislike.

Talk with them cheerfully   of things which give them pleasure   but when words might give offence   it is better
to hold oneself silent.

Neither maintain opinions   on matters you have not perceived   as for gossiping and whispering   be on your
guard, I tell you.

Do not associate with slaves   except during household 20
affairs   they will draw you into disgrace   as perhaps I
have told you.

Sandamane na wayinga   wasoyua kuitunga   ziumbe wasio changa   wata kuwakurubiya.

Mama pulika maneno   kiumbe ni radhi tano   ndipo apate usono   wa akhera na duniya.

Nda Mngu na mtumewe   baba na mama wayuwe   ya tano nda mumewe   mno imekaririwa.

Nawe radhi mumeyo   siku zote mkaayo   siku mukhitariwayo   awe radhi mekuwiya.

Na ufapo wewe mbeye   radhi yake izengeye   wende uitukuziye   ndipo upatapo ndiya.

25 Na siku ufufuwayo   nadhari nda mumeyo   taulizwa atakayo   ndilo takalotendewa.

Kipenda wende peponi   utapekwa dalihini   kinena wende motoni   huna budi utatiwa.

Keti naye kwa adabu   usimtie ghadhabu   akinena simjibu   itahidi kunyama'a.

Enda naye kwa imani   atakalo simukhini   we naye sikindaneni   mkindani huumiya.

30 Kitoka agana naye   kingia mkongoweye   kisa umtandikiye   mahala pa kupumuwa.

Kilala siikukuse   mwegeme umpapase   na upepo nasikose   mtu wa kumpepeya.

Kivikia simwondowe   wala sinene kwa yowe   keti papo siinuwe   chamka kakuzengeya.

Chamka siimuhuli   mwandikie maakuli   na kumtunda muili   kumsinga na kumowa.

Mnyoe umpalilize   sharafa umtengeze   mkukize mfukize   bukurata wa ashiya.

35 Mtunde kama kijana   asioyua kunena   kitu changalie sana   kitokacho na kungiya.

Go not about with foolish people   who know not how to
   control themselves   as to persons who are immodest   avoid
   any contact with them.
Little mother, listen to this counsel   for a woman there are five
   blessings   whereby she may get peace   in the next world
   and this.
They are of God and His Prophet   her father and mother, she
   must know them   the fifth is her husband   much has this
   been affirmed.
Let your husband be content with you   all the days that you
   dwell together   on the day on which ye are chosen   may
   he be happy and attribute it to you.
And should you die before him   do you seek his blessing   that 25
   you may go forth exalted   thus shall you find the right road.
And on the Day of Resurrection   the award is with your husband   he will be asked what he shall wish   and as he wishes
   it will be done.
If he wish that you go to Paradise   you will forthwith be
   brought there   if he says that you go to the fire   without
   escape you will be put there.
Live with him befittingly   do not provoke him to anger   if he
   rebukes you, do not answer back   try to control your tongue.
Keep faith with him   what he desires do not withhold   you
   and he, dispute not together   a quarreller is always hurt.
When he goes out take leave of him   and when he returns 30
   pleasantly greet him   then set ready for him   a place of
   ease-taking.
When he rests do not betake yourself off   draw near to him,
   caress him   and for cooling air let him not lack   someone
   to fan him.
When he sleeps do not arouse him   and don't speak with a loud
   voice   stay there, rise not from your place   so that if he
   wakes he has to search for you.
When he awakes delay not   prepare a meal for him   and take
   care of his body   perfuming him and bathing him.
Shave him that his skin be smooth   and let his beard be trim-
   med   let him enjoy ablution and incense   morning and evening.
Look after him like a child   who knows not how to speak   One 35
   thing you must look well to   the household expenses and
   income.

Mpumbaze apumbaye   amriye sikataye   maovu kieta
yeye   Mngu atakuteteya.

Mwanangu siwe mko'o   tenda kama uona'o   kupea na
kuosha cho'o   sidharau mara moya.

Na kowa na kuisinga   na nyee zako kufunga   na yasimini
kutunga   na firashani kutiya.

Nawe ipambe libasi   ukae kama harusi   maguu tia ku-
gesi   na mikononi makowa.

40 Na kidani na kifungo   sitoe katika shingo   muwili siwate
mwengo   ya marashi na daliya.

Pete sitoe zandani   hina sikome nyaani   wanda siwate matoni   na nshini kuitiya.

Nyumba yako i nadhifu   mumeo umsharifu   wakutanapo
sufufu   msifu ukimweteya.

Moyowe alipendalo   nawe ufuate lilo   yambo limtuki-
alo   siwe mwenye kumweteya.

Ukutiwapo kutoka   sharuti ruhusa taka   uonapo meu-
dhika   rudi na kuiketiya.

45 Fuata yake idhini   awe radhi kwa yakini   wala sikae
ndiani   saa ya nne ikasiya.

Wala sinene ndiani   sifunue shiraani   mato angalia tini   na
uso utie haya.

Rejea upesi kwako   ukakae na bwanako   utengeze matandi-
ko   mupate kuilaliya.

Na bwanako mtukuze   sifa zake uzeneze   wala simshuru-
tize   asoweza kutukuwa.

Akupacho mpokeye   na moyo ufurahiye   asilotenda kwa
yeye   huna haja kumwambiya.

50 Uonapo uso wake   funua meno uteke   akwambialo lishi-
ke   illa kuasi Jaliya.

Be gay with him that he be amused   do not oppose his authority   If he brings you ill   God will defend you.

My child, be not a sloven   do as you see done   to sweep and
wash out the bathroom   do not scorn to do it at once.
As to bathing and perfuming yourself   and plaiting your
hair   and stringing jessamine blossoms   and strewing them
upon the coverlet.
Do you adorn yourself with finery   that you remain like a
bride   put anklets upon your ankles   and bracelets upon
your arms.
And necklace and clasp   remove them not from your neck   to 40
your body deny not the fragrance   of rosewater and dalia
powder.
Remove not the rings from your fingers   nor lack henna on your
fingernails   cease not to put wanda below your eyes   and
upon your eyebrows.
Let your house be well kept   so that you honour your husband   when people foregather there   then will they bring
you praise.
That which he desires in his heart   do you also follow that   as
for a matter offensive to him   do not be the one to indulge in it.
Whenever you need to go out   be sure to ask leave   when
you see that he is vexed   return and sit yourself at home.
Wait upon his permission   that he may be truly content   do 45
not loiter by the way   when the fourth hour has passed.
And do not gossip by the way   nor uncover from within the
shiraa   let your eyes be downcast   and your countenance
modest.
Return quickly to your home   that you may sit with your
lord   make ready cushions and rugs, so that you may take
your ease together.
And exalt your husband   spread his praises abroad   but do
not make obligations for him   which he cannot fulfil.
That which he gives you, accept from him   with a heart that
rejoices   what he does not (ask) of his own accord   you
have no need to tell him.
When you look upon his face   reveal your teeth in a smile   that 50
which he tells you hold to it   except to rebel against the
Highest.

Mama sinoe ulimi   nioleza wako umi   naliowa nyaka
kumi   tusitete siku moya.

Naliowa na babako   kwa furaha na ziteko   tusondoleane
mbeko   siku zote twaloka'a.

Siku moya tusitete   ovu langu asipate   na lake lisi-
nikute   hata akakhitariwa.

Yalipokuya faradhi   kanikariria radhi   kashukuru kafawidhi   moyo wangu katushiya.

55 Tangu hapo hata yeyo   siyanyamaa kiliyo   nikumbukapo
pumbayo   na wingi wa mazoeya.

Watu wakipulikana   milele hukumbukana   illa wenye
kushindana   milele huiyutiya.

Mausio ya mvuli   Allah Allah ya'amili   na nduguzo na
ahali   wapende nakuusiya.

Uwaonapo sahibu   ambao wakunasibu   wakikwambia
karibu   angusa kukurubiya.

Na wachandika chakula   uchambiwa nawe nla   wala si-
weke muhulla   nyuma nyuma kurejeya.

60 Wala sifanye kiburi   nla hata ushakiri   usiyakuta si-
kiri   ukambwa na kondolewa.

Watu wote wa umini   kwako na wawe wendani   sipende
masalatini   washinde ukiwepuwa.

Sipende wenye jamali   na utukufu wa mali   fukara uka-
wadhili   cheo ukawavundiya.

Akupendao mpende   akuizao mwenende   kwa zema mvunde-
vunde   la'ala akaridhiya.

Na ayapo muhitaji   mama kwako simuhuji   kwa uwezalo
mbuji   angusa kumtendeya.

My child, be not sharp-tongued   be like me, your mother   I was married ten years   yet we did not quarrel one single day.

I was wed by your father   with happiness and laughter   we did not abase our mutual respect   all the days that we lived together.

Not one day did we quarrel   he met with no ill from me   and from him none did I encounter   until the time when he was chosen.

And when death came   he repeatedly told me his content   and resigned himself in peace to God   while my heart was filled with grief.

From that time unto this day   I yet cease not from lamenta- 55 tion   when I remember the ease   and plenty of our accustomed life.

If people heed one another   for ever they share fond memories   but those who strive against each other   regret it for eternity.

The instructions of your husband   with faithful care discharge them   and your kindred and relations   love them, I adjure you.

Whenever you see friends   who are your equals by birth   if they bid you welcome   hasten to visit them.

And if they lay out a meal   and you are asked, eat it then   but do not leave a long delay   before returning to your home.

And do not be discourteous   eat until you are satisfied   if not 60 yet content, do not confess it   when told that the dish be removed.

All people who are safe to trust   at your home, then let them be friends   do not be fond of quarrelsome people   overcome them by avoiding them.

Do not love those who affect elegance   with the arrogance of wealth   while it despises the poor   and disparages to them their lot.

She who loves you, love her   she who dislikes you, go to her   by kindness disperse her ill-feeling   mayhap she will be appeased.

And when there comes one in need   my child, to you, do not embarrass her   with what skill you are able   hasten to assist her.

65 Mama haya yasikize   tafadhali sinipuze   utaona nafuuze za
akhera na duniya.

Tamati maneno yangu   kukuusia mwanangu   sasa tamu-
omba Mngu   anipokelee duwa.

Kwani yote tunenawo   mwana adamu ni puwo   Mola
ndiye awezawo   kupoteza na kongowa.

Nakuomba we Manani   unitilie auni   ninenayo ulimini na
yote nisoyatowa.

Yote nimezoyanena   Rabbi takabali minna   na yasalieyo
tena   nakuomba nitendeya.

70 Niwekea wangu wana   na umbu langu mnuna   yakue yao
maina   yenee majimbo piya.

Rabbi waweke nduzangu   na wana wao na wangu   wenee na
ulimwengu   kwa jamali na sitawa.

Na jamii isilamu   Mola wangu wa rahamu   matakwa yao
yatimu   nyoyo zikifuahiya.

Ya Allahu wangu wana   nimekupa ni amana   watunde
Mola Rabbana   siwate kuwangaliya.

Nimekupa duniani   watunde uwahizini   unipe kesho
peponi   mbee za Tumwa Nabiya.

75 Wangalie kwa huruma   uwongoze ndia njema   uwepulie
na tama   za akhera na duniya.

Kwako kuomba sikomi   wala sifumbi ulimi   ya Mufarrija
l-Hammi   nikomesheza udhiya.

Nisimeme muhitaji   nipa hima sinihuji   ajili bi l-faraji ya
afua na afiya.

Nondolea ndwee mbovu   yaloningia kwa nguvu   dhambi
zangu na maovu   ya Rabbi nighofiriya.

Kwetu yangawa mazito   kwako wewe ni matoto   nepulia
uvukuto   unepuke mara moya.

My child, hearken to these words   I pray you do not ignore 65
me   you will behold the advantage of them   for the life to
come and this.

This is the end of my words   directing you, my daughter   now
I will entreat God   that He receive of me a prayer.

For all that we have said   a child of Adam is but empty folly   the
Lord, He it is who is Powerful   to destroy and to preserve.

I pray to Thee, O Beneficent One   grant to me aid   for the
words that are upon my tongue   and for all that are in my
heart.

All things of which I have spoken   O Lord, receive in trust for
me   and as to those which remain unsaid   I pray thee, grant
me favour.

Take for me into Thy care my children   and my kinsman, a 70
young brother   that their names may endure   and spread
abroad in all lands.

O Lord, preserve Thou my kindred   and their children and
mine   may they increase in this world   with help and prosperity.

And the company of Islam   O my Lord of mercy   may their
needs be fulfilled   that their hearts may rejoice.

O Lord God, my children   I have given to Thee in trust   protect them, O Lord and Master   cease not to look after them.

I have given them to Thee in this world   that Thou protect and
cherish them   grant them to me hereafter in Heaven   in
the presence of the holy Prophet.

Look upon them with compassion   guide them in the right 75
path   remove them from the troubles   of the next life and
of this.

To Thee I cease not to pray   nor do I still my tongue   O
Comforter and Protector   bring me to the end of my suffer-
ings.

As I stand a suppliant   yield to me readily, force not upon
me   a death without blessings   of pardon and salvation.

Remove from me the evil malady   which has forcibly seized
upon me   my sins and ill-doings   O Lord, forgive to
me.

Although things be hard for us to bear   yet to Thee they are
but small matters   take from me the fever of sickness   mayest Thou relieve me speedily.

80 Nakuomba we Latifa   unondolee mikhafa   kwa Yaumu li-
Arafa   na idi ya udhihiya.

Kwa siku hizi tukufu   za kuhiji na kutufu   niafu Rabbi
niafu   unishushize afuwa.

Ya Allahu ya Allahu   ya Rabbahu ya Rabbahu   ya Ghayata
Raghbatahu   nitika hukwamkuwa.

Nakuomba we Rabbana   bi'asmaika l-husuna   tisaa wa
tisaini   mia kupungua moya.

Nipulishie walimu   wakinambia fahamu   dua hini isilamu   akiomba hurudiwa.

85 Nami mjao dhaifu   mwenye nyingi takalufu   nakuomba
takhafifu   Rabbi nitakhafifiya.

Nakuomba tahisiri   mambo nisiyokadiri   unegeshe kulla
kheri   ovu ukinepuliya.

Ya Rabbi nitimiliza   mambo nisiyoyaweza   wala moya
nisowaza   amba yatasikiliya.

Rabbi unifurahishe   mambo mema unegeshe   maovu
uyagurishe   tusikutane pamoya.

Uniweke duniani   miongo ya wahusini   nifapo nende peponi   makao ya hafidhiya.

90 Tungile utungu hunu   kwa zahimu na zitunu   kwa kadha
yako Dayanu   na hukumuzo Jaliya.

Tungile nili sakimu   moyo usina fahamu   usomeni isilamu   mukiongozana ndiya.

Na sababu ya kutunga   si shairi si malenga   nina kijana
muyinga   kapenda kumuusiya.

Kapenda kumnabihi   la'ala katanabahi   kamfuata Illa-
hi   pamwe na wake rija'a.

Somani nyote huramu   maana muyafahamu   musitukue
laumu   mbee za Mola Jaliya.

95 Somani mite ya nganu   mtii waume wenu   musipatwe
na zitunu   za akhera na duniya.

Mwenye kutii mvuli   ndake jaha na jamali   kulla en-
dapo mahali   hutangaa na kweneya.

I pray to Thee, the All-Benevolent   ward off from me fears   by 80
  reason of the Day of Arafat   and the Festival of the Sacrifice.
By these glorious days   of the Pilgrimage and the Kaaba   save
  me, O Lord, save me   send down to me deliverance.
O God O God   O Lord O Lord   O Fulfilment of all
  desire   answer me as I call upon Thee.
I call upon Thee, O Lord God   by Thy beautiful Names   nine
  and ninety   one hundred less one.
So let me hearken to the learned   as they tell me, Know
  thou   this prayer of the Faith   if one prays, ever is it granted.
And I, who am Thy poor handmaiden   one burdened with 85
  many troubles   I pray Thee, lighten them   O Lord, do thou
  unburden me.
I pray to Thee in haste   as to matters of which I cannot
  judge   do Thou bring to me every happiness   mayest Thou
  deliver me from evil.
O Lord, fulfil for me matters   which I cannot accomplish   nor
  can I think of even one of them   that they shall come to pass.
Lord, do thou cause me to rejoice   bring the good near to
  me   remove the evil from me   so that I do not meet with it.
Keep me safe in this world   among the number of the Faithful   that when I die I may go to Paradise   the abiding-place
  of the Saved.
I have composed this poem   amid trouble and grief   by Thy 90
  dispensation, O Judge   and by Thy decrees, All High.
I have composed it in sickness   my heart is without understanding   read it, O true believers   that you may follow the
  true path.
And the reason for composing   is not poesy nor minstrelsy   I
  have a young innocent child   and I wish to instruct her.
And I desire to warn her   that mayhap she shall realize   and
  follow the Lord God   together with her man.

Read, all you women   so that you may understand   that you
  may bear no blame   in the presence of God the Highest.
Read, you who are sprouts of wheat   obey your menfolk   so 95
  that you may not be touched by the sorrows   of the after-life
  and of this.
She who obeys her husband   hers are honour and charm
  wherever she shall go   her fame is published abroad.

Mwenye kutunga nudhumu   ni gharibu mwenye hamu   na
ubora wa ithimu   Rabbi tamghofiriya.

THE SAIYIDS

Serjeant, writing on the Saiyids of Hadramawt,[1] states: 'Saiyid writers say that the great emigration to Africa took place in the 14th/8th and 15th/9th centuries . . . Saiyids entered Africa . . . at Mogadisho and points on the Kenya coast—early Swahili poetry shows the influence of Hadrami verse-forms, and in some cases is actually composed by Hadrami Saiyids.'

These are the Saiyids in descent from Sheikh Abu Bakr b. Salim, whose birth-place was Tarim in Hadramawt and who died in A.D. 1584. In the introduction to his edition of *al-Inkishafi*,[2] Hichens has provided a genealogy based upon information from the late Sir Mbarak Ali Hinawy of Mombasa showing that at least four poets whose work is at least partially extant were descended from Sheikh Abu Bakr. Of these, Saiyid Aidarus, great-grandson of Sheikh Abu Bakr, was the author of *al-Ham-ziyah*, written in 1749, an extremely difficult poem to translate; Saiyid Abdallah b. Ali b. Nasir, who lived *c*. A.D. 1720–1820, came of the line of Sheikh Abu Bakr's son Ali, whose great-great-grandson, Ali b. Nasir, was Saiyid Abdallah's father. Saiyid Abdallah is the author of the *Utendi wa Inkishafi* (*al-Inkishafi*) and of the *Takhmis ya Liyongo* (see Chapter 4, p. 188). Another poet descending from the line of Sheikh Abu Bakr's other son, Husein, is Saiyid Abu Bakr b. Abd al-Rahman, known popularly to the Swahilis as Saiyid Mansab; he was born at Lamu *c*. A.D. 1828–9, studied law and theology at Mecca as a pupil of Saiyid Ahmad Dahlan, and continued his studies in Hadramawt under Saiyid Aidarus b. Umar al-Habshi and Saiyid Abd al-Rahman b. Muhammad al-Mashur. Saiyid Mansab wrote several homiletic poems of which at least ten are extant. And finally, Saiyid Sheikhan b. Ahmad b. Abu Bakr al-Husein is the author of a long homiletic poem upon the due observance of Islam, composed in A.D. 1895, in which the author states that the poem was revealed to him in a dream by his ancestor, Saiyid Abu Bakr.

[1] R. B. Serjeant, *The Saiyids of Hadramawt*, Inaugural Lecture, School of Oriental and African Studies, University of London, 1957, p. 24.
[2] William Hichens, *al-Inkishafi*, London, Sheldon Press, 1939.

She who composed this poem   is one lonely and sorrowful   and the greatest of her sins   Lord, Thou wilt her
forgive.

The poem most familiar to scholars of Swahili is probably Saiyid Abdallah's *Utendi wa Inkishafi*, not least because it has been well edited by Hichens[1] and for some years was the only Swahili poem provided with a complete translation, notes, and glossary for non-Swahili readers. Whether this poem should in fact be regarded as *primus inter pares* is doubtful, for even Hichens, generous as he was in his estimate of the poem, wrote in his Foreword:

This work, holding so eminent a position in the field of Swahili literature, not unnaturally came early to the notice of European scholars, who, though not without some misconceptions, were disposed to assess it 'as a great, if not the greatest, religious classic of the race'. That view might now be modified in some degree by the claims of other great compositions which have more recently come to light, though not in a manner which would depose the Inkishafi from a place in the forefront of Swahili classical literature.[2]

The early attention given to *al-Inkishafi* by European scholars can be explained without primary reference to the merit of the work. One would hesitate to use the word 'great' in reference to any Swahili poem, while not denying the considerable merit that poems like *al-Inkishafi* most certainly possess. As more Swahili poems come to light one is able to make comparisons that were denied to earlier European scholars, and the most that can be said of *Inkishafi* is that it is a very good example of poems of its kind. This is not to deny the esteem in which the work has been regarded by Swahilis. It is a mistake to suppose that even Swahili scholars were ever in the position to make a critical appraisal of the whole corpus of Swahili poems. They valued those poems in their possession and could be uncritical in some instances. *Al-Inkishafi* was rightly esteemed by the people with the most influence and perhaps with the best judgement, but there is no reason to suppose that it was the only poem of its kind that was valued by the leaders of Swahili religious life.

Even so, Hichens is justified in quoting Sir Mbarak Ali Hinawy who wrote:[3] 'The leading Muslim theologians in East Africa have greatly valued the poem; and it was the practice of some not

---

[1] Loc. cit.   [2] pp. 8–9.   [3] p. 8.

only to memorize the whole of it, but to carry copies of it with them.' It should be added that *al-Inkishafi* is not the only poem which the theologians and copyists knew by heart. At the turn of the century, about A.D. 1900, the well-known poets and copyists, Muhammad Kijuma and Mwalimu Sikujua, were both able to repeat by heart more than one Swahili poem from earlier times.

To omit the *Inkishafi* from any survey of traditional Swahili poetry would be indefensible, but by including it with other comparable poems it may be possible to see the poem in better perspective than before.

Utendi wa Inkishafi

This poem is a homiletic on the inevitability of death, the transitoriness of even the richest forms of life, and a warning to the human soul against the danger of eternal damnation. Hichens calls it 'a soliloquy of mortal defection', but this is hardly so, for the poet speaks well of those who have died. The particular feature distinguishing this poem from others of its kind is the application of the homily to the downfall of the sultanate of Pate. Other poems of this kind lack any illustration of the doctrine expounded. That is why so often they seem to us so dull; undiluted doctrine without reference to actual events makes dull reading, though the Swahilis seem to have preferred it that way. *Al-Inkishafi* was written after Pate had fallen to ruin and at a time when the once-lively houses still stood, desolate and void. The ruins of Pate were evidence of the truth of the poet's theme, the vanity of this transitory life. When the poem was written, probably between A.D. 1810–20, the Swahilis of Pate and Lamu could remember well some of the prosperity of Pate, the downfall of which served the poet as a moral to his homily.

The poet's uncle Talib, dying in 1755, would have lived to see the turbulent reign of the Patean sultan, Bwana Tamu Mtoto, when through political intrigue, sedition, and assassination the ancient sultanate fell to final disruption, to pass in 1814 into the control of the Mazrui governors of Mombasa, and thence, a few years later, under the rule and finally into the domain of the sultans of Zanzibar. As a youth the poet may have heard of the glories of Pate from his uncle and from his father Ali.

The title of the poem is given in verse 8 as *Inkishafi*, a derivative of the Arabic verbal *kashaf*, which means 'to uncover or examine'.

Hichens gives the interpretation 'he revealed himself to himself', and from this uses an English title for the poem, viz. *The Soul's Awakening*. This is not strictly a proper title for the poem. Hichens's translations from Swahili are usually too rhapsodical. Perhaps a better rendering would be simply 'self-examination'. The poet looks into his own heart, and addresses his heart and his soul.

The poem opens in the manner proper to all of the longer traditional Swahili verse, by setting forth the Attributes of Allah, with a prayer for the Holy Prophet, his Companions, and kindred. Then (in vv. 6–10) he explains the design of his work, to write a poem, likened to a string of pearls, whereby, from its regard, both he himself and all who heed his counsel may turn from sin to the good life. He then exhorts his heart to abandon the follies of mortal life, and mingling parable with exhortation reaches the climax of his theme in verses 33–54 where he depicts the glories of Pate, contrasting them with the pathos of its fall. In verses 65–77 he expounds on the penalties awaiting those who do not accept the counsel of righteousness, and he describes the punishments which await the sinful in the Seven Hells of Islam.

As Swahili poems usually open with formal invocations upon the Names and Praise of Allah and the Prophet, so it is customary for them to conclude with verses, bringing the work to its stated end, often with a prayer and frequently with the subscription of the author's name, coupled with a request to readers of the poem to correct errors, in doing which they shall be held blameless and praiseworthy. The *Inkishafi* does not conclude in this way, and it may be considered an unfinished work. Hichens is probably right in supposing that the last two verses are an interpolation. Of the seven degrees of the Muslim purgatory Saiyid Abdallah deals only with six; no mention is made of Saqar. It is difficult to suppose that the poet would have omitted a verse upon it from his scheme of the work. Upon that verse the final movement of his theme must have turned, in which would have been held forward the promised rewards of the righteous. The author expressed his purpose of 'weaving a rosary' and we may conclude, with Hichens, that his intention was to compose a homily of not less than ninety-nine verses, which is the number of the beads of the rosary of Islam, a number hallowed by its associations with the Exalted Names of Allah.

Hichens's description of the prosody of the poem is unacceptable. He regards the *utendi* verse-form as a later development from the long-measure verse and states that 'the verses are properly to be regarded as linked in pairs'. There is no evidence at all to show that the *utendi* verse-form was of late development, but rather the reverse. In shorter Swahili poems verses are often linked by various devices, but in the *tendi* this does not happen.

Utendi wa Inkishafi

Bismillahi naikadimu   hali ya kutunga hino nudhumu   na
ar-rahmani kiirasimu   basi ar-Rahemi nyuma ikaye.

Nataka himdi nitangulize   ili mdarisi asiulize   akamba
himdi uitusize   kapakaza illa isiyo nduye.

Ikisa himdi kutabalaji   ikituzagaa kama siraji   sala na
salamu kiidariji   tumwa Muhammadi tumsaliye.

Na alize thama banu Kinana   na sahaba wane wenye maana   tu-
salie wote ajmaina   sala na mbawazi ziwaaliye.

5 Allahumma Rabbi mkidhi haja   msalie Tumwa aliyekuja   na
tauhidiyo Mola wa waja   akatusomesha tafsiriye.

Kwimakwe kwisa kuzikamili   himdi na sala kaziratili   niya-
dhihirishe yangu makali   ambayo moyoni nikusudiye.

Makusudi yangu ya kudhamiri   nda kutunga koja kilida-
wiri   mivazi ya duri ikinawiri   mikinda ya lulu nyuma
nitiye.

Tatunga kifungo kwa kukisafi   nikipange lulu kulla tara-
fi   na ina nikite inkishafi   kiza cha dhunubu kinipukiye.

Kitamsi kiza cha ujuhali   nuru na mianga itadhalali   na
ambao kwamba ataamali   iwe toba yakwe aitubiye.

10 Kwimakwe kwisa dibaji yangu   penda kuuonya na moyo
wangu   upitwe na hawa ya ulimwengu   hila za rajimi ziu-
ghuriye.

The measure of each *kipande* in the *Inkishafi* is of eleven *mizani* or vocal syllables, a common measure in homiletic verse. The transliteration given below follows the Swahili-Arabic script as found in Hichens's edition, and it will be seen that it differs in many instances from the transliteration provided by Hichens. The translation avoids the turgid and rather bombastic style favoured by Hichens.

The Poem Inkishafi

I put first 'In the Name of God'   as I compose this poem   and I write 'The Merciful One'   and after that 'The Benign One'.

I want to put praise first   lest the curious ask   saying, Have you deprived us of the praising   and so spread a wrong that has no like?

Praise having been offered   illuminating us like a lamp   prayers and peace follow on   let us pray for the Prophet Muhammad.

And for his kinsfolk of the clan Qinan   and for his four named Companions   let us pray for them all together   may prayer and compassion leave their mark on them.

O my Lord Allah, Granter of requests   let us pray for the 5 Prophet who came   and who of Thy One-ness, O Lord of slaves   taught us the meaning.

When the full measure is complete   of setting in order prayer and praise   let me make clear my treatise   which I purpose in my heart.

My inner intention   is to make a necklace, entwining it   shining with large pearls   and to put little pearls at the end.

I will make a clasp by correcting it   arranging the pearls on every side   and let me call its name *Inkishafi*   so that the darkness of sins be withdrawn from me.

May the darkness of ignorance be effaced   and light and radiance give forth brightness   and whosoever reflects (on what I write)   let it be pardon to him who repents.

My preface is now ended   I wish to give counsel to my 10 heart   which is overcome by the lusts of the world   with the wiles of Satan which deceive.

Moyo wangu nini huzundukani   likughurielo hela ni nni   hunelezi nami kalibaini   liwapo na sura nisikataye.

Moyo wangu nini huitabiri   twambe u mwelevu wa kukhitari   huyui dunia ina ghururi   ndia za tatasi huzandamaye.

Hunu ulimwengu bahari tesi   una matumbawe na mangi maasi   aurakibuo juwa ni mwasi   kwa kulla khasara ukhasiriye.

Ni kama kisima kisicho ombe   kwenye mtapaa mwana wa ng'ombe   endao kwegema humta pembe   asipate katu kunwa maiye.

15 Au enga vumbi la muangaza   wakati wa yua likichupuza   mwenda kulegema akilisoza   asione kitu ukishishiye.

Au enga meto limetukapo   wakati wa yua lilinganapo   mwenye nyota hwamba ni mayi yapo   kayakimbilia akayatwaye.

Chenda akaona mwako wa yuwa   mai alotaka akayatuwa   asifidi yambo ila shakawa   ikawa mayuto yasimsiye.

Khasaisi zote na matakawo   shida na shakawa likupetewo   ni dunia siyo uipendawo   yenye dhuli nyingi na makataye.

Dunia ni jifa siikaribu   haipendi mtu ila kilabu   i hali gani ewe labibu   kuwania na mbwa hutukizwaye

20 Kwami ina illa ilio mbovu   ilikithiriye ungi welevu   ni kalifu mno kuta kiwavu   kupa watu ngeya ikithiriye.

Wangapi dunia waipitewo   wakataladhudhi kwa shani lawo   ikawasumbika zitala zawo   wakanguka zanda waziumiye.

Tandi la mauti likawakuta   wakauma zanda wa kuiyuta   na dunia yao ikawasuta   ichamba safari munipukiye.

Ichamba hayati ndio safari   yakomele tena ya kuusiri   bidhaa ya ndewo na takaburi   mtandile kwangu nishuhudiye.

O my heart, why dost thou not awake?   but what is it that
deceives thee?   Thou dost not explain to me for me to discern
it   if it have a countenance may I not reject it?

O my heart, why dost thou not explain it?   Let us say thou art
clever to discriminate   but knowest thou not that the world
is vanity?   Why dost thou follow its turmoiled paths?

This world is a raging sea   it has coral reefs and much insub-
ordination   who rides it knows it is a tyrant   responsible
for every loss.

It is like a well without a bottom   a place where the tossing
bull   who approaches it breaks his horns   without succeeding at all in drinking its water.

Or look at the dust in a ray of light   when the sun rises   if 15
one gets near to grasp it   he sees nothing he can hold on
to.

Or look at the mirage when it glistens   when the sun is at the
meridian   the thirsty one says, There is water   and runs to
take of it.

When he goes he finds only the sun's fire   (not) the water he
wants, so he rends himself   gaining nothing but trouble   and
so it is unceasing remorse for him.

All vices and hardships   the difficulties and troubles which you
have had   (they come from) this world which you love   with
its very base condition and its troubles.

The world is corrupt, cleave not unto it   it loves not man but
only the infidel   How does it come about that you, so able to
comprehend   should fight with dogs and be (thus) profaned?

For me it possesses only what is evil   it abounds in much cun- 20
ning   it is very fierce at striking a glancing blow   dealing
men a coup de grâce over and over again.

How many who have passed through this world   enjoying life
after their fashion   and (the world) upset their apple-cart (lit.
their deliberations)   and they fell only to gnaw the finger of
repentance?

The noose of death met up with them   and they gnawed their
fingers in remorse   and their world obliterated them   saying, Depart, keep away from me.

(The world) says, Get going, this is it   this is the end of further
tarrying   The merchandise of pride and arrogance   you
have dealt in it, I can witness.

Mvi wa manaya ukawafuma   akatumbukia katika nyama   nasi-
we mwatami mwenye kwatama   amwamba ni ani yalikuwaye.

25 Wakazisalimu umri zawo   hadimu ladhati achenda nawo   pasi
mkohozi akohowawo   au mwenye kwenda asiridhiye.

Zituko zingapi hutanabahi   ukanabihika hukunabihi   utaata
lini ya usafihi   nambia ukomo na usikiye.

Hiki ewe moyo kievu changu   hukengeuki nusuha yangu   huza
akherayo kwa ulimwengu   kuna hadawa mno ukhitariye.

Nisikia sana nikwambiapo   roho enga taa katika pepo   haizi-
wiliki izimikapo   sasa mi huona izimishiye.

Au enga moto kururumika   ulio weuni katika tuka   paka-
shuka wingu katika chaka   ukawa kuzima usiviviye.

30 Ewe moyo enda sijida yake   hela tafadhali unabihike   shetani
rajimi asikuteke   kesho kakuona kuwa kamaye.

Hunu ulimwengu uutakawo   emale ni lipi upendeawo   hauna
dawamu hudumu nawo   umilikishapo wautendaye.

Hakuwa mtume Sulaimani   maliki wa insi na ajinani   walim-
futeye ukamukhini   akiwa mwingine humtendaye.

Watoto wangapi uwawenewo   ukawayakini kupona kwawo   sasa nyumba za ti ziwatetewo   katika luhudi iwafundiye.

Uwene wangapi watu wakwasi   walo wakiwaa kama shama-
si   wa muluku zana za adharusi   dhahabu na fedha wakhi-
ziniye.

35 Malimwengu yote yatwatiile   na dunia yao iwaokele   wa-
chenda zitwa zao zilele   mato mafumbuzi wayafumbiye.

Wakimia mbinu na zao shingo   na nyuma na mbele ili miyongo   wakaapo pote ili zitengo   asikari jamu wawatandiye.

The arrow of death pierces them   (death) enters deep into their
mortal flesh   Don't let the wide-mouthed be so aghast   saying, Who is it? what has happened?

Rendering up their lives   the depriver of pleasure (death) walks 25
with them   without (so much as) a cougher who coughs   nor
one who from the Journey can refrain.

How many alarums were alerted   You were warned (but) you
were not ready   When will you stop this presumption?   Tell
me the end of it and listen.

By this my beard, O heart   thou art not converted by my
counsel   thou dost barter thy future life to the world   by
too much deception and you have chosen it.

Listen well to what I tell you   O soul, behold, a lantern in the
wind   nothing can prevent its being put out   at once you
see it has been extinguished.

Or look at the roaring fire   in the forest-glade in the thickets   a
cloud comes down in the hot season   and (the fire) is put
right out and you cannot revive it.

O heart, kneel prostrate before Him   Come then, please take 30
heed   lest the accursed Satan laugh at you   and tomorrow
see you even as he is himself.

This world that thou desirest   what is its good that you so
love   it has no eternal quality, it does not last   If thou
hadst dominion (over it) what wouldst thou do with it?

Was not the prophet Solomon   ruler of men and of jinns   yet
did not (earth) banish him and cheat him?   If it were another,
what then would (earth) do to him?

How many children (of earth) have you seen   and been certain
of their subsequent happiness   but now the houses of the
earth (i.e. graves) enfold them   in the sepulchre which en-
shrouds them?

How many rich men have you seen   who shone like the
sun   who had control of the weapons of war   and stored
up silver and gold?

All the world paid them homage   and their world was straight 35
ahead for them   they walked with heads held disdain-
fully   and eyes closed in scorn.

Swinging their arms and arching their necks   while behind and
in front crowds accompanied them   everywhere they live
there are seats of honour   and troops of soldiers attend them.

Nyumba zao mbake zikinawiri   kwa taa za kowa na za
sufuri   masiku yakele kama nahari   haiba na jaha iwazingiye.

Wapambiye sini ya kuteuwa   na kula kikombe kinaki-
shiwa   kati watiziye kuzi na kowa   katika mapambo
yanawiriye.

Zango za mapambo kwa taanusi   naapa kwa Mungu Mola
mkwasi   zali za msaji kwa abunusi   zitile sufufu zisitawiye.

40 Kumbi za msana ili kuvuma   na za masturi zikiterema   kwa
kele za waja na za khudama   furaha na nyemi zishitadiye.

Pindi walalapo kwa masindizi   wali na wakandi na wape-
pezi   na wake wapambe watumbuizi   wakitumbuiza
wasinyamaye.

Kwa maao mema ya kukhitari   juu la zitanda za majodori   na
mito kuwili ya akhadhari   kwa kazi ya pote wanakishiye.

Misutu mipinde wakapindiwa   juu la firasha kufunikawa   maji
ya marashi wakikukiwa   itiri na kaa waipashiyc.

Ukwasi ungapo na tafakhuri   wakanakiliwa ili safari   washu-
kiye nyumba za makaburi   fusi na fusize liwafusiye.

45 Sasa walaliye mji shubiri   pasipo zuliya wala jodori   ikawa
miwili kutaathari   dhiki ya kaburi iwakusiye.

Zitukuta zao hutawanyika   usaha na damu hawa itika   pua na
makanwa bombwe hushuka   haiba na sura zigeushiye.

Wasiriye wote kula kwa dudi   na kuwatafuna zao jisadi   na
mtwa na tungu huwafisidi   na nyoka na nge wawatatiye.

Nyuso memetefu zikasawidi   launi ya duba au kiradi   zitamazakiye zao juludi   mifupa na nyama ikukutiye.

Nyumba zao mbake ziwele tame   makinda ya popo iyu wengeme   husikii hisi wala ukeme   zitanda matandu walita-
ndiye.

Their lighted houses were aglow   with lamps of crystal and
    brass   the nights were as the day   beauty and honour sur-
    rounded them

They decorated (their houses) with choice porcelain   and every
    goblet was engraved   and in the midst they put crystal
    pitchers   amongst the decorations that glittered.

The rails for the decorations to please the eye   I swear by God
    the All-Wealthy   were of teak and of ebony   placed rank
    upon rank in order to look fine.

The mens' halls hummed with chatter   and the harem cham- 40
    bers rang out with laughter   with noise of talk from
    slaves and servants   merriment and shouts of joy waxed
    loud.

And while they lay down for rest   they had masseurs and fanners
            and gay-robed women, the minstrels   singing melo-
    dies ceaselessly.

On lovely couches well-chosen   upon beds of padded
    cushions   with pillows of green at head and foot   worked
    with braided skein.

Folded fabrics they arranged   above the divans to cover
    them   they were sprinkled with rose-water   attar and
    sandal-wood they anointed themselves with these.

Yet even though wealth has its boasting   they were taken on
    the great Journey   and descended to the mansions of the
    grave   where the crumbling earth demolished them.

Now they lie in a town of finger's span   with no fine curtains 45
    nor cushions   and their bodies are destroyed   for the con-
    straint of the grave has come upon them.

Their perspiration is at an end   the pus and the blood oozes out
    of them   maggots pass down through noses and mouths   the
    beauty and the countenances are transformed.

They have all become food for insects   who eat their bodies   the
    termites and the ants lay them waste   and the snake and the
    scorpion have them encoiled.

Their radiant faces are become dark-hued   the likeness of a bear
    or of a baboon   their skins are lacerated   their bones and
    flesh are shrivelled.

Their lighted mansions are uninhabited   the young of bats
    cling up above   you hear no whisperings nor shout-
    ings   spiders crawl over the beds.

H

50 Madaka ya nyumba ya zisahani   sasa walaliye wana wa
nyuni   bumu hukoroma kati nyumbani   zisiji na kotwe
waikaliye.

Wana wa zipungu wapende zango   na wana wa ndiwa humia
shingo   na kupija mbawa matongotongo   ziku na zitati
waliwashiye.

Nyumba kati zao huvuma mende   kumbi za msana hulia
ngende   yalifiye vumi makumi ya nde   kuwa mazibala yali-
siriye.

Ziwanda za nyumba ziwele mwitu   ungi wa matuka na kutu-
kutu   milango ya ndia yatisha mtu   kwa kete na kiza kili-
fundiye.

Kwamba husadiki hwamba mbwongo   enda nyumba zao
uzinde shingo   ukita hwitikwi ila ni mwango   sauti ya mtu
itindishiye.

55 Moyo huyatasa kunabihika   zituko zingapo huyaidhika   hata
masikizi ya kupulika   naona kwa haya yafuatiye.

Sasa moyo pako tauza nawe   nelezato sana nami nelewe   wa
wapi wazazi wakuzaawe   nambia walipo kawamkiye.

U wapi Ali bin Nasiri   na muwamu wake Abubakari   mwinyi
Idarusi na Muhudhari   wendelepi kuwe mbonya ndiaye.

Mimi nakwambia nipulikiza   watezewe nyumba za jizajiza   zi-
sizo muanga na muwangaza   ndio mashukio walishukiye.

Wapi wa Kiungu wayaza kumbi   na mashekhe mema wake
Sarambi   walaliye nyumba za vumbivumbi   ziunda zamiti
ziwaaliye.

60 Wa wapi ziuli wa Pate Yunga   wenye nyuso ali zenye mianga   wangiziye nyumba za tangatanga   daula na ezi
iwaushiye.

Kwali na mabwana na mawaziri   wenda na makundi ya asikari   watamiwe na nti za makaburi   pingu za mauti
ziwafundiye.

Kwali na makadhi wamua haki   wahakiki zuo wakiha-
kiki   waongoza watu njema tariki   wasiwe kwa wote
waitishiye.

The wall-niches for porcelain in the houses   are now the resting- 50
place for nestlings   owls hoot within the house   mannikin
birds and ducks dwell within.

Young vultures perch on the rails   and young doves arch their
necks   and flap their wings in lazy fashion   wild pigeons
and swallows have built there.

In the houses the cockroach rustles   the cricket calls in the mens'
halls·   stilled is the hum in the ante-rooms   for silence and
darkness encloses all.

The courtyards are overgrown with bush   with lots of weeds
and liana   people fear the outside doors   for silence and
darkness cover them.

If you do not believe and say it is a lie   go to their houses and
turn your neck   if you call you get no reply but an echo   the
voice of men has come to an end.

O heart, you have not yet understood   when alarums come, are 55
you not perturbed?   yet you have ears to hear   I consider,
for these matters which follow.

So now, my heart, for your part I will ask you also   explain to
me entirely so that I can understand   Where are the parents
who bore you?   tell me where they are, that I may greet them.

Where now is Ali b. Nasir   and his brother-in-law Abu
Bakr   and Sharifs Aidarus and Muhadhar?   where did they
go yonder?   show me the way they went.

I tell you so listen to me   they have been made mock of in the
darkest of mansions   where there is no light nor brightness   these are the resting-places to which they have descended.

Where is Kiungu and those who filled the halls?   and the good
Shaikhs of Sarambi?   they sleep in the mansions of the
dust   the grave-boards strain hard upon them.

Where are the brave men of Pate sultanate   men of noble and 60
shining mien?   they have been forced into the mansions of
the eternal sands   sovereignty and might have been removed
from them.

There were lords and viziers   who went with troops of soldiery   wide-yawning graves opened up for them   the fetters
of death enshackled them.

There were judges, dispensers of justice   students of books who
proved things   leaders of people in the right paths   yet they
were called and all have answered.

Aimi wa wapi wake zidiwa   zituzo za mato wasiza ngowa   wasiriye wote kuwa mahuwa   sasa ni waushi waliushiye.

Moyo ya kwambia ya watu sawo   kalamu ya Mungu iwape-
tewo   nawe wa yakini kuwa kamawo   au una yako uya-
shishiye.

65 Moyo taadabu sipeketeke   ata ya jauri haki ushike   wendo
wachokoka nawe wokoke   moto wa jahimu usikutwaye.

Yua siku ya nti kubadiliwa   na mbingu sabaa zikageuwa   uka-
telelezwa mwezi na juwa   hari na harara zisitusiye.

Siku ya maini ndani kuwaka   na paa za watu kupapatuka   ukim-
biliepi pa kukushika   mbonya malijaa nitagmiye.

Tafakari siku ya kwima kondo   ya kuaridhiwa kula kiten-
do   pindi madhulumu atapo ondo   achamba ya Rabbi
namua naye.

Namua na huyo menidhilimu   kwa hukumu yako iliyo nyu-
mu   Mungu Jabari akahukumu   amtendeleo amlipiye.

70 Na malipwa yao wadhilimuwa   si dhahabu timbe si ya kufu-
wa   fedha hawatwai na wangapowa   ila hasanati ni malip-
waye.

Aso hasanati wala thawabu   hufungwa kitaya kama rika-
bu   akatwekwa dhambi za maghusubu   akambiwa haya
mtukuliye.

Moyo tafakari na Jahanamu   wenye silisia na azmamu   pindi
ya dayani akiukimu   unene labeka niitishiye.

Uye ukivuma na kuta panda   ukita sauti kama ya punda   mjani
akwepe sura za yonda   ndimi na ziyali zimtatiye.

Kuna na hawiya pulika sana   ni moto mkali hau makina   asi
angiapo hula kitana   huona pumuzi zimsiziye.

75 Moto wa sairi ufahamuto   ni moto mkali katika nyoto   ni
mngi wa moshi na mitukuto   majoka na pili waikaliye.

Ah me, where are the dove-like women   balm for the eyes,
    soothers of passion?   they are all gone and departed   now
    they have gone and faded right away.

O heart, these things of men I state   the Pen of God has written
    their fate (lit. got them)   and you, for certain, will be even as
    they   unless you have your own (belief, Islam) to which you
    hold fast.

O heart, beware, be not a firebrand   abandon false pride, hold 65
    to the right   your friends are saved, so be thou saved also   lest
    the fire of Hell take you.

Know that earth's day shall be changed   and the seven heavens
    will be moved from their place   the moon will be stilled and
    the sun   but fire and heat will not cease from us.

The day of the burning spleens inwardly   and people's roofs
    being torn off,   where will you flee for succour?   show
    me a refuge that I can depend on it as well.

Consider the day when the multitudes shall stand   for every
    deed to be revealed   the time when the oppressed shall bend
    the knee   saying, O Lord, judge between him and me.

Judge me, for this man has oppressed me   by your judgement
    which is strict   and God the All-Powerful will judge   As he
    did him ill, so shall he pay.

The recompense for them who are oppressed   is not the nugget- 70
    gold nor washed gold   they take no money though they be
    given it   in nought but virtue is their payment.

And he who has neither merit nor reward   is fastened by the
    jaw like unto a horse   and is made to carry the sins of the
    oppressed   and is told, Come on, carry them for him.

O heart, take thought of Jahannam   with its chains and
    ropings   when the Judge doth proclaim to it   it says, I am
    here, let me give forth answering cry.

Cometh the trumpet's fearsome blast   sounding like the voice
    of an ass   the sinner cringes, with the face of an ape   the fire
    and the flames engulf him.

Then there is Hawiya, listen hard   it is a fierce fire, it has no
    repose   when the rebel enters it he tastes conflict   he finds
    his breath fail him.

The fire of Sairi, understand it well   it is a fierce fire in 75
    flames   there is much smoke and bubbling   serpents and
    pythons dwell there.

Na moto wa ladha nao pulika   moto ukitiwa mara huwaka   huona manofu yakikwambuka   waona ziungo ziungushiye.

Fahamia tena sio Hutama   motowe muwashi na kungu-
ruma   huvunda mifupa hupisha nyama   bongo na
wasakha limshushiye.

Sasa takhitimu tatia tama   atakofuata na kuyandama   tapata
khatima na mwisho mwema   Rabbi twakuomba tujaaliye.

Rabbi mrahamu mwenye kutunga   namezokhitimu mja
malenga   Sala na salamu ni zao kinga   Rabbi takabali
ziwashukiye.

SAIYID MANSAB

Saiyid Abu Bakr b. Abd al-Rahman, of Lamu, is known popularly as Saiyid Mansab, which strictly is a title and not a name.
He wrote a number of adaptations in Swahili verse of Arabic
works of theology and law. According to Sir Mbarak Ali Hinawy,
Saiyid Mansab asked the Liwali of Lamu, Abdallah b. Hemedi, to
arrange for the publication of a collection of his verses. The
Liwali asked an Indian merchant, one Jaffer Dewji, to take the
manuscripts for this purpose to Bombay. The merchant later
reported that all the manuscripts had been lost at sea. There are
probably only about ten copies of work by Saiyid Mansab extant,
that is, of separate poems, and these copies are said to have been
made from the originals before the latter were sent to India.

Saiyid Mansab was appointed Kadhi at Zanzibar by the Sultan
Saiyid Majid, but returned to Lamu after the death of the Sultan.
He was later appointed Kadhi at Lamu by the Sultan Saiyid
Barghash. He died at Lamu on 20 Shaaban, A.H. 1340/18 March,
A.D. 1922.

Perhaps the most interesting of Saiyid Mansab's Swahili poems
is his abridged maulid called in Swahili *Maulid Barzanji*. Sir
Mbarak Ali Hinawy, while still Liwali of Mombasa, allowed me
to make a photostat copy of this work in 1950.

And the fire of Ladha, also, listen   if cast in that fire at once you
burn   you find that lumps of flesh come off   you see your
joints split apart.

Know again about this same Hutama   its glowing fire with its
roaring   it breaks the bones, it rives the flesh   the brains
and pus gush out.

Now I will end, now I put the ending   he who follows and
attends these words   shall gain at length a good end   O
Lord, we pray Thee, grant us this.

O Lord, bless him who is the composer (of this poem)   and he
who has finished (these verses is) a humble bard   Prayer and
peace be their safeguards (who read them)   O Lord, let thy
favour come down to them.

Maulid Barzanji

The popularity of the *Maulid Barzanji* among the Muslims of
East Africa has been noted by Dale, who wrote as follows:[1] 'One
of the most popular books in Zanzibar is a book called Maulid
Barzanji, a kind of Gospel of the nativity of Muhammad. . . .
Amongst its readers are the principal Kadhi and the leader of
prayers in the principal mosque'.

During the month of Rabi al-Awwal, when the birthday of the
Prophet is celebrated, and on other days, it is customary for the
Qur'ān and extracts from the *Maulid Barzanji* to be read in private
houses as well as in mosques. In Zanzibar this has become a
traditional procedure.[2] The *Maulid* is read most frequently in
Arabic and in its full form, but sometimes also in the abridged
Arabic version and in the version by Saiyid Mansab in Swahili.

Brockelmann[3] mentions an abridged Arabic version, *Muhtasar
Maulid al-B.*, found in Tunis. Ja'far b. Hassan b. Abd al-Karim b.
Muhammad al-Hadim b. Zain al-Abidin al-Barzanji al-Madani
was born in Medina in the year A.H. 1101/A.D. 1690, and was
Preacher at the Prophet's Mosque at the same place. He was a
mufti in Muslim law according to the Shafi rite. He died in the
year A.H. 1179/A.D. 1766.

Snouck Hurgronje has commented[4] upon the popularity of a

[1] G. Dale, *The Peoples of Zanzibar*, London, 1920, p. 65.
[2] *Zanzibar Gazette*, News Suppl., xlii (1933), p. 159.
[3] Brockelmann, *Geschichte der arabischen Litteratur*, Suppl. 11 (1938), pp. 517–18.
[4] C. Snouck Hurgronje, *The Achehnese*, vol. i, p. 212, Leydem, 1906.

collection of *maulids* both at Mecca and throughout the whole Indian coastal regions. He reported that this collection was published in a single volume handsomely lithographed at Cairo by Hasan at-Tochi Ahmad, and that this volume contained the Maulid by Ja'far al-Barzanji, written in verse.

Although the full Arabic version is known in East Africa, the abridged version is more commonly used. According to Sir Mbarak Ali Hinawy, this was the work of Barzanji's grandson, Zain al-Abidin b. Muhammad al-Hadi, and is the version upon which Saiyid Mansab based his own poem.

In describing the contents of the full Arabic version, Dale writes as follows :[1]

Great wonders appeared at the Prophet's birth. Crosses were broken, there was a miraculous light which flashed from Arabia and illuminated the Palace of the Persian king, and the sacred fire of the Zoroastrians was extinguished. When Halima was conveying Muhammad to her home, her ass, which owing to a famine had lingered and loitered on

---

Maulid Barzanji
Bismillahi l-rahmani l-rahim

Bismillahi l-rahmani 'ahmadu llaha musta'ini
Thumma salla 'llahu fi kulli hini   'ala Muhammadi
   Sayyidi 'umma.

1 Tayitia kati ya wasifuwo   henda hazipata tatuko zawo   illa
   sitayua kwa lugha yawo   tanena kiamu mutafahamu.

2 Tayatafsiri maulidina   nalikhitasiri ya Sayidana   naye
   mefupiza ya Maulana   Shekhe Barzanji mwenye karama.

3 Ni mukhutasari hunu jalili   nimewita ina la tafawuli   hitewa
   iksiri Rabbi kabuli   ngwa tutimiliza tumezosema.

4 Sondoe baraka huizidiza   tawasala kwao una ijaza   yatakond-
   okea ya kutukiza   wa khaswa fatiha mukizisoma.

5 Safidi mahala pakusomeya   ufanye uzuri nguo mpiya   na ndu-
   zo ipese kuhudhuriya   muwashe na taa mutabasama.

[1] G. Dale, op. cit., p. 65.

the way to Mecca, fully recovered its vigour owing to its precious burden, and completely outdistanced the asses of the other women who had accompanied Halima to Mecca. Halima had no need of a light in her house because of the light that streamed from the forehead of her foster-child.

It will be seen that these events are omitted in the abridged poem, but the central theme and the purpose of the poem remain the same as in Dale's description of Barzanji's work in Arabic.

Saiyid Mansab's poem consists of an introduction in Swahili of fourteen verses; these are followed by a verse of invocation in Arabic and in Swahili, then the poem proper of fifty-five verses is placed interlinearly with the Arabic verses; finally, there are eight Swahili verses to conclude the work. At the end, the copyist, Abdallah b. Rashidi b. Muhammad b. Rashid al-Mazrui, writes in Arabic to give his name and the date of writing. The measure is in eleven *mizani*. There is a chorus in which the faithful were expected to join.

The Maulid of Barzanji

In the Name of God the Merciful, the Compassionate

In the name of God the Merciful, I praise God
May God bless at all times   Muhammad the Lord of
    the people.

I will include myself among those who praise   so that I may 1
    follow in their steps   but I will not use their language   I will
    speak Kiamu and you will understand.
I will translate the story of the Birth   it is an abridgement con- 2
    cerning our Master   he (the writer) has shortened (the story)
    of our Lord   by the gifted Shaikh Barzanji.
This abridgement is an honoured work   and I have called it by 3
    the proper name   praying that God will make it accept-
    able   that He may fulfil what we have said.
Do not take away the blessing but increase it   for those who 4
    pray there is reward   all that you dislike will depart from
    you   and especially if you recite the fatiha.
Clear the place where the poem is recited   make it look pleasant 5
    with new cloths   and your brethren should be in atten-
    dance   light the lamps and you will be happy.

6 Kwamba muliopo pana sharifu   mpeni chetezo atie pefu   fatiha musome kwa utatufu   kisa muitoe yangu nudhuma.

7 Kwanda nda Mtume na nduze wote   pili nda sahaba tumwa yo yote   kisa mawalii walo popote   penye Barazanji na sisi nyuma.

8 Na faida zake za duniani   takaosomewa mwake nyumbani   kahati na baa hazimuoni   hepuliwa mawi kapowa mema.

9 Haingii mtu nyumba ya huyo   husuda fitina hepuwa nayo   na baraka nyingi watiliwayo   talipwa gharama mwaka mzima.

10 Hakungia meza wa kuandikiwa   huko kaburini kisailiwa   tafunza jawabu ya kumwokowa   iwe ni zitangu zilizo zema.

11 Tamvika nguo Mola mkwasi   za stibraki na za sandusi   ndizo afkhari ya malbusi   ende kiyongoya na kuisema.

12 Na kwa shurutize ya kusomewa   pamwe na Mtume hufufuliwa   malaki shadhidi pamoya huwa   wakafufuliwa wapindi nyama.

13 Kheri toa tamu hatta kahawa   udi na marashi ni kheri towa   wa khaswa wakati tumwa kuzawa   huwa tafawuli na taadhima.

14 Wallahi nambayo ya hashiyani   Sayduna Shata meyabaini   sikuzidi neno kangalieni   nimewata mangi sikuyasema.

Bismillah l-rahmani l-rahimi
Alhamdu lillahi l-ladhi kad aujada   min nurihi nuran bihi 'amma al-huda.

Kulla sifa njema ndake Moliwa   ambao kwamba ye umemuzowa   katika nuruye nuru metuwa   na kwa sababuye tuvuke 'amma.

1 Memurehemu ye wake Moliwa   pame na alize mezowavuwa   na sahaba zake walonakiwa   mwida kudhihiri yao nujuma.

2 Tumwa ni rehema yetu ziumbe   ni neema kuu kwetu iwembe   hushukia sote hata dhurumbe   fadhilize nyingi Mola karima.

If there is a Sharif where you are give him a thurible for him to 6
put incense in recite the *fatiha* in a proper manner and
then start on my composition.

First it is offered to the Prophet and all his kin secondly to the 7
Companions and to all other Prophets and then to the saints
wherever they may be where Barzanji is and we stand behind.

And the earthly benefits of this recital for him who has the 8
work read in the house evil and misfortune do not come to
him separate from evil things he receives the good.

Into that person's house no one will enter jealousy and discord 9
will be kept far from him and many blessings will be
granted for one complete year expenses will be paid.

Never will darkness enter in in the grave when he is being 10
interrogated he will be taught the answers that will save
him so that he will find lovely gardens.

God the infinite Giver will clothe him with silk garments of 11
finest quality these are proud dresses and he may go gaily
in them and speak of them also.

And by following the rules for the recital he will be raised from 12
the dead by the Prophet the angels will be there as witnesses they will be raised a new body.

It is better to offer something sweet or even coffee aloe wood 13
and rose water had better be sprinkled especially at the time
when the Birth takes place it serves as a good omen and a
gesture of respect.

By God what I say is right Saiyid and Shatwa have approved 14
it I have added nothing, look and see but I have omitted
many things.

In the Name of God the Merciful, the Compassionate
Praise be to God who created from His Light a Light with
which guidance was made general.
Every good praise be to God who has created Him He
has chosen a Light in His Light and because of Him
may we reach guidance.

May God bless Him giving mercy together with His family who 1
are saved and also his noble Companions as long as a star
appears.

The Prophet is our blessing, we mortals He is manifold help to 2
us everywhere He pours down upon all creatures the
great goodness of the Blessed God.

Kipokeo

Mola nushito kwa swalawati　kaburi ya Tumwa kwa dai-
mati　ishushe salamu ya yako dhati　kushuka kwa hizo
kuwe dawama.

3 Menena Moliwa kwa kulla mbeya　　　kuta la nuruye uwe
nabiyya　kipendi changu ni Muhammadiya　　tumwa
mtukufu mwenye makama.

4 Ni mukhuburiwa wa kulla siri　mwana wa mtindwa mwenye
fakhari　ni Abdullah mutatwahari　pango ya masitu mbwene tu mwema.

5 Namwita mtumwa wa Mutwalibi　kwa huyo ni abbi wa tumwa
bibi　naye mbwa hashimu mpe gharibi　wa kuulizwaye kwa
kulla ema.

6 Abdu Manafi ni jadi wawo　na hini nasabu kuyua hawo　ni
lazima yetu itupesewo　tumwa kumuyua baba na mama.

7 Mola memukhusu Mwana Amina　kwa kumpa radhi kwa kulla
hina　kuwa ndiye mama wa Nabiyyana　mefurahi kwayo
furaha tama.

8 Metukua mimba ya jauhari　pasina uzito pasina shari　kutu-
wili kwake kwali sururi　urefu wa muda hata kukona.

9 Usiku wa mimba yaliyoingiya　ya firdawsi jannati aliya　yali-
funguliwa milango piya　kwa ziniwa safi za tasnima.

10 Mimba ikitimu nyezi tisiya　　　kuzaliwa kwake mekuru-
biya　mwenye kutumwa metuyiliya　kutujazi sote majazi
mema.

11 Kupijani kiye walikingiya　siti Mariamu siti Asiya　alomi-
miniwa ukamingiya　uongofu ulio tama.

12 Hapo wakingiya Mwana kazaa　　　kwa barazi tumwa akiza-
gaa　kheri ya ziumbe mezotufaa　mezokuwa pweke kwa
kulla ema.

Kipokeo

Mola nushito . . .

13 Iwe mukhubiri wa kulla siri　salamu tukufu ndako kathiri　kipendo cha Mungu Tumwa Bashiri　hukushukia we nyingi
rehema.

Chorus

> God perfume with Thy blessings   the grave of the Prophet for ever   Of Thy free will bring down peace   that it may be so for all time.

His God has spoken to every man   that the Wall of His Light 3 should be the Prophet   my Beloved is Muhammad   the glorious Prophet who is my Agent.

He is the One informed of every secret   the last born of great 4 fame   it is Abd Al-Lahi who has been cleansed   in a cave of the forest I have seen only good.

I mention Abd al-Muttalib   for he was his paternal grand- 5 father   And he is of Hashim, give him the preference   he is asked for every good thing.

Abd Manaf is an ancestor   and to know his lineage   that is 6 something we should know   for the Prophet to know of His father and mother.

God gave permission to Lady Amina   by giving her blessings 7 all the time   to be the Mother of the Prophet   she is happy with a real happiness.

She conceived a precious jewel   with no heaviness nor mis- 8 hap   her waiting for the Birth was cause of happiness   the length of the time until it was completed.

On the night of her conception   the noble paradise of Firdaw- 9 si   its gates were opened wide also   and became as delight- ful as a watering-place.

When the nine months were fulfilled   and His birth was at 10 hand   the Sent One came to us   to fill us with all His blessings.

There they came entering   Lady Mariamu and Lady Asiya   to 11 him was outpoured   all glory in its completeness.

And when they entered she delivered   with the pains and cries 12 of, O Prophet   the best of all creatures who have benefited us   He is unique in His goodness.

Chorus

> O God, perfume . . .

O One informed of every secret   let peace be yours abun- 13 dantly   the Beloved of God, Prophet and Messenger   much mercy descend upon you.

14 Uliposhushia mwezi dhahiri   zikasitamana zote kamari   siya-
muonapo mtu mzuri   uso wa furaha kama hashima.

15 Wewe yuwa ndiwe kamari   wewe ndiwe nuru yiu la nuri   wewe ni kimiya cha kulla kheri   wewe ndiwe taa ya nyoyo
njema.

16 Kijuju kikavu na baa mwitu   zataka nusura kwa tumwa
wetu   na take nusura kwa kulla mtu   hapakuzawani kwa
kwanda kwema.

17 Kwa kuzawa huku tumwa nabiyya   tumetawasali ngwa tuepu-
liya   fitina ya dini na ya duniya   ngwa tubadiliya kwa kulla
ema.

18 Hapana asili iteketewo   ila kwa hini ya wayukuwo   Hasani
Huseni bwana ni wawo   sala na salamu ndenu daima.

19 Na kuzawa kwake ukutayapo   sunna kusimama kwa wali-
opo   ndipo adabuye itimiapo   mezokokoteza kulla alama.

20 Malaki mbinguni walitunguwa   kwa kumrehemu akichemuwa   baada himda ya msafiwa   kamwazizisha mwenye
adhama.

21 Yalotupa ada waliyaona   siku ya kuzaa ni mangi sana   kuwa
ni msinji wa hino dina   ukawika kwayo na kusimama.

22 Na kuzawa kwake kuwiye Makka   alohui nyoyo zikahuika   nti
mukhtari yenye baraka   kampendelea hapo Alima.

23 Ina la sharafu lenye jamali   bibiye memwita kwa tafawuli   awe
Mahmuudu kwa kulla hali   kwa ziumbe pia awe ni mwema.

24 Mola wa ziumbe memtendeya   aloyatumai bibiye piya   na
nafusi yangu ndakwe fidiya   yamuhimidiwa kwa kulla ema.

Kipokeo
Mola nushito . . .
25 Tumwa mtukufu alomwamsa   kwanda ni mamake sabaa
kisa   wamenena hayo wenye siyasa   litejemewalo waloli-
sema.

When the full moon shone down   all (other) moons were 14
extinguished   I have never seen so lovely a person   with
such a happy face of great dignity.

You are the sun and the moon   you are a light beyond all 15
light   you are the elixir of every blessing   you are indeed
the lamp of good hearts.

The dry stick and the evil in the forest   these need help from 16
our Prophet   help is needed by every man   for there was
no one born by beginning good.

By this Birth of the Prophet   we have prayed through Him to 17
be saved   from religious and secular discord   that we may
be changed for the better.

There is no purer ancestry   than this of your grandchild- 18
ren   Hasan and Husein, they are noble   blessings and peace
be yours for ever.

And when you mention His Birth   it is traditional for those 19
present to stand up   that is how good manners are enacted   it
is what every learned man has stipulated.

And the angels in Heaven spoke   by blessing Him as he 20
sneezed   after the praise of God by the Holy One   and the
Lord raised Him to high rank.

Those who made an offering saw (wonders)   on the day of the 21
Birth (the miracles) were many   that was the foundation of
this religion   by that it was strengthened and by that it survives.

And His Birth was at Mecca   He who created souls and gave 22
them life   the chosen place full of blessings   and the wise
One favoured Him there.

The noble Name which has its beauty   His grandfather called 23
Him it according to the prediction   that He should be Mah-
mud (praised) in every circumstance   and be good also to all
created beings.

The Lord of Creation has done for Him   all that his grand- 24
father hoped for   and my own self is faithfully His   who is
praised for every good quality.

Chorus

     O God, perfume . . .

The one who suckled the Holy Prophet   first it was His mother 25
for seven months   worthy men have related this   and what
they have said is certainly undeniable.

26 Kisa ni Thuweiba ni wa piliwe   na Mwana Halima ni wa tatuwe   na hini saada ikadiriwe   nda Sayidatina Mwana Halima.

27 Mwaka wane wake kenda Madina   yeye na mamakwe kuzuru Bwana   kulipa fadhili ndiyo mungwana   alokuanda zema hulipwa zema.

Kipokeo
     Mola nushito . . .
28 Tumwa mwombezi ngazi hukweya   hakuna daraja aso-ingiya   ukamili wake mesikiya   hata hakupata wa kum-wandama.

29 Kwa kiwiliwili na roho yake   mekwenda usiku na kanga zake   nyingi ajabu za Mola wake   mezoona sana na kuzisema.

30 Mepanda Buraki malaki tini   akinenda naye ali nyaoni alikita-raji daraja thani   yao masayidi awe imama.

31 Pindi ya baiti li-Makadasi   wakusuiyepo kenda upesi   akawa-salisha a-'azzu n-nasi   ngazi ya furaha kendea sama.

32 Kenda kuonyeshwa kuu ajabu   zipindi zitatu zake thawa-bu   kama khamsini ukihasibu   yake makusudi yawe timama.

33 Kadiri ya kaba kawusini   khitilafu nyingi wana zuoni   maana kuruba si iwazini   kumuona Mungu Mwenye adhama.

34 Yakumuona Mola mato ya kitwa   na moyoni mwakwe pasi ghalatwa   yahifadhi huyo ndiye wasitwa   kauli kawiyya wali-zosema.

35 Wallahi billahi alimwambiya   nena utakalo takutendeya   na usoyaomba takuzidiya   kwa mahaba yangu na kwa rehema.

Kipokeo
     Mola nushito . . .
36 Alimwamrisha Mola wake   pa kupajuriya mfano wake   naye kwa yandama amri yake   kangia Madina ni mahashuma.

Then the second is Thuweib   and Lady Halima is the third   and 26
this happiness was predestined   the Lord meant it for Lady
Halima.

And in the fourth year they went to Madina   He and His 27
mother to pay homage to the Lord   To repay goodness is a
gentlemanly act   for who has done you good deserves goodness.

Chorus

O God, perfume . . .

The Prophet and the Intercessor climbs the stairs (of rank)   there 28
is no height to which he does not climb   we have heard of
His completeness   and there has been no one to follow Him.

In His body and His spirit   by night He went in wakeful- 29
ness   many wonders of His God   He saw plainly and nar-
rated them.

He rode Buraq with the Angel beneath   with him under His stir- 30
rup He went   expecting to enter Heaven's second grade   that
He might be the Imam of the other prophets.

Up to the House of Jerusalem   where they intended to go 31
quickly   and He led the prayers of the mightiest people   the
ladder of happiness leading to the heavens.

He went to be shown great wonders   His reward for the three 32
times of prayer   is fiftyfold if you count it   so that his aim
be fully accomplished.

For the distance of a bow's length   there is much dispute on 33
this amongst the learned   because its distance is not certain   to have seen the Lord of Glory.

To have seen the Lord with the naked eye   and in His mind there 34
was no doubt   He is the Protector and the Mediator   that is
a confirmed word which they tell.

By God I swear He (God) told Him   Say what you want and I 35
will do it for you   and what you do not ask for I will grant
you   through my Love and my Mercy.

Chorus

O God, perfume . . .

His Lord ordained Him   to follow His example   and He 36
obeyed His command   and entered Madina firmly supported.

37 Kwa ulinganawe ukatanga'a   hunu islamu ondoa ba'a   kamtaka
   Mungu mwenye mafa'a   kanda msikiti msinji mwema.

Kipokeo
     Mola nushito . . .
38 Tumwa mustafa kheri Nabiyya   alipita watu sura tabiyya   hana
   mfano hata mmoya   memuweka pweke kwa kulla ema.

39 Ni mweupe mno mezongiliya   wekundu katiti wawaridiya   ki-
   moche wasitwa chalo tengeya   kama kinua shua nyingi neema.

40 Radhi ya mtume hutaipata   illa awe radhi Muumba nyota   na
   la maaswala ukilinieta   ataghadhibika hutamwe jema.

41 Nyingi khaswaiswi sitoziweza   kuzikumenganyazimenimeza
   kisa kwa mitume amemaliza   amekuwa mwiso ndiye khatima.

Kipokeo
42   Mola nushito . . .
   Na hapa nakoma makusudiwa   kutunga shairi Tumwa kuzawa   utukufu wake hawakupawa   Tumwa mirsali
   mutakadama.

43 Twakuomba Mola uteketewo   iwe mwenye mwiso uzenje-
   wawo   iwe mwenye mwando uandilizawo   ngwa tujazi
   naswi majaza mema.

44 Na tutumai tupe karimu   tupe naswi Mola yako karamu   kwa
   upaji wako ulio umu   ni zawadi zetu zisizokoma.

45 Utuneemeshe utuzoweze   zinyoke nafusi na shahawaze   zi-
   funguwe nyoyo uziongoze   zimezofunguka hawakwandama.

46 Tukikurejea tukubaliye   na ndia ya haki tuwafikiye   jamii ya
   dhambi tughoforiye   za kukusudia na za kutiya.

47 Utuneemeshe kulla afiya   ya kulla maradhi yalotekeya   tupe
   Mola tupe kumiminiya   umetuzoweza zake neema.

And through His example it spread   this Islam drives away 37
    evil   He prayed to God the Lord of Power   and started a
    mosque, a good foundation.

Chorus

    O God, perfume . . .

The chosen Prophet, best of them all   in countenance and con- 38
    duct he surpasses them all   He has no like, not one   He is
    placed alone for every good.

He is very fair of hue   with the slight redness of the rose   of 39
    medium height, the best of heights   and He is dewy with
    much grace.

The blessing of the Prophet you will not receive   unless the 40
    Creator of the stars be willing   and when you do a sinful
    deed   He will be angry and you will be kept far from good.

Many other matters I shall not be able (to tell)   for to relate 41
    them burdens me   but He is the last of the Prophets   and
    He has put an end to the line.

Chorus

    O God, perfume . . .

And now I bring my intention to an end   of composing a poem 42
    on the Birth of the Prophet   glory like His was not re-
    ceived   by any of the prophets who preceded Him.

We pray to Thee, O Holy One   Thou art the One who ends 43
    all things   Thou art the One who beginneth all things   Lord,
    reward us with Thy blessings.

And we trust that Thou wilt give us grace   give us also, O God, 44
    of Thy goodness   of Thy generous bounty which is in-
    finite   gifts without end.

And bless and train us   make straight our passionate lives   open 45
    our hearts and lead them aright   for locked are the hearts of
    those who do not follow Thee.

And if we come to Thee do Thou accept us   and lead us to the 46
    right path   and redeem all our sins   the sins of intention
    and the sins of ignorance.

And bless us all with good health   (free from) all diseases that 47
    have appeared   O God grant us, grant us an outpour-
    ing   Thou who hast accustomed us to Thy goodness.

48 Pambo la amani pamba Moliwa   uzivike nyoyo kwa kuzu-
    nguwa   kwa nuru ya pambo zinawiriwa   saa nda suudi iki-
    tuandama.

49 Na kwa dini zetu tuthubutishe   kwa yakini yako utukawi-
    she   tuyachayo yote usituegeshe   twayayua yako hapo
    kiama.

50 Kheri ya ziumbe kituombeya   jamii maovu hutuepukiya   janati
    adni tutaingiya   twekewe zitaka za watu wema.

51 Aloijirisha neema hini   mshukuru Rabbi umuawini   umjaaliye
    yuu na tini   firasha kabuli yatakusema.

52 Walotuajiza utatujibu   tukikuomba we Mola wahabu   husunu
    khatima twaitulubu   ulotuajiza tujibu hima.

53 Sala na salamu ya Maulana   imezotakata nda Sayidana   mwo-
    mbezi wetu dunia dina   kheri ya ziumbe mwonya mwema.

54 Na alize wote na sahabaze   mwida kusukika miti tanduze   miti
    nyumunyumu itezetcze   pepo ya mmande pindi kuvuma.

55 Tamma maulidi kuyafasiri   Mungu na tueneze kwa kulla
    kheri   ametuepulia na kulla shari   ngwa tuhasinisha yetu
    khatima.

1 Utughoforiye dhunubi piya   za kukusudia na za kutiya   na
    baba na mama ndugu namoya   na muuminina na isilama.

2 Tayilinda Mola kukushiriki   kupisa moyoni au nutuki   kuwa
    la kasidi au sitaki   tuhifadhi nayo na kutwe jema.

3 Turehemu Mola zamani hizi   wapenda adui lakutukhizi   nasi
    kuondoa hatwawezi   ishushe muweza yako neema.

4 Epue fitina ni kama hini   dini na dunia ziko zamani   kama tulo
    hapo mahasharini   ngwa tuokoa Mola sote salama.

5 Tarehe Hijira kumuwaghamu   ni thalatha mia tisia amu   na
    nyaka alifu za maalumu   na thani Rabii kuzawa Tumwa.

O Lord adorn us with the embellishment of peace   and cover our
hearts with Thy protection   with the light of Thy embellishment they shine   happy is the home where peace follows with us.

And make us firm in our religion   with Thy certainty make us 49
more sure   keep us away from all that we fear   we know
that they are there on the Day of Resurrection.

The best of all mortals shall plead for us   for all evils to be kept 50
from us   we shall enter the gardens of Eden   and gain a
place amongst the good people.

He who obtains for us this bounty   thank God for Him, the 51
Helper   and grant Him in either this or the next world   a
good resting-place, say we.

Thou wilt answer as Thou hast told us   when we pray to Thee, 52
Beloved Lord   we long for a goodly ending   grant quickly
our prayers as Thou hast said.

The prayer and peace of our Lord   be upon our pure Mas- 53
ter   our Intercessor in this world and the next   the best of
all creatures, our guide to what things are good.

And to all His kin and His Companions   as long as the branches 54
of the trees are bent   and the stretched trees sway   while
the east wind blows.

This is the end of translating the story of the Birth   may God 55
grant us all good things   He has kept us from evil   may He
give us a good ending.

Redeem us also from all sins   both those of intention and those 1
of ignorance   our father and mother and brothers also   and
all the believers in Islam.

I will guard myself, O Lord, against associating Thee   either 2
in my heart or by word   either deliberately or involun-
tarily   protect and guard us from such evil.

Have mercy on us, Lord, in this our day   our enemies love what 3
distresses us   and we are unable to drive them away   so
bring down, Almighty, Thy grace.

Take away strife of this sort   religion and the world are of old 4
time   as though we are now at the Resurrection Day   may
the Lord save us all and grant us peace.

And the date of the Hijra by counting   is three hundred and 5
nine years   and a thousand known years   of Rabii-i-Thani
from the Birth of the Prophet.

6 Nalo khitasiri na kufaisiri   mimi Mansabu ali fakiri   wa
  mdirahmani li-mashuhuri   ali Huseini bunu Salima.

7 Idadi za baiti za arabiya   ni arobaini pamwe tisiya   kazidiza
  sita pakuzaliya   wala siazabi aliosema.

8 Nimetafusiri moya kwa moya   na muda shuruti nimezitiya   na
  mwiso ukuu kuyangaliya   lulu kwa dhahabu ndiyo khatima.

Kad katabahu bi kulam al-fakiri ar-rajij afuu mawlahu Abdallah
b. Rashidi b. Muhammad b. Rashid al-Mazrui bi yadihi. Tarehe
Hadi 2, 1311.

ACROSTIC POEMS

    An essential part of Muslim religious education is the teaching
of Arabic so that believers may be able to read the Qur'ān. The
composition of acrostic poems in which the Arabic alphabet provided the framework, as it were, of the poem may well have had
a utilitarian purpose, quite apart from the poet's intention to
amuse or to exercise his skill.
    The best exponent of this type of verse was a member of a
well-known family of Saiyids in southern Arabia, Saiyid Umar b.
Amin b. Umar b. Amin b. Nasir al-Ahdal, who was Kadhi
of Siu on the East African coast about A.D. 1856 and who
left a number of poems on religious themes. His poem known as
Wajiwaji, for instance, is an acrostic in *takhmis* verse-form, and is
presented in our next chapter (pp. 192–201).
    Using the *utendi* verse-form rhyming *aaab* he wrote a poem, the
title of which is given in the last verse, viz. *ya dura mandhuma*, a
Swahili rendering of the Arabic words al-Durr al-Manzum, or
'Strung Pearls'. Such a title is frequent in Arabian literature, for
the Arabs liken the verses of a poem to strung pearls, and prose

---

Dura Mandhuma

1   Alifu   ا Andika mwandishi khati utuze
                   ا Isimu ya Mola utangulize
                   ا Utie nukuta na irabuze
                     Wasiilahini wenya kusoma.

And he who has abridged and translated this   it is I, Mansab, 6
  God's pauper   son of Abdul Rahman the famous   descending from Husein son of Salim.
The total number of verses in Arabic   is nine and forty   and 7
  six have been added to the story of the Birth   nor is it untrue
  what he has said.
I have translated it literally   and I have followed certain con- 8
  ventions   and when at the end I look at its length   pearls
  with gold indeed is its end.

Written by the pen of the pauper who hopes for the pardon of
his Lord, Abdallah b. Rashidi b. Muhammad b. Rashid el-Mazrui,
with his hands, Date, Thal-ka-adi 1311.

---

they liken to unstrung pearls. The manuscript copy which formed
the basis of the following transliteration is pasted on two pieces
of cardboard and was written by Muhammad Kijuma, the copyist
and poet. Each verse is written as a single line and the poet takes
the Arabic alphabet as the basis for the beginning of each of the
first three *vipande* of a verse. This means that the first syllable of
these *vipande* begins with a sequent letter of the Arabic alphabet
together with the vowel-signs fathah, kisra, and damma respectively. The syllabic measure is eleven *mizani*.

In setting out the transliteration of this poem the *vipande* are
written as separate lines and the sequent Arabic letter has been
given, together with the Swahili name for the respective letter, in
order that the reader may see more clearly the device employed.
It is necessary to add that the orthography employed in standard
Swahili (which is the one adopted in the transliteration) ignores
the distinction between the sounds represented by certain Arabic
letters. It will be clear from the transliteration which letters these
are.

Strung Pearls

Write ye, scribe, and keep steady your writing   1
Preface it with the Name of God
And put the dots and vowels in place
That the readers may not find fault with it.

2   Bei   بَ Ba'ada ya ina kulibutadi
                  بِ Bijahi Rasuli tutahamadi

                  بُ Bushura ya pepo nasi tufidi
                       Mola atujaze majaza mema.

3   Tei   تَ Tauba ya mja akitubiya
                  تِ Tilika Rasuli ni kumsaliya

                  تُ Tubuni ziumbe hini duniya
                       Kesho siratini uwe salama.

4   Thei   ثَ Thawabu kiumbe akiitaka
                   ثِ Thiki moyo wako kutozunguka

                   ثُ Thubutisha ta'a yake Rabuka
                       Atakujaziwe majaza mema.

5   Jimu   جَ Jannati na'imu fi li-jinani
                   جِ Jini na insi waitamani

                   جُ Jumla ya watu hawaioni
                       Illa kwa ambao watenda zema.

6   Hhei   حَ Hapo mizani ikikunduwawa
                   حِ Hisabu za waja wakipimiwa

                   حُ Hoja haifai uyapotowa
                       Illa kwa amali kutakadama.

7   Khe   خَ Khasara nda mja alokhitari
                  خِ Khitiyari yake nyumba ya nari

                  خُ Khussu sa'a moya utafakari
                       Nyumba ya jannati na ya jahima.

8   Dali   دَ Dalili ya mja kitaka jana
                  دِ Dini ya Rasula hushika sana

                  دُ Dunia daniya akaiona
                       Kuwa kitu duni kisicho kima.

After starting with the Name   2
With honour let us praise the Prophet
That we may earn the happiness of Paradise
And God bestow upon us His blessings.

The repentance of a poor mortal, if he repents   3
Is to ask in prayer for the Prophet to be blessed
Repent ye, O created beings on this earth
So that tomorrow on the way to heaven you may be safe.

If a created being wishes for reward   4
Then steady your heart that it go not astray
Make sure of your obedience before the Lord
And He will give you abundantly of His blessings.

Plenty in the gardens of Paradise   5
Both spirits and mortals yearn for it
But a number of people will not see it
Only those who do good things.

When the scales are placed in readiness   6
To measure the actions of subject beings
No excuse is acceptable though it be advanced
But only preceding actions are taken into account.

A great loss is to the poor mortal who has chosen   7
Whose choice is the house of fire
Just set aside one hour in which to think
Of the house of Paradise as against that of Hell.

The sure sign of a mortal's desire for Paradise   8
Is that he observes meticulously the religion of the Prophet
And that he regards the world as something lowly
As a worthless thing without value.

9   Dhali   ذَ Dhahabu na fedha na wata-pamba
                 ذِ Dhihizini mwako sifanye umba

                 ذُ Dhulikari-nini alizokumba
                    Kisa mwiso wake kazisukuma.

10   Rei   رَ Raha ya dunia isikughuri
                 رِ Riba na maovu ukakithiri

                 رُ Roho itokapo ni mashahari
                    Wapija mayowe na kulalama.

11   Zei   زَ Zawadi ni zipi za kutufata
                 زِ Zilizali hizo hutazipita

                 زُ Zuhudi ya ta'a huyaieta
                    Mbona upumbeeo bunu Adama

12   Sini   سَ Safari ni nzito mwendo baidi
                 سِ Si ya mtu kwenda aso zawadi

                 سُ Sumbuko la ndia likishitadi
                    Nakuchea kuwa mtu wa nyuma.

13   Shini   شَ Sharia hunena aso thawabu
                 شِ Shida na mashaka yatamshibu

                 شُ Shufaa ya Tumwa li-mahabubu
                    Huwa mbali naye na kumwegema.

14   Sadi   صَ Sali la jihimu mambo mazito
                 صِ Siyaha na zite katika moto
                 صُ Sura uwakao kwa mivukuto
                    Hari mteu na kunguruma.

15   Thadi   ضَ Dhamirini mwako usisahawu
                 ضِ Dhiki za motoni udharawu

                 ضُ Dhurubu mithali kama hiyawu
                    Wadhurubio wote ulama.

Gold and silver and well-dressed women   9
Make no image of them in your mind
Alexander the Great had the monopoly of them
But in the end he put them aside.

Let not the pleasures of this world deceive you   10
Nor keep increasing evils and usury
When the soul comes into its own it is the Resurrection Day
You will cry out and appeal in vain.

What are the gifts that go with us?   11
The quakes of hell you will not avoid
You have not yet brought with you the detachment of obedience
Why are you so weak-minded, O child of Adam?

The journey is difficult and the way is long   12
It is not the journey for one without gifts
When the hardship of the road increases
I fear that you may be among the last.

The Law says that he who is not rewarded of God   13
Is sure to be met by difficulties and doubts
The intercession of the Beloved Prophet
Is far from him and cannot support him.

It is a dreadful thing to burn in hell-fire   14
The yelling and the groaning in the fire
The way it burns and is inflamed by blowing
And how it is bubbling and roaring.

In your inner thought do not forget   15
Or scorn the distress of hell-fire
Just think over it and make similitudes
Similitudes (of hell) which all learned men give.

16   Twei   ظَ Tabaki za moto pindi zichaka
                   ظِ Tini na majiwe yatapishika

                   ظُ Tumaa ni ipi wewe kokoka
                      Mbona upumbee bunu Adama.

17   Thwei   ظَ Dhalimu wa hapa ulimwenguni
                   ظِ Dhili ya 'arishi hakai tini

                   ظُ Dhuluma humpa kwenda motoni
                      Nyumba ya majoka kama milima.

18   'Aini   عَ Akirabu wengi waso mithali
                  عِ Idhimu motoni meno makali

                  عُ Usati za Mola wakiwasili
                    Huwanyang'anyia kwa kuwauma.

19   Ghaini   غَ Gharibu wambaye ambapo Mngu
                   غِ Ghibu nepukia matoni mwangu

                   غُ Ghururi potofu za ulimwengu
                    Na zikunusuru na Jahanama.

20   Fei   فَ Fahamia mambo nalokuwasa
                 فِ Fi li-isirari ukiyapisa

                 فُ Furaha za nyoyo ukiyafusa
                    Yeo siye mbee huna rehema.

21   Kafu   قَ Kalibi u nani upotezeye
                  قِ Kitali cha Mola uteuziye

                  قُ Kurubia ta'a ukakamiye
                    Ufie dinini mwake Hashima.

22   Kyafu   كَ Kamwe sikuoni kukiri uja
                  كِ Kiza cha johali ukapambaja

                  كُ Kulla amali mbi henda kungoja
                    Kheri tangulize amali njema.

When all the degrees of hell-fire are burning   16
The soil and the rocks beneath get burnt
What is your hope of escaping?
Why are you so negligent, O child of Adam?

The transgressor here in the world   17
Does not dwell under the shadow of the Throne
His transgression will send him into hell-fire
Into the house where snakes are piled up like mountains.

Plenty of scorpions without number   18
Large ones therein with sharpened teeth
When God's disobedient ones arrive there
The snakes will scramble to bite them.

What will you answer, O stranger   19
When God says, Disappear and get out of my sight
Let arrogance and worldly delusions
Save you from the fire of Hell?

Remember what I forbade you to do   20
But in private you did those very things
Following the pleasures of your heart
Now get away from me, there is no mercy for you.

O my heart, what art thou to go thus astray   21
Choosing to fight with thy Lord?
Get near to obedience and be hard at it
That you may die in the religion of the revered One.

I have never found you professing submittance   22
And you embrace rather the darkness of ignorance
Every evil action goes before to await your arrival
It is better that you should send forward your good deeds.

23   Lamu لَ Labuda moyowa nimekwambiya
                 لِ Likwangamizalo ni maasiya

                 لُ Ludhu billahi nakuusiya
                     Kesho siratini uwe salama.

24   Mimu مَ Mauti sidhani yana muhula
                مِ Milele ziumbe hufa ghafula

                مُ Muumini hapa chenda kilala
                    Sipambaukiwi nili mzima.

25   Nunu نَ Nawe siliwae ukaikuwa
                نِ Ni haki mauti yafaridhiwa

                نُ Hyumanyuma ta'a ukikutiwa
                    Ufie dinini mwake Hashima.

26   Wau وَ Wallahi billahi thama taalahi
              وِ Wisipo waadhi watinabahi
              وُ Wulati amri wake Illahi
                 Hukunyang'anyia kwako kuuma.

27   Hei هَ Hadi li-mudhili mwenye kwongowa
             هِ Hiba na 'atia tupe 'afuwa

             هُ Huda li-bushura alotongowa
                Kesho siratini tuwe salama.

28   Ya يَ Ya Rabi twaomba waume wake
            يِ Yiu la ghorofa ukatuweke

            يُ Yule afurahi yule ateke
              Tukitanaamu na kuterema.

29   Na aliyotunga bunu Amini
               'Aini na mimu rei mwisoni
               Nazo baiti ni thalathini
               Isimu ya Dura Mandhuma.

Perhaps, O my heart, I have told you   23
That what ruins you is your apostasy
Submit to God I solemnly charge you
That tomorrow on the way to Heaven you may be safe.

Do not think there is any time limit in death   24
Always created beings die with suddenness
A believer is he who thinks here when going to sleep
I will not see the dawn again alive.

Don't be forgetful and make yourself arrogant   25
Death is to be expected and is prescribed
Keep yourself by obedience when it meets you
That you may die in the religion of the revered One.

I swear, swear and swear by God   26
Unless you pay heed and act upon this advice
Those in power in the next world
Will scramble for you to hurt you.

O reformer, O vanquisher, who leads men in the way   27
Grant us gifts and rewards with forgiveness
He who leads us is Guidance Himself and Good News
That tomorrow we may be safe on the way to Heaven.

Both male and female we pray you, O God   28
Place us above the upper room
So that that one may rejoice and that one may laugh
That we may be at ease and rejoice.

He who has composed this is the son of Amin   29
'Aini and *mimu* with *rei* at the end
And the verses are thirty in number
And the name is Strung Pearls.

SWAHILI *TENDI* AND EAST AFRICAN HISTORY

Swahili poetry is itself a part of the history of East Africa in the sense that it reflects the contribution made by the Saiyids from southern Arabia and Hadramawt to the cultural and religious life of the Muslim community. It also enshrines a certain amount of oral tradition which, even when it is not founded on historical happenings that can be proved to have taken place (as in the tradition of Liyongo), is part of the cultural heritage. The poetry has historical implications. Has it anything more direct to offer the historian? Are there any poems dealing with events in East Africa, supplementing historical evidence that the historian may acquire from other sources?

Dr. Freeman-Grenville has written:[1]

The . . . poem *al-Inkishafi* gives not only a portrait of Swahili society but tells about its culture in such a way as to illuminate the dead bones of the (historical) monuments. Sheikh Mbarak Ali al-Hinawy's edition of the *Utenzi wa al-Akida* is without question a work of first-class historical importance, for it makes clear beyond all shadow of doubt the connection between poetry and history. It is regrettable that it is out of print. We have not got nearly enough documents of this kind. There is very much which is not in print. I have notes of more than sixty documents known to different writers which are not available.

Most Swahili historical chronicles are either in Arabic or Swahili prose. While the *utendi* verse-form is adequately suited for the narration of historical events, we find that only in the nineteenth century did Swahili poets begin to use this medium for describing events in East Africa which they had either experienced themselves or about which they were informed by their elders. Early Swahili poetry had no East African reference whatsoever. It is perhaps unfortunate, from the historian's point of view, that nineteenth-century Swahili poetry with reference to East Africa can only supplement most of the information that the historian can quite well obtain from other sources. The idea that Swahili poems pre-dating the nineteenth century may exist which could shed a positive light, not elsewhere to be obtained, on East African history is most improbable. Even *al-Inkishafi* belongs to the nineteenth century and only supplements what we already know from the prose chronicles of the sultanate of Pate. It is an

[1] G. S. P. Freeman-Grenville, 'Swahili Literature and the History and Archaeology of the East African Coast', *J. E. African Swahili Committee*, No. 28/2, p. 19.

exaggeration to call the *Utendi wa al-Akida* a work of first-class historical importance'. It presents no single fact that is not known from other sources, and, indeed, one must first know the history in order to understand what the poem is all about. For students of Swahili poetry it is fortunate that ample historical evidence exists to enable them to understand the historical *tendi* dealing with East African events.

These factors should not detract from the interest even of those *tendi* which deal with historical events that are well-documented in other sources. *Tendi* have been written about the First World War, and especially of the fighting then in East Africa, about the Maji-Maji rebellion in East Africa in 1905 and about wars in the nineteenth century, and although they include local references that add colour and supplement the broad outline of events, they are not to be regarded as serious historical documents. They may serve a historical purpose inasmuch as often they are personal accounts of what actually happened, as in the case of *Utenzi wa Vita vya Maji-Maji*,[1] and they help to fill in the picture which already is recognizable enough. Much of the nineteenth-century verse in shorter poems of a different verse-form from the *utendi* is about local events which are not documented elsewhere and are therefore difficult to interpret, but when a poet contemplated the writing of a *utendi* of at least a hundred verses it was usually on a theme of wider reference.

As an example of nineteenth-century *tendi* with reference to East Africa, the *Utendi wa al-Akida* is transliterated from the manuscript copy lent to me by Sir Mbarak Ali Hinawy.

Utendi wa al-Akida

Sir Mbarak Ali Hinawy has provided an account[2] of the life of Muhammad b. Abdallah b. Mbarak Bakhashweini, known to the Swahili as al-Akida. In the same book he gave a transliteration of the *Utendi wa al-Akida* based on the same manuscript used in the transliteration that follows. The author of the poem was Abdallah b. Masud b. Salim al-Mazrui, who was born A.H. 1212/A.D. 1797 and who died at Takaungu in A.H. 1312/A.D. 1894. He was the

---

[1] Abdul Karim b. Jamaliddini, *Utenzi wa Vita vya Maji-Maji*, Supplement to th *East African Swahili Committee Journal*, No. 27, June 1957.

[2] Mbarak Ali Hinawy, *al-Akida and Fort Jesus, Mombasa*, London, 1950.

author of other *tendi*, notably the *Hadithi ya Barasisi* and *Hadithi ya Hasina*, of which there are copies in the Library of the SOAS.

When Saiyid Said, Sultan of Zanzibar, succeeded in ridding Mombasa finally of the Mazrui governors of Fort Jesus in about 1837–8, he appointed Abdallah b. Mbarak, al-Akida's father, to be akida or commandant of Mombasa. One of the Sultan's Baluchi generals, Jemadar Tangai b. Shambe, took over the military command. At about the same time, Muhammad, who was to become al-Akida, was born in the Fort, but while Muhammad was still an infant his father died, leaving him under the guardianship of Jemadar Tangai. When Muhammad was old enough he recommended him to the Court of Zanzibar to fill the post of akida and Muhammad was appointed to his father's office, under the direction of the Jemadar. Eventually he was made wali of Mombasa.

Suud b. Said al-Maamiry, an accomplished poet, was leader of the political faction in Mombasa against al-Akida. Pretending to leave for Mgau in what is now Tanganyika Territory, he sailed instead for Zanzibar and there intrigued against al-Akida who was called to Zanzibar by the Sultan to give an account of himself. On his return to Mombasa, al-Akida had revenge upon the people of Mombasa by ill-treating them. They in their turn reported their complaints to the Sultan. They had the support and sympathy of Mustafa, son of al-Akida's friend and former foster-father, Jemadar Tangai, and with Mustafa's support went that also of his Baluchi garrison.

The Sultan's wazir, Muhammad b. Suleiman al-Bu-Said, was sent to Mombasa in 1874 to proclaim al-Akida's deposition. Al-Akida, on being summoned to attend a meeting for this purpose, presented himself with his full bodyguard. The wazir read the Sultan's proclamation of deposition and then handed the document to al-Akida, who replied that he would obey but that he first

---

Utendi wa al-Akida

Bismillahi awali   utakapo hino kweli   biladi ya Sawahili   hai-tufai kukaa.

Hakimu hakimu wetu   hakimu mzawa kwetu   huzuwiliwaje kitu   asiweze kukitwaa.

Lakini si mwaka mwema   washabihi na kiyama   yaum al-hasra wa nnadama   pulikizani jamaa.

wished leave to go back to the fort for the keys in order to hand them over formally. Once returned to the Fort he had the gates closed and barred. He summoned his second-in-command, Said b. Ali al-Adwan, and expressed his intention to fight and over-power the Baluchi garrison together with Mustafa, the com-mandant. Fighting ensued and al-Akida was eventually persuaded by his father-in-law to leave the Fort. Al-Akida made his formal apologies to the wazir, and thinking that he was once more in control of the fort, he expelled the Baluchi garrison from it to be scattered in the town.

The Sultan, Saiyid Barghash, decided to remove al-Akida from his office and from the fort. Early in January 1875, he sent to Mombasa three dhow-loads of Omani Arab soldiers under the command of his amir, Seif al-Amur, accompanied by al-Akida Matar b. Muhammad al-Husni. Al-Akida sent orders commanding all his soldiers to be inside the fort that night. Next morning, 14 January 1875, he attacked the Sultan's forces, ordering that Mombasa was to be burned to the ground. Al-Akida's men were routed and he retired to the fort, barricading himself in. Two British men-of-war, H.M.S. *Rifleman* and H.M.S. *Nassau*, were sent from Zanzibar to Mombasa with orders to evict al-Akida from Fort Jesus. After an ultimatum, the commanding officer put a preliminary warning shot across the fort, which was returned by a salvo of ball. The gun-boats then fired at the fort, causing many casualties. Al-Akida surrendered and the commander was compelled to put him under arrest and take him to Zanzibar as a prisoner. From Zanzibar he was deported to Mkelle. From there he later went to Madagascar and married Birira-Vun, the Sultana of Bisina. He returned to Zanzibar in 1888, but his efforts to be reinstated proved fruitless. He died in Zanzibar *c.* A.D. 1894–6.

Al-Akida

First in the Name of God   if you want the truth   the Swahili
    country   is no place for us to live in.
Ruler, our ruler   ruler born in our country   how could any-
    thing be withheld   from him that he could not seize?
But the year is not good   it is like a day of awakening   to
    sorrow and repentance   listen, brethren.

Ni mwaka wa ijuma'a   mwishoni una khada'a   una ungi wa
ba'a   nanyi mutajioneya.

5 Ulingiya na fitina   ya watu kutoonana   na maroho kutoa-
na   pasi kisa nawambiya.

Hadha akhiri zamani   raia hayumkini   kuteta na Sultani   asiweze kurudiwa.

Kisa cha Bakhashweini   tawaeleza yakini   na mwanzowe
ujueni   ni fitina zaweleya.

Liwali ali ni mtu   na kupendeza kwa watu   na kwa Sayyidi ni
kitu   mno sana kajeteya.

Lakini kulla hakimu   hapendwi ni watu amu   hakosi wake
dhalimu   maovu kumwandaliya.

10 Katiliwa Muhammadi   ufitina kwa Sayyidi   ukakuwa na
kuzidi   na miyali ukatowa.

Kampeleka Maulana   waziriwe wa maana   kwenda kutazama
sana   ambalo akisikiya.

Kuwasili marikabu   ilikuja na jawabu   hapana tena
kujibu   Sayyidi ametukiwa.

Mtu aliomo ndani   Muhammadi bin Suleimani   mjumbe wa
Sultani   ndiye amezotiwa.

Kushukakwe forodhani   akipanda darajani   jamii ya Wakilindini   wote wakamwandamiya.

15 Wazee walo biladi   wakamwambia Saidi   al-Akida ni
fisadi   ni kheri kumjuliya.

Akanena ana nini   au yuna yambo gani   hata kwao Dauani   hawezi kunitaadiya.

Wazee wakanyamaza   watafuta la kuwaza   wachamba kuganz-
aganza   Saidi ametukiwa.

Kawauza muna nini   au muna yambo gani   mulilo nalo ne-
nani   mimi tawatimiziya.

Tulilo nalo ni moja   twapenda tukidhi haja   utuondolee
huja   hino ilotungiliya.

20 Jaza ya Bakhashweini   yote ajua Mannani   Rabi Mola
ngwamlaani   sote tukimuamba'a.

Kauliye Sultani   na twendeni barazani   khamsa wa khamsini   askari wameka'a.

Akenda itwa liwali   kaja zake kwa ukali   hata akija ni
kweli   barazani akaka'a.

It is a year beginning unluckily   and ending with deception   a
year of much trouble   as you will see for yourselves.

It came in with strife   want of friendliness   and destruction of 5
souls   all, I say, without cause.

In these last days of the good old world   a subject cannot
be allowed   to quarrel with his Sultan   and go un-
punished.

The tale of Bakhashweini   I will relate exactly   understand
that its beginning   is the strife that you know of.

The Wali was a man   beloved by the people   a man in whom
the Sultan   had great confidence.

But there is no ruler   who is loved by all   there is sure to come
an evil person   who seeks to do him ill.

And so Muhammad   was slandered to the Sultan   and the 10
friction increased   until discord flared up.

Our great lord sent   his special minister   to investigate the
reports   that had reached him.

When the ship arrived   it brought the reply   there was nothing more to say   the Sultan was angry.

The man in the ship   was Muhammad b. Suleiman   the Sultan's envoy   he it is who was on board.

When he landed at the Customs   and came up the steps   all
the Kilindini people   followed him in a crowd.

The elders of the town   told Said (the Sultan)   al-Akida is a 15
bad man   it is better to beware of him.

He asked, What is the matter?   What has he done?   Whatever
(he may have done) in his own home Dauani   he cannot deal
threateningly with me.

The elders were silent   not knowing what to think   they kept
on hesitating   till the great man was annoyed.

He asked them what was the matter   what had they to say   Say
what you have to   and I will consider it.

We have only one thing to say   Our wish is this   that you take
away from us the trouble   that has come upon us.

What Bakhashweini deserves   is known to God Almighty   may 20
the Lord God curse him   and deliver us all from him.

The Sultan's command   was to go to the Court   five and
fifty   soldiers were waiting there.

The Wali was sent for   he came in a rage   when he arrived he
saw how it was   and sat down in his place.

Akatolewa waraka   akapokeya haraka   mikononi kaushika   ndani akaufunuwa.

Akiufunua ndani   masomoye kwa yakini   nda kutolewa ngomeni   sikae tena asiya.

25 Kauli ikamutoka   ya ulimiwe hakika   funguo nenda zitaka   nije nazo zote piya.

Kaondoka takhubiri   akenenda kwa jeuri   mshuko wa adhuhuri   lango akajifungiya.

Akamtoa Khalifa   kamfunge Mustafa   kheri uradhiwe kufa   ela huku nileteya.

Enenda hima shawishi   kawafunge Mabulushi   kisha umwambie shishi   anti ni kiarabiya.

Enenda al-Adwani   simba wangu mwenye kani   kama wwewe simuoni   katika askari piya.

30 Ndipo hatoa shaka   kwa moyo wangu hakika   wabulushi tawashika   wake na waume piya.

Katamka al-Adwani   al-Akida una nini   punguza zako huzuni   bulushi takushikiya.

Wabulushi tawashika   na pingu nitawavika   chumba cha Wadi Mataka   ndicho takachowatiya.

Kaondoka kwa ajili   akenda kwa tasihili   akifika ala wali   Mustafa kajifungiya.

Bunduki ikatakata   wengine wakajifita   jemadari kenda tata   risasi inamngiya.

35 Ai huu uvundifu   sisi ndio maarufu   walakini mbili safu   ndipo tukavundikiwa.

Ramadhani Kazabeka   haya ndiyo ulotaka   hapana tena kwepuka   kwani imetekeleya.

Mustafa akafungwa   nusura kupigwa panga   ela Rabbi kaminga   chumbani akenda tiwa.

Auladi Bakhashweini   wakanadi ngomeni   ni nani leo ni nani ambaye atatujiya.

Haihati haihati   kutoka katika kuti   tastahabu mauti   lakini siji tolewa.

40 Kutoka sitakubali   kutolewa ni muhali   japo kusanyika mali   siwezi kuyapokeya.

Mimi kuzawa ngomeni   jamii Wakilindini   na waliomo mjini   wote nimewazoweya.

He was handed a letter   which he took hurriedly   he grasped
it   and tore it open.

When he opened it   he saw the order which had been written   that he should leave the Fort   and live there no more.

Then he spoke   with his tongue and said   I am going for the 25
keys   and I will bring them all here.

He went off, I tell you   he went off arrogantly   just after mid-
day   and barricaded himself within.

He sent forth the Khalifa   Go and capture Mustafa   face death
itself   to bring him to me.

Go quickly, sergeant   and arrest the Baluchis   then tell him
(Mustafa)   Shishi anti, it is Arabic.

Go, Al-Adwan   my brave lion   I have none like you   among
all my soldiers.

So shall I remove doubt   entirely from my heart   I will seize 30
the Baluchis   women as well as men.

Then spoke al-Adwani   al-Akida, what is the matter?   Grieve
not so much   I will take the Baluchis.

I will seize the Baluchis   and put them in chains   in the cell
of Wadi Mataka   there will I put them.

He set off to do so   going in a hurry   when he got there (he
found him) eating rice   and Mustafa was enchained.

Rifles were fired   some people hid themselves   As the Jemadari crouched down   he was hit by a bullet.

Alas this destruction   we are a famous people   but because 35
we are divided (lit. in two ranks)   that is why we are
destroyed.

Ramadhani Kazabeka   these are the things you wanted   there
is no escape from them now   for they have come upon us.

Mustafa was imprisoned   he was almost slain by the sword   but
God protected him   and he was put in a cell.

The people of Bakhashweini   called out in the Fort   Who is
it today?   who is it?   Who (dares) to approach us?

Never, never   far be it from me   I will prefer death   rather
than be forced out (of the Fort).

I will not agree to come out   to force me out will be diffi- 40
cult   even though you may collect riches   I will not
accept them.

I was born in the Fort   The Kilindi folk   and all who are in
the town   I am familiar with them all.

Nawauza wa Mvita   kwani kutakuja vita   walakini muna
tata   nyote zimewatatiya.

Mwambieni Shekhe Sudi   mtoto wa ba-Saidi   kwani ni
nyingi juhudi   laala katatanyuwa.

Kwani ndiye babangu   mume wa mamangu   kanifanyia
mizongu   hata nikauzuliwa.

45 Kawaga kwenda Mgawu   mimi nikamdharawu   kanama
nisufahawu   fitina enda itiya.

Kanitiliya fitina   mno ikashikamana   nisipate ya
kunena   kwa Sayyidi hitungiya.

Hitokeya kwa Sayyidi   nisiupate muradi   kama kitwana
fisadi   aliyefanya khatiya.

Naliliya nguvu zangu   kuteta na walimwengu   kumbe vile
kuna jungu   kubwa mno napikiwa.

Nilisema haidari   sitatoka Zinjibari   haiyonea khatari   kui-
kosa Mombasiya.

50 Nilipokuwa Unguja   nilidhani sitakuja   sitarudi huku
haja   Mvita haiwasiliya.

Nina watu nataraji   kisha ni hawa wa miji   lakini kwangu
hawaji   fedha ningejiwapiya.

Tawajaalia fungu   nililopawa ni Mungu   niwape nao wenzangu   nao wapate tumiya.

Niwapatapo wa miji   ingekuwa kwangu huji   mithili ya Rambi Saji   ambavyo nimetukiwa.

Salimu jifunge sana   tuje tufe kiungwana   ijapokuwa
mtana   usikhofu ni mamoya.

55 Salimu nakae papo   ndipo mahali nijapo   nimuwaewae ja
popo   asijue pakungiya.

Muhammadi akadumu   ngomeni mwe na zihamu   za rijali na
harimu   lango hataki funguwa.

Akendewa kwa makozi   ya watu wema azizi   awate ya upuuzi   nasaha akakata'a.

Muhammadi katamka   siwati nililoshika   mlango toani
shaka   si mwenye kuufunguwa.

Akawatoa ngomeni   mabulushi masikini   kwa unyonge na
huzuni   nyandoni wakaeneya.

60 Zikaenea khabari   zikafika Zinjibari   Sayyidi kata-
fakari   kwa khadaa kumtowa.

I ask the people of Mombasa   Why should war come?   When
you are all entangled   you are all involved in trouble.

Tell Sheikh Suud   the son of the Saiyids   because so much is
involved   he can by no means disentangle affairs.

For he is as my father   the husband of my mother   he has
spun this web around me   until I have been deposed.

He left to go to Mgau   and I thought nothing of him   not 45
realizing he was bent on mischief   going to tell tales.

He involved me in discord   and it stuck hard   so that I had
nothing to say   that I could make up before the Sultan.

I appeared before the Sultan   without getting my intention   like a corrupt slave   who had done wrong.

I grieve for my efforts   in striving with people   when lo a pot
(of trouble)   very big indeed was being brewed for me.

I said to myself   I will not leave Zanzibar   and I saw that I
was in danger   of losing Mombasa.

When I was in Zanzibar   I thought I would not come   I will 50
not return (but) I came   and I reached Mombasa.

I am expecting some people   they are elders of the town   but
they do not come to me   I would give them money (if they
came).

I would grant them a share   of what God gave to me   I
should give it to my companions   for them to use.

When I get the townspeople   it would be for me a matter of
questioning   like Rambi Saji   so great is my anger.

Salimu make ready   so that we may die like men   even if it
be by daylight   fear not, it is all the same.

Let Salimu stay right there   that is where I am coming   let me 55
fly round him like a bat   till he knows not where to go.

Muhammad remained   in the Fort with the crowd   of men
and women   and refused to open the gate.

There went to him groups   of good and honourable men   (to
beg him) to cease from his folly   but he refused their counsel.

Muhammad declared   I will not go back on what I have
decided   about the gate have no doubt   I am not the one
to open it.

He drove them from the Fort   the poor Baluchis   in humiliation and sorrow   they were scattered about the villages.

The news spread   and reached Zanzibar   The Sultan pon- 60
dered   how to get him out by a trick.

Kwa siku chache kupita ikaja njema bukhuta na amani aka-
pata ndipo hapo kajitowa.

Baada ya siku kuduru kuwasili Sefu Muru na akidawe
Mataru na jeshi ya askariya.

Katambuwa Muhammadi kwamba hino ni jihadi atashi-
kwa bilyadi kiwata kujiteteya.

Akasema sina budi mji nitaufisidi sifurahishi hasidi hari-
dhika kukhadawa.

65 Kanadi Bakhashweini askari wa ngomeni wasibakie
mjini jua lishapo kutuwa.

Akafanyiza shauri na ndugu na maamini wakinena kwa
fakhari na manenoye ni haya.

Madufaa tumepanga bunduki zetu zalenga kulla aliye
muinga ndiye atayetujiya.

Kulla aliye mwerevu japokuwa ana nguvu akawa ni
mshupavu si kweli atatujiya.

Kwani hino ni khasara yendemene na tijara jamii umm
il-kura nawaje huku jama'a.

70 Musidhani nda Gaeti hakuhimili mauti nawambia siwa-
fiti mimi tajihimiliya.

Mutaona jeshi jeshi ndia kuu kama moshi musidhani ni
ubishi kwa haya nalowambiya.

Kulla aliye tangu mwenya kite na utungu ni mani nane
za pingu ndizo takazomtiya.

Kila aliye aduwi tamgeukia tuwi maana hanitam-
buwi ndipo akanitezeya.

Haya ndiyo masemoye Muhammadi na nduguye kulla
tandamana naye shauri lao ni moya.

75 Lakini ni mlakule na walao wasilale wakae mato vivile hata
sabaha kungiya.

Akalifungua lango nisemayo si uwongo haja yangu si ma-
tango lolote tajitendeya.

Akazimwaya pagaro akamba rero ni rero musidhani muna
charo mjini tutaingiya.

Nisemayo si ubishi ndiani kwenele moshi tukaona jeshi
jeshi kanama ni aduiya.

After a few days   there came good gifts   and a pledge of peace   then he came out of the Fort.

After the day's round   there arrived Seif the Sour   with his akida Mataru   and an army of soldiers.

And Muhammad realized   that this is war indeed   without doubt he will be captured   unless he defends himself.

He said I must   get the town on my side   I will not rejoice the enemy   and consent to be tricked.

Bakhashweini proclaimed   that of the soldiers of the Fort   none 65 must remain in the town   after the setting of the sun.

He had a consultation   with his brothers and other faithful men   they spoke boastfully   and this is what they said.

We have placed the cannons in position   our guns are set   only he who is a fool   will dare to come to us.

Every sensible man   even though he be strong   would be only a fool   to come upon us so.

For this is a great loss   which follows along with great gain   and I call upon all Muslims (lit. the family of the Mother of Cities)   to come and join us here.

Do not think it is like Gaeti   who was not equal to death   I 70 tell you without hiding anything   I will certainly face it.

You will see regiment upon regiment   on the highway like smoke   Do not think this is boasting   what I am telling you.

Everyone who is first   with moaning and anguish   with twenty-four pounds of chains   that is what I shall put him in.

To every man who is my enemy   I shall change into a leopard for him   it is because he does not know me   that he trifles with me.

This is how they talked   Muhammad and his brother   and all who followed along with them   were of the same mind.

But this is a gamble   and those who sleep must not sleep   they 75 must keep watch   till the morning comes.

He opened the gate   (and said) what I say is no lie   I have no need of idle words   all I want I shall do.

He poured out his carriers   saying, Today is the day   Do not think there is a journey ahead   for we are going into the town.

What I say is true   the road was filled with smoke   we saw hosts of men   and lo they were the enemy.

Hebu jitunzeni sana   si usiku ni mtana   tujitoe kiungwana   isiwe ni kukimbiya.

80 Wakawa kama jaradi   mji wakaufisidi   wakafanya na
taadi   mno kwa kuukiliya.

Kawasili Mwingereza   ya nasaha kwamweleza   akamba
sitasikiza   lolote talonambiya.

Akatukiwa Mzungu   kamwambia kwa utungu   hutaki
maneno yangu   hata moya kusikiya.

Akanena Adumeri   sasa ni lipi shauri   la kusema Zinjibari   ambalo limelekeya.

Tatengeza manowari   itambae na bahari   uovu amekhi-
tari   lazima kumtendeya.

85 Tamsukuma kombora   simpigi barabara   talipisha kwa ishara   laala akalekeya.

Akafanya masahara   ngome haina ishara   wale ndani
wakang'ara   wakapiga heriya.

Likenda tena kombora   likapiga barabara   likatia kuu
dhara   na roho zikapoteya.

Kateremsha bendera   kaikweza juu mara   kuonya wale
ishara   ya kwamba twaangukiya.

Ukanyamaza mzinga   vijana wakajifunga   wakaja pwani
kuenga   ngomeni wakajitiya.

90 Akatoka Muhammadi   roho yenele baridi   kwako nataka
ahadi   Adumeri nitendeya.

Napenda unidhamini   unibakishe ngomeni   au kwake
Sultani   tukifika niombeya.

Adumeri kabaini   nendapo kwa Sultani   ukawa hu mkononi   hilo halikuelekeya.

Tungie marikabuni   twende zetu dalheini   kifika kwa Sultani   tapata la kumwambiya.

Wakateremka pwani   wakaingia melini   wakifika Ungu-
jani   akamwambia tuliya.

95 Yeye akashuka pwani   akenda kwa Sultani   Muhammadi umo
ndani   bwana nimekuleteya.

Tumekuja kwa ahadi   nitakalo sinirudi   naye yu juu ya
kaidi   na miye namwombeya.

Utakalo umepata   nami ni wa kufuata   unamtoa mata-
ta   yaliyo kumtatiya.

Now look after yourselves   it is not night but day   let us go
forth like noblemen   let there be no running away.

They were like locusts   and they destroyed the town   and they 80
behaved with violence   intent on evil.

An Englishman arrived   and gave him good advice   and he
said I will not listen   to anything you say to me.

The European was vexed   and said to him sharply   You do
not like my words   not one do you hear.

The Admiral spake   Now what advice   should we give in
Zanzibar   about what should be done?

I will arrange for gunboats   to creep up by sea   he has chosen
evil   and he must suffer for it.

I shall attack him with shell   but I shall not aim to hit   the 85
shot shall pass as a sign   perhaps he will give up.

He took it in jest   the Fort had no sign (of damage)   those
inside rejoiced   and blessed their good fortune.

Another shell came over   and hit the target   and it caused
great damage   and lives were lost.

He lowered the flag   hoisting another at once   to show them
a signal   that we have surrendered.

The firing ceased   the young men made ready   and came
ashore to look   and entered the Fort.

Muhammad came out   his heart was very cold   I want your 90
promise   Admiral, that you will do something for me.

I want you to stand surety for me   and leave me in the Fort   or
if we go to the Sultan   when we arrive intercede for me.

The Admiral explained   If I go to the Sultan   and you are not
in my hands   that would be wrong.

Let us go on board   and sail at once   when we get to the
Sultan   I shall find something to say.

They went down to the shore   and went on board   when
they reached Zanzibar   he told him not to worry.

He went ashore   and went to the Sultan   (who was told) 95
Muhammad is inside   Sir, I have brought him to you.

We have come according to promise   do not refuse my request   he is under arrest   and now I ask pardon for
him.

What you ask has been granted   and I will follow your counsel   you have got him out of the difficulties   which sur-
rounded him.

Simuweke Zinjibari   namuonea khatari   kwani ni ali
 shari   ataharibu raiya.

Tamati nimezokoma   mwisho wangu wa kalima   kwa
 haya niliyosema   sikubaki hatta moya.

Love-Song

In contrast to these serious religious and historical *tendi* is a
love-song in measure of six *mizani* to which Hichens gave the
title, *Liyongo na Mmanga*. Two manuscript copies of this poem
were collected by Werner from Muhammad Kijuma, one written
on a scroll (No. 47795 in the Library of the SOAS). Hichens
sought to identify the Arabian maiden, whose charms the poet
eulogizes in somewhat embarrassing detail, with Kundazi, the
woman who betrayed Liyongo by removing his weapons as he
slept, but this is a very doubtful connexion. There is no evidence
to connect this poem with Liyongo, and it is more likely to have
been modelled on an Arabian original, for poems of this type are
found in Hadramawt. The author is unknown, and the complete
poem has forty-nine verses, the last ten of which recount metaphorically the consummation of the poet's love.

Love-Song

Pijiani mpwasi   pembe ya jamusi   kwa cha mtutusi   au
 mwananiga.

Upije na pembe   iliayo jumbe   muwangi uwembe   kwa
 ya ndovu-kanga.

Vumi lende mbali   lamshe ahali   wake na wavuli   waje
 gangaganga.

Waje wakele ti   wambeja banati   tupani sauti   tumsifu
 mmanga.

5 Tupani baiti   tukizitafiti   jema ziweke ti   mbi tukitenga.

Kisa kuziona   baiti kufana   yatupwe kunena   zakwe
 mwanamanga.

Basi tuwakifu   yasiwe marefu   sifa tusanifu   zakeye
 miyanga.

Do not keep him in Zanzibar   I foresee danger there for
   him   for he is a mischievous person   and will harm my
   subjects.
Now I have come to the end   my tale is finished   I have said
   all there is to say   and there is nothing left to say.

The *utendi* verse-form has never been freely employed for
love-songs nor for poems of light relief. Even today it is used for the
same purposes as formerly, namely, for narration and for didactic
themes. Where love-songs are included in Swahili epics they are
usually in a different verse-form from the main body of the story.
In the nineteenth century the quatrain, verse with eight *vipande*,
became the popular verse-form for expressing sentiments loving
and otherwise, and this may be regarded as a more indigenous
product than the *utendi*.

The first twenty-five verses of the *Love-Song* illustrate sufficiently the nature of the poem, which is a catalogue of the physical
charms of the beloved. As a love-poem it does not have the
human interest, nor the skill of selection, the personal angle of
much of the later love-poetry in quatrain form, and this may well
be because the poet is too consciously following the pattern of
similar Arabian poems.

Love-Song

Sound to the distant coast-line   the buffalo-horn   with (rod)
   of buck-thorn   or of the green-dove tree.
Blow the ivory horn as well   that cries to the Sultan's house   let
   the skies resound   to the curved ivory horn.
Let the blast go far   and wake up the kinsfolk   the youths and
   the women   to come hasting hither.
Let them come and be seated   the fair maids and daughters   lift
   up your voices   let us praise the maid of Araby.
Give forth your verses   as we choose them well   setting down 5
   the good ones   and rejecting the bad.
And when we have seen   that our verses scan well   be they
   flung forth to tell   of the maid of Araby.
Thus may we arrange them   so that they are not too long   let
   us sing the praises   of her glowing delights.

Ta kwanda kitwani   nduza sikiani   hariri laini   zakwe
nyele singa.

Kitwache huramu   ni kama ruhamu   au jaizimu   taole
kuzinga.

10 Yakwe masikiyo   apulikiyayo   yatendele tawo   kama
kombe-nanga.

Uso wake mwana   utengee sana   na pasiyaona   huota
miyanga.

Nshize zifene   nta zilingene   shina lifungene   kama lalo-
funga.

Ni nyeusi mno   zizidiye wino   zitaliye kono   ya tando
za mnga.

Mato avikapo   khasa avuwapo   mtu akiwepo   hutisha
kuyenga.

15 Puwaye ajabu   zifungu huribu   nisita hesabu   mwenye
kuziwanga.

Sitaajabuni   kuliko Mannani   hatta ishirini   zifungu
hupanga.

Zakwe zitefute   zizidiye zote   ya mkatekate   mafuta
yakinga.

Miyomo myembamba   asipoifumba   atakapo kamba   hwe-
lewa muyinga.

Kamba takwambaye   tatongoa iye   ajabu menoye   humo
yengayenga.

20 Si ya akhadharu   si ya shamaru   hufana na nuru   iwaayo
Manga.

Si ya mkakasi   si rangi nyeusi   ni kufana basi   kuwa
wanda Manga.

Kanwa huradidi   nyushi za mkadi   au za zabadi   yangawa
nafunga.

Ulimi upesi   wake ni fanusi   khassa kidodosi   hudengemu
yanga.

Shingoye ni refu   muwandi sharifu   ipambewe mkufu   kama
za kutunga.

25 Ni hidaya jema   umbile karima   iyaliye nyama   yakwe
mitulinga . . .

Verse of four *vipande* in the measure of six *mizani* is seldom
found in long poems. There are a number of short poems in

Take first her head   my brothers, hearken   soft and silken   are
  her tresses.
The head of the maiden   it is like marble (for smoothness)   or
  like (a shell?)   in its curving profile.
Her ears   as she listens   swell in (sweet) curves   like the 10
  cups of a shell-fish.
The maiden's face   is beautifully made   such as never else-
  where has been seen   it blooms with light.
Her eyebrows so neat   are matched   as though they join
  where they meet   where (the long brows) grow.
They are very black   much blacker than ink   like the tendrils
  that branch   from the *mnga* tree's spread.
From her drooping glances   if she lift up her gaze   anyone
  present   would fear to look.
Her nose, 'tis a wonder   its arches sweep high   to count them 15
  I fear   I dare not try.
Yet be not amazed   if by Allah I swear   in a score of
  arches   her nostrils are raised.
Her cheeks   are beyond all compare   (treated) with simsim
  oil   and with cosmetics rare.
Her lips are narrow   unless she brings them together   and
  when she wishes to speak   even a fool can understand.
When she speaks, what can I tell you?   what can I declare   of
  the wonder of her teeth   as they quiver on the brink (of her
  lips)?
They are not leaf-green   nor of the colour of the rose   but are 20
  like the light   that shines in Araby.
They are not many-hued   nor black in colour   but compare   with the kohl of Araby.
Her mouth breathes out   the perfume of pandamus   or of
  sweet musk   even when her lips are closed.
She has a ready wit   her tongue sparkles with fun   and when
  she hesitates in speech   it sounds clearly in the air.
Her neck is as slender   as a noble bamboo   and it is adorned
  with a chain   like those that are strung (with gems).
It is a thing of wonder   a creation of beauty   granted to her 25
  body   where the shoulders (curve). . . .

---

this measure, including the one recorded first by Taylor, as
follows: [*see over, page 146*]

Shairi la Mkata

1 Mkata haisi   kula na mkwasi   achanza kula swi   hulia kitwani.
2 Mkata kamwite   aje tule sute   aje ale mate   ni mwawi chanoni.
3 Mkata ha haya   akitwa yuwaya   na damu za tawa   zi-jele nyaani.
4 Uso wa mkata   u matitatita   kwa ndaa na nyota   iliyo moyoni.
5 Ukata si umbe   kupata kiumbe   humtenda ng'ombe   aka-lishwa yani.
6 Ukata si kitu   upatapo mtu   akiwa sharifu   hana buru-hani.

The Poem of the Poor Man

1 A poor man knows not   how to eat with a rich man   if he begins to eat fish   he eats the head.
2 Invite a poor man and he comes disreputably   he comes licking his lips   he is an upsetter of the platter.
3 The poor man has no reserve   if he is called he comes   with the blood of lice   in his finger-nails.
4 The face of a poor man   is furrowed   by hunger and thirst   that is in his vitals.
5 Poverty is no state   fit for mortal man   it makes him a beast   to be fed upon grass.
6 Poverty is no right thing   when a man gets it   though he be nobly born   he has no power with God.

In the Hichens Papers (Library of the SOAS), scripts by Muhammad Kijuma contain two poems of this type relating to the Liyongo tradition. One is the *Shairi la Ndoto*, 'The Dream Song', another version of that taken down by Werner in 1913 from the blind poet of Witu, Mzee b. Bisharo al-Ausiy, a native of the Bajun coast north of Lamu. Kundazi is mentioned as the name of the woman who betrayed Liyongo. The poem opens with Liyongo dreaming of a plot by his cousin to betray him.

Shairi la Ndoto

1 Nili kwangu ndele   nami totomile   ndosele mbwele   kili-pacho wazi.

Ndoto ndoseya   toshee miuya   kuuawa nduya   mwana wa 2
    shangazi.
Kondoka tikima   nguu kaiyuma   moyo ukanima   kamwita 3
    Kundazi.
Kundazi amwawo   katwaliye ngawo   na msu ndona- 4
    wo   pamwe na shirazi.
Kinoo ndeteya   msu chuga chiya   nuo ninoeya   utishao 5
    mwazi.
Ninoe kipate   makali ya nete   payewepo pite   sitoe zimizi. 6
Payewepo nyime   moyo usimame   niwe ng'ombe 7
    dume   kiuka cha mbuzi.

The Dream Song

I was at home asleep   and I was deep in slumber   I dreamed a 1
    fevered dream   that gave clear foresight.
I dreamed a dream   that I was surprised by danger   being 2
    slain by my kinsman   my father's sister's son.
I awoke with a start   my strength mocked me   my heart stood 3
    still   and I called Kundazi.
Kundazi tiptoed in   and took away my shield   and the 4
    sword that I had   together with a lantern.
Bring me the whetstone   I fear to be without a sword   let me 5
    sharpen the scabbard   that it alarm the slayer.
Let me hone until it gets   a keen cutting edge   wherever they 6
    approach   I will not cease to resist.
Wherever they oppose me   let my heart stand firm   let me 7
    be as a strong bull   leaping over the goat-house.

The other short poem said to be related to Liyongo was called
by Hichens *The Warrior Song*. It is clearly of very early origin.

The Warrior Song

Sikai muyini   hawa kitu duni   nangia mwituni   haliwa
    na mngwa.
Mngwa kinipata   kaninwa mafuta   ni ada ya vita   kuua-
    wa na ngwa.
Mwanangwa ni fili   hafi kwa ulili   ela fumo kali   liu-
    walo mwangwa.
Mwanangwa ni fiya   hufa kwa bidiya   akenda akiya   huyo
    si mwanangwa.

I dwell not in the city   to become a worthless object   I go into the forest   to be eaten up by the alien.

If the alien seizes me   and devours my flesh   well, that is the fortune of war   to be killed by the enemy.

A nobleman is like an elephant   he does not die in bed   but by the keen-edged sword   which kills in battle.

A nobleman is a spitting cobra   he dies hard   if he comes and goes   this is no nobleman.

Before going on to consider other verse-forms, it may be of interest to see how the modern poet, writing in roman script, can retain much of the spirit and poetic mould of the earlier didactic *tendi*. Nothing has quite taken the place of the earlier Swahili romance epics, but of *utendi* didactic verse some modern poems compare quite favourably with the earlier work. The most versatile Swahili poet today is Shaaban Robert of Tanga. In his *tendi*,[1] one addressed to a girl and another to a boy, called *Utendi wa Hati* and *Utendi wa Adili*, he is directly in the tradition of earlier writers,

---

Utendi wa Hati

Leo nataka binti   ukae juu ya kiti   ili uandike hati   ndogo ya wasia.

Mimi kwako baba   hati hii ya huba   andika iwe akiba   asaa itakufaa.

Bado ungali kijana   na dunia ngumu sana   kukufunza kuona   ni jambo la welekea.

Kwa faidayo mtoto   kwanza andika vito   vya kima na uzito,   ufananishe tabia.

5 Ulimwengu na adha   njiaze kadha wa kadha   itunze kama fedha   hati utabarikiwa.

Dunia ina aibu   hati hii dhahabu   tunza kama sahibu   itakupa manufaa.

Usifanye tashtiti   na watu kuwasaliti   hati hii yakuti   nakupa kama hidaya.

Kama utaikariri   hati na kuifikiri   utaona ni johari   ndipo hakutunukia.

[1] Shaaban Robert, *Pambo la Lugha*, Witwatersrand University Press, 1948.

and it is difficult perhaps to realize that these poems were written only about 15 years ago, not 150 years past.

Note that in the rhymes Shaaban Robert adopts the practice already exemplified in the *Utendi wa al-Akida* in the preceding pages of rhyming -*ea* with -*iwa* or with -*aa*. In the Swahili-Arabic script the rhyming consonant should be the same, so that to rhyme -*ya* with -*wa* or with -'*a* (the inverted comma standing for the Arabic letter 'ain which has consonantal value in rhyming positions) is *guni*, i.e. it is defective verse. But in the nineteenth century these rhymes were used quite often, but never by the best writers. Shaaban Robert is not really concerned with reproducing the rhyme of consonant plus vowel in words that end in semi-vowel plus vowel or in a double vowel, but if he had been writing in the Swahili-Arabic script, his rhymes, in many instances, would not have been perfect. This is not necessarily a modern characteristic, for, as has been said, some writers in the mid-nineteenth century departed from the strict rhyming convention of identical Arabic consonants.

Utendi—Poem of the Written Homily

Today I want you my daughter   to sit on a chair   and write
    a moral homily   a small one of exhortation.
I am father to you   so this treatise is from love   write so that
    it may be something in reserve   perhaps it will be of use to
    you.
You are still young   and the world is very hard   to teach you
    to understand   is a sensible thing.
For your good, child   first set out the gems   of value and
    weight   compare their character.
The world and its worry   its ways are various   as if it were 5
    money do you attend to it   this homily and you will be
    blessed.
The world is dishonourable   but this treatise is golden   mind
    it as a friend   and it will be of great use to you.
Do not be provocative   nor betray people   this homily is like
    a sapphire   I give it you as a gift.
If you copy it out   this homily, and think over it   you will
    find it like a jewel   that is why I have made you a present of it.

Hati iwe zamaridi   katika yako fuadi   ambaa na ufi-
sadi   utiao utu doa.

10 Hati hii ni lulu   iweke utafaulu   wema hawatahulu   baraka
kukuombea.

Kuombea njema dua   mtu hujaliwa   siri kuzitambua   na
heri kumfikia.

Aombewaye laana   dua zikizidi sana   wokofu huwa hana   ila
kuangamia.

Mungu hutia kabuli   katika zetu kauli   maamuzi ya
kweli   ndiye anayetoa.

Na sauti nyembamba   hupaa kama kwamba   mbawa zime-
pambwa   kwenda tusikojua.

15 Hasa imethibitika   kabisa bila shaka   neno likitamkwa   katika hewa hupaa.

Hupaa hata ng'ambo   aliko mwelewa mambo   wala hapana
jambo   yeye asilosikia.

Hati haya isemayo   fananisha na radio   sauti iendavyo
mbio   toka mbali kukujia.

Hati hii muktasi   tunza kama almasi   jihadhari na matu-
si   kinywa ovyo kutoa.

Tena uwe azizi   kila unapobarizi   hati hii feruzi   kama
utaangalia.

20 Dunia ni mvurugo   japo hati ni ndogo   ukiitunza mite-
go   mibaya utambaa.

Hati usione nzito   nakupa huba mtoto   itakuletea
pato   mwangaza wa dunia.

Mtoto ishiketo   cheche huzaa moto   mto huanza kijito   tone
bahari na ziwa.

Weka na kuihifadhi   kwako iwe kama radhi   mambo ya hii
ardhi   watu wengi husumbua.

Hati hii ni mali   kwa mtu wa akili   ifanye kama kipuli   siku
ya kujikwatua.

25 Fanya kama kipini   bora hakina kifani   itaongeza uoni   hati
ukishikilia.

Nakupa iwe hereni   pambo la masikioni   hati iweke moyoni   siku moja itafaa.

Shikamana na ibada   kutimiza kila muda   kesho ina
faida   ikisha hii dunia.

This treatise is like an emerald   in your heart   keep away from
  vice   which blemishes our human nature.

This homily is like a pearl   wear it and you will succeed   good 10
  people will not omit   to pray for you to be blessed.

By praying good prayers   a person is granted   to know the
  secret things   and happiness comes to him.

But he who is accursed   even if prayers be increased   he has
  no salvation   but will be destroyed.

God gives acceptance   to our words   true judgements   it is
  He who gives them.

And a small voice   ascends up as if   wings had been
  spread   going whither we know not.

It has certainly been established   without any doubt at all   that 15
  if a word (of prayer) be uttered   it ascends up into the sky.

It goes up to the other side   where He is the Omniscient   nor
  is there any matter   which He does not hear.

These things this homily says   compare them to the radio   the
  way that sound travels fast   coming to you from afar.

This homily is a summary   care for it as a diamond   guard
  yourself against abuse   coming from an evil mouth.

Then be dignified   whenever you have guests   this homily is
  like turquoise   if you look into it.

The world is a turmoil   even though this treatise is small   if 20
  you observe it, then   you will avoid wicked traps.

Do not think this homily heavy-going   I give you love, my
  child   it will bring you profit   the light of the world.

My child hold fast to it   a spark produces fire   a river begins
  in a stream   a drop of water (becomes) a sea and a lake.

Put it safe and look after it   let it be for you like a blessing   the
  things of this world   trouble many people.

This homily is wealth   for an intelligent person   treat it like
  a pendant   on a day when you make yourself smart.

Treat it like a nose-ornament   fine and without compare   it 25
  will increase (in worth) in a binding   when you hold this
  treatise.

I give it to you to be as an ear-ornament   a decoration for the
  ears   place this homily in your heart   one day it will be of
  use.

Hold fast to worship   fulfilling every time (of prayer)   tomorrow it will prove advantageous   when this world is done.

Dini mali ya roho   mwilini kama joho   unapoteza uroho   na
anasa za dunia.

Hati hii ni nuru   shika nakuamuru   Mungu atakunu-
suru   akuepushe na baa.

30 Jifunze na elimu   uwe mtu taalam   halali na haramu   uweze
kupambanua.

Elimu kitu kizuri   kuwa nayo ni fahari   sababu hum-
shauri   mtu la kutumia.

Hati nakupa kafara   weka ni kitu bora   utaokoka madhara   na mengi ya udhia.

Upishi mwema kujua   na mume kumridhia   neno analokw-
ambia   kwako itakuwa taa.

Na mume msishindane   wala msinuniane   jitahidi mpa-
tane   ndiyo maisha ya ndoa.

35 Fanya kila hali   la mume kulikubali   ila lisilo halali   kukataa si hatia.

Nyumba yako i nadhifu   kwa kufagia uchafu   kila mdudu
dhaifu   asipate pa kukaa.

Ziko nyingine amali   kujifunza ni halali   taabu ziki-
kabili   uwe umejiandaa.

Zikikukuta tayari   taabu hazihasiri   wala huwezi kukiri   kukushawishi vibaya.

Taabu zikikukuta   waweza nazo kuteta   njia ya kupita   lazima zitakwachia.

40 Lakini zikikuona   huwezi nazo pigana   zitakusumbua
sana   hati inafunua.

Tia katika moyo   nia ya maendeleo   hati hii ni cheo   kushinda ovu andaa.

Maovu yanavizia   na mtu kujiandaa   kuweza kuyazuia   tuzo
bora hupewa.

Hati nakupa ni ngao   ndiyo usiseme siyo   siyo ukasema
ndiyo   kubatilisha vibaya.

Kutumika ni sharti   wajibu kila binti   usingoje bahati   yote
kukutendea.

45 Watu wengi huclelewa   kwa kungoja kutendewa   bahati
wakaumbua   zingatia sana haya.

Wakati tanabahi   mtu sharti kuuwahi   lakini kuu-
sihi   kungoja ni kupotea.

Religion is the wealth of the soul   it is like a cloak for the body
  you lose your soul   because of the pleasures of the world.
This homily is as a light   observe it I command you   God will
  preserve you   and deliver you from evil.
Learn and be educated   become a scholar   so that the lawful 30
  and the unlawful   you may be able to distinguish them.
Education is a fine thing   to have it is splendid   because (by
  it) you can advise   a person what to do (lit. use).
This homily I gave as an offering   put it safe for it is an excellent
  thing   you will be saved from harm   and from much trouble.
Knowing how to cook well   and to satisfy your husband   in
  what he tells you   that will be as a lamp for you.
And do not oppose your husband   nor sulk with one
  another   try to agree together   that is what marriage should be.
Arrange everything   that your husband will agree to   but what 35
  is not lawful   you will not be blamed for refusing that.
Let your house be tidy   by sweeping away the dirt   every
  smallest (lit. weak) insect   don't let him have a place to stay.
There are other chores   it is lawful to learn them   so that if
  trouble confronts you   you will have prepared for it.
If you meet with trouble   then trouble will not bring you
  loss   nor can you admit then   that to persuade you (like
  this) is bad.
Should troubles confront you   you can face up to
  them   a way of escape   they will surely leave
  for you.
But if (troubles) find you   unable to fight against them   they 40
  will annoy you greatly   this homily reveals it so.
Have in your heart   the will to progress   this homily is a
  measure   prepare to oppose evil.
Evil things prevent success   and for a person to prepare himself   to be able to hinder (evil)   he receives a fine reward.
This homily I give you, it is a shield   do not say no for yes   nor
  yes for no   to waver is bad.
To serve is a thing of obligation   it is proper for every daughter
  don't wait for your luck   or for everything to wait upon you.
Many people delay   by waiting to be served by others   and 45
  they spoil their luck   remember well these things.
The time, remember   a person must observe it   but to in-
  treat it   to wait is to be lost.

Wakati huteleza   una nuru na giza   wapo wanaopoteza   kwa
kungojeangojea.

Hati unayopewa   kama utafanya nia   daima kushiki-
lia   huzami utaelea.

Majivuno hayafai   yanaleta uadii   japo mtu humjui   kum-
dunisha hatia.

50 Usishiriki uwongo   ijara upate hongo   mtu mwongo msu-
ngo   masuto mengi hupewa.

Masuto si mazuri   yanapunguza kadiri   jitahidi kuji-
bari   mbali na madoa.

Jambo usiloliona   haifai kunong'ona   hiyo ndiyo fitina   mngwana ya kujitoa.

Ulimi kulainisha   neno likafurahisha   ni furaha ya maisha   kila wakati tumia.

Ulimi wa pilipili   hutenga watu wawili   kuishi mbalimbali   hii hasara sikia.

55 Ulimi ulio tamu   hupendeza wanadamu   cheko na tabasamu   unalosema hupewa.

Hupendeza wasikizi   wakati wa maongezi   hili jambo
azizi   wajibu kuliana.

Ulimi mzuri mali   huvuta walio mbali   kusikiliza kauli   namna unavyotoa.

Tena nakupa fununu   sikiliza sana nunu   kila lililo
tunu   kulipata fanya nia.

Usoni kuwa na haya   juu ya jema na baya   na akili ya
kutua   pambo katika dunia.

60 Mawili haya ghali   kukosa usikubali   joharize mtu
mbili   ni akili na haya.

Hizi tunu thabiti   ashikaye madhubuti   hakosi kupata
kiti   cha heshima kukalia.

Hati yasema kwamba   mwanamke zampamba   nje na katika
nyumba   akiwa azitumia.

Ujitenge na kutu   inayoharibu utu   mwanamke hawi
kitu   aibu akiingia.

Mke nguo nyeupe   doa katika utepe   jihadhari usiipe   hai-
himili madoa.

65 Kupenda watukufu   kwa kumilki sarafu   na fukara
kukashifu   hati yasema vibaya.

Time slips by   there is light and darkness   there are those who
   get lost   by waiting and waiting.
This homily that you are receiving   if you make up your
   mind   always to hold fast to it   you will not sink but float.
Self-esteem is of no avail   it brings enmity   even if you do not
   know a man   to belittle him is wrong.
Have nothing to do with lying   the reward of lying is black- 50
   mail   a liar is uncouth   he gets charges brought against him.
Accusations are not good   they lessen one's rank   try to keep
   yourself   far from blemishes.
A thing that you do not see   it doesn't do to whisper about
   it   this indeed is a source of discord   the well-born keep
   out of it.
To soften the tongue   and to make people happy by your
   speech   is the joy of life   do this always.
A peppery tongue   separates two people   so that they live
   far from each other   this is a loss, understand.
A sweet tongue   pleases people   by a laugh and a smile   they 55
   accept (lit. receive) what you say.
It pleases the hearers   at conversation-time   this is an excellent thing   it is proper to have it in mind.
Good speech (lit. a fine tongue) is wealth   it attracts those afar
   off   to hear your voice   the way in which you use it.
I will give you something else to think of (lit. a rumour)   listen
   well little sister   every thing which is of value   make up
   your mind to get it.
To be able to blush   about things good and evil   and to have
   sense to settle down   these add lustre to the world.
There are two things of great worth   don't agree to be without 60
   them   the two treasures of a man   they are sense and shame.
These are outstanding gifts   he who holds firm to them   does
   not fail to receive a chair   of respect for sitting on.
This homily says that   (these two things) decorate a woman   both
   outside and inside her house   if she has (lit. uses) them.
Keep yourself from the rust   that destroys your womanhood   a
   woman is nothing   if she gets involved in scandal.
A wife is like a white cloth   but a spot on the cloth   be careful
   not to give it   for it cannot endure spots.
To love those in high place   by having money   and to dis- 65
   parage the poor   my homily says this is bad.

Penda wenye cheo   na wanyonge uwe nao   hayo ndiyo mapo-
keo   mema mtu kutumia.

Kila mtu msharifu   dunia ni badilifu   shida sana kuarifu   mtu
atayekufaa.

Mwema hujiharibu   ikampasa adhabu   na mbaya aki-
tubu   dhambi zake hufutiwa.

Kitu bure heshima   mpe baba na mama   kila mtu mzima   na
walio nawe sawa.

70 Ukosefu wa adabu   ni jambo la aibu   wajibu kujita-
nibu   mbali nalo kukaa.

Mpungufu wa adabu   duniani ana taabu   hakaribishwi
karibu   marafiki humwambaa.

Iweke moyoni hati   ubora wake thabiti   hapana tofauti   heri
itakujia.

Tumbo la rutuba   umepewa kama huba   uzae mama na
baba   kustawisha dunia.

Tumbo hili dhahabu   huzaa wenye thawabu   na wengine
wa ajabu   hupata kuzaliwa.

75 Kwa hivi una uzazi   kuuguza na ulezi   hutaka maanga-
lizi   bora hati yakwambia.

Tena kujitegemea   ni ngao ya ukiwa   siku ya kubakia   peke
yako hufaa.

Peke yako ukiwa   wajibu kukaza nia   tendo likishari-
kiwa   sifa yake hupungua.

Sifa ya peke kubwa   vigumu sana kuzibwa   hata kama iki-
kabwa   ushahidi itatoa.

Sifa ya wengi shirika   lazima kugawanyika   ya peke joho
huvika   mmoja mteuliwa.

80 Katika maisha yetu   ana chango kila mtu   japo kidogo si
kitu   toa unachojaliwa.

Chango mbaya uvundo   wajibu kutenga kando   bora hua-
cha uhondo   daima kukumbukiwa.

Love people of rank   but do not despise (lit. be with) the humble   for this is the tradition   a good one for a man to follow.

Every high-born person   on this earth is changeable   it is very difficult to know   the person who will benefit you.

The good man destroys himself   and is deserving of punishment   and the evil man when he repents   has his sins wiped out.

Respect costs nothing   so give it to your father and mother   and to every adult person   and to whom you have all alike.

Failure in good manners   is a matter of shame   one should 70 examine oneself in this   and be far from it.

The bad-mannered person   has trouble on earth   he is not welcomed   his friends withdraw from him.

So take to heart this homily   it is of proven worth   there is nothing different (from what I have said)   happiness will come to you.

A fertile womb   have you received for love   for you to bear a mother and father (i.e. in their turn)   to make the earth prosper.

This womb is gold   it gives birth to the gifted   and others of great wonder   get to be born.

And so you have motherhood   nursing and raising (chil- 75 dren)   these things need care   my homily had better tell you this.

And then to be independent   is the shield of loneliness   when you are left   quite alone it will be a good thing.

If you are alone   you should make up your mind (to endure)   an act that is shared   lessens its praise.

A thing done alone has great praise   it becomes difficult to stop (its being praised)   even if its praise is cut off   it will still produce its own evidence.

The praise of a thing done with others   is bound to be divided   but done alone it is like a cloak   that covers the chosen one.

In our lives   each person has a contribution to make   even 80 though it be small that matters not   give what you have been granted.

A bad contribution (to life) stinks   keep aside from it   good deeds make a feast   always to be remembered.

Tendo bora hudumu   kufutika ni vigumu   baya kwa wanadamu   halina pa kukaa.

Umekuta dunia   vema imeandaliwa   karimu kukupo-
kea   shukurani zako toa.

Umekuta wasafiri   walioipa kwa heri   wameiweka vi-
zuri   nawe zidisha stawa.

85 Kukinai jifundishe   kidogo kikutoshe   kikubwa siji-
zoeshe   kukujia kwa hatia.

Pato lako la halali   japo kitu dhalili   bora kuliko mali   fedheha inayotia.

Hati fanya kikuba   moyo wako utashiba   dunia ina
ghiliba   kama hukuangalia.

Hati hii ni kufuli   kinga yako ya mwili   shauku kitu
batili   kwa uzuri kuchafua.

Uzuri wako wa sura   kufanya uwe imara   sharti uwe na
busara   ya kuambaa hadaa.

90 Na ubaya wa sura   unaweza kuwa bora   kama unayo fikira   ya matendo ya murua.

Zamu moja twaishi   ikisha haturudishwi   maisha ya fawai-
shi   acha kuandamia.

Ewe binti tajiri   siku zote jihadhari   kutengana na
kiburi   mali huota mbawa.

Na binti maskini   usiache abadani   kujizidisha thamani   kwa
kuwa mwaminiwa.

Binti wa mkubwa   watu usiite mbwa   fahari inapozibwa   nawe
utasimbuliwa.

95 Na binti wa mdogo   waweza kupata togo   kwa kufuata
mwigo   wa matendo ya murua.

Hati nawapa wote   tunzeni kama pete   mazao mema
mpate   mfurahie dunia.

Dunia jengo lake   la mume na mwanamke   kazi hii
mshike   hata kufanikiwa.

Ijengeni kwa tofali   wote watu wawili   hata iwe kamili   iwari-
dhishe kukaa.

Kazi hii itendeke   pasiwe na pekepeke   wajao nyuma wach-
eke   kuona imetimia.

100 Wakatabahu beti   mtenzi wa hati   ni Shaaban Robert   jina
mwaarifiwa.

A good deed lasts   to wipe it out is difficult   but an evil deed
   towards men   has no place to remain (in the memory).

You have met with the world   it is ordered well   it is generous
   in its reception of you   so offer your thanks.

You have met with pilgrims   who have said goodbye to it (the
   world)   they dealt well with it   and so increase your own
   prosperity.

Learn to be content   be satisfied with little   be not accus- 85
   tomed to plenty   for it will bring you into wrong-doing.

Your profit is lawful   even though it be a poor one   it is better
   than wealth   which brings shame.

Make my homily to be like a canopy   and your heart will be happy
   the world will get the better of you   if you don't take care.

This homily is like a lock   it is protection for your body   to
   desire a worthless thing   for beauty's sake is defilement.

The beauty of your face   if you want it to last   then you must
   have wisdom   to avoid deception.

And if your face is plain   you can make it beautiful   if you 90
   think   of honourable deeds.

We have finished one turn (i.e. the daughter's turn, and next will
   be the son's)   so then we don't have to go back   to a pur-
   poseless life   do not follow after that.

O my daughter, rich (in blessings)   always be careful   to keep
   clear of pride   for wealth grows wings.

And O my poor daughter   never never stop   increasing your
   worth   for you are trusted.

O my big daughter   don't call people dogs   when prosperity
   is halted   you will be greatly troubled.

O my little daughter   you can gain affection   if you follow the 95
   example   of good deeds.

I give this homily to everybody   look after it like a ring   so
   that you may bear good fruit   and be happy on this earth.

The world is a place   for a man and a woman to build   so take
   to this work   until you come to prosper.

Build it with bricks   both man and woman together   until it
   be complete   and satisfy you as a home.

Let this work be done   without any fuss   so that those who
   come after may be happy   in seeing that it is done.

He who has written the verses   of the Poem of the Written 100
   Homily   is Shaaban Robert   a name that you know.

Utendi wa Adili

Kijana lete kalamu   nina habari muhimu   napenda uifahamu   dadayo kesha zamuye.

Zamuye imekiwisha   baki kujikumbusha   leo nataka maisha   yako nawe tuongee.

Mungu akiniamuru   nataka nijikusuru   nikupe yasiyodhuru   yakufae baadaye.

Moyo wangu tamimina   kwako leo kijana   kila lenye maana   uchague mwenyewe.

5 Habari niliyo nayo   nataka nikupe leo   tia katika sikio   moyoni mwako ikae.

Sitaki ikuponyoke   moyoni mwako iweke   itakuja siku yake   ya kutaka utumie.

Mnyama afunza kinda   taaluma ya kuwinda   yapasayo kutenda   sina budi nikwambie.

Hasha kuwinda wetu   hakuna faida kwetu   lakini vipo vitu   mtu lazima ajue.

Kuna mambo maalumu   ambayo yalazimu   kila mwanadamu   kupata fununuye.

10 Kwanza mche Mungu   mtengeneza ulimwengu   juu akaweka mbingu   nyota zituangazie.

Ameweka kwa mkazo   mbingu bila nguzo   himidi wake uwezo   yana ajabu mamboye.

Na ardhi katandika   chini kama mkeka   na mito kutiririka   mchana na usikuwe.

Mito huitiririsha   majangwa kuneemesha   na mvua isikonyesha   kwayo hukoma kiuye.

Ardhi ina maki   kizikwacho hakinuki   na mbegu hubariki   huu wote uwezowe.

15 Tena kwa hekima   kasimamisha milima   mikubwa imesimama   hana mshabahawe.

Ameweka na bahari   pana hazina kadiri   ili vyombo kusafiri   hayakauki majiye.

Hewa haina mpaka   ndege huri huruka   wanyama hutononoka   porini kwa neemaye.

Baharini samaki   na kila mahluki   wake ana riziki   toka kwake yeye.

Utendi—The Poem on Good Conduct

Young man bring a pen   I have something important   that I
  want you to understand   your sister has had her turn.
Her turn is finished   now it is for you to remind yourself   that
  today I want us   to talk about your life.
God commanding me   I want to make an effort   to give you
  what does not hurt   but what will be of use to you in the
  future.
I will pour out my heart   to you today, young man   so that
  everything sensible   you may choose it yourself.
What I have   I want to give you today   listen to it care- 5
  fully   so that it may dwell in your heart.
I do not want it to escape you   lay it to heart   the day will
  come   when you will want to use (what I say).
An animal teaches its young   the skill of the hunt   what
  should be done   I must tell you.
To chase our (children) away   is of no use at all   but there are
  things   that a person must know.
There are special things   which are necessary   for every
  human being   to get an idea about.
First, reverence God   the Arranger of the Universe   who 10
  placed the heavens above   and the stars to give us light.
He has placed firmly   the heavens without any pillars   worship then His power   for His works are wonderful.
And He set out the earth   beneath like a mat   and rivers to
  glide along   by day and night.
He makes the rivers to flow   making desert-places to flourish   so
  that where rain does not fall   thirst may be quenched by
  them.
The earth is deep   what is buried does not arise   and He
  blesses seeds   all this is from His power.
Then with wisdom   He caused the hills to stand   big (hills) 15
  stand up   He has no compare.
He has also placed the sea   there are treasures untold (in it)   so
  that ships may journey   and its water does not dry up.
The sky has no limit   birds fly free   animals get fat   in the
  bush by His grace.
Fish in the sea   and every creature   all His (created beings)
  have sustenance   which comes from Him.

Ajua yote kwa ghibu   bila kusoma kitabu   ni bwana wa
thawabu   wajibu aheshimiwe.

20 Amemilki elimu   kila kitu afahamu   kwake hapana
gumu   asilojua mbinuye.

Yeye ni mfafanuzi   dunia kwake i wazi   wala hakuna ta-
tizi   itatizayo kaziye.

Amemilki na nguvu   juu ya ushupavu   ambayo hakuna
mwivu   aliye sawa naye.

Nguvuye haina mwisho   haiingiwi na chosho   wala
hakuna tisho   lilegezalo moyowe.

Kabisa hashindiki   wala halinganiki   katika yake milki   hai-
pimiki enziye.

25 Ana mapenzi kweli   hana kidogo batili   kila siku mka-
bili   kuomba ufanikiwe.

Mwombe daima Rabi   akusamehe madhambi   mwanadamu
ni vumbi   makosa desturiye.

Bwana wa mahakimu   mpende simuhasimu   kila analohu-
kumu   hana rufaa mbelee.

Ni mjuzi wa habari   mwelewa kila siri   wala hana ghururi   kusahau mbali naye.

Lugha amedhibiti   duniani za umati   haimpiti sauti   asi-
yojua maanaye.

30 Roho yake mpe yeye   atunze isipolewe   shetani kama
mwewe   kupoa amaliye.

Amewatukuza watu   juu ya kila kitu   wajibu kila mtu   heshima amfanyie.

Kukaa naye karibu   kwa mawazo wajibu   Mungu mtu
haharibu   ila aanze mwenyewe.

Ni mwonaji aona   vyote kwa bayana   dunia nzima haina   mwonaji kamaye.

Pili tii mfalme   wa kike na wa kiume   bila ya kinyume   utii uwatendee.

35 Mfalme kajaliwa   uwezo maridhawa   analolitaka kuwa   li-
takuwa uelewe.

Tatu baba na mama   wataka taadhima   na kila lililo jema   ukiweza watendee.

Tunza pasimee gugu   kati yenu ya vurugu   baba yako ni
mbegu   uliyochipuka wewe.

He knows of things that are far away   without reading a
book   He is Lord of Gifts   He should be respected.

He rules over knowledge   He understands everything   for 20
Him there is nothing hard   of which He does not know its
shape.

He is the Revealer   the whole world is open to Him   nor is
there any complication   to mess up His handiwork.

He rules with strength   over obstinacy   and no one jealous
of His strength   is at all equal to Him.

His strength has no end   it does not tire   nor is there any
terror   that can weaken His heart.

He is altogether undefeatable   as well as incomparable   in
His domain   His power is immeasurable.

He has true love   and not the least variableness   always the 25
one who faces Him   to pray is blessed.

Pray always to the Lord   for Him to forgive your sins   man
is as the dust   he is an habitual sinner.

Lord of Lords   love Him and do not antagonize Him   whenever He passes judgement   there is no appeal afterwards.

He knows everything   He understands every secret   He has
no passing arrogance   and He never forgets.

He has protected the languages   on earth of great number   there
is no sound   of which He does not know the meaning.

Give Him the soul that is His   let Him care for it so that it does 30
not become cool   Satan like a hawk   it is his job to make
(the heart) cool.

He (God) has exalted people   in every particular   it is only
proper then for people   to do Him honour.

To dwell near Him   in thought is proper   God does not
destroy a man   unless the man begins it first.

He is the seer who sees   all things clearly   in the whole
world there is no one   who sees as He does.

Secondly obey the king   either the king or the queen   without
being contrary   pay them homage.

The king was granted   power in plenty   so that what he wishes 35
to come about   it will come about, understand.

Thirdly for your mother and father   you need respect   and
every good thing   if you can do it for them.

See that no weed grows   amongst you to mess things up   for
your father is the seed   from which you burst forth.

Mama amefanya kazi   katika wako uzazi   yakupasa kumuenzi   hata upate radhiye.

Watu hawa wana deni   kwako la hisani   litie mwako moyoni   daima likumbukie.

40 Nne fanya taaluma   kujifunza kusema   neno linalochoma   bila udhuru sitoe.

Usitumie lafidhi   kwa watu inayoudhi   lugha humpa hadhi   kutumia ajuaye.

Kila kukipambazuka   viungo vyako hutaka   ulimi kutotamka   baya visiumie.

Kila kukicha tazama   viungo vyako husema   ulimi nena mema   pigo lisitujie.

Lugha mbaya hasara   inawakisha hasira   na kuleta madhara   hiyo yache pekee.

45 Usiseme usafihi   watu ukawakirihi   hauna masilahi   acha usitumie.

Ambatana na adabu   uwe nayo karibu   ina mazao ajabu   shika usiachie.

Ukiwa na ghadhabu   jifanye kama bubu   kimya ni utibabu   wa hasira uelewe.

Tano lililo adhimu   ni kujifunza elimu   ina mwanga maalumu   elimu kwa elewaye.

Maisha bila elimu   hayafai mwanadamu   sababu mambo magumu   mengi sana mbelee.

50 Milango wazi adimu   kwa asiye na elimu   kwa mwenye nayo gumu   hujifungua wenyewe.

Ingawa dunia pana   nyembamba sana huona   mtu asiyeona   kwa akili na machoye.

Elimu aliye nayo   amepata ufunguo   mbele ya mazuio   katika maishaye.

Onyo kwa mafunzo   silifanyie mzozo   wapewa iwe nguzo   mafunzo ugemee.

Kadhalika mwalimu   mkuza yako fahamu   naye ana sehemu   heshimayo apewe.

55 Ana madai ya haki   kwako ya urafiki   sababu alishariki   ujingani utolewe.

Yote atakayo kwako   hayapunguzi mfuko   ni kumbukumbu kuwako   bainayo na yeye.

Your mother has laboured   at your birth   so it behoves you
to respect her   so that you win her approval.

These have a debt   which you should pay for their kindness   have it always in your heart   remember it always.

Fourthly take steps   to learn how to speak   a word that 40
pierces   do not speak it without some excuse.

Do not speak with an accent   that upsets people (i.e.
affected)   speech gives respect   to him who knows how to
use it.

Every morning   your body (lit. joints) wishes   that your
tongue should not speak   lest hurt be done.

Every evening, look   your body says   speak good things, O
tongue   in case we get beaten.

Bad speech brings damage   it enflames anger   and brings
injuries   so leave it alone.

Do not speak impudently   insulting people   (for then) there 45
is no reconciliation   don't do it.

Be well-mannered   always have good manners   for this brings
amazing results   so keep to this and do not give it up.

If you are angry   make yourself as though you were
dumb   silence is a balm   for anger, understand.

Fifthly what is pleasing   is to become educated   this is a
special light   is knowledge for him who understands.

A life without knowledge   is no good for a man   because
there are difficult things   many of them ahead.

The open door (lit. doors) is rare   for the unlearned   but the 50
learned (with a) difficulty   is able to solve it.

Though the world be wide   he finds it very narrow   does the
man who does not see   with his mind and with his eyes.

Whoever has knowledge   has got a key   to any hindrances
before him   for the difficulties in his life.

Advice by lessons   do not make it a quarrelling matter   you
receive it to be a pillar   tap (i.e. benefit from) your lessons
then.

Likewise your teacher   he is your benefactor, understand   and
he has his part   so let him receive your respect.

He has legal claims   on you of friendship   because he was 55
devoted (to you)   to take you out of (your) ignorance.

All that he wants from you   costs you nothing   it is a reminder
of what there is   between you and him.

Ingawa hili waona   kuwa dogo sana   lakini lina
maana   akupaye mpe naye.

Aliyokupa si haba   amekupa ya kushiba   fadhili hii
kuiba   kubwa sana aibuye.

Sita ukioa mke   kwa mapenzi mshike   simfanyie makeke   ila
akuanze yeye.

60 Hata hivyo ukiweza   samahani kufanyiza   faida itafu-
liza   kuwajia yeye nawe.

Ni tone samahani   la asali moyoni   hutia furahini   mpewa
na atoaye.

Mkeo mpe heshima   muhesabu kama mama   mzaa watoto
wema   ulivyozaliwa wewe.

Watoto wako wapende   katika moyo wagande   na uwezalo
litende   liwafae baadaye.

Wafunze taamuli   kila namna adili   kabla kuwapa
mali   watoto watumie.

65 Hazina na ulegevu   kwa mtoto upotevu   mpe funzo la
nguvu   kuamsha akiliye.

Ndugu wapende sana   wapendezwe kukuona   binti zao na
wana   wote wakufurahie.

Jinalo liwe kwao   bora katika mioyo   likitajwa masikio   yao yapendezewe.

Patana na masahibu   ulio nao karibu   kwao uwe muhibu   wa
mbali wakuanie.

Huyu kumpenda yule   ni asili ya umbile   upeke jambo
tule   huchukiza uvundowe.

70 Uwe kwa rafiki zako   kitu cha makumbuko   ukiwapo ama
huko   daima ukumbukiwe.

Jengole ni matendo   ambayo hayana fundo   ndiyo yajengayo
pendo   haya yazingatie.

Jina la machukio   huchukiza masikio   na kuvimbisha mioyo   jihadhari usipewe.

Mfano wake tatoa   hili ninalokwambia   ili upate elewa   shina na matawiye.

Jina la uhaini   kubeli si kifani   kusikiwa atamani   juu
yake litumiwe.

75 Hili kwa kufananisha   nadhani hapa latosha   mengine
linganisha   mwenyewe baadaye.

Though you find this   to be a small matter   yet it has
    much meaning   for what he gives you, give him (something
    back).
What he gave you is not small   he has given you enough to
    satisfy   to steal such kindness   is a great shame.
Sixthly if you marry a wife   cleave to her with love   don't
    annoy her   unless she begins it first.
Even so if you can   bring about forgiveness   mutual benefit 60
    will arise   between you and her.
Forgiveness is a drop   of honey in the heart   it brings
    joy   for the receiver and the giver.
Respect your wife   treat her as a mother   the mother of good
    children   as you were born yourself.
Love your children   clasp them to your heart   and do what
    you can   for what may help them in the future.
Teach them to be thoughtful   and every kind of good man-
    ners   before you give them money   for them to use.
Slackness with money   for a child is fatal   teach him in a 65
    practical   manner to arouse his understanding.
Love well your brethren   that they be pleased to see you   and
    their sons and daughters   let them all be happy with you.
Let your name be with them   well in their hearts   so that if it
    be mentioned   in their ears, they may be pleased.
Agree with your friends   who are near   be affectionate with
    them   so that the distant ones may speak well of you.
For this person to love that one   is the most natural thing   lone-
    liness is a wretched thing   its odour offends.
Be towards your friend   someone to remember   whether with 70
    them or not   always be remembered.
The building is done with deeds   which have no ill-feel-
    ing   these are the things that build love   think on these
    things.
The name of bad-temper   offends the ears   and breaks the
    heart   be careful not to be called such.
I will give an example   of what I am saying   so that you can
    understand   the root and its branches.
The name of treachery   nothing like it does the good per-
    son   wish to be heard   being used about himself.
This for an example   is enough I think here   make other com- 75
    parisons   yourself afterwards.

Penda na watu wote   aliye mbali mvute   ila kuamini
wote   hili sana liambae.

Hadhari usiache   siri yako ifiche   ila watu wachache   wapa-
sao wajue.

Na ukiweka ahadi   kutimiza jitahidi   inabatilisha
sudi   ahadi kwa avunjaye.

Ahadi ni heshima   kabla ya kuisema   wajibu kuipima   ndipo
kinywani utoe.

80 Ahadi usibadili   ila iwe batili   sababu ni halali   mtu jema
achague.

Msaada ukiweza   kutoa ni mwangaza   ambao utatu-
kuza   jinalo lisipotee.

Kutaka yote wewe   wengine wasipewe   hakuna heri mwishowe   hilo usikusudie.

Njia isiyo adili   iliyo na ukatili   hawendi makubeli   nawe
usisafirie.

Mashavu yasikuvimbe   bure na watu ugombe   fahamu jino
pembe   kila mtu mchekee.

85 Uso wa tabasam   dalili ya ukarimu   kiburi uhasimu   la
kwanza lichague.

Na uso wa furaha   huvuta karibu jaha   usionyeshe jeraha   la
pigo mbali nawe.

Ukidai kuwa bora   jua watiwa fora   hajipi sifa bora   mtu
ila apewe.

Tumika kwa adili   kazi msingi wa mali   uvivu husumu
mwili   usiandame rahaye.

Raha ya uvivu mbaya   umaskini huzaa   acha kuikaribia   usi-
sikize witowe.

90 Kazi yako idhibiti   ipe jicho na dhati   ukitoka katikati   wa-
muzi jina wachie.

Kwa waamuzi wa haki   waone hulaumiki   wa batili iwe
dhiki   kutaka doa utiwe.

Kabla sijakwisha   habari ninawapasha   kosa mkisahihi-
sha   ndiyo adili yenyewe.

Kama mwaona adili   kuweka yastahili   niombeeni Jalali   amani yake nipewe.

Love all men   the one far from you draw him near   but do
  not believe in everybody (indiscriminately)   keep clear of that.

Go on being cautious   hide your secret   except from a few
  people   who ought to know it.

And if you make a promise   try to keep it   success is
  destroyed   for whoever breaks promises.

A promise is honourable   before you make it   you should consider it   and then speak it.

Do not change a promise   unless it is cancelled   this is a 80
  proper reason (for changing it)   for man to choose.

If you can help   by giving, that is a light   by which you will
  exalt   your name that it be not lost.

For you to want everything   without others getting something   brings no happiness in the end   so do not purpose
  this.

An ill-mannered way (of life)   which is a cruel one also   good
  people do not follow it   so neither should you.

Do not puff up your cheeks   for nothing, and quarrel with
  people   understand that at a misplaced tooth   people laugh.

A smiling face   is a sign of generosity   contend with 85
  pride   and choose the first of these.

And a joyful face   attracts honour near   do not show the
  wound   of an attack (made) far from you.

If you claim to be superior   know that you will lose the
  game   no one praises himself   but one receives it (from
  others).

Work honourably   for work is the foundation of wealth   laziness poisons the body   do not follow after its comfort.

The bliss of laziness is bad   it brings forth poverty   come not
  near it   do not listen to its call.

Do your work well   give it your whole attention   if you leave 90
  it in the middle   leave to the critics a (good) name.

For the good critics   to see that you are not to be blamed   for
  uselessness (and) it become (a source of) trouble   wanting to
  stain your character.

Before I finish   I want to tell you this   if you correct a mistake   that is quite proper.

If you think it right   to consider (lit. place) it (i.e. this homily)
  deserving   pray to the Almighty for me   that I may be
  given His peace.

Niombeeni Karimu   anipe nami karamu   mambo yaliyo
tamu   katika hazinaye.

95 Hazina yake haishi   shida haikorofishi   nami kwake mta-
shi   niombeeni nipewe.

Niombeeni maisha   afya kuninadhifisha   umri wangu
ukisha   peponi nami nitiwe.

Kama mbaya itupeni   sina ghaidhi moyoni   mwandishi
Shaaban   Robert babangu miye.

Msidhani mahuluti   kabila sikusaliti   Mwafrika madhubuti   vingine nisidhaniwe.

Sikuchanganya nasaba   kwa mama wala kwa baba   inga-
waje ni haiba   mimi sina asiliye.

100 Si Mwarabu si Mzungu   Hindi si jadi yangu   naarifu
walimwengu   wadadisio wajue.

Pray to the Generous One   that He may give me gifts   things
 that are pleasant   from His store.

His store does not fail   shortage does not ruin it   and I am 95
 an urgent suppliant towards Him   pray then for me that I
 may receive (what I ask).

Pray for my life   that health may keep me clean   and that
 when my days are done   I may be put in Paradise.

If there is evil throw it away   I have no anger in my heart   the
 writer Shaaban   whose father is Robert, that's me.

Do not think unkindly   I have not betrayed my tribe   I am an
 honest African   do not think of me otherwise.

I am not of mixed lineage   neither on my mother's nor my
 father's side   however fine (other lineage) may be   I am
 not sprung from it.

I am no Arab nor a European   I am not of Indian descent   I 100
 tell this to the world   so that the curious may know.

4

LONG-MEASURE VERSE

LONG-MEASURE is the characteristic metrical mould of some of the earliest-known forms of Swahili poetry. Long-measure verse usually consists of a single line or strophe divided, not always medially, by a caesura (Sw. *kituo*), and with an end-rhyme to each line. In some poems of this type an internal rhyme upon the caesura is designed to respond to the terminal rhyme of the line, making the single strophe into a rhymed couplet.

GUNGU SONGS

The most popular form of long-measure verse is that with a syllabic measure of ten *mizani*. Examples are found in the Taylor Papers in the Library of the SOAS in Swahili-Arabic texts written and transliterated into roman script by the copyist, Muhammad Kijuma. These poems include marriage-songs and serenades reflecting the gracious days before the passing of the Arab citadels on the East African coast. Muhammad Kijuma's collection includes two poems already recorded by Bishop Steere,[1] *Utumbuizi wa Mwana Mnazi* and *Mama nipeeke haoe*, which Steere describes as song-accompaniments to the *gungu* dances. He found these dances and their accompanying songs still popular in 1869, but by that time much of the glory of the setting had departed. Steere recounts[2] 'that it is the custom to meet about ten or eleven o'clock at night and dance on until daybreak. . . . The men and slave-women dance, the ladies sit a little retired and look on. . . . Each piece takes a long time to sing, as most of the syllables have several notes and flourishes or little cadences to themselves.'

The titles *Gungu la Kufunda* and *Gungu la Kukwaa* are translated by Steere respectively as 'The Pounding Figure' and 'The Hesitation Dance', implying that the word *gungu* had special reference to a form of dance. Steere wrote: 'the names refer to the sort of steps in which the songs are danced. . . . the first figure (*la kufunda*) is danced by a single couple, the second by two couples.'

---

[1] Steere, *Swahili Tales*, London, 1928, pp. 472 et seq.   [2] Ibid., preface, p. xii.

While this may be true of the particular dances mentioned here, it is likely that the term *gungu* itself applied to the whole ceremony at which dancing and the composition of enigma verses were the principal activities. Sacleux in his Dictionary states that the term *gungu* applies to an old dance with a song relating to the story of Liyongo, and that in Mombasa it was performed once a year on the Siku ya Mwaka at the grave of the Shekhe wa Mvita; in Zanzibar, he says, it was performed at weddings.

A loose sheet in the Taylor Papers gives an extremely interesting text from Lamu concerning the enigma verses at the *gungu* ceremony:

'Huku Amu walipokwenda wakitaka fanya gungu, hupeleka upatu kwa shaha na fedha ndani yakwe na tambuu nyingi na maji na sukari.

'Nalo gungu ni patu kubwa lapigwa. Nda asili lile patu latoka Shirazi. Na gungu sharti nda harusi.

'Basi shaha huweta wale washairi wenziwe walio tini yakwe, wakaja wakagawanya upatu. Wakisha gawanya hutunga shairi. Shaha akafunga nyama. Maana ya kufunga nyama ni kufunga nyama kwa fumbo. Na lile shairi hawaambiwi maana yakwe lile fumbo, huwatajia tu.

'Wakenda wakanza ile jawabu wakwe majumbani mwao, hatta usiku iklandikwa gungu kule hamsini.

'Huyo shaha hutoa ule wimbo wake wa kufunga nyama, basi akafungua. Akatoka mtu kujibu. Basi akiwa anamfungua nyama shaha hupigapiga upanga, maana kumtambulisha kwamba nyama unamfungua wewe. Yule mwenyewe akajua nyama namfungua, basi hutunga wimbo wa kujisifu.

'Na akitomfungua, yule shaha humtungia wimbo wa kumvika guni, maana kumtokoza, kumtahayarisha kwamba nyama hukumfungua, hukumjua nyama. Basi huwa na huzuni sana, na wengine hulia.'

'Here at Lamu when they went wishing to perform the *gungu* ceremony, a dish-shaped gong was sent to the Shah containing money, much betel, water, and sugar.

'And the *gungu* is a big dish-shaped gong which is beaten. The gong with its gifts originated from Persia. For a *gungu* ceremony there must be a wedding.

'And so the Shah calls his friends the poets, who are his

subjects, and they come and divide up the gifts in the gong. When they have shared them, a poem is composed. The Shah ties up an animal. The meaning of "tying up an animal" is tying up an animal by (composing) an enigma. They are not told the meaning of the enigma in that poem, the poem is just read out to them.

'And they used to go and begin to solve the enigma in their houses, writing at night as many as fifty *gungu* songs.

'The Shah gives out his "tying up the animal" song and then unties it. And there appears a man to answer. If he unties the animal (i.e. solves the enigma) the Shah beats a sword, this is to let him know that he has untied the animal. And so he composes a song to praise himself.

'And if he does not untie it, the Shah composes a song *kumvika guni*, to tease him, to make him ashamed that he did not untie the animal and did not know the animal. And so the man is very sorrowful, and some even cry.'

The use of the *upatu*, a dish-shaped gong, during wedding celebrations is mentioned by Velten,[1] but the *gungu* ceremony is not specifically mentioned by him in the texts he collected. It is likely that the *gungu* ceremony was not an integral part of a Swahili marriage, but that at most marriages *gungu* songs were sung, whether or not the ceremony described in the above text took place. No verses clearly recognizable as belonging to this practice survive, at least no verses that plainly are enigma verses, but since the majority of *gungu* songs were composed to explain or suggest a solution, the enigmatic character of the subject-matter may not be apparent. Certainly there are many Swahili poems which are not understood even by the Swahilis themselves, but whether these are enigma poems or poems with difficult topical allusions and obsolete words it is impossible to say.

Manuscripts clearly relating to the *gungu* ceremony either describe the general setting or are song-accompaniments to a dance. Included in the *Utendi wa Liyongo* by Muhammad Kijuma is the long-measure poem describing the setting. It would appear that in Steere's day the song-accompaniments and the dances were performed outside the context of marriage celebrations. Some of these *gungu* songs do make frequent reference to the story of Liyongo. The following example, with internal rhymes, is from

[1] *Desturi za Wasuaheli*, Göttingen, 1903, p. 114.

a copy in the Taylor Papers. It consists of the irregular number of eleven *vipande* of fourteen *mizani*.

Pijia pembe ya nyati

Pijia pembe ya nyati mke yenye tawo.

Mama niliko hatezame umbuji kwawo   kukuteneke washorongwa na nyemi zawo.

Yeo ni siku ya kunyema wasikiyewo   mshika gogo na towazi yeo ni yewo.

Kumbuke Mbwasho na Kundazi na Fumo kwawo   uta na zembe silahaye atukuwewo.

Uta ni baba ndiyo ni mama azaziyewo   siisi kama na kunena siku ya yewo.

Tupate radhi ya wazee wazazi yewo   vuani mato mutezame wambuji u mmbuji yewo.

Enda kaweta Mringwari walinda nini.

Play the buffalo horn

Play the curved horn of the she-buffalo.

Lady, from where I am let me behold the festive array
    there   where the players are met together with joyful clamour.
Today is the day for merry noise, hear them today   the drumstick player and the cymbals, today is the day.
Remember Mbwasho, Kundazi and the spearlord at their homeland   the bow and the spear-heads, his arms that he bore.
The bow is his father or it is (like) his mother who nurtured him   I know not what to say or speak on this day of days.
Let us seek a blessing from our elders, our parents, today   raise your eyes and see the fair maidens, you are beautiful today.
Go and call them, Mringwari, for what are you waiting?

A slightly longer fragment by the same copyist, Rashidi b. Abdallah, in the Taylor Papers is carelessly written, but is of special interest because it mentions the plot of the *kikoa* meal when Mringwari intended to shoot down Liyongo as he climbed the tree to pick the fruit. The syllabic measure is irregular, but most probably the original was in fifteen *mizani*. This poem is called by Hichens *The Song of Shagga*, and for convenience we may retain the title here.

The Song of Shagga

... mtezi na Mbwasho na Kundazi   pijiani pembe vikoma mle na towazi.

Mmbeja mwiwa kumbuke mwana wa shangazi   yu wapi simba ezi ali kana mtembezi.

Fumo wa Shagga sikiya shabah mitaa pwani   fumo wa Shagga chambia waTwa mfungiani.

Kikaze muwi nguo nawapa za kitwani   mkapatia na mikumbuu viunoni.

Papa kitambi kamwinde huo manyikani   wasi washinda ila ye pweke manyikani.

Kenda wambieni kasite yuu tumuyeni   ye yufite ngozi kiyungwa shake la buni.

Nikila tapo na zipopo za mwituni   wachamba kila tiwiye tule kikoa wa sisi al-sultani.

Achamba hila kikoa mkata muno talipani   achamba tashukume wivu la ngaani.

Tule cha yayi tafuma wivu la ngaani   kafuma ngaa wachamba huyu si mtu yunga jini.

Liyongo Fumo hukufilike Liyongo koka hudani . . .

... the performer and Mbwasho and Kundazi   beat the horns, the state drums and the cymbals.

Fair lady, discerning one, remember the cousin   where is the mighty lion who is as a wanderer?

The Lord of Shagga hearing rumours from the coastal settlements   the Lord of Shagga speaking to the Twa, (saying), Tie him up.

Fix it and to the killer I give you head-cloths   and you shall get cinctures for your loins.

Flap the hand-cloth and hunt this person in the wilds   where none dwells except he alone in the bush.

Go, I tell you, and hide, and let us leave him for dead up aloft   he is hiding at Kiyungwa in Ngozi in the miserable haunts of the Buni.

Eating wild-fruit and the areca-nut of the forest   they said, Eating a bad thing? Let us eat a sharing-feast, we who are the Sultan's people.

And he said, If I eat a sharing-feast, what shall I, a poor man, pay? and he said, I will shake down the ripe fruit of the top-most branch.

Let us eat of the choicest, I will pierce the ripe fruit of the topmost branch and he shot down the topmost branch, and they said, This is no man, he is like a jinn.

Liyongo the Spearlord is not slayable, Liyongo escapes by divine guidance . . .

*   *   *

MAVUGO WEDDING-SONGS

Another type of wedding-song is unrhymed and non-metrical (i.e. no measure of vocal syllables). These are the *mavugo* wedding-songs which take their name from the *vugo* or buffalo-horn which, beaten with a wooden rod to make it resound, formed the accom-paniment to the prose-poem and marked the pace of the rhythm. Verse of this type may be described as rhythmic prose, and may be the earliest type of indigenous Swahili songs recorded, though no external evidence can be adduced to establish this. No date can be assigned to *mavugo* songs in the Swahili-Arabic script, but reliable Swahili scholars, like Sir Mbarak Ali Hinawy (from whose collection the following examples were taken) have been of the opinion that the origin of these songs is in the remote past.

The following example begins with a conventional opening:

Pani kiwanda niteze polepole mtu mweni
Huno utumweni wangu si wenyeji wenu
Mtu mweni utimbile kisima kuwanywesha wenyejiwe mayi
Akima kupata mayi akapija panda
Aketa wana wanyema ndooni muole
Wana wanyema wakiya wakima na kulia
Ya kushindwa ndiyo eda ya waume.

Give me a courtyard that I, a stranger, may play,
For this my service is not as your citizenship.
A stranger dug a well that he might give the citizens to drink,
Having found water he stood and blew a horn,
And he called the good people, Come and see.
And the good folk came and stood and cried,
It is the lot of men to be left some hope.

*   *   *

The *mavugo* songs are not so Arabicized as the more cultured verse. Another example is as follows: [*see over, p. 178*].

Huyu yuwaya yuwaya mtelea nguu
Aya atukule pembe
Na pembe mwana nyema
Atukuziye akitua mzigo kitwani.

This one comes, she comes swift of foot
She comes carrying gleanings
And the gleanings are a lusty babe
She carries it until she lowers the burden from her head.

★   ★   ★

SERENADES AND PRAISE-SONGS

Not all long-measure verse can be definitely associated with
weddings, but this does not exclude the possibility of their being
gungu songs. Some are love-songs and others clearly deal with a
subject that is only indirectly related to marriage. References are
made to the Liyongo story.

The next example, from the Taylor Papers, is a serenade. As in
other poems of this type there is no internal rhyme.

The Swahili houses, like the one mentioned in the poem, had
stout walls of dressed coral-rock and were usually of more than
one storey (Sw. *msana*). In the upper stories, the windows of
which overlooked an inner courtyard, were the chambers of the
harem, sometimes provided with a latticed balcony overlooking
the roadway. On the lower or ground floor were the entrance hall
or vestibule, to which access was given from the street by one of
the massive carved wooden doors which are still an ornament of
some of the bigger houses, and the reception hall, where guests
foregathered.

The furnishings of the reception rooms consisted chiefly of
cabinets and balustrades of carved ebony, teak, and other hard-
woods, and these, with the supporting plinths and pillars of the
doorways, were sometimes inlaid with mother-of-pearl or silver,
or were studded with gold and silver. In the walls were niches
for placing pieces of crystal and china-ware, pitchers, bowls, and
other utensils both for ornament and for use. In the sleeping-
chambers of the upper stories were beds, also of carved woods,
canopied with silken and other hangings; and these with the
linens and coverlets of the beds were perfumed with attars, ambergris, aloe-wood, and other fragrancies.

The text from which the two following serenades are taken was written by Muhammad Kijuma (Taylor Papers).

Serenade 1

Ewe mwana siliye   ukaliza wako walimbezi.
Ukaliza wenye kukweleya   na wapisi wa ndiya wenezi.
Ukaliza mwana wa washaka   muwate kite shake na uzi.
Ewe mwana nyamaa nkutuze   nguo njema za kwetu Hijazi.
Nikwambike mkufu na shangwe   la dhahabu kazi ya Shirazi.   5
Kuwakie nyumba kuu nyeupe   ya chokaa na mawe ya kazi.
Kupambie kwa zombo za kowa   waowao wanika maunzi.
Wa kangange wa ngoi wa nana   wa uziwa wa Shaka na Ozi.
Wakuteshe wema wazaziyo   na wamia wali tumbaizi.
Na wamia kitinda ngamiya   ng'ombe wangi kondoo na mbuzi.   10
Kuwa mama mamangu kuwa   nikuonye yangu ni mapenzi.
Nikuonye mahaba makuu   uyaone kwa yako maozi.
Uyaone mato ukivuwa   kulla yambo liwe waziwazi.
Kulla yambo yema kutendcya   kwa fadhili zakwe muwawazi.
Kwa fadhili zakwe la rehema   ziwawao mfano wa mwezi.   15

Serenade 1

O lady, be calm and cry not   but sing to your suitors.
Sing to those who guide you   and to the discerning passers-by.
Sing to the son of Shaka's people   cast aside your grief and sorrow and distress.
O lady, be calm, let me give you gifts   fine clothes from our homeland the Hejaz.
Let me adorn you with a chain and beads   of gold devised in   5 Shiraz.
Let me build for you a great white house   of lime and stone.
Let me furnish it for you with furnishings of crystal   so that they who see it will be astonished by its construction.
Spread beneath with rushes soft   from the lake-sides of Shaka and Ozi.
Let me satisfy your good parents   and let them rest at ease with minstrels' songs.
Let them lie at ease (with food of) the young of camels   and of   10 many oxen, sheep and goats.
Because, my lady, O lady mine   let me tell that you are my beloved.

Let me tell you of my love so great   that you may see it with
your own eyes.
Lift up your eyes and see   that everything may be plain to you.
Every good thing Will I do for you   by the goodness of
Almighty God.
15 By His goodness and compassion   that shines brightly like the
bright moonlight.

★   ★   ★

Another serenade from the Taylor Papers recalls the attempts
by Daud Mringwari to kill Liyongo:

Serenade 2

Ewe mwana nyamaa siliye   kasikia Fumo wa Bauri
Kasikia Fumo yu mukenge   mudanganya yuu la namiri
Yuasiye jinni yuasiye   hata mwizi Fumo Mringwari
5 Ata shake muwiwa siliye   ukaliza yangu yakajiri
Washorongwa wapozewe mali   kumuzinga Fumo wa Bauri
Akateza Liyongo na waTwa   na mwiwa Mbwasho kamshamiri
Wakenende wasowene simba   yushishiye msu hanjari
Wakarudi kwa umoya wawo   kamwambia Fumo Mringwari
Hawezeki Liyongo ni moto   si kiumbe huyule ni nari.

Serenade 2

O lady, be calm, weep not   listen about Fumo wa Bauri.
Hear of Fumo the refugee   who could outwit even a leopard.
Who defied the jinn who defied   even the impostor Fumo
Mringwari.
Stop crying, gentle one, weep not   wait for my story to take effect.
5 The players were made to accept money   to surround the Lord
of Bauri.
And Liyongo was dancing with the Twa   and dear Mbwasho
gave him warning.
So they went but did not find the lion   who wields sword and
scimitar.
And in one body they returned   and told Fumo Mringwari.
Liyongo is unassailable, he is a fire   he is not mortal, he is a
flame.

★   ★   ★

In irregular ten *mizani* is an interesting poem from the Hichens
Papers, referred to by him as *The Wine Song*, and once again it is
associated with the Liyongo tradition:

The Wine Song

Ewe mteshi wa uchi   wa mbata ulio utungu
Nitekea wa kikaskini   tesheweo ni ngema wangu
Nitekea wa kitupani   uyayongao kwa zungu
Nitekea ulio nyunguni   ulopikwa kwa kunyinywa nyungu
Hishirabu nikema kuwewa   nilitake embekungu langu   5
Embekungu la mani ya tuma   mpiniwe mba tungutungu
Embekungu kangika changoni   pangikwapo siwa na mavungu
Pangikwapo magoma ya ezi   na mawano mawano ya bangu.

O tapster of soured wine   from the sheath of the withered palm,
Draw wine for me in the pipkin-jar   that was tapped by my own winester.
Draw wine for me in the little flask   that makes a man stagger and sway.
Draw wine for me in wine-jar   hot-mulled and dregged of its lees.
When I am well wined I stand   demanding my keen-edged 5 sword,
My keen-edged sword with its guard-leaves of steel   and its hilt of mtupa wood.
My keen-edged sword that hangs from the peg   where the war-horn and trumpets hang.
Where are slung the state-drums   and the rack-edged spears of battle.

*   *   *

There are a few interesting fragments surviving in the Taylor Papers which may have formed part of longer poems in the Liyongo tradition. A fragment popularly ascribed to one of the followers or kinsmen of Saiyid Abu Bakr b. Salim of Hadramawt, c. A.D. 1600, may be referred to as *The Lament*. Abu Bakr is said to have sought a wife among the women of Ozi on the Tana River, but had her eventually from the people of Shaka. The song is held to have been sung by the people of Shaka as against the Ozi folk who had turned away so estimable a suitor:

The Lament

Ai mwezi kuwawato kuwawia makutani
Kuwawia Shaha Shagga   Shaha Ozi yu gizani
Chui ho ho chui kimango . . .

Ah! how brightly shines the moonlight, gleaming on the walls,
Gleaming on the Shah of Shagga   darkness Ozi's walls empalls.
Leopard, ho! ho! thou mighty leopard . . .

*   *   *

Another fragment may be referred to as *The Bathing Song*. By
tradition, during his exile from Shagga on the mainland, Liyongo
visited regularly a place called Gana to bathe in the lake said to
have existed there. The Pokomo tradition of Liyongo's bathing
at Gana is given in *Pokomo Grammatik* (Neukirchen, 1908, p. 136).
Werner in *BSOS*, vol. iv, p. 253, gives a fragment of a song by a
woman of Witu in 1912 which may also commemorate Liyongo's
journeys to Gana, but the song as heard by Werner goes on to the
opening lines of the *Song to Saada* which is included in the *Utendi
wa Liyongo*. The blind poet, Mzee b. Bisharo, subsequently a-
mended the woman's version for Werner and repeated the tradition.

The Bathing Song

Noa chifua na nguoza mbwenepo mayi   hateka chinwa nisisaze
     kasia nyota.
Aniombao nisiize nduu na mbasi   sina la kwamba nambe nini
     tama nisiize.

I bathe and wash my clothes wherever I behold water   I draw of
     it and drink, nor do I cease until I have quenched my thirst.
Whoever begs a draught of me I do not refuse, be he kinsman or
     friend   I have no word to say, what should I say, I could not
     refuse him the dregs.

*   *   *

Then there is the interesting *Bow Song*, once again associated in
popular tradition with Liyongo. This song is in irregular long-
measure of fifteen *mizani* and is from the Hichens Papers.

The Bow Song

Sifa uta wangu wa chitanzu cha mtoriya   upakwe mafuta una-
     wiri kama chiyo.
Mwanzo chondoka nifumile nyoka umiyo   hafuma na ndovu
     shikilole kwa mautiyo.
Hafuma kungu na kipaa chendacho mbiyo   wanambia hepe
     Mwana Mbwasho nasha matayo.

Praise my bow with haft of the wild-vine   let it be dressed with oil and shine like glass.

When first I set out I shot a snake through its throat   and I shot an elephant through its ear as it trumpeted.

Then I shot a piebald crow and a duiker running away   and they tell me, Stand aside, son of Mbwasho, lay your weapons aside.

*   *   *

Songs in praise of trees have been written in long-measure and have had a propagandist value in the development of Swahili agriculture. The Swahili chronicle, *Khabar Pate*, tells of one such period in the late twelfth century when Ahamed I of Shagga is said to have encouraged extensive development in the planting of cultivated fields. To this end poems were written extolling the virtues of the pomegranate (*kuthmani*), the betel-palm supplying the areca-nut (*mtambuu*), the teak-wood tree (*msaji*), and, of course, the coco-nut tree (*mnazi*). The following poem on the coco-nut palm was found by Muhammad Kijuma in the house of one Bwana Kombo and is now in the Taylor Papers:

Sifa ya Mnazi

Pani kiti nikae kitako   niwambie sifa ya mnazi

Mti huu unzapo kumeya   makutiye yanga panga wazi

Baadaye hushusha kigogo   hutoleza mapanda na mizi

Hatimaye huvyaa matunda   matundaye inakwitwa nazi

Huyangua hwambua makutiye   hapikia wali na mtuzi

Kifuvuche hatonga upawa   kapikia Saada muwandazi

Na takize hamwaya jaani   katakura yimbi mtakuzi

Makumiye hasokota kamba   haundia sambwe na jahazi

Makutiye hazibia nyumba   hazuia pepo na fusizi

Kigogoche hafanyia mlango   hazuia harubu na mwizi.

Praise of the Coco-nut Tree

Give me the minstrel's seat that I may sit   and tell you of the praises of the coco-palm.

This tree when it begins to sprout   its leaves spread outwards widely.

Then it thrusts forth its bole   and puts forth its leaf-sheath and its spreading roots.

Lastly it brings forth its fruits   and its fruits are known as coco-nuts.

They are plucked down and stripped of their husks   and cooked with boiled rice and sauces.

From the empty shell they carve a ladle   and the hand-maiden
    Saada cooks with it.
Its grated nut, squeezed free of juice,   is scattered on the midden
    and the cock scratches for it there.
Its fibre they plait into cord   for the rigging of clippers and
    dhows.
With its fronds they thatch a house   and ward off the winds and
    the wind-swept sand.
Of its trunk they make a door   to resist the enemy and the
    robber.

*   *   *

Some manuscripts of this poem append two lines on the dum-palm, useful for its fronds and bole rather than for its fruits, though these have been eaten in time of famine, as, for instance, in the story of Liyongo:

Ukisifu sifa ya mnazi   ya mkoma mle uliwee
Ya mkoma shinale ni moya   kule yuu tanzu zienee.

When you praise the virtues of the coco-nut palm   the virtues
    of the dum-palm are therein displayed.
The bole of the dum-palm is as one   and at its crest the branches
    widely wave.

The comparison between the dum palm and the coco-nut palm is amusingly employed in a lively poem with the measure of ten *mizani* from Muhammad Kijuma's collection in the Taylor Papers. This is a poem on marriage, extolling its virtues to the wife. The similes of the good wife, compared to the provident coco-nut palm, and of the bad wife, compared with the dum palm, and of wives generally who are like the tall borassus with its acrid fruit or the spiny but immaculate mnga borassus, are favourite devices with Swahili poets.

Sifa ya Ndoa

Pani kiti nikae kitako   niwauze neno wandaniwa
Niwauze sababu na kisa   nini wake kuiza kuowa
Mke hawi ila kwa mumewe   wanginewe nini kutukiwa
Mwanamke ni mwenye mumewe   haibudi na kusitahiwa
Wako mume mshiketo sana   wake nduze watatenda ngowa
Wake nduze hupanda mnazi   na mkoma tunda wachanguwa
Twakuona wapanda mtapa   na mvule mnga na mtuwa

Mtu ndia hwenda na rafiki   mwenda pweke haina sitawa
Akinenda katika umuri   mara mtu huchomwa na mwiwa
Au jito kungia mtanga   kahitaji mwenye kukutowa
Ni waadhi nawaonya mpwasi   na mkata sanda kongolewa
Heri shuka isiyo kitushi   kama shali njema ya mauwa.

In Praise of Marriage

Give me the minstrel's seat that I may sit   and ask you a word, my friends.

Let me ask for what reason or rhyme   women refuse to marry?

Woman cannot exist except by man   what is there in that to vex some of them so?

A woman is she who has a husband   and she cannot but prosper.

Cleave unto your man   and his kinsmen will become jealous

His kinsmen have planted coco-palms   but the fruit they reap is dum-palm nuts!

We think you plant the borassus palm   the teak, the mnga and the solanum tree.

When man goes on his road he goes with a friend   for he who walks alone has no good fortune.

As man goes through life   soon he is pierced by the thorn (misfortune).

Or the sand-mote enters his eye   and he needs a friend to remove it.

Likewise I give you advice, the rich man   and the poor man join hands across the shroud.

Better a loin-cloth without disgrace   than the fine-flowered shawl of shame.

★   ★   ★

Dialogue poems are usually in verse of eight *vipande* (the quatrain) in Swahili, but the following long-measure poem is in fact a dialogue between a wife and her mother on the universal theme of the aggrieved wife. This poem also is from the Taylor Papers:

The Aggrieved Wife

Mamangu we hunambia kwamba   ukae naye sana mumewo
Mkhadae kwa ada na esha   umpoke kulakwe na nguwo
Kula nala na nguo navaa   siyo mume unindoziewo
Lakini nani yule mumewo   akupaye kulakwe na nguwo
Namwiza yuna tabia mbi   na khuluka ni kama jogowo
Kula kwake kwa maneno mawi   na nguoye ina masumbuwo

Kucha kucha silali kwa tenge   kutendea inda na mpewo
Hunambia ondoka tutete   tusikize wanzi wapitawo
Tusikize wawinda wa mwitu   na wa pwani wendao mwambawo
Nawauza munambie kweli   hali ndiyo watu wakaawo
Nizuiwe na wangu wandani   hapa mtu mmoya ayawo
Nizuiwe na wangu wazazi   sina nyumba moya ningiawo.

(*Wife*)   Mother, always have you said to me   dwell well with
          your man.
          Placate him according to custom and duty   that you
          may receive from him clothing and food.
          As for eating, I eat, and clothes I wear   but not from
          the man to whom you have wed me.
(*Mother*) But who is the man   who gives you clothes and food?
(*Wife*)   I deny him for he has an evil nature   and he is lustful
          as a chanticleer.
(*Mother*) To eat at his house with evil words   and wear his
          clothes must cause him annoyance.
(*Wife*)   From morn till eve I rest not from alarms   and from
          his hasty fault-finding extreme.
          He tells me, Wake up and let's have an argument   let
          us listen to our friends passing by.
          Let us listen to the hunters from the bush   and the
          fisher-folk going to the shoals.
          I ask you, tell me the truth   is this how people live?
          I am prevented from seeing my friends   no one ever comes
          I am hindered from meeting my parents   nor is there
          a single house I may visit.

*   *   *

By the rules of Arabic prosody it was held that the terminal
rhymes of all verses in a poem, however long the composition
might be, must rhyme together. In verses with an internal rhyme,
therefore, once the poet had committed himself to a rhyme in his
first line, he was bound to it throughout the poem. Preference
was given to verse in which the internal rhyme did not respond
to the end-line rhyme. This was an important development in
Swahili verse, and a considerable amount of modern verse is still
written according to this rhyming system. An example from the
Papers of Sir Mbarak Ali Hinawy (in the Library of the SOAS)

has the first four lines in six *mizani* and the last two lines in irregular ten *mizani*.

Yallah mwenye ezi

Yallah mwenye ezi   Mola wa kadimu
Mjayo mjazi   zipungue hamu
Sina usingizi   wala tabasamu
Kwa nyingi simanzi   pamoya na ghamu
Niondolea Muwawazi   nitakao jamii yatumu
Yote siri ni wewe mjuzi   ulotakamali nirehemu.

Allah, I confess me   Eternal Lord, I pray,
Thy poor servant, bless me   and take my grief away.
Ne'er does sleep caress me   nor laughter cheer my day.
Sorrow doth oppress me   and grief with me doth stay.
Compassionate Lord, redress me   all my needs, Lord, thou can'st allay.
Thou knowest all things, Lord, O bless me   and grant me mercy, I pray.

*   *   *

When, as in the above example, the internal rhyme responds to the sequent rhymes on the caesura (Sw. *kituo*), the tendency is for the grouping of lines in verse-formation, and not, as in early long-measure illustrated in this chapter, for each line to be regarded as a separate verse. There is no reason to believe, however, that in Swahili verse-formation developed historically from long-measure verse with rhymes. The direct influence of specific Arabian models has to be borne in mind, and these in their turn have been modified by Swahili writers. Perhaps the most notable of these Arabian models, certainly in relation to long-measure verse, is the *takhmis*.

THE SWAHILI *TAKHMIS*

In Arabian prosody *takhmis* is the form of poetical composition in which each stanza is of five lines rhyming *aaaab* and with no medial rest. The last two lines of each stanza are usually adopted from the work of an earlier poet, and the first three lines serve as a contemporary frame for the older piece and as a gloss or exposition of its theme. Swahili poets from among the Hadrami Saiyids adopted this five-line pattern, though their verses are not in every instance of dual authorship.

Takhmis ya Liyongo

The earliest example of the *takhmis* in Swahili is by Saiyid Abdallah b. Nasir, the author of *al-Inkishafi*, and is based upon traditional songs concerning the legendary hero, Liyongo, and more especially upon what Hichens has called *The Dungeon Song*. A scroll manuscript of this poem, wrongly described as an *utenzi*, was presented by Taylor to the British Museum (No. Or. 4534), and is the only manuscript in the Swahili-Arabic script in the Museum. The same poem was transliterated by Steere in his *Swahili Tales*, and he wrote: 'The translation (i.e. transliteration) into the current Swahili of Zanzibar was made by Hassan b. Yusuf and revised by Sheikh Muhammad b. Ali to whom I was indebted for a copy of the original with an interlinear version in Arabic'.

This mention of an interlinear version in Arabic is worth noting, for it implies the existence of a poem in Arabic which formed the basis for the Swahili version. Examination of the Arabic interlinear version has shown that it does not vary much from the Swahili version. This is therefore the only known poem in Arabic dealing with a subject that has direct African references concerning Swahili tradition. From this it may be said that the Liyongo tradition found expression by at least one Saiyid in Arabic. The Swahili references exclude any possibility that the Arabic version is based again on any Arabic original in southern Arabia.

An edition of this *takhmis* from three collated manuscripts was published by Meinhof in 'Das Lied des Liongo', *Zeitschrift für Eingeborenen-Sprachen*, Bd. xv, pp. 241–65. Meinhof adopted a number of Steere's mistranslations, though his transliteration, so far as it is possible to judge in his collation, is quite faultless. The three manuscripts employed in Meinhof's edition were M., in the

---

Takhmis ya Liyongo

1 Nabudi kawafi takhamisi kiidiriji
Niidhihirishe izagale kama siraji
Ili kufuasa ya Liyongo simba wa miji
Ai wajiwaji naza waji kisiza waji   ma'a kadiliza kisikiliza mwa-
   nangwa mwema.

British Museum, W., written in 1914 for Werner by Muhammad Kijuma at Lamu, and B., a text in the possession of Büttner in Berlin.

In the last two verses of the poem the author is named and his lineage given, Saiyid Abdallah b. Ali b. Nasir, descended from Abu Bakr b. Ali through his son Ali, whose great-great-grandson was Ali b. Nasir, the poet's father. The place of origin of this well-known Hadrami family is stated in the poem to have been Tarim, a fact that is amply verified from Arabian sources.

The poem is held by Hichens to have been based upon a *Dungeon Song* sung by Liyongo at the *gungu* ceremony when he made his escape from Shagga's gaol. No separate manuscript of the *Dungeon Song* has been found, so that it is not possible to take the last two lines of the verses as comprising a separate poem of different authorship, although Hichens did so. There is no proof of this, and it is perhaps better to take the whole poem as the work of Saiyid Abdallah rather than to assert, with Hichens, that a poem actually by Liyongo is preserved within it. In manuscript copies the scribes invariably write the last two lines of each verse in a *takhmis* as a complete strophe, i.e. as one long line, but this is the usual practice and cannot be accepted as evidence for the separate authorship of the two last lines. Certainly the poem refers to an occasion when Liyongo was held captive by Daud Mringwari. Verse eleven, in which the hero invokes the vengeance that would be his were he not shackled, leaves no doubt as to the circumstances around which the author has composed a homiletic in order that men may observe the knightly code of a warrior-prince.

Since the work has been published in full in Meinhof's edition, it may suffice here to give the first twelve verses (there are twenty-eight in all) in order to exemplify the character of this *takhmis* poem.

The Liyongo Takhmis

I begin my five-line verses putting them into rhyme   so setting 1
   them forth that they shine like a lamp   to tell of Liyongo the
   lion of cities.
Yes, it is a homily that I begin and bring to its ending   How
   shall I set it out so that I may complete (this poem on) the good
   nobleman?

2 Pindi uonapo ali shari mume mwendo
Pindua mtima ujitile kani na vindo
Uwe ja namiri tui mke katika windo
Mwanangwa mbonaye mbuzi wako katika shindo   ukemetwe
pembe na mkami akimkama.

3 Akhi ewe mbuya twambe mambo yakujelele
Huyi muungwana shati ari aiondole
Nakuchea kufa mwenye cheo kavilekele
Mtu huonaye muhakara kwakwe wimile   asiradhi kufa na mayu-
to yakaya nyuma.

4 Napa kwa injili na zaburi ili kiapo
Si mkengeufu pindi shari limbwagazapo
Nalekeza moyo katokoza shari lilipo
Mtetea cheo mwenye cheo ateteapo   hambiwi niawi hata roho
na ingatama.

5 Naitenda mja kwa wenzangu kapata sono
Wala sina wambo siwenendi kwa mavongono
Bali sikubali lenye dhila na matukano
Ni mwofu watu nishikwapo naoa mno   ni muwi wa kondo
sikiapo mbi kalima.

6 Sibwagazi kondo msi lango kapija kifa
Ili kusifiwa kwa ambazo ni tule sifa
Nitegemezapo kondo zito tende hakhafa
Ni mwana shajii mpendeza nyemi za kufa   kwa kuta mpco na
aduiwa kunisema.

7 Mbonapo harubu chiugua nawa na afa
Kawa na furaha ja harusi ya mzafafa
Kaekeza moyo kwa Muungu nisikhilafa
Ni mwana asadi mtanganya moyo wa kufa   kwa kucha khazaya
na adui kumbona nyuma.

8 Napa kwa Muungu na Muungu ndiye kiapo
Nampenda mtu pindi naye anipendapo
Bali nduu yangu pindi ari ambwagazapo
Ninga mwana kozi sioneki niwakuapo   ni muwi wa nyuni nawa-
kua katika yama.

Whenever you see a fellow your friend in misfortune   set your 2
heart and commit yourself to be strong and stand firm   be
like a leopard (like) a leopardess in the hunt.
O nobleman what do I see? Your goat in trouble   caught by
its horns with a milker milking it?

Oh my brother let us tell of matters that give respect   the man 3
of gentle birth is bound to cast away evil   to fear death is not
fitting for a person of rank.
How can a man behold the rising of shame   and yet be unwilling
to die before remorse comes?

I swear by the Word and the Psalter and it is an oath indeed   I 4
am no waverer when evil overwhelms me   I direct my heart
and scoff at evil wherever it is.
He who strives for honour is honoured as he strives   he is not
told, You are mine, even though his soul is expiring.

I make myself a slave to my friends that I may gain friend- 5
ship   nor do I slander or run to them with complaints   but
I do not submit to abuse nor to occasion for humiliation.
I am gentle and yield gently when people hold me   but I am a
warrior-slayer when I hear ill-word's infamy.

I do not plunge into war without a reason for smiting my 6
breast   to be praised by those whose praise is worthless   but
when I bear the brunt of battle I make little of it.
For I am a brave young man well-pleased with the cries of (the
enemy) dying   fearing only a victor and anything that my
enemy may say to my shame.

When I see the fray even though I am ill I become well   and I 7
become happy like a bridegroom in the bridal procession   I
turn my heart towards God nor do I rebel against Him.
I am as a lion proud to die   fearing only disgrace and that my
enemy should find me in the back-ranks.

I swear by God and God is indeed someone to swear by   that 8
I love any man as long as he loves me   but if my own kinsman should bring evil to me.
Then I am like a young eagle indiscernible as I swoop down   I
am like a killer of birds seizing them out of the flock.

9 Wallahi nithika saya yangu si maongope
   Teteapo cheo kiwa mwiu nawa mweupe
   Nimpapo uso aduiya shati akupe
   Ninga mwana tai shirikene na mwana tope   na mlisha yani
      zenye tani na zingulima.

10 Laiti kiumbe pindi mambo yakimpinga
   Papale angani aduize akawainga
   Awavunda paa na mifupa ya mitulinga
   Ningali kipungu niushile katika anga   kala nyama toto hata
      simba mkuu nyama.

11 Ningatindangile kwa sayufu na kwa sakini
   Na msu mkuli kiupeka yuu na tini
   Kavuma ja mwamba usokanile na kani
   Illa muu yangu yo mawili kuwa pinguni   na shingoni mwangu
      niweshiwe peto la chuma.

12 Ningashahadiza Kuruani yangu kalima
   Illa uketeze kuwa nyimbo Mola karimu
   Wama huwa bikauli shairi kalila ma
   Tufutufu mayi kizimbwini yanganguruma   kamwezi kwima
      liushapo wimbi Ungama . . .

Not more than five or six *takhmis* poems have survived, for
preference was given by Swahili poets either to verses of four or
eight *vipande*. The *takhmis* of Saiyid Umar b. Amin al-Ahdal,
Kadhi of Siu, is an acrostic, usually referred to as *Wajiwaji*, in
which the fourth line of each verse begins with a sequent letter of
the Arabic alphabet. The text that follows is based upon my
edition of the poem in the *Bulletin of the SOAS*, vol. xiii, part 3
(1950), pp. 759–70.

Wajiwaji

1   Bismillahi nabtadi yangu nudhuma
        Na alhamdu kiiratili kama kusoma
        Sala na salamu nda Mtume na walo nyuma
   Alifu   Ali na sahaba na dhuria wenye karama   na wafuweseo
           wafuwasi tariki njema.

By God I swear that these words of mine are not just proud boast- 9
    ings   when I strive for honour though I be black I become
    white   and when I turn my face to my foe he must give way.
I am like a vulture in strife with an antelope   or with a beast on
    the grass-plains or on the high mountain peaks.

Alas for the creature when things go badly against it   when 10
    there in the sky he sees his enemies   he breaks their skull and
    shoulder-blades.
I am like a vulture that soars in the sky   preying upon small
    creatures and upon great beasts like the lion as well.

I would thrust my way through with sword and cutlass   swing- 11
    ing my keen-edged sword high and low   I would thunder as
    the heavens in undenied rage.
But both my legs are confined in shackles   and around my neck
    I am gripped by an iron ring.

I would have the Qur'ān witness to my words   but that it is 12
    denied by the Bountiful God to serve as a poem   'It is not as
    the word of poets O ye of little faith'.
When the swirling waters of the deep leap up-roaring   no man
    can withstand the up-leaping billows of Ungama's foam . . .

Wajiwaji

In the Name of God I begin my poem   with Praises setting it in 1
    order for reading   prayer and peace belong to the Prophet
    and all who follow after
The kinsmen and the Companions and gifted descendants   and
    those who have followed, the followers in the right way.

2   Nduza na wendani pulikani nina shauri
        Penda kuuonya moyo wangu kwa ushairi
        Utaghafalie hawandami ndiya ya kheri
Bei   Bahati nda mja mwenye moyo wa tafakuri   asa nami
        kawa kama soyo mwelewa mema.

3   Moyo siwe pite kama jura mwenda wazimu
        Kwanda tafakari umbo lako ulifahamu
        Ni tono la mayi lalokaa likawa damu
Tei   Tabaraka Llahu kaliumba Mola karimu   katia mifupa na
        mishipa ngozi na nyama.

4   Ndiyo yalokuwa si maneno ya ati ati
        Na nyezi tisia matumboni walimo kati
        Ukaruzukwa kwa masiku na mtikati
Thei Thama wapunguzi wateshele hawakupati   kukupa
        chakula wangafisha zao huruma.

5   Zikisa kutimu nyezi kenda zaloandikwa
        Ukapiswa ndiya za mashaka zisopitika
        Ukaya kwa raha pasi shida na kusumbuka
Jimu Jamii ya watu walioko wakatamka   allahuma sali wa sali-
        mu wa taslima.

6   Ukisa kuzawa ukaweza kuta kishindo
        Utunushiyelo ni kwa Mola kupija kondo
        Na kumsikiza mambo mawi yenye uvundo
Hhei Haramu hukuwa shaakiru zake zitendo   ushishie fumo
        hungurumza liketetema.

7   Ushishie ngao kama kwamba una jununi
        Huwaliza kondo kumpija Mola Manani
        Hela ukiteta zita zako zamdhuruni
Khe   Khasara inawe utetapo wenda motoni   nyumba jizajiza
        na uvundo usio koma.

8   Wataka kuteta na mateto siyo yawawo
        Wateta na mtu kwa chakula chake na nguwo
        Hela zituruku na makazi ukaziewo
Dali Dabiri mangine ukafanye yako makawo   nti zake gura
        situlie ukasimama.

Brethren and friends listen for I have something to say   I want 2
   to admonish my heart in verse   for it has forsaken the way of
   happiness
blessed is the slave whose heart loves contemplation   would
   that I were like him who appreciates good things.

O heart be not foolish or ignorant like one insane   first consider 3
   your creation and understand it   it is but a drop of water
   changed into blood
blessed be God the Most Bounteous who created it   and formed
   it into bones and veins, skin and flesh.

That is what it was, there was no uncertainty about it   and for 4
   nine months you were deep in the womb   being nourished
   night and day
while the midwives marvelled at not being able to reach you   to
   feed you even though they hid their kind concern.

At the completion of the nine months decreed   you were led 5
   through dangerous and impassable ways   and you came out
   blissfully without trouble or difficulty
the company of the people present acclaimed   God is great and
   may peace and prayer be upon the Prophet!

Once you are born you dare to make a commotion   what you 6
   desire is to make a quarrel with God   and to bring evils and
   malodorous charges against Him
you were never grateful for all that He has done   spear in your
   hand, brawling and trembling with anger.

Holding a shield as though you were mad   considering conflict 7
   against the All-Kind God   well then, if you fight will your
   quarrel bring him harm?
you are the loser, for to hell will you go if you fight   to pitch-
   dark abode with unceasing stench.

You see a quarrel without a reason   you quarrel for His own 8
   food and raiment   Very well then, do without them and give
   up your dwelling-place
look out for another place and make that your abode   leave
   His domain without further delay.

9   Ukisa kugura nti zake usizikaye
Chakula na nguo ukawata usitumiye
Hapo ndipo zita umeweza kuteta naye
Dhali Dhati ya mateto utakalo kaifanyiye   akusukapo hina
shaka wamsukuma.

10   Ela uli mumo yuu lati tini mwa mbingu
Huwezi kuteta ni muongo nafusi yangu
Kheri ufuase taa yake Moliwa Mungu
Rei Rahimu Ghafaru mfuasi hupata fungu   na kuwatutiza
waja wake fi li-kiyama.

11   Kheri ufuate uwe pote la wafuasi
Lo lote liyalo uridhie usikikisi
Usikasirike kisirani haikupasi
Zei Zamani za nyuma kwali watu wenye ziasi   lo lote liyalo
huridhia likiwegema.

12   Kwanda tanabahi ufikiri yamezopita
Mitume teule Mola wetu aloiyeta
Hapa duniani kuongoza japo wa zita
Sini Sambe walihiti ndio huja ya kuwakuta   mauti ni siku
zikomapo mtu hukoma.

13   Kupambaukiwa sifurahi na kutwelewa
Ukamba umri uko mbee nalondikiwa
Hizi siku zote zipitazo huhasibiwa
Shini Sharuti uyuwe kula siku hupungukiwa   zikomapo siku
na umri wako hukoma.

14   Zundushanye ito siwe kama ulo ndeoni
Ulao zileo au ulo usindizini
Umri hupita kamwe huzundukani
Sadi Sahibu muovu ufenyeo kuwa mwendani   wa kukuliwaza
na sirata mustakima.

15   Hiko upetecho kifahamu umechopata
Usambe umri uko mbee huya ukuta
Wangapi watoto kuliko we wamezopita
Thadi Dhahika mashibu hatta yeo huyaiyeta   toba hungojani
ushengee uhali mama.

When you have left His domain never to dwell therein   and 9
    have renounced food and raiment never to use them again   only
    then dare you make conflict with Him
a real combat which you seek, then engage upon it   no doubt
    you can retaliate if He so much as pushes you.

But so long as you remain on earth under the canopy of 10
    Heaven   you dare not fight know ye, my false self   better
    far to follow the light of Almighty God
the follower receives his share from the Merciful Forgiver   who
    heaps rewards on the faithful on the resurrection day.

Better to follow and be a slave of the faithful   and submit to 11
    whatever befalls you without complaint   do not be angry for
    anger ill becomes you
in times gone by they were righteous people   whatsoever befell
    they were content as it drew nigh them.

Take care first and consider the past   the chosen prophets whom 12
    God has brought   here on earth to lead us against the
    enemy
do not say they sinned and so met with what befell them   death
    comes on the appointed day and a man is no more.

Do not rejoice when dawn and evening come upon you   nor 13
    boast that your decreed life still lies ahead   all these passing
    days are counted
you must realize that each passing day lessens the time   for
    when the days come to an end your life ends with them.

Open your eyes and be not like one intoxicated   who takes 14
    strong drink or is in sleep   life passes by and never do you
    realize
the evil companion whom you make your friend   he it is who
    lures you away from the right path.

The life you have had, think well upon it   and say not that your 15
    life is still to come and (the end) not yet near   how many
    younger men than you have passed away?
Even at this obvious old age you have not as yet   repented for
    what do you wait in this state of anger?

16   Ajali husonga nyuma yako hukufukuza
            Na usoni mwako Sheitani hukupambaza
            Kwa hili na hili mfahamu hukuangamiza
    Twei   Tabibu mshiri ni ambao aloyokoza   hapa duniani na
            akhera kenda salama.

17   Yenye kukokoza ukitaka kuyafahamu
            Siwe na zitimbi na nduguzo wana adamu
            Safi moyo wako yambo iwi usizuumu
    Thwei   Dhahiri ushike arikani za isilamu   shahada na sala na
            zakati hija sauma.

18   Hija na zakati hukupasa kwa sharutize
            Nikuwa na mali na saumu usangamize
            Shahada na sala sura zote zikupasize
    'Aini   'Ala kuli hali ukiweza usiziweze   sharuti utende fara-
            dhize ni mahatuma.

19   Hizi nguzo tano ukidumu kuzishika
            Sala ukasali kwa wakati usiyatoka
            Ukafunga tumu ukahiji ukapa zaka
    Ghaini Ghafaru dhunubi akujazi hapana shaka   kwa amali hiyo
            na shahada ukilisema.

20   Ukitoyatenda mambo sayo yakupesewo
            Ukaipumbaza yamlezi mla zilewo
            Umeikupiza ufahamu yuwa wendawo
    Fei   Fazaa ni bora ya mauti yakungojawo   kufa ni ndiyare
            mtu hendi kauya nyuma.

21   Ukinuka kufa ukigura ya duniani
            Nyumba ukitiwa tini mwati mwa ufukoni
            Ukiwa na mali uwasiye ulimwenguni
    Kafu   Karaba hunena walioko makaburini   tondokapo hapa
            tuze mali twawanye kima.

22   Hawasikitiki kufa kwako hawaku ali
            Watindie zite mashughuli yao ni mali
            Wataka kwawanya himahima kwa tasihili
    Kyafu   Kafani na nguo zakoshezwa zikiwa ali   ini huwatinda
            kama kwamba ndao mapema.

Fate presses upon you from behind, it runs after you   and facing 16
    you is the Devil deceiving you   by this and that remember
    that he is destroying you
a clever physician is the one who cures himself   both here upon
    earth and in the next world he goes in peace.

If you really want to know what will save you   stop intriguing 17
    against your brethren the children of Adam   let your heart
    be clean and do not think of evil things
hold fast in public to the pillars of Islam   the creed and the
    prayer, alms-giving, the pilgrimage and fasting.

The pilgrimage and alms-giving are of obligation   provided 18
    that one has the means, but do not away with fasting   nor
    recitation of the creed nor prayer, for all these things you must
    perform
in any case whether you are indisposed or not   you must fulfil
    the duties prescribed for they are of obligation.

If you continue to hold fast to these five pillars   praying without 19
    leaving off before the appointed time   keeping Ramadhan,
    taking the pilgrimage and giving alms
the Forgiver of sin will most certainly reward you   for what
    you have done and for your confession of faith.

If you fail to do what you should   playing the fool like a 20
    drunkard   you will have made trouble for yourself, so know
    where it leads
disquiet is better than the death that awaits you   death is a long
    road, no one goes and is able to return.

When you are dead and departed from the world   and placed in 21
    the sepulchre beneath the ground   if you have any wealth left
    behind in the world
the relations there at the cemetery will say   When we leave here
    let us sell his property and divide the proceeds.

They are neither sorry nor care about your dying   the mourning 22
    at an end, their concern is for your property   they wish to
    divide it at once without delay
and if the shroud and the burial-cloths be valuable   their inmost
    feelings are stirred as if the things belonged to them already.

23

       Karaba na mbasi kaburini wakutiyapo
       Ukawa we pweke usione mtu kuwapo
       Neno la Munkari na Nakiri watongoapo
Lamu   La kutia huma na baridi yenye kitapo   kwa kucha
       zimondo za motoni simbo za chuma.

24

       Kuna na fazaa bora mno yalosifiwa
       Zaidi mauti na kaburi kuhadithiwa
       Nayo siku hiyo huitwa siku ya kufufuwa
Mimu   Mato ya paani hayaoni yangafumbuwa   hakutambu-
       wani mzaliwa hayui mama.

25

       Baada ya kwisa kufufuwa kuna hisabu
       Na kuwaziniwa amalimbi na za thawabu
       Mtu enushao hasanati hana adhabu
Nunu   Na ambao kwamba zainama una ikabu   huenda ole
       wake nyumbani ya Jahanama.

26

       Hapo pana nida siratini ndoni upesi
       Watu watapita kama kali pepo za kusi
       Na wangine tena watapita kama farasi
Wau   Wangi watapita kama kwamba ni mahabusi   wapitao
       ndia zenye nyeta na mingulima.

27

       Hapo siratini watu wangi takao teya
       Mmoya kupita wangukao zaidi miya
       Na kuanguka huku ni sharuti kusikiliya
Hei   Hawiya Sakaru na Jahimu kududumiya   kwa kucha
       Sairi Jahanama Ladha Hutama.

28

       Walo akhiyari Siratini hawataona
       Shida na fazaa ila nuru zake Rabana
       Hali nyuso zao hunawiri kama mtana
       La illaha illahuwa tawajazi katika janna   kwa fadhili
       zake Mola wetu majazi mema.

29

       Tamati waadhi idadiye alifu bee
       Na mwenye kutunga ni 'aini mimu na ree
       Ibunu Amini musidhani uzo uzowezee
Ya   Yale kuweleza wajiwaji na uwelee   aonao kosa akitoa
       hana lawama.

When relatives and friends have placed you in the grave   and 23
   you are left alone with no one there at all   and the Angels
   Munkar and Nakir begin to interrogate you
you feel feverish and cold with trembling   from fear of Hell's
   flames and the beating with iron rods.

There is another disturbance, far better, which is praised   more 24
   worthy than death or the grave to be related   and that is the
   day called the Day of Resurrection
watching eyes see nothing though they be opened wide   no one
   is recognized, not even a child by its mother.

After the Resurrection then comes the Judgement   when evil 25
   actions are weighed against the good   the man who abounds
   in good works has no punishment
but he whose evil outweighs the balance has trouble   woe to
   him, for he goes to the dwelling of Hell.

There is a call on the way to Hell, Come quickly   people will 26
   go through like a fierce wind from the south   others will
   pass like galloping horses
many will pass as though they were prisoners   making their
   way through paths along cliffs and precipices.

Many people will slip on that road to eternity   for every one 27
   that passes by a hundred will fall   while that fall must carry
   them down
deep into the pits of Hawiya, Sakaru and Jahimu   for fear of
   Sair, Jahannam, Laza, and Hutama.

The chosen ones on that road will not find   any trouble or 28
   confusion, but they will see the light of the Lord   while their
   faces shine bright as the day
He who is God Alone will reward them in Paradise   by His
   kindness, our God, the Bestower of good.

Concluded is this poem, while the verses are the number of the 29
   alphabet   and the composer is 'Aini, Mimu, and Rei   son of
   Amini, do not consider him to be experienced
he means to explain in a poem what you may understand   and
   whoever finds a mistake is not to be blamed for correcting it.

In his poem, *Dua ya Kuombea Mvua*, Sheikh Muhyi 'l-Din adopted a modification of the *takhmis* verse-form by introducing internal rhymes in each line. The end of the verse is still marked by the end-verse rhyme, but the primary *vipande* rhyme together throughout each verse. The caesura divides each line into *vipande* of six and nine *mizani* respectively, the first example noted here of a caesura which is not exactly in medial position. Strictly speaking this poem is not a *takhmis*, but it is most certainly a development or modification of the *takhmis*.

Dua ya Kuombea Mvua

1 Nanza kubutadi   kwa Isimu yake Karima
Kuomba Wadudi   Mtukufu Mwenye adhama
Tumwa Muhammadi   nasalia kiumbe chema
Nipate miradi   ufurahi wangu ntima   siku ya tanadi   waja
asi wakilalama.

2 Na alize thama   wateule wenye ajiri
Wenye sifa njema   simba zake Tumwa Bashiri
Na siku ya kwima   kondo zetu ndio shururi
Ndio wenye shima   waketele dhuli na ari   siku ya kiama
waokene na Jahanama.

3 Nikomele tama   dibaji sitaikithiri
Nina mambo mema   nayawaza kiyafikiri
Mbwene makulima   yadhiika kwa nyingi hari
Naomba rehema   kwa Wahabu Mwenye amuri   nituze
mtima   kwa rehema yake Karima.

4 Ai Subuhana   Mola wetu uso shirika
Ndiwe Rahamana   Muwawazi usio shaka
Warehemu wana   na wazee wenye mashaka
Waijua sana   hali yetu kati ya chaka   juwa la mtana   kula
siku lisilo koma.

5 Tu waja dhaifu   mlangoni pako twemele
Kwa nia yakafu   shida yetu Rabbi yondole
Hatuna wokofu   mtatuzi uyatatule
Kwako ni khafifu   ni mafupi yangawa male   mwingi wa lutufu
Muwawazi wawi na wema.

Sheikh Muhyi 'l-Din al-Waili (A.D. 1798–1869), Kadhi of Zanzibar, was the Kadhi honourably mentioned by Burton[1] for his proficiency in Arabic. He was responsible for writing the copy of *Kitab as-Sulwa fi-Akhbar Kulwa*, which the Sultan of Zanzibar, Saiyid Barghash, presented to Sir John Kirk, who in turn presented it to the British Museum.[2] The present writer has edited the poem for *African Studies*,[3] but the translation given below has been modified from that first provided.

Prayer for Rain

I begin to write through His Name the Bountiful One to 1
 beg the Beloved the Glorious and Most High the Prophet
 Muhammad I pray to the best of beings
that I may obtain my desire and be glad in my heart on the
 Day of Resurrection when disobedient servants moan.

Together with His family the chosen who have reward who 2
 are of good fame the lions of the Blessed Prophet and who
 in the day of challenge in our battles with evils
are the ones of quality refusing humiliation and disgrace who
 on the Day of Resurrection are saved from Hell.

I have come to a stop and will not increase the preface I have 3
 some good matters which I ponder and think about I have
 seen the plantations being ruined with drought
I ask for mercy from the Great Giver of the law that I may
 rest my heart content by the mercy of the Generous One.

Glory be to God our God who has no associate Thou art 4
 the Merciful One the indisputable Disposer have mercy
 on the children as well as on the troubled elders
You are well aware of our position in this drought the sun
 throughout the day (shining) every day without ceasing.

We are weak mortals at your door we stand with one 5
 intent our trouble, Lord, remove we have no salvation undo what is entangled
for these are light matters they are small though (for us) they
 are important O full of kindness Thou art Disposer to
 both good and bad.

[1] *Zanzibar*, vol. i, p. 423. [2] Or. MS. No. 2666, written in Arabic.
[3] Lyndon Harries, 'A Swahili Takhmis', *African Studies*, vol. ii, No. 2, pp. 59–67.

6 Rabbi tuawaze   tungaasi kwa rehemayo
Situpatilize   kwa makosa tuyakosayo
Tupe barakaze   Muhammadi ndiye Tumwayo
Na wote nduuze   waombezi na mambo sayo   utunyeshe-
leze   mvua nyingi yenye rehema.

7 Tuletee mvua   tuondolee nyota na juwa
Ndiwe mwenye kuwa   ufishao na kufufuwa
Hali waijuwa   huhitaji kuarifiwa
Hasha kuemewa   ni amuri kuni ikawa   wala kutendewa
Jala Rabbi mwenye adhama.

8 Wengi waayisi   kwa mateso kuwa tawili
Wana asiwasi   kwa madhambi yao thakili
Rabbi tunafisi   Muungwana uso mithili
Mwengi wa ukwasi   tupe nasi utujamili   na yawe
mapesi   iwe kuni yako kalima.

9 Saya tutakayo   hako mtu katu muweza
Wala mwenye nayo   ila wewe Mwenye maiza
Na tutamaniyo   kutindiwa ni yetu aza
Kwa yote twambayo   tutendee ili majaza   tushukuru
kwayo   ifurahi yetu mitima.

10 Muomba Wadudi   havi shaka twaa yakini
Apata muradi   na matako yake moyoni
Pindi akinadi   ja Ayub Rabbi masani
Katu kamurudi   mja kwake mwenye maani   hata Namo-
rodi   kafiri mbi ashosilima.

11 Kwa yote masimu   twakuomba Mola Karimu
Kwanza ni Adamu   mtumeo na muungamu
Na wote kiramu   wandikao kula kalamu
Loho na kalamu   na zuozo zote kadimu   na wenye masi-
mu   mawalii na waja wema.

O Lord dispose us well   though we have rebelled (do it) of 6
  Thy mercy   take not vengeance on us   for the wrongs we
  commit   give us His blessings   Muhammad who is indeed
  your Prophet
And those of all his brethren   for us beggars who ask for
  such   cause the rain to pour down   for us an abundance
  of blessed rain.

Bring the rain for us   take from us the thirst and the sun   Thou 7
  art the Self-Existing One   who puts to death and who re-
  vives   Thou knowest our state   thou needest not to be
  told
nor ever to be discommoded   thou hast only to command and
  it is done   nor art thou dependent on others   most glorious
  and powerful Lord.

Many are blemished in body   because of the prolonged suffer- 8
  ing   they are in despair   because of their weighty
  sins   Lord save us   O Lord of incomparable rank
O most rich   grant us our request and be kind to us   and
  lighten our burdens   let it be done by thy word of command.

For these things we want   there is none at all who is able   nor 9
  any who possesses them   except Thou the All-Powerful   and
  what we long for   is the cessation of the torment
for all that we say   grant us these things as favours   that we
  may be grateful for them   and our hearts be glad.

He who supplicates the Beloved   there is no doubt and you can 10
  be sure   he achieves his purpose   and the wishes of his
  heart   should he call out   like Job, Lord, I am in trouble
never will He refuse   the one who comes to Him for any purpose   even Nimrod   the evil infidel who never became a
  Muslim.

By all who are highly named   we beg you, O Generous 11
  God   first by Adam   your prophet and confessor   and
  by all the blessed   who record every word from on high
by the tablet and the pen   and all your ancient writings   and
  by the famous   the saints and the good servants.

12 Rabu tutubiye   ya nusuha yenye nadama
   Utughofiriye   kuu dhambi iwe lamama
   Nawe uneneye   uduuni yako kalima
   Tutawasaliye   kwa Isimu yako adhama   dua naipaye   na
   kabuli ije kwa hima.

13 Dua naitimu   kwa hamudi na taadhima
   Na iwe naamu   na kabuli ije kwa hima
   Wapate naimu   na ajiri wenye kusoma
   Sala na salamu   na mbawazi zendee Tumwa   na wote kira-
   mu   Sahabaze wenye dhimama.

14 Rabbi takabali   na kabuli iwe ajili
   Yote tajamali   tutakayo kwa tasihili
   Hatuna amali   tutendayo yenye kabuli
   Ila kwa ajili   na rehema zako dalili   ndio tawasuli   maomb-
   ezi yetu wafama.

15 Twataka amani   ya ghadhabu zako Jabari
   Huku duniani   na Kiama siku ya nari
   Tutie Peponi   tusakini katika dari
   Utupe hisani   wake wema wa kukhitari   nao wilidani   watu-
   pambe mbele na nyuma.

16 Na mwenye kuomba   kutendewa ni yake jaza
   Hata mwenye kwimba   jaza yake yawa kutuzwa
   Siuze muomba   Muungwana mwenye maiza
   Wallahi mi namba   aombaye Mola Aziza   kula matilaba   yu-
   wapewa na nyingi neema.

17 Nami ningatunga   siyajui ni kutamani
   Sijui kupanga   lulu njema na marijani
   Hatauwa shanga   makuruto usho thamani
   Kwa nyote malenga   muonapo penye lahani   kamuwi
   wajinga   mufanyapo mwapata mema.

18 Na mwenye maani   ya utungo wa tawasuli
   Jina tabaini   mufahamu yake asili
   Ni Muhiyidini   bunu Shekhe mja dhalili
   Ni bunu Kahtani   jadi yake bunu Waili   ndio Ara-
   buni   waungwana asili njema.

This type of verse is closely related in form to regular five-line
verse in which the last primary *kipande* rhymes with the secondary
kipande of the preceding lines.

Lord we repent our ways   with real and true contrition   grant 12
us forgiveness   let our great sin be our lament   for you
have said   Give me your requests   that is what you said
so we supplicate   by your exalted Name   let the prayer
ascend   and your acceptance come quickly.

Let the prayer be complete   by praise and glory   let it be, 13
Yes   and sanction come quickly   that they may receive
grace   and rewards, those who read
let prayer and peace   and compassion be for the Prophet   and
for all the blessed   His Companions who have the promises.

O Lord do accept   and let acceptance come quickly   favour 14
us in everything   in what we want and that quickly   we
have no good deeds   nothing we do has your approval
but for your sake   and by your mercies   this is the supplication   our true prayers.

We ask for peace   from your wrath O Powerful One   here on 15
earth   and at the Resurrection the day of dread   place us in
Paradise   let us rest within that roof
give us your favours   choice women and good   together with
boy-servants   to adorn us before and behind.

And for the one who begs   his reward is the granting of his 16
wishes   even for a singer   his reward is to be given gifts   so
let alone the supplicator   of the noble and all-powerful God
by God, as for me I say   he who begs of God Most High   every
request   he is granted with much grace.

And though I do compose   I know not the art, it is only a desire 17
I do not know how to arrange   the good pearls with the
coral   I only choose beads   that are smooth and worthless
and for all ye minstrels   when you see where there is a mistake   correct the foolish error   for when you do this you
are rewarded.

And he who had the idea   of composing this supplication   I 18
will mention his name   that you may know his origin   it is
Muhy-ed-din   son of Shaikh, a humble being   son of Kahtan
his lineage is Bin Waili   it is in Arabia   free men of good stock.

5

THE QUATRAIN

THE most popular verse-form in Swahili for topical and specific themes has undoubtedly been verse of eight *vipande* with alternate rhyme and a measure of eight *mizani* to the *kipande*. Although in the scripts verse of this type is written either as a single line or in two lines, we may for convenience regard it as a quatrain. This verse-form owed much less to Arabian sources for its subject-matter than either the *utendi* or the *takhmis*. It became the popular medium for expressing themes that were original in the sense that they were not borrowed from Arabian sources. Almost every subject within the orbit of Swahili experience has been used as a theme for poems in quatrain form.

The topical nature of many of the allusions makes it often very difficult to translate the earlier quatrains. Quite often references are extremely local and probably contemporaneous, and the particular occasion that gave rise to the composition has passed out of living memory. Manuscripts are usually without any kind of annotation or even titles to the separate poems. One collection of poems in roman script, belonging to Sir Mbarak Ali Hinawy (photostat copy in Library of the SOAS), has general headings, such as *Mashairi ya Malalamiko* (Poems of Lament), *Mashairi ya Mapenzi* ('Love Poems'), but in Arabic-Swahili scripts Swahili poems do not have a title.

The outstanding composer of quatrains in Swahili is Muyaka b. Haji al-Ghassaniy (A.D. 1776–1840), who lived in Mombasa. A collection of his poems was prepared by Hichens (*Diwani ya Muyaka*, Witwatersrand Press, 1940) and included a Swahili preface in which an attempt was made to associate particular poems with known events in Mombasa as well as in the life of the poet. Hichens was indebted to Sir Mbarak for most of the information in the preface. The historical account given there corresponds largely with information about Mombasa under Mazrui rule to be gained from other sources. The poems are in the Taylor Papers, but without historical notes and, for most of the poems, with insufficient explanations of difficult terms in Taylor's own transliteration. By collaboration with Sir Mbarak it was possible for Hichens to identify certain poems with definite events, but some of the verse of a more personal character is identified, with somewhat less credibility, with particular events in the poet's personal life. In any case, sufficient connexion is maintained between the poetry and the background to show that Muyaka's poems were often written for a specific occasion and for a special purpose.

Muyaka aimed at encouraging the Mazrui rulers of the Fort at Mombasa and their followers in opposing the overlordship of Saiyid Said, the Sultan of Muscat. Muyaka's contemporaneous verse expressed something of the spirit of the Mazrui; his poetry is not only a commentary on the times, but also a reflection of contemporary emotion. Muyaka was a friend of the Mazrui governors of Fort Jesus, Abdallah b. Hamed (Governor from 1814–23) and Salim b. Hamed (Governor from 1826–35). Abdallah was the first of the Mazrui governors to refuse to pay tribute to Sayyid Said, Sultan of Muscat, who claimed rule over the coastal settlements of East Africa. When Abdallah successfully invaded Pate in 1819 and placed a contingent of soldiers at Lamu, the Sultan was moved to take action against him.

The following poem was intended to strengthen the Mazrui in their determination to resist the Sultan:

Mugogoto wa zamani

Mugogoto wa zamani   ule muukumbushawo   1
Na uoneke ngomani   ukihimu watezawo
Wake na makao nduni   nduni namba si ya yewo
Yunga na Kiwa-Neewo   na Mkongowea weni.

Jifungetoni masombo   mshike msu na ngawo   2
Zile ndizo zao sambo   zijile zatoka kwawo
Na tuwakalie kombo,   tuwapigie hariwo
Wakija tuteze nawo   wayawiapo ngomani.

Na waje kwa ungi wawo   tupate kuwapunguza   3
Waloata miji yawo   ili kuja kujisoza
Na hawano waiyewo   wana wa Mwana Aziza
Sijui watayaweza   au ni kuongeza duni.

4   Wajile wajisumbuwa   hawa na wana wa Manga
     Kutaka lisilokuwa   ni maana ya ujinga
     Kulla siku twawauwa   na kuwakata kwa panga
     Mwaka huno ukizinga   hawaji tena mwakani.

1 The former threatenings   which you remember   giving rise to
a state of war   hastening the participants   to the women
and those in readiness   I say it will not be today.   You of
Pate and Lamu   and the fortress rock of Mombasa.

2 Fasten well your loins   take hold of sword and shield   Those
are indeed their sailing-craft   they have come from their
land   so let's join with them in ill-temper   let us hail them
as they approach   When they come, let us make a game of
them   when they begin to fight.

3 Let them come in their great number   so that we can make them
decrease   those who have left their towns   to commit sui-
cide for nothing   And those who have come (include)   the
sons of Queen Aziz   I don't know if they will succeed   or
merely add to their wretchedness.

4 Let them come (for) they bring trouble on themselves   these
(from Zanzibar) and the Arabs   To want something that
cannot be   this is the meaning of folly   Each day we will
kill them   and cut them up with swords   When this year
comes to an end   they will not come again next year.

★   ★   ★

Another poem in the same spirit challenges the Sultan's forces
in Zanzibar:

Tumwe ukifika Zinji

     Tumwe ukifika Zinji   Zinji la Mwana Aziza
     Wambile waje kwa unji   unji tutawapunguza
     Hawatatupiga msinji   jengo wakalitimiza
     Wakija wakitekeza   maneno ni ufuoni.

     Wakija wakitekeza   katika nyamba na fungu
     Wataona miujiza   vituko vya ulimwengu
     Wambaje watayaweza   kuvumilia matungu
     Wemapo simba wa bangu   maneno ni ufuoni.

Wemapo simba wa bangu   wenye utambo na vimo
Watalia ole wangu   wangie ndani mwa shimo
Watakatika manungu   mtemo hata mtemo
Panga zao na mafumo   hazifai ufuoni.

Messenger, when you reach Zanzibar   the Zanzibar of Queen
  Aziz   Tell them to come in great number   we will decrease
  their number   They will not attack our foundation   and
  complete (the ruin of) our building   If they come and carry
  out their plan   the matter will be settled on the beach.

If they come and carry out their plan   in the reefs and sand-
  dunes   they will discover wonderful things   The shocks of
  this world   What do you say?   Will they be able   to
  endure the hardships   When they stand, O lion of battle   the
  matter will be settled on the beach.

When they stand, O lion of battle   men of strength and stature
  they will cry out, Woe is me   Let them go into a pit   They
  will be cut in pieces   cut by cut   Their swords and
  spears   are of no use on the beach.

★   ★   ★

This poem is an example with linked verses, see p. 249.

In 1828, during the governorship of Salim b. Hamed, Sultan
Sayyid Said once again succeeded in taking the fort, but his
soldiers were held in siege by the Mazrui. Food was withheld
from them and they were reduced to eating the leather of their
footwear, paper, rats, and snakes. Those who survived starvation
within the fort were killed as they surrendered to the Mazrui.
Fort Jesus has frequently been the scene of conflict and Mombasa
the place of stirring events. There are many poems about Mombasa itself, including the following which is found also in Taylor's
African Aphorisms, pp. 81–82. A version in the Swahili-Arabic
script by Muhammad Kijuma is in the Taylor Papers.

Kongowea ja mvumo

Kongowea ja mvumo   maangavu maji male
Haitoi lililomo   gongwa isingenyemele
Msiotambua ndumo   na utambaji wa kale
Mwina wa chiza mbwi chile   mtambuzwa hatambuli.

Kongowea aridhi mbi   ukenda usijikule
Ina mambo tumbitumbi   wajuzi hawajuvile
Mara huliona wimbi   lausha nyuma na mbele
Mwina wa chiza mbwi chile   mtambuzwa hatambuli.

Mteza wa Nyalikuwu   kugeua mageule
Humvundanga maguwu   asende mwendo wa kule
Akawa paka mnyawu   mnyau paka mwele
Mwina wa chiza, &c.

Gongwa nda Mwana Mkisi   Mvita muji wa kale
Usitupile viasi   ukenda enda kwa pole
Inika chako kikosi   maninga vyema sivule
Mwina wa chiza, &c.

Mvita mji wa ndweyo   ivumayo kwa kelele
Ilitutile tutiyo   panga za masimba wale
Haishi vingurumiyo   na kwangusha mwanzi mle
Mwina wa chiza, &c.

Mombasa is like a roaring surf   in dead-calm and at spring-tide
It vents not forth what is in it   Mombasa could not be peace-
ful   You who do not recognize its war-cries   and its manner
of old   the abyss of that deep gloom   (even) the notorious
knows it not.

Mombasa is evil ground   if you go (there) don't be
proud   (Mombasa) has innumerable affairs   those who
know them (are as if) they did not know   But suddenly they
see the billow   surging fore and aft   The abyss of that
deep gloom, &c.

He who plays with Mombasa   in order to make changes   it
smashes his legs   so that he cannot go even as far as
there   and he becomes a cat   a grimalkin a sick cat   The
abyss of that deep gloom, &c.

Mombasa is Queen Mkisi's place   Mvita the old town   Exceed
not your proper limits   when you go there go softly   Bend
your back   but lift not altogether your eyes   The abyss of
that deep gloom, &c.

Mvita city of pride   that roars with noise   has brandished
aloft its swords   the swords of lofty lions   It never ends its
sudden alarums   and the beating of the drums of war   The
abyss of that deep gloom, &c.

*   *   *

The following two poems by Muyaka refer to sickness in
Mombasa, the first, according to a note in Taylor's papers, to
an epidemic of small-pox:

Kongowea yauguwa

Kongowea yauguwa   kwa kite na uuguzi
Kwa mambo kuyageuwa   kugeua mageuzi
Rabi ngwaipa afuwa   na kuiafu si kazi
Kutanani wamaizi   shauri jema mtende.

Wamaizi kutanani   welewa wana wa Gonga
Wenye urembo na shani   waungwana wa kutunga
Mwime na mikono tani   muombe lenye muwanga
Zisiwe nyoyo kuzinga   shauri jema mtende.

Mombasa is sick   with groanings and sick-nursing   for things
to be changed   to change the changeable   Lord give it
health   for you to give it health is no task   Meet together
you learned men   and put a good plan into effect.

You learned men meet together   O clever sons of Mombasa   who have splendour and glory   free men of invention   Stand with hands on (patient's?) back   and pray
where it gives him pain   Let not men's hearts waver   put a
good plan into effect.

*   *   *

Kongowea cha kigewu

Kongowea cha kigewu   kigeugeu geuka
Haitawali mnyawu   mnyau mwana wa paka
Humvundanga maguwu   maguu yakavundika
Kuinamako kwinuka   pindi ingawa mwakani.

Ingiapo kuuguwa   Kongowea hujisuka
Hata ikapata dawa   ndwele yakwe ikondoka
Ambapo haijapowa   hukusa watu mashaka
Kuinamako kwinuka   pindi ingawa mwakani.

Mombasa is a place of change   never constant never the
    same   A grimalkin does not rule there   no grimalkin off-
    spring of a cat   The place smashes a man's legs   and his
    legs are broken   What is bent low is lifted up   though it be
    the year after next.
When it enters a period of sickness   Mombasa rouses itself
    until it gets the cure   and the sickness departs   while it is
    not yet cured   it involves people in doubts   What is bent low
    is lifted up   though it be the year after next.

*   *   *

During the governorship of Fort Jesus of Salim b. Hamed, the
Sultan of Muscat agreed with the people of Lamu to attack Pate.
The Mazrui under Salim went to the help of the Pateans in 1834
against the Sultan and his Lamu contingent. In this connexion
Hichens gives six verses of a poem in his preface to *Diwani ya
Muyaka* and attributes the authorship of four of the verses to the
people of Lamu and of the other two verses to Muyaka who was
writing on behalf of the Mombasans and the Pateans. The six
verses are in the Taylor Papers, but with no reference to dual
authorship. This raises the question of the authorship of dialogue
verse. In the case of the poem mentioned, it is likely that the six
verses were written by Muyaka himself. They are as follows:

Watumba mji wa kale

Watumba mji wa kale   mwakalia kandokando
Jivuteni muje mbele   tuonyeshane zitendo
Muwaone watasile   nguo wafungene pindo
Siku ya kutinda ſundo   tutaonana fundoni.

Wallahi twapa kwa Mungu   na Mtume Muhammadi
Ndoni munene matungu   mubadilike jisadi
Muwe karamu ya tungu   na tai kuwafisidi
Na tamaa ya kurudi   kwenu siifikirini.

Na kwamba mwataka kuya   hayataki mshawasha
Kwanda fanyani wasiya   na wana kuwaridhisha
Wake wapeni zifaya   muda wa maeda kwisha
Mkija tutawashusha   mashukio ya zamani.

Nami niko Pate Yunga   nifuete Ahamadi
Kati si mwenye kuzinga   ahadi yangu sirudi
Tambo zenu mngapinga   hazitangui ajadi
Siku ya thuluthi hadi   tutaonana fundoni.

Kwamba uko Pate Yunga   naswi tuko Kiwa Ndeyo
Sikae ukaipanga   hutafidi muradiyo
Mume huyu akasonga   haneni yeo ni yeyo
Ole ni waoleweyo   watundao misituni.

Atani wa Kiwa Ndewo   maneno mangi atani
Msinene mupendawo   yawatokayo kanwani
Siku ya msu na ngawo   na risasi matavuni
Mtakwambiwa semani   la kunena msijuwe.

(*Lamu*) Ye baggages of Mombasa Old Town   you skulk on the side   drag yourselves come forward   let us show one another deeds   See them perplexed as they are   they have folded the cloth for the burying   On the day of settling the contention   we shall meet in mutual resentment.

By the Name of God we swear by God   and the Prophet, Muhammad   Come and speak bitter things   be changed in the body   become as feast for the ants   and let the eagle destroy you   And (as for) desire of returning   to your native land do not entertain it.

And that you want to come   it needs no persuader   First make your dying request   and satisfy your children   Give the women the necessary things   until the mourning shall end   When you come we will throw you down   with the humiliations as before.

(*Pate*) And I am here in Pate   I have followed Ahmadi   I am no falterer in the ranks   I do not forsake my oath   Though your prancings block the way   they do not annul our purpose   On the third day   we shall meet in mutual resentment.

(*Lamu*) That you are in Pate   well, here we are in Lamu   I do not stay idle while you line up   you will not fulfil (lit. redeem) your plan   A man comes who overwhelms   he does not say today is the day   O woe on the betrothed   who make their gain in the bush-country.

(*Pate*) Let alone you men of Lamu   Enough of many words   Do not speak as you please   with vain words from the mouth   On the day of the sword and the shield   with bullets in the cheek   then will you be told, Speak up   but what to say you will not know.

       ★   ★   ★

DIALOGUE VERSE

Sequences of dialogue verse are found in nineteenth-century Swahili quatrains. It is not always possible to know if the dialogue verse is actually of dual authorship, but dual authorship can generally be attributed to poems in which a theme is developed in a fairly long sequence of verses and similarly answered. What Hichens has called *The Forge Song* is a dialogue between Muhammad b. Ahmad al-Mambassy who sent seven verses of poetry to Suud b. Said al-Maamiry, the latter sending eleven verses in reply. It is known that religious leaders and poets used to debate in verse some point in dispute. The dispute between Abu Bakr b. Bwana Mengo and Ali b. Sheikh Abdullah concerning the custody of a young girl (referred to as *dura* or love-bird) is probably of dual authorship and runs to sixty verses. Both of the parties to the dialogue were well-known men, an important factor in confirming dual authorship. Similarly, a dialogue between Ali b. Athman, also known as Ali Koti, and Mwalimu Musa al-Famau, discussing the duty of prayer in adverse circumstances, as, for instance, when there is no water for the ceremonial ablutions, is probably of dual authorship. The poem has forty verses and each asseveration consists of at least four or five verses.

There is no reason to doubt that some Swahili poets corresponded with one another in verse-form. The opening lines by each of the parties to the dialogue usually comprised the kind of formula associated with the sending and receiving of a communication. In the scripts belonging to Sir Mbarak Ali Hinawy there is a dialogue poem of thirty-five verses in which Sheikh Ali b. Saad of Lamu writes to Bakari Mwengo of Pate (both well-known men) seeking legal advice for a mother of children who had been neglected by her husband; also a dialogue of eighteen verses between Muhammad b. Ahmad al-Mambassy and Suud b. Said al-Maamiry, the authors of *The Forge Song*, discussing the legal status of a Zigua family who had come to live in Mombasa; and in contrast to these is a dialogue poem of ten verses in which Muhammad b. Tubwa of Wasini talks with his cat.

Not even the most ardent cat-lover would dispute the single authorship of this last example of dialogue verse, and there are clearly other poems in which the dialogue is the invention of a single poet. A good example is the poem included in Sacleux's

Dictionary in which the dialogue is between the Kadhi or Judge and the sorcerer's client. The whole of this poem was written by Sheikh Muhyi 'l-Din, the Kadhi of Zanzibar. Before exemplifying dialogue verse from other sources, we may consider some of Muyaka's short dialogue poems. One appears in the *Diwani*, but as two separate poems with another poem, *Sili*, quite unrelated to the dialogue, dividing the dialogue. This is a love-poem with linked verses.

Risala wa Kongoweya

Risala wa Kongoweya   muyumbe mwenye maana   1
Nakutuma fikiliya   kanisalimie sana
Mwambie la kumwambiya   tumiwe kwako ni bwana
Musiwate kuonana   kwa hii siku ya lewo.

Musiwate kuonana   mupene yaliyo ndani   2
Ndani silofitamana   mafito yalo moyoni
Moyoni mwangu naona   sijui mwako mwandani
Mwandani ngia ndiani   kwa hii siku ya lewo.

Kwamba risala afika   mjumbe wa Kongoweya   3
Ingekuja na waraka   mwema akakuleteya
Au angelitamka   maneno akakwambiya
Lakini hapana ndiya   ya kuonana na wewe.

Lakini hapana ndiya   ya muwanga ilo wazi   4
Ndipo akalimatiya   kuja kwako matembezi
Penyenye ya kupenyeya   siioni kwa maozi
Ndipo hafanya ajizi   ya kuonana na wewe.

Ndipo hafanya ajizi   ningelikutokeleya   5
Pasi kuona manyezi   hatakasa yangu niya
Ila nawacha walinzi   walindao kula mwiya
Ndipo hajizuiliya   nisionane na wewe.

Ndipo hajizuiliya   moyo ungatoa weza   6
Kinyume haushikiya   kisha nikauliwaza
Nisiche kuukwemeya   kwani upate punguza
Kwa kukosa muwangaza   wa kuonana na wewe.

7 Kwa kukosa muwangaza muwanga ungazaga'a
  Huona kikuu kiza nilipo nikianga'a
  Usambe vyanipendeza kwa hilo sikukata'a
  Napenda sikuliwa'a la kuonana na wewe.

8 Napenda sikuliwa'a mwandani mwangu mpenzi
  Kwa wema ulinitwa'a kwa huruma na mbawazi
  Huwaje kukuwamba'a kwa leo nyakati hizi
  Tafanyaje makatazi ya kuonana na wewe.

9 Tafanyaje makatazi kwako wewe mwananinga
  Ndiwe lulu ya mbazi ipendezayo kutunga
  Ikapangua simanzi zamani za kujifunga
  Kukuata ni ujinga kutoonana na wewe . . .

(*Lover*)

1 Messenger from Mombasa O go-between with a purpose I will send you to reach her and take my greetings of love Tell her what there is to tell I am sent to you by my lord do not fail to meet him on this very day.

2 Do not fail to meet exchange what is in (the heart) what is not hidden within altogether (in) the secrets of the heart I see into my own heart I do not know yours beloved Beloved take the pathway on this very day.

(*The Beloved*)

3 To say that a messenger arrives a Mombasan envoy but would that this came with a letter and brought you good news or that if he had spoken it he had told you (fair) words but there is no way of meeting for you and me.

4 But there is no way clear and plain that is why she delayed coming to you walking A secret place to go in by I do not see it with my eyes that is why I delayed our meeting you and I.

5 That is why I delayed or I would have appeared to you without any aversion and with a clear intention But I fear my guardians who keep watch the whole time That is why I withheld myself so that we did not meet you and I.

That is why I withheld myself   though my heart was will- 6
ing   Afterwards I took courage   and then I consoled my
heart   fearing not to lift up my heart   though it came to
be weighed down   from failing a way of escape   for meeting
with you.

For failing a way of escape   may the light shine brightly   Thou 7
seest thick darkness   where here the light (of my love)
shines   Say not these things please me   for I never denied
my love   I love and was not forgetful   about our meeting you and I.

I love and was not forgetful   my own dear beloved   In thy 8
goodness thou tookest me   from pity and compassion   How
could I then impoverish thee   today at this time   How
could I make any refusal   of our meeting you and I.

How could I make any refusal   to you my green pigeon   You 9
are indeed a pearl of compassion   pleasing to cherish   Grief
has disarranged my pearl   when it was being fastened   To
leave you is folly   (O the sorrow at) our not meeting you
and I . . .

★   ★   ★

A short dialogue poem by Muyaka b. Haji in the Taylor Papers
concerns a debtor and his friend. This poem is probably incom-
plete, because it has none of the conventional greetings and ends
abruptly :

Nilime mnda Nogizini

Nilime mnda Ngozini   ule wangu mujuawo
Pata kata ishirini   ni mbili zipungushewo
Nawauza hutendani   nionyani zitendwawo
Mke yuataka nguwo   nami nawiwa kikanda.

Karejee Ngozi mbambe   winike yako maungo
Mpiga na ti ni yembe   huinua nlilo kongo
Mke mrai au mpembe   kwa kweli au kwa uwongo
Deni ongeza kiwango   mwenye deni takulinda.

Nlirejee Ngozini   halitanganya na kongo
Alijile mwenye deni   kanikamata mafungo
Ambe siswi mndani   tatunda yembe na kongo
Nimwongezeze kiwango   yuizize kunilinda.

Huyo yulaliye shari   mwamkie na mapema
Utake watu jifiri   wawepo muyi mzima
Wakutakie saburi   ya mwaka kwenda kulima
Mdeni kaliwa nyama   enda usiate panda.

Kusenye watu muyini   tangu usiyanambiya
Kumuonya mwenye deni   yangu hakuyaridhiya
Amba silindi mwakani   singoji mwezi kusiya
Kesho ukitopimiya   tatunda yembe na mnda.

(*Debtor*) I tilled my plot in Ngoziland   my farm that you know
of   and I got only twenty pecks   less two pecks for tithing-
dues   I ask you what's to be done   show me what to
do   my wife wants clothes   and I am in debt for a bag of
grain.

(*Friend*) Go back to Ngozi's soil   and bend your back   He
who digs the ground with a hoe   raises crops from the furrow   Flatter and outwit your wife   with truth or with
lies   Add interest to your debt   and your creditor will
wait for you.

(*Debtor*) I went back to Ngoziland   and wrought with the
earth's furrow   then my creditor came   and seized me by
the shirt-tail   He said we stay in the plot   I will sell your
hoe and your plot   I offered him more interest   but he
refused to wait.

(*Friend*) That man plans evil   so pay him at the earliest   A
crowd of people is what you need   let the whole village be
there   Let them demand for you grace   of a year for you to
go and cultivate   Should a debtor be eaten like meat?   Go
and do not yield your ground.

(*Debtor*) The people in the village gathered together   long before you told me this   (they went) to advise my creditor   but
he would not rebate my debt   He said, I will not wait until
next year   I will not wait until the end of the month   If
you don't pay by tomorrow   I will impound your hoe and
your plot.

In dialogue verse the final rhyme is usually the same throughout the poem, though examples occur in which the verses of each of the participants have their own terminal rhyme. The poem already illustrated beginning, *Risala wa Kongoweya*, is an example of the latter type, and so is the poem on exorcism by Sheikh Muhyi 'l-Din, Kadhi of Zanzibar, though in this poem by the Kadhi there is a defective rhyme and some of the *vipande* are lacking in the version given by Sacleux. Another manuscript of this poem was lent to me by Sir Mbarak ali Hinawy and the following is the transliteration. For convenience the poem may be referred to as the *Poem of the Judge and the Sorcerer's Client*.

The Judge and the Sorcerer's Client

In order to understand the subject of this poem one must know something of traditional Swahili belief in spirits and of the method of exorcizing them. No less than eight different spirits are named in the poem and the ceremonies involved in exorcising five of these are described in Swahili texts in Velten's *Desturi za Wasuaheli* (Göttingen, 1903), pp. 144–67. It was believed that the *mganga* or witch-doctor, during the drumming and dancing, called the spirit into the head of the patient, *kuchuchia pepo kichwani*, and the head of the sick person being treated was referred to as *kiti cha pepo*, the seat of the spirit. The following extracts from Velten provide an interesting commentary on the poem:

'Mwanamke akiwa na homa siku tatu hujitia pepo kutaka kupungwa. Wazee wake yule mwanamke wakimwona mtoto wao mgonjwa humwambia mumewe, Mkeo pepo wa bibi yake amemrithi, ndiye anayemwuguza, sababu alipokuwa mdogo tulimpandisha kichwani bibi yake pepo wake, tukasema naye, Mlee huyu mtoto hata akikua, akipata mume tutakupa chano chako; na sasa bibi yake amekufa, pepo anataka chano chake, amemshika mjukuuwe.

'Mumewe atamwita mganga atazamie ubao, Nini kinamwuguza mke wangu. Atajibu, hana kitu ila pepo basi. Atajibu mume, Nataka umfanyie dawa. Mganga atajibu, Kwanza tumfunulie nyungu tumtezame hali yake. Na hiyo nyungu namna mbili; kuna nyungu ya mawe na nyungu ya mvuke.

'Nyungu ya mawe huokotwa vidurazi . . . huleta mawe saba wakafanya moto, na yale mawe huungua. Tena hujenga banda la jamvi. Akaja yule mgonjwa, hukaa juu ya kiti, likachimbwa shimo; kisha huja mtungi wa maji akafunikwa uso yakazimwa yale mawe na maji ndani ya shimo, moshi wake humpata yule mgonjwa, hutoka na jasho.

'Nyungu ya mvuke, huchuma majani ya mvuke yakapikwa katika mtungi hata yakawiva, moshi wake huinamia yule mgonjwa, akatokwa na jasho. Na maji mengine ya ule mvuke humpaka maungo mazima.

'Muda wa siku saba kila siku jua linapotua hata jua kutua hufanya nyungu, hukaa saa moja ndani ya ile nyungu. Na yule mwanamke hufurahi nyungu inapokwisha, sababu karibu ata-pungwa. Ikesha nyungu hufanya mashauri ya kumpunga, hum-wambia yule mganga, Huyu ndiye mteja wako, wapashe habari wateja wako, twataka kufanya ngoma . . . Mara litajengwa banda, ikiwa shamba au mjini; jina lake banda hilo kilinge.

'Jioni mwanamke yule hupelekwa kilingeni, napo kilingeni hupambwa chano. Katika chano hutiwa ndizi, sukari, mua, mayai mabichi, mkate na kulla kitu cha tamu. Mwanzo wa esha hurembwa uso yule mwenye pepo, humtona madoadoa meusi meupe na mekundu. Mara huanza wimbo wa kumchuchia yule pepo apande juu ya kichwa, na watu wanapiga ngoma. Na watu huitikia, labda muda wa saa nzima. Akipanda pepo hujitingisha maungo mazima; mara yule mganga hutaranya, maana husema na yule pepo. Na maneno hayo hajui mtu ila yule mganga na mwele wake. Fundi ataamuru ngoma kupigwa sana, pepo mara atasi-mama kucheza. Na watu wote walio wanachama wanacheza, na mshindo wa ngoma ukawapata, wengine wanaanguka kilingeni, wakenda majumbani kwao wagonjwa wanataka kupungwa nao.

'Na muda wake hiyo ngoma siku saba, usiku na mchana kucheza. Na yule pepo anapokuwa hodari kucheza, hupata tunza kwa watu, lakini tunza hizo si zake, mwenyewe mganga na wapiga ngoma na zumari . . . Kila ukapigwa mshindo wa ngoma, pepo akacheza, watu humweka mapesa juu ya kichwa.

'Hata siku ya sita ndio siku ya kutaja jina lake la yule pepo, ndio siku ya fedheha kujulikana yeye pepo au si pepo, maana hutaja jina la kijini, hapana mtu alijuaye. Akisha taja, watu hufu-rahi sana.

'Siku ya saba ndio ya kukomoa. Huchinjwa mbuzi pwani, hukusanyika na pepo wote kunywa damu ya yule mbuzi. Na asiyekunywa damu hiyo hana pepo; na wasio pepo kichwani, wakiona wenzao wanakunywa damu, wote pepo huwapanda kichwani. Wakisha kunywa damu, pepo atabebwa apelekwe nyumbani kwake, amekuwa mzima.'

'If a woman is ill for three days she has a spirit and needs to be exorcized. The woman's parents, when they see her ill, tell her husband, As for your wife, the spirit of her grandmother has taken possession of her (lit. inherited her), it is the spirit who is making her ill, because when she was small we had the spirit of her grandmother to climb into her head, and we told it, Bring up this child until she has grown, and when she gets a husband we will give you your offering; and now her grandmother is dead, so the spirit wants its offering, it has taken hold of her grandchild.

'Her husband will call the witch-doctor for him to consult the divining board (saying), What makes my wife ill? He will answer the husband, There is nothing the matter except for a spirit. The husband will reply, I want you to treat her with medicine. The witch-doctor will reply, First let us prepare the vapour-pots for her so that we can see her condition. And these pots are of two kinds: vapour-pots from stones and vapour-pots from leaves (lit. vapour).

'For the vapour-pots from stone ant-hills are found . . . they bring seven pieces (of the ant-hill), make a fire and the pieces of solid earth are burnt. And they build a hut of matting. And the sick person comes and sits on a chair, and a hole is dug; then a potful of water is brought and the woman's face is covered and those pieces of earth are cooled by the water in the hole, and the steam comes up to the patient and she perspires.

'As for the vapour-pots from leaves, they gather vapour-leaves and these are cooked in a pot until they boil, and the sick person leans over the steam and perspires. And the water is used for anointing all her limbs.

'For the space of seven days each day from dusk until sunset they do this vapour-bath, they stay a whole hour in the vapour-bath. And the woman is glad when the vapour-baths are finished, because soon she will be exorcized. When the vapouring is over, they arrange to exorcize her, and so they tell the witch-doctor, This woman is now your client, so tell your clients (members of a guild of the exorcized), we want to have the dancing . . . At once a hut will be built, either in the field or in the village; the name of this hut is *kilinge*.

'At evening-time the woman is taken to the *kilinge* and there at the *kilinge* the platter of offerings is prepared. In the platter are placed bananas, sugar, sugar-cane, fresh eggs, bread and every sweet thing. At the beginning of the evening prayers the face of the person possessed is made up, they apply black, white and red spots. At once they begin the song for calling the spirit into the head of the patient, and the drums are beaten. And the people respond (in song), perhaps for a whole hour. As the spirit rises, the patient shakes her whole body; then the witch-doctor utters unintelligible sounds, that is, he speaks to the spirit. And no one knows these words except the witch-doctor and his sick patient. The leader orders the drums to be beaten hard, and at once the possessed person (lit. the spirit) stands up to dance. And all members of the guild dance and when the sound of the drums affects them some fall down at the *kilinge* and they go home ill, wanting themselves to be exorcized.

'This dancing goes on for seven days, night and day they dance. And when the possessed person becomes energetic in the dance (lit. clever) she receives gifts from the people, but these gifts are not hers, but the witch-doctor's and the drummers' and the instrument players' . . . Whenever the drums sound the possessed one dances, and people put money on her head.

'The sixth day is the day for naming the spirit, it is a day of shame for the spirit to be known as a spirit or not, for the name of a jinn is called out, for no one knows it. When he has been mentioned, the people are very glad.

'The seventh day is the day of freeing the person of the spirit. A goat is slaughtered on the sea-shore, and they all gather together with the person to be freed to drink the blood of the goat. And whoever doesn't drink of the blood is not possessed; and those who have no spirit in their heads, when they see their friends drinking the blood, become possessed in their turn (lit. the spirits climb into all their heads). When they have finished drinking the blood, the person who was possessed is carried on the back and taken to her house, for she is quite well.'

The above account gives a general picture of the ceremony of exorcism. The details vary according to the type of spirit to be exorcized. In some instances the physical symptoms of an illness were identified with the presence of a clearly known spirit, and the treatment varied and was enacted accordingly. In the poem that follows the following spirits are mentioned by name: Kitanga, Kitimiri, Pangwa, Koikoi, Madungumaro, Ringwa, Matari, and Rewa. Of these the ceremonies associated with the exorcism of Kitimiri, Pangwa, Madungamaro, Matari, and Rewa are described in detail in Velten's book.

Some of the spirits, for example, Kitimiri and Matari or Tari, are described specifically as of Arabian origin, and it would be wrong to suppose that this belief in spirits and their exorcism was confined to the non-Islamic peoples of East Africa. In his poem, Sheikh Muhyi 'l-Din is not addressing a pagan audience; he is writing to a Muslim and for Muslims. Velten's informant, a Muslim, gives the following story, which shows what an attraction these practices had for Muslims as well as pagans, and that the more devout, like Sheikh Muhyi 'l-Din himself, were at considerable pains to dissuade their fellow Muslims from taking part in these ceremonies.

'Zamani moja naliugua mbavu na maungo yote, akaalikwa mganga kunifanyia dawa. Akaniletea mivuke ya dungumaro siku saba, kesha akawaambia wazee wangu ya kama Mtoro amepatikana na dungumaro, sasa msimpe rukhsa kula nyama ya kondoo wala nyama iliyokangwa na vitunguu. Wazee wangu wakayasadiki maneno yale. Siku moja amesema, Sasa hali yake njema, lakini tumpunge, pepo apate kumtuliza. Maneno yale ya mganga wakayakiri wazee wangu.

'Mwalimu wangu aliposikia maneno yale ya kutaka kupungwa akanikataza, akaniambia, Wewe huna haya? Utacheza katika uwanja watu wote wakuone? Nikatahayari kwa maneno yake, nikawajibu wazee ya kama mimi sitaki kupungwa. Mama yangu akafanya hofu ya kukataa kupungwa. Na yule mganga aliposikia akanipigia marufuku kondoo nisile, akasema, Iwapo atakula kondoo, Mtoro atakufa.

'Siku moja mwalimu wangu amealikwa karamu na mimi pamoja. Na yule Mwarabu alichinja kondoo. Mwalimu akaniambia, Hii nyama ya kondoo, utakula? Nikamjibu, Sijui. Akaniambia, Tawakali Mungu, hakuna pepo, upuuzi. Nikala nyama ya kondoo. Nilipofika nyumbani nikamwambia mama, Leo nimekula kondoo. Moyo wake ukashtuka sana, akaniambia, Kwa nini umekula kondoo? Hutaki roho yako? Basi nikakaa yapata siku

tano au sita, sikuumwa na kichwa wala mguu, na hata leo nipo
hapa.'

'There was once I had a bad side and all my joints were aching,
and the witch-doctor was invited to make medicine for me. And
he brought me the Dungumaro medicines for seven days, and
then he told my parents that I was possessed by Dungumaro, so
they must not give me permission to eat mutton nor any meat
fried with onions. My parents believed these words. One day he
said, Now his condition is good, but let's exorcize him, so that
the spirit may quieten down. My parents accepted these words of
the witch-doctor.

'When my (Muslim) teacher heard these things about wanting
to have the spirit exorcized, he refused me permission, and said
to me, Have you no shame? Will you dance in the courtyard for

---

Kadhi

1   Ghofira Mola Jalali   asa takughoforiya
      Uiatapo tabili   muda ya mwaka mmoya
      Itarudi yako hali   upungue na udhiya
      Ya wadeni kukujiya   kwako wewe kudabiri.

2   Kasha ya watenda kazi   ujira hula batali
      Hawauwati uizi   huiba la ukalili
      Kesha watimba mizi   wataka kuku awali
      Pasijc pita kabuli   huwa wamekuhasiri.

3   Talii katika vyuwo   ufunue ukisoma
      Unionye wapungwawo   majini wacheza ngoma
      Illa ni huo wambwawo   urongo unaeosemwa
      Moto zakwe zikikoma   hapana kutahayari.

4   Nanyi bure mwapa mali   hao hawana uganga
      Wapisha nao feeli   wari wanaowapunga
      Akanushao si kweli   amedumu na ujinga
      Kwanza wapunga Kitanga   na wapunga Kitimiri.

all the people to see you? And I was ashamed by what he said, and I told my parents that I didn't want to be exorcized. My mother was afraid about my refusing to be exorcized. And when the witch-doctor heard he told me that I was forbidden to eat mutton, and he said, If ever he eats mutton, Mtoro will die.

'One day my Muslim teacher was invited to a feast and I was invited with him. Our Arab host slaughtered a sheep. My teacher said to me, This meat is mutton, will you eat it? And I answered him, I don't know. He said to me, Trust in God, there are no spirits, it's just foolishness. And so I ate the mutton. When I reached home I told my mother, Today I have eaten mutton. She was much upset, and said to me, Why have you eaten mutton? Don't you want your soul (to be safe)? Well, I went on for about five or six days, and I had no pain in my head nor in my leg, and up to today, here I am.'

The Judge

Forgiveness, Almighty God   perhaps He will forgive 1
   you   when you give up your prognostications   for the space
   of one year   your (former) state will return   you will have
   less trouble   from debtors coming to you   seeking you out.

The (money-)box of the workers (the sorcerers)   (they get) 2
   wages for doing nothing   they do not leave off thieving   they
   steal what is of no account   when they dig for roots   (but)
   first they demand a fowl (in payment)   and no sooner have
   they your consent   than they are making you angry.

Read in the books   open and read them   show me (where I can 3
   find about) the exorcized   (about) jinns and dancers   (there
   is nothing) except what you are told   the falsehood that you
   are told   when his (the sorcerer's) fires are over   is there
   no one ashamed?

You give them money for nothing   they have no medical 4
   knowledge   you make room for their misdeeds   (with) the
   girls whom they exorcize   whoever denies that this is not
   true   continues in ignorance   first they exorcize the spirit
   Kitanga   and they exorcize the spirit Kitimiri.

5   Thabitisha kwa yamini   na chamba huzini nawo
     Wari wa kuja ngomani   wateje uwapungawo
     Hwendi nao faraghani   sirini hwingii nawo
     Na chama walala nawo   yamini ikuhasiri.

6   Yakiri maneno yangu   kwa hivi nikwelezavo
     Kwani kweli ni utungu   watu ndivo wanenavo
     Iwa radhi ndugu yangu   na kama wanena sivo
     Nambie ndivo yalivo   la kweli huwakasiri.

7   Amuri yakwe Manani   kiumbe alitendalo
     Lipitalo duniani   nalo aliamurulo
     Kuna na lake Shetani   la Muungu hili silo
     Kwa kweli ulitendalo   kupunga heri kukiri.

8   Saburisha moyo wako   uiate hiyo kazi
     Utazame hali yako   kadiri ya kumi mezi
     Daraja kuu na mbeko   Mola takayokujazi
     Zikuepuke za uzi   utague ya hariri.

Sorcerer's Client

9   Risala andama ndiya   fika kwa bwana nyumbani
     Enenda kaangukiya   aiwate kasarani
     Hayo aliyosikia   urongo wa majirani
     Mwenye kutaka amani   akiri yali moyoni.

10   Twapenda tukae nawe   uwe kanzu niwe kaba
     Maovu yatuambiwe   ndiyo yangu matilaba
     Sitambui kwako wewe   kwangu mimi nina msiba
     Yanizingile mahaba   ni yapi mwako moyoni.

11   Twapenda tuwe uliko   kwa dawamu na milele
     Wenye heshima na mbeko   kwa yetu mapana na male
     Pasi maneno ya mwiko   nami niyafurahile
     Ama sivyo nisilale   ni yapi mwako moyoni.

Affirm on oath   and if it be said that you fornicate with 5
them   the women clients who come to the dance   the clients
whom you exorcize   (affirm then that) you do not go with
them in private   that you do not go in with them in secret   and
if it be said you sleep with them   may the oath cause you hurt.

Confess my words   what I have explained to you   for the 6
truth is bitter   that is what people say   be content my
brother   and if they say what is not so   tell me how things
really are   (the word) of truth will make them angry.

(There is) the law of God   and what the created being 7
does   what happens on earth   (besides this) there is what
He commands   and there is also (the word) of Satan   this is
not of God   so truly what you do   in exorcising, it is better
to confess it.

Make patient your heart   leave off this work   look at your- 8
self   in about ten months   (there will be) honour and respect   God will fill you with all blessings   to keep you
from trouble   so choose things that are lawful.

Sorcerer's Client

Messenger, follow the way   go to the master's house   go and 9
prostrate yourself   that he may leave off anger   these things
he has heard   are neighbours' lies   the person who wants
peace   confesses what is in his heart.

We want to live together with you   as closely as a robe and its 10
lining (lit. you be the robe and I the lining)   the evil things you
have spoken against us   this (refutation) is my intention   I
do not recognize you   as for me, I am bereaved   my friendship wavers   what are these things in your heart?

We want to be where you are   for ever and ever   having 11
respect and honour   that are both broad and deep   without any prohibitions   for then would I rejoice in these
things   but if not, may I get no sleep   what are these things
in your heart?

Kadhi

12   Tatu wenzio wajapo   kwako wakikusudiya
      Wakiona upungapo   kiumbe kutenda haya
      Sibabu hupungi pepo   wateje wamenambiya
      Sharti kitu kuingiya   au ni kwa ujasiri.

13   Hasa ya hawa waganga   jamii Mabaramaki
      Makoikoi na Pangwa   wajiwapo sisadiki
      Madungumaro na Ringwa   ndiyo kwanza mazandiki
      Ambao ni wanafiki   kwanza wapunga Matari.

14   Dalili tawambiani   kama mwataka ambiwa
      Mutunzeni Halifani   kwa siku anayojiwa
      Kwanza hupita Kokoni   ili kubadili hewa
      Kizabu pepo ya Lewa   na pepo ya madogori.

15   Zaka mwenye kuitowa   na kusali kwa ibada
      Ukiwa na ndwele hupowa   na baraka ikazidi
      Na amali kutubiwa   hali budi hali budi
      Ya nini kujitahidi   kupunga kwa mazumari.

16   Sasa basi tawambiya   niwalete mashahidi
      Watu wa kushuhudiya   mukifanya ufisadi
      Wadi Kongo wasikiya   Asumani na Saidi
      Na wa tatu Wadi Budi   yeye naye Ambari.

17   Shahidi huyo wa mwisho   ushahidiwe thabiti
      Ndiye mshika mugwisho   wateje kuwatafiti
      Akizengea mafusho   kulla panapo kwa mti
      Weka vema wari ati   aliona akakiri.

18   Dhahiri ukimwona   hana analotamani
      Mwate angie kunena   au awe ugangani
      Huwa kama Hamana   au la kama Firauni
      Ukomo wa darajani   kwa haliye ujabari.

19   Radhi mukitaka yangu   ziumbe mupulikawo
      Wazuieni kwa pingu   jamii watoto hawo
      Na amaniaye Mungu   huepuka na matawo
      Na mwenye akanushawo   si islamu ni kafiri.

The Judge

When three of your associates come   to your place intend- 12
ing   to see you when you exorcize   what a thing for a created
being to do   for you do not really exorcize spirits   the
clients have told me   they must make a payment   or it is
foolhardy (for them to go?)

Especially amongst these sorcerers   (are those of) the family of 13
the Barmecides   (who profess to exorcize) the spirits of Koikoi and Pangwa   when they are 'under the influence' I do not
believe it   (and the exorcizers) of the spirits Dungumaro and
Ringwa   they are absolute impostors   who are hypo-
crites   they (profess) to exorcize the spirit Tari.

I will tell you the proof   if you want to be told   look at Hal- 14
fani   on the day when he is 'under the influence'   first he
goes along Kokoni   to get some fresh air   (oh) to lie about
the spirit Lewa   and the spirit of the dogori dance.

The one who gives alms   and who prays at worship   if he is 15
ill he recovers   and the blessing is increased   and this business of being medically treated   it must it must (be as I
say)   why then make such efforts   to exorcize with wind-
instruments (for the dance)?

So now I will tell you   let me bring witnesses   people to bear 16
witness   that you act viciously   Kongo's sons, you understand   Asmani and Saidi   and the third is Budi's son   and
he is Ambari.

This last witness   his witness is certain   he is the holder of the 17
wand   examining the clients   looking for leaves for the
fumigation   wherever there is a tree   place the women
clients well, is it?   he saw (these things) and confessed.

It is plain that if you see him   there is nothing he desires   so 18
leave him to speak   or else let him go to the exorcism   (in the
first instance) he is like Haman (the quiet, calm minister of
Pharaoh)   or (in the second instance) like Pharaoh (proud
and self-centred)   at the very limit (lit. the end of the
bridge)   because of his pride.

If you want my blessing   O created beings who listen   prevent 19
them with chains   the whole lot of these children   and whosoever believes in God   keeps himself without reproach   and
whosoever denies this   he is no Muslim but an infidel.

20 Dharari yako ni nini   kusuduku kama haya
    Ujuao Kuruani   ziada ya sura miya
    Jambo lisilomkini   wewe ukasudukiya
    Ukaingiwa udhiya   billeli wa nahari.

The Forge Song

Three manuscript copies of the dialogue poem referred to as
The Forge Song are in the Taylor Papers and they correspond very
closely to the version given in Sir Mbarak Ali Hinawy's book,
al-Akida and Fort Jesus, Mombasa. The occasion which gave rise
to this dialogue poem was the departure from Mombasa to Zanzibar of the poet, Suud b. Said al-Maamiry, leader of the Mombasan
faction against the Governor of the Fort, Muhammad b. Abdullah
b. Mbarak Bakhashweini, known as al-Akida. Suud's purpose was
to influence the Sultan of Zanzibar to recall al-Akida and in this
he was supported by some of the most prominent citizens of
Mombasa. Amongst them was the poet, Muhammad b. Ahmad
al-Mambassy, who was at that time (*c*. A.D. 1872–3) staying with
Sheikh Abdallah b. Jabir at Mgoli, Pemba. On hearing of Suud's
arrival in Zanzibar he sent him his poem of seven verses, giving
advice and encouragement.

Sir Mbarak Ali Hinawy's explanation may be given here of the
metaphors employed in the poem:[1]

'Suud is encouraged to get into touch immediately with the officials
of the Sultan's court and to ask them to smooth the way for a favourable
reception of his address. But he must remember that giving the Sultan
an account of Muhammad b. Abdullah's conduct is only one step
towards the success of their plot. "The tempering of the tongs does not
mean that the sword is forged" (verse 1). Suud must persist until he
achieves his end.

'Further, Suud is familiar with the language of intrigue, here referred
to as the "abjadi" method of writing; he must be cautious in what he
says, and he must not expect his sympathizers to express their attitude
openly, although they are weaving the sling that will fling a stone to
slay this bird of prey, al-Akida (verse 2).

'Let him remember other men of high office like al-Akida who
eventually were deposed and disgraced. Al-Akida, whatever his resis-
tance, is not undefeatable (verse 3).

'Let him recall Bori, the ruler of Sadani in the time of Sayyid Majid,

[1] Mbarak Ali Hinawy, *al-Akida and Fort Jesus, Mombasa*, pp. 53–54.

What necessity have you   to believe in things like these?   (you) 20
who know the Quran   with more than its hundred chap-
ters   a matter which is impossible   (why) do you believe
in it   and so go in for trouble   by night and day?

---

and Mwereka-mwanamchief of the Zigua, with their army of slaves and
their allies, the Shambala. They rebelled against the Sultan and were
defeated, and they are examples of what befalls those who abuse their
authority (verse 4).

'Let him think also of Mwana Kingwaba, who had succeeded
Mwereka-mwana, and who had gone the same way. Let Suud be
patient and cautious; when the time came to strike, then he and his
supporters could strike hard, and the régime of al-Akida would be
destroyed (verse 5).

'Let him remember also the fate of Abdallah Mwaketa, a chief of the
Digo tribe who had defied Sayyid Majid. Mwaketa had claimed the
small island of Maziwe, near Pangani, as the boundary between his
territory and that of the Sultan, and had declared that in his own territory he was independent of the sultanate. Suud would recall what had
occurred. Sayyid Majid had despatched an emissary, Hemed b. Suleiman, with presents and fair words. Mwaketa accepted the invitation to
board the Sultan's ship, believing Hemed's story that he would be
taken to Zanzibar to pay his greetings to Sayyid Majid. As soon as the
vessel had put to sea and was beyond Maziwe island, Mwaketa was
seized, thrown overboard and drowned near the very place which he
had claimed to be the boundary of his territory. Yet he had possessed
a large and strong army.

'Finally Muhammad reminded his friend Suud of the downfall of the
family of Sheikh Mataka of Siu, who had once controlled the destinies
of Siu, Faza and Pate, yet had finally seen their lands subdued and their
power destroyed by the sultanate of Zanzibar. All these once powerful
men who had tried to assert their independence on the Coast had been
overcome by those whom they had sought to oppress; and Muhammad b. Abdullah also, if he tyrannized over the people of the land,
would meet the same fate.'

Suud b. Said sent a reply of eleven verses to Muhammad b.
Ahmad, the real meaning being cloaked by what were apparently
nothing more than instructions to his dhow-captain, telling him
how to take his ship in safety from Zanzibar to Pemba and to
deliver his respects in person to Muhammad. The last six verses
are addressed directly to his friend, Sheikh Muhammad, and they

assure him that Suud is persevering with his plans for deposing
al-Akida and that he is confident of ultimate success.

Strictly speaking these are two separate poems, but it is

The Forge Song
Sheikh Muhammad b. Ahmad

1   Risala siwe ajizi   enenda kwa wenye chewo
      Ukenda siwe mkazi   mtafute mwendaniwo
      Mwambie eshe simanzi   dira ashike ziliwo
      Kuno kuzima kwelewo   haiwi kwisha uhunzi.

2   Ayuha Shekhe Suudi   sikiza nikwambiawo
      Yakwelea abjadi   tusiufunue mwawo
      Sione kimya kuzidi   mlinzi asuka tewo
      Kuno kuzima kwelewo   haiwi kwisha uhunzi.

3   Kumbuka utayaona   mangapi yapisiyewo
      Ya watu wenye maana   ni kipi kikomo chawo
      Haile ngoma ya wana   sijaona ikeshawo
      Kuno kuzima kwelewo   haiwi kwisha uhunzi.

4   Bori na Mwereka-mwana   walina Wazigua wawo
      Walina wangi watwana   na Wasambaa ni wawo
      Walipoleta khiyana   mbonya nami mwiso wawo
      Kuno kuzima kwelewo   haiwi kwisha uhunzi.

5   Yu wapi Mwana Kingwaba   akomele sambe nawo
      Kuna siku ya dharuba   kumbukani ivumawo
      Mwana hatajua baba   mja hatajua kwawo
      Kuno kuzima kwelewo   haiwi kwisha uhunzi.

6   Mwaketa alina simba   akenenda kwa matawo
      Mrima akauwamba   pasiwe na apitawo
      Mabwana wakamkumba   Maziwe mpaka wawo
      Kuno kuzima kwelewo   haiwi kwisha uhunzi.

7   Kwalina wana Mataka   na ubora walinawo
      Na ungi wa mamlaka   na Sawahili ni yawo
      Husuda yaliwashika   waliliwe hata lewo
      Kuno kuzima kwelewo   haiwi kwisha uhunzi.

customary to regard the separate asseverances of a dialogue poem as constituent parts of a single dialogue poem. *The Forge Song* must be regarded as one of the best of its kind.

The Forge Song

Sheikh Muhammad b. Ahmad

Messenger do not tarry go to the people of rank go now 1 and do not delay seek out your friend tell him, Do not worry go where the compass points the cooling of the tongs does not mean the end of the forging.

Hail Sheikh Suud hear what I say to you you know the 2 clues to Abjadi the speech which cannot be free do not think the watch grows tardy the watchman weaves a sling the cooling of the tongs does not mean the end of the forging.

Consider, you will see how many who have passed on of 3 men of renown how came their end? it is like a childrens' dance I have not seen it last till morning the cooling of the tongs does not mean the end of the forging.

Bori and Mwereka-mwana they had their Ziguas they had 4 many slaves and the Shambaa were theirs when they brought rebellion show me their end the cooling of the tongs does not mean the end of the forging.

Where is Mwana Kingwaba? he is finished and no longer 5 speaks there is a day of storms remember how it roars the child knows not his father nor the slave his home the cooling of the tongs does not mean the end of the forging.

Mwaketa also was a lion making his tortuous way and he 6 sealed up the Mrima country so that no one could pass by but his masters attacked him Maziwe was their boundary the cooling of the tongs does not mean the end of the forging.

There were the sons of Mataka and the splendour that was 7 theirs and their abundant authority for the Swahili country was theirs but envy came upon them so that they are lamented even today the cooling of the tongs does not mean the end of the forging.

Suud b. Said

8   Tumi peleka jawabu   risala ulonijiya
       Utokao kwa sahibu   anipendao kwa niya
       Bisha siche aziyabu   sikhofu kulimatiya
       Kamwambie yatweleya   kama sikwisha uhunzi.

9   Ngojea zije za juwu   uwandike Manga Pwani
       Na tanga utie kuwu   legeza punde demani
       Usafiri kwa pashawu   singie Mkokotoni
       Mwana iwate joshini   makusudi ni ya Ngezi.

10   Mwana wishapo kujuwa   nambiya nami nijuwe
       Jua huwa limetuwa   tahadhari na Maziwe
       Hata ukiifunuwa   ni sharuti upinduwe
       Umande ukunyakuwe   tanga moya hata Ngezi.

11   Kangie kwa Mabaoni   ndio mlango wa kweli
       Uwambaze pwanipwani   ufulizie Mgoli
       Kwa Shekhe wa Arabuni   mwenye jaha na jamali
       Mwambie sio dalili   ya kuwa kwisha uhunzi.

12   Ukima kusikiliya   Mgoli kwa Shekhe letu
       Enda kwa kunyenyekeya   uuwate utukutu
       Yeye atamuzengeya   Muhamadi mwana kwetu
       Zijapo zimwa kitutu   haiwi kwisha uhunzi.

13   Ewe Shekhe al-Mambasi   sikiza nikwambiawo
       U mtu wa kumarisi   kwa akili na mabawo
       Naona kuna ruwasi   ya tutu na kiapiwo
       Kweli kuzima kwelewo   haiwi kwisha uhunzi.

14   Usidhani nimekoma   kuunda kupiga mbawo
       Mimi sijile kutuma   nauandama mwambawo
       Fahamia nanguruma   Shaha nimeshika mwawo
       Kweli kuzima kwelewo   haiwi kwisha uhunzi.

15   Ndugu naiyona kesha   ya ile ngoma ya wana
       Waso mayi ya kunwesha   wala kulisha zijana
       Siku nendao egesha   kwa ladu njema za puna
       Taiondoa fitina   niukomeshe uhunzi.

Suud b. Said

Messenger take an answer   to the envoy who came to me   who 8
came from my friend   who loves me entirely   work to
windward fearing not (to miss) a fair wind   nor fear to be
becalmed   tell him we understand   that I have not finished
the forging.

Wait for the north-west wind   and set sail for Manga 9
Pwani   hoist the great lateen   slack the mainsail tackle
ready   make bold your way in the wind   heave not to at
Mkokotoni   leave Mwana to windward   steer for Ngezi (in
Pemba).

And when you sight Mwana   tell me so that I may know   by 10
then the sun will have set   so beware of Maziwe (the
swell)   but once in the lee (of Maziwe island)   you must
luff your sail   let the landwind take you   a straight course
(single sail) to Ngezi.

Go in by Mabaoni Channel   that is the proper way in   then 11
hug the coast   and make straight for Mgoli   to the Arab
Sheikh   a man of honour and good manners   tell him that
there is no sign   that the forging is finished.

When you arrive   at Mgoli at our Sheikh's place   go with 12
humility   leaving aside any nervousness   he will look for
him   for Muhammad that son of our town   even though
our tongs be quenched   the forging is not finished.

O Sheikh of Mombasa   listen to what I say   you are an astute 13
person   clever with the diviner's tray   I see there is
a kind   of drumming with mens' calling for joy in the
dance   truly the cooling of the tongs   is not the end of the
forging.

Do not think I have finished   putting the planks together   I 14
have not come for profit   I travel along the shore   understand, I am roaring   I am like the orator at the *mwao* song-
festival   truly the cooling of the tongs   is not the end of the
forging.

Brother I think it will last the night   that dance of the 15
children   yet they have no water to drink   nor food for the
young people   on the day when I make my vessel fast   it
is with sweetmeats   that I will heal the strife   and put an
end to the forging.

16   Jamii wote wateje   wameenea pagaro
       Wakiulizwa mwambaje   hunena twataka charo
       Wakiambiwa wangoje   hunena rero ni rero
       Lijapo uswa gandaro   haiwi kwisha uhunzi.

17   Ngome haikuwaweka   Rashidi na Selemani
       Nao wali wakiwaka   kama jua la vitwani
       Wali na nyingi tafaka   mingarizo kwa imani
       Wakauka kiwandani   ikawa kwisha uhunzi.

18   Kwali na nikwa mitambo   na mangi mno marima
       Waloshikwa ni ulimbo   waliokoka salama
       Wamesaa wa mgambo   yao nyungu yanguruma
       Kweleo na zingazimwa   haiwi kwisha uhunzi.

A number of poems by Muyaka b. Haji express the idea that his verse is a message to the beloved. These are not dialogue poems, though the opening lines or line may take the conventional form of dialogue poetry. The following is an example:

Risala wangu bashiri

    Risala wangu bashiri   leo napenda kutuma
    Enenda ndiwa huuri   mwenye cheo na heshima
    Fika ukamhubiri   haya takayotuma
    Namuapia Karima   siupati usingizi.

    Wishapo mpa salamu   ndiwa asio mfano
    Mwema wa kutakalamu   fasiha yakwe maneno
    Ni mwema wa tabasamu   mchache wa makutano
    Hasa himuwaza mno   siupati usingizi.

    Wishapo mkurubiya   ndiwa mwema wa mangani
    Enda kwa kunyenyekeya   upomoke maguuni
    Kisha umweleze piya   yangu yaliyo moyoni
    Mato yangu hayaoni   kwa kukosa usingizi.

My message of greeting   today I want to send   Go then to my gracious lady   of rank and esteem   Get there and tell her   the message I send   I swear by The Beneficent One?   I get no sleep.

The whole group of the wizard's clients (i.e. Al-Akida and his 16
followers)   are fully armed   when asked, How say
ye?   they say, We want to get going (lit. a caravan, a journey)   when told to wait   they say, Today is the day   though
the nail-rack be removed   this is not the end of the forging.

The Fort did not put them (in safety)   Rashidi and Sele- 17
mani   they were firebrands (lit. burning)   like the sun on
(our) heads   they had many guns   and weapons to trust
in   but into the open they came   and that was the end of
the forging.

They had many a trap with bait   and many a pit (made 18
ready)   those who were stuck in the birdlime   escaped
safely   now there remains to the rulers   a pot (of trouble)
for them that rumbles   for although the tongs be cooled   this
is not the end of the forging.

When you have greeted her   my matchless dove   accomplished
in speech   gracious in words   whose smiling presence   seldom favours public assemblies   (tell her) in truth for thinking
upon her so much   I get no sleep.

When you have approached her   my heavenly dove   go in
humility   fall down at her feet   and so tell her   what
I have in my heart   My eyes go blind   for I get no sleep.

★   ★   ★

Muyaka's poems on domestic life are often personal and express
true relationships. Take, for instance, the poem inspired, according to a marginal note in the Taylor Papers, by Muyaka's trouble-
some second wife:

Usinambie papale

Usinambie papale   mama na baba waliko
Na watu wajee tele   hajua shauri lako
Leo ni pweke tukele   na washauri hawako
Hili langu ndilo lako   au una jinginele.

Wanizidia matungu   kuongea sikitiko
Kutoshusha moyo wangu   kwa hali ya pujuliko
Ni ipi khatia yangu   niliyoikosa kwako
Hili langu ndilo lako   au una jinginele.

Unambiapo si tuwa   muungwana mwenye mbeko
Mtukufu wa mruwa   mwelewa wa matamko
Sifanye isiyokuwa   nitoa langu sumbuko
Hili langu ndilo lako   au una jinginele.

Kwamba huna huja nami   usinionye vituko
Nijinyamele sisemi   kwako wewe sina suko
Satui wangu ulimi   si nyemi sina kiteko
Hili langu ndilo lako   au una jinginele.

Don't stand there and tell me   where your mother and father are   or that your people are numerous   and that they know how to advise   Today there's just the two of us   and your advisers are not here   What I have to say is for you   or have you something else to suggest?

You make me more bitter than before   to speak together is a sorry business   I can hardly get my breath   because of this wretched battle of words   What exactly is the thing I am supposed   to have offended you about?   What I have to say is for you   or have you something else to suggest?

When you tell me there is no quarrel   O free-born mother   O well-mannered lady   O lady of choice speech   Do not make such empty pretence   but remove the cause of my annoyance   What I have to say is for you   or have you something else to suggest?

If it be that you have no need of me   well then, don't keep on nagging me   I have gone all quiet without saying a word   nor do I disturb or annoy you   I make no discord with my tongue   no clamour, I don't even laugh   What I have to say is for you   or have you something else to suggest?

*   *   *

The following is a poem by Muyaka b. Haji in which a mother speaks to her refractory daughter:

Alipokwenenda kwawo

1   Alipokwenenda kwawo   mamaye alimwambiya
Nipa fedha au nguwo   nataka kwenda tumiya
Nikosapo hivi lewo   nipa kisu tajitiya
Huzunguka akiliya   kwa maana ya uketo.

Ndipo mamaye kawaza   pamwe na kuzingatiya   2
Fedha zako umesoza   na leo zimekwishiya
Kisu sitakukataza   twaa upate jitiya
Mbele zangu nondokeya   wende na ukiwa wako.

Ulipogeuka nondo   nguo ukazingiliya   3
Kakakaka kwa vishindo   usisaze hata moya
Leo wanuka uvundo   wambeja wakukimbiya
Mbele zangu nondokeya   wende na ukiwa wako.

Ulijigeuza nyama   kama simba ukiliya   4
Watumwa ukawegema   ukawala wote piya
Pasi kuona huruma   kutoa wahurumiya
Mbona hukuzingatiya   enda na ukiwa wako.

Si mimi naliokupa   uketo huo sikiya   5
Kwamba utakuja hapa   nipate kuondoleya
Naapa thama naapa   sina la kukutendeya
Mbele zangu nondokeya   wende na ukiwa wako.

Tamati nalikomele   ni hayo nalokwambiya   6
Hapahitaji kelele   na kujirisha mabaya
Na kwamba yakutukile   sema yapate neleya
Zidi radhi kuniweya   wende na ukiwa wako.

When she went home   she said to her mother   Give me 1
money or clothes   I want to go and use them   and if I fail
to get them today   well, give me a knife for me to stab
myself   She wanders about crying   because of her plight.

Then her mother thought   and remembered as well   You 2
have wasted your money   and now today it is all finished
up   I shan't refuse you a knife   so take it and stab
yourself   Go from before me   go away with your loneliness.

When you were like a moth   in a cocoon of new clothes   you 3
were in a hurry to make a sensation   (and used up your
clothes) without leaving one   But today you just stink   the
well-dressed women run away from you   So go from before
me   go away with your loneliness.

You became like an animal   crying out like a lioness   You 4
depended entirely on your slaves   and consumed them
all   without pity   without having compassion on them   O
why didn't you think?   Go away with your loneliness.

5 It isn't I who gave you   this trouble, understand   That you
   have come here   so that I might rid you of your trouble   I
   swear and swear again   I can do nothing for you   So go
   from before me   Go away with your loneliness.

6 I have come to the end   and it is as I have told you   There is
   no need for a noise   nor for you to cause trouble   And if
   these things (that you have done) displease you   well say so
   for me to understand   Ask my pardon   or else go away with
   your loneliness.

★   ★   ★

In this last poem the first verse is introductory to the rest of the
poem and has a different terminal rhyme. One feels that poems of
this type are only part of what must have been much longer
works, though no long poem in quatrains telling a consecutive
story has been found. There are many poems of only one verse
each in the early manuscripts and these are often unintelligible
without the extensive annotation which neither the manuscripts
nor informants provide. Taylor's own notes often leave serious
gaps. In the following single-verse poem addressed by metaphor
to a sweetheart, Muyaka's allusions are explained by Taylor. Had
they not been, the poem, like so many others, would have been
quite untranslatable.

Tanzi za nyama tanzi

Tanzi za nyama tanzi   tanzi mkivumiza
Kukanya wakurufunzi   sote vyatusangaza
Tujile na yetu runzi   twatafuta vya kuwaza
Wakurufunzi mwauza   au ni mituzi yenu.

This verse was written at a time when grain was the medium
of exchange. The word *tanzi* was a greeting to professional
hunters, meaning, 'Have you had any luck?'; the literal meaning
is 'a trap, a noose, a loop'. If the answer was *Za maji*, it meant
'I have got nothing', but if the answer was *Za nyama*, it meant 'I
have had luck'. The verse may be translated as follows:

You display your bag of game; for professionals to refuse to sell
is amazing to us all. We have come prepared to barter with our
grain. We don't know what to think (lit. we are seeking things
to think of). Will you sell, you experts of the gun, or is it your
own relish?

★   ★   ★

Muyaka is reputed to have been a man of very simple tastes who bothered very little about his personal appearance. His old clothes were sometimes the subject of jesting by the better-dressed. In the following poem Muyaka attacks the dandies of Mombasa, and he has composed his verses to be reminiscent of his tattered clothes, for we see that the final rhyme is faulty, unlike his other verses which normally have a regular terminal rhyme throughout the poem, i.e. at the end of each stanza.

Tao la nyanje mwaowa

Tao la nyanje mwaowa   na kwamba nali hivuta   1
Nyote mngelia ngowa   mkiniona hipita
Nyoyo zingependezewa   upindo hiukokota
Mpiga konde ukuta   huumiza mkonowe.

Nangojani silivuti   tao la nyanje mwaowa   2
Upindi siukokoti   nti ukalewalewa
Matengoni hiwa kati   kulla mtu akajuwa
Hatambi na kutambiwa   mato nisiyafumbuwa.

Wanyanje wa Kongoweya   wavutapo nyanje zawo   3
Huvuta wakisinziya   hawajui wenzi wawo
Wendapo katika ndiya   ulimwengu kwamba mbwawo
Na kwamba moyo ni chuwo   ningekupa ukasome.

Wote wanyanje mwaowa   wali watijika nawo   4
Unyanje wawasumbuwa   watozeni nyanje zawo
Mno mno walishowa   na kutengeneza mavawo
Wamepigwa ni jangawo   kwa baa zao ni mbovu.

You have seen the dandy's gait   If I were to walk like them   you 1 would all weep with envy   seeing me passing by   You would be so pleased to see me   drag the border of my garment   Who strikes his fist on a wall   hurts his hand.

For what do I wait? that I do not mince along   with the gait of 2 a dandy you have seen   nor do I drag my cloth along on the ground   so that it sways along   When I am in people's houses   every man knows   I strut not proudly and without being told   May I not keep my eyes open?

3 When the dandies of Mombasa   walk about in their finery   they
   mince along with eyes half-closed   not knowing their
   friends   When they go along the road   they act as if the
   world were theirs   But if the heart were a book   I would give
   it you to read.

4 You have seen all the dandies   they could be mentioned by
   name   Their foppery annoys you   so make them give up
   their fine attire   Far too often they have married   and so
   prepared more fine clothes   Doubtless they have troubles of
   their own   troubles rotten to the core.

★   ★   ★

THE USE OF A REFRAIN

Swahili poets have experimented with many variations and
adornments of the accepted form of the regular quatrain. The
chief of these have been the use of refrains or choruses, the inclusion of proverbs (though in some instances the proverbs derived
from the verse), and such devices as the repetition or reversal of
hemistichs.

The use of a refrain was, of course, borrowed from Arabic.
Elkott has written[1] of Arabian poetry: 'Arabs always favoured a
line that vividly and compactly expressed a moral or an axiom in
a proverbial way. In their oratory, in their moments of exaltation
and in situations that needed some laconic and effective remark,
they usually resorted to such lines. An argument could triumph-
antly be brought to an end, and an adversary made to feel himself
at a loss, by the simple means of the rival throwing in one of those
disarming lines at the right moment.' The same could be said of
the Swahilis. In earlier verse in Swahili the refrain was sometimes
written in Arabic, especially in religious Swahili poetry. The use
of a refrain is still a very popular device in modern Swahili poetry
in the vernacular press.

A fixed refrain in the last *kipande* of each verse provides the
greatest freedom for rhyming in the other *vipande*, since, of course,
the rhyme of the final *kipande* is fixed throughout the poem
whether a refrain is used or not. As soon as a refrain of more than
one *kipande* is adopted, the poet is restricted in his rhymes, and
in his desire to break free from this restriction he may often produce verses defective in rhyme.

[1] A. Elkott, 'Arab Conception of Poetry', Thesis for Ph.D. London, p. 146.

The poet may at times prefer a restricted rhyming scheme, as, for example, in the poem by Muyaka in which he chooses to use a refrain in both the first and the final *kipande* of each verse:

Mwandani wako mwandani

Mwandani wako mwandani   ukitaka umujuwe   1
Ngia naye safarini   wenende mwendo wa kuwe
Au muate nyumbani   ukatembee ukawe
Atoapo kuwa mwewe   huyo ni wako mwandani.

Mwandani wako mwandani   ukitaka mfeeli   2
Mtima utie kani   utumie yakwe mali
Umuonapo haneni   hakuregeza kauli
Ha shabihi ha mithili   huyo ni wako mwandani.

Mwandani wako mwandani   ukitaka mjuato   3
Mpishe ndia yakini   zenye miwa na tototo
Au ukambwage zani   ambayo kwamba ni nzito
Akuonyapo mapito   huyo ni wako mwandani.

A friend your true friend   if you wish to know his worth   go 1
with him on a journey go to some distant place or else leave
him behind at home   and go out on a loitering stroll   If he
watches like a hawk (on your behalf)   that one is your true
friend.

A friend your true friend   if you wish to hurt his name   de- 2
ciding wrongly   to use his wealth   when you see that he
says nothing   nor rebukes you without equal is his fame   that
one is your true friend.

A friend your true friend   if you wish to know him well   take 3
him along some known path   full of brambles and thorns   or
involve him in some mischance   of a serious nature   If he
still shows you the ways to pass   that one is your true friend.

*   *   *

REGULAR VERSE

The term 'regular' is applied in the technical sense to poems in which the penultimate *kipande* rhymes with the one immediately preceding it. The term applies to verse of any number of *vipande*

from three to ten. Not one of the poems by Muyaka b. Haji
in the Taylor Papers—and there are nearly 300 of them—breaks
this strict convention. Modern poets, however, frequently write
irregular verse. Of the thirty-five poems by Shaaban Robert in
Pambo la Lugha, only two are in regular form, the author pre-
ferring to rhyme all of the first *vipande* to a line with a different
rhyme from all of the second *vipande*. In relation to the earlier
poetry, poems of this type are defective (*guni*), though modern
writers may not regard them as such. The following example is
by Shaaban Robert:

Ziaka tupu hutisha

Ziaka tupu hutisha   likiwa na mfuniko
Adui atakupisha   njiani kila wendako
Bila ya kudhihirisha   nia kwa tamko
Stadi kubahatisha   hatambui siri yako.

Ziaka bila mshale   likifunikwa hutisha
Hudhaniwa imo tele   mishale ya kufisha
Ulimi vile vile   siri yake hudumisha
Usipomwaga nenole   ovyo katika maisha.

An empty quiver frightens   if it has a cover   An enemy will
let you go by   on the road wherever you go   without
making known   his intention by word   Though he be
clever at guessing   he does not know your secret.

A quiver without arrows   if it is covered it frightens   It is
thought to be full of them   of arrows that make afraid   The
tongue in like manner   it can keep its secret   unless it spills
the matter out   and that is foolishness in the life of a person.

*   *   *

This poem discards the important convention that the final
kipande should rhyme throughout the poem. If the rhyming convention were observed, then all of the second *vipande* would have
the same rhyme in this type of verse, but the poet does not in this
instance wish to accept this restriction.

Modern poets favour the use of a refrain, but when they employ
a refrain in the last two *vipande*, they frequently write defective
(*guni*) verse. Note the following example by Kaluta b. Abedi:

Kweli yataka hodari

Kweli yataka hodari   aseme ikimupinga
Ni chungu kama shubiri   wengi uwongo hutunga
Iwazingapo hatari   wengi kweli huikenga
Hawi mkweli mkenga   kweli zama za hatari.

Hawi mkweli mkenga   akengaye hako shwari
Hawi shwari kuikinga   wala si njema hadhari
Si hadhari kuipinga   kweli inapodhihiri
Hawi kweli mkenga   kweli zama za hatari.

Truth needs a stable character   one who speaks it though it thwart him   It is as bitter as aloes   and many fabricate lies   when danger surrounds them   many cheat the truth   A cheat is not a true man   (but better) truth in times of danger.

The true man is not a cheat   and the one who cheats is not at peace   He is not calm to check the lie   nor for him is caution a good thing   It is not prudent to contradict   the truth when it is made evident   The true man is no cheat   (but better) truth in times of danger.

★   ★   ★

The first verse in this poem is regular, but the second verse is *guni*, because the second *vipande* do not rhyme with the penultimate *kipande*. Though the earlier verse scarcely ever breaks this convention, the use of a whole-line refrain inevitably restricts the rhyming-pattern. The following example of regular verse is by an unknown author and is in the Hichens Papers:

Nalipawa ulimwengu

Nalipawa ulimwengu   nanyi mkiangaliya
Hikosa sina matungu   ndivo ulivo duniya
Mja huondolewa fungu   naye alihitajiya
Amuri ikinijiya   hifuata tatendaje.

Kwani amuri ni nzito   ukiiza hukujiya
Kukukosa we ni pato   kiumbe huzingatiya
Ulimwengu ni utoto   hau mwanzo ukasiya
Amuri ikinijiya   hifuata tatendaje.

I was bestowed of mortal life   and (when I die) do ye behold   missing (things) will not make me grieve   for it is the way of the world   The slave is deprived of his life's portion   when he is needed   When my time comes   what shall I do but follow the command?

For the decree is weighty   if you refuse it will come to you all the same   If it miss thee (for a while) that is a gain   but the created being bears in mind   that the world is a dependency   and whatever begins must have an end   When my time comes   what shall I do but follow the command?

*   *   *

A refrain of the last two *vipande* in Arabic was occasionally employed in the earlier verse. Refrains of the last four *vipande* are infrequent, but they were sometimes used. In the following example from the Hichens Papers the proper order of the last two *vipande* is transposed, because the poet has found difficulty in making the rhyme correspond with the sense:

Ule dari ukandika

Ule dari ukandika   hata tone lisitone
Dongo likaporomoka   linti ligendemene
Ungeshika kuteteka   mbele yakwe ni mavune
Bandika ukibanduwa   ukibandika vingine.

Wahadau la shirika   ni yeye hako mwingine
Mkuu ni rama nyoka   hapazwa tusimuone
Ungeshika kuteteka   mbele yakwe ni mavune
Bandika ukibanduwa   ukibandika vingine.

You mortared the roof with lime   so that not a drop of water could drip down   but the mortar fell out   before it was set firm   If you decide to quarrel   there are consequences to come   It is as if you unfasten the roof of your house   in order to fasten it up again.

My God Who is Alone   it is He unrivalled by any other   great and merciful and steadfast   lifted high above mortal domain   If you decide to quarrel (repeated refrain) . . .

*   *   *

LINKED VERSES

Poems in which successive verses are linked together by the repetition in each successive verse of a terminal measure of the preceding verse bear out the fancy that verses are like strings of pearls in a necklet, graced with clusters of large pearls, the rhymes, at intervals. This Swahili concept, taken from the Arabs, is mentioned in a number of poems, for example, in verse 7 of *al-Inkishafi*.

There are two types of linking, namely, the simple or 'continued' verses, called *mashairi ya nyoka*, lit. snake-verses, and the reversed or 'turned-line' verses, known as *mashairi ya mapinde*, lit. turned verses.

The most common expedient in *mashairi ya nyoka* is linking by repetition of the penultimate *kipande*, and this is usually combined with the grace of a refrain in the final *kipande*. A poem from the Hichens Papers will illustrate this as follows:

Kusumbuani si kwema

Kusumbuani si kwema   ewe mzuri tausi
Mwenye cheo cha heshima   ndoo hima kwa upesi
Tuambiane kalima   zituc zetu nafasi
Wajua sina kiasi   jinsi nikupendawo.

Wajua sina kiasi   hali yangu waijuwa
Nakupenda we halisi   unishize moyo ngowa
Hiwa nina wasiwasi   ni wewe wa kunituwa
Nda nini kunisumbuwa   jinsi nikupendawo.

To annoy you is not good   O you lovely peacock   O most nobly ranked   come quickly   let us speak to one another   and so comfort ourselves   You know that I have no limit   in my love for you.

You know that I have no limit   as for my state you know it   I love you truly   so solace my passion   While I am in this state of disquiet   it is you who can pacify me   Why do you leave me thus distressed   loving you as I do?

     *   *   *

The following poem by Muyaka b. Haji exemplifies the same use of a refrain in 'continued' verses:

Baada Dhiki Faraji

1   Kwa heri mwana kwa heri   nenda zangu ngezimaji
    Nimeazimu safari   kwa pepo za maleleji
    Kwa malenge na shuwari   natawakali mpaji
    Baada dhiki faraji   hakuna lisilokuwa.

2   Baada dhiki faraji   wasemi waseme lewo
    Nasafiria mbiji   yenye kamba na uwawo
    Nitafika vitongoji   kwa Twaka ndio makawo
    Muombe mwanza mkwawo   hakuna lisilokuwa.

3   Muombe mwanza mkwawo   mpa wema na waovu
    Atupe tutashilewo   kutupa swi si mapevu
    Atupe kula na nguwo   kwa uwezowe na nguvu
    Atwondolee utovu   hakuna lisilokuwa.

4   Atwondolee utovu   wajawe tu mashakani
    Tusione uemevu   wa ukata duniani
    Zipate nyoyo utuvu   zisiwe la kutamani
    Mambo pia kwa Manani   hakuna lisilokuwa.

5   Mambo pia kwa Manani   fikiri uzingatile
    Ondoa hamu moyoni   ujingani usingile
    Tutatoka sumbukoni   tusumbukalo milele
    Si male kwakwe si male   hakuna lisilokuwa.

6   Si male kwakwe si male   nawe wata kisirani
    Matungu uvumilile   tuombe Mola Manani
    Nendako nisikawile   nirejee autani
    Iwe urembo na shani   hakuna lisilokuwa.

7   Iwe urembo na shani   Mola apendapo huwa
    Atwondolee huzuni   na mwenye ndwele kapowa
    Na huu umasikini   si ila wala si tuwa
    Aweza kuuondowa   hakuna lisilokuwa.

1 Farewell my son farewell   I go my way to Ngezimaji   I mean
to take my journey   in the season of changing winds   In
storm and calm   I put my trust in the Great Giver   After
trouble there is consolation   there is nothing which has not
always been.

After trouble there is consolation   let the speakers speak of it 2
today   I journey in a sea-going vessel   having ropes and
planks   I will reach the villages   at Twaka that is where
I live   Pray to the Lord   there is nothing which has not
always been.

Pray to the Lord   the giver to the good and the evil   that He 3
may give to us who are perplexed   giving to us in our
immaturity   for Him to give us food and clothing   by His
power and strength   that He may take from us our shortcomings   There is nothing which has not always been.

That He may take from us our shortcomings   His servants in 4
dire distress   that we may not bear the burden   of poverty
in the world   that our hearts may be tranquil   that they
may not be lustful   All is in God's hands   There is nothing
which has not always been.

All is in God's hands   consider and bear in mind   Remove 5
anxiety from the heart   enter not into folly   We will come
out of trouble   which plagues us for ever   With Him the
waters are not deep not deep   There is nothing which has
not always been.

With Him the waters are not deep not deep   so do you put 6
away anger   endure what is grievous   let us pray to God the
Beneficent   Whither I go let me not tarry   let me return to my
fatherland   may it be glorious and wonderful   There is
nothing which has not always been.

May it be glorious and wonderful   when God wills so it 7
is   May He take sorrow away from us   and let the sick be
cured   then this poverty   is neither disgrace nor blemish   He is able to remove it   There is nothing that has not
always been.

*   *   *

A rare device is linking by repetition of the final *kipande* as the
first *kipande* of the next verse. The following example from the
Hichens Papers will illustrate this :

Nenda na ukiwa wangu

Nenda na ukiwa wangu   nikaapo hakumbukwa
Mema na maovu yangu   yalipo yakamulikwa
Yakakusanywa vitungu   kulla nyumba pakapekwa
Sirudi nyuma hatekwa   nenda na ukiwa wangu.

Nenda na ukiwa wangu   na kungi kufurahiwa . . .

I go in solitude   but where I stay I am remembered   My good
and evil deeds   where they exist they are put to the test   and
gathered together   in every house to be put to the test   So
I don't go back to be laughed at   I go my way in solitude.

I go my way in solitude   and life is filled with happiness . . .

*   *   *

A good example of reversed or 'turned-line' verse is the poem
beginning, *Simba ndume na wambiji*, in the Taylor Papers and by
Muyaka b. Haji. The poem has nineteen verses and is extremely
difficult to translate in its entirety. The opening verses illustrate
the use of 'turned' lines:

Simba ndume na wambiji

Simba ndume na wambiji   sikizani tatongowa
Niketele vitongoji   na safari za mashuwa
Leo nakumbuka mbiji   ya kutweka na kutuwa
Ai pato na mpewa   litakapo kukutana.

Ai mpewa na mpato   lipalo mtu kukuwa
Angawa mwana mtoto   wa kutishika kachewa
Akiwa na upasito   wa kutamani ukiwa
Ai ndwele na afuwa   litakapo kukutana.

Au afuwa na ndwele . . .

Lion-hearts and ladies gentle   listen and I will proclaim   I have
dwelt in villages   and made journeys by boat   but today I
remember one barque   in foul and fair   Ah! the blessing
and the blessed   when they both do meet.

Ah! the blessed and the blessing   What fills man's soul with power
Even though he be a puling infant   frightened by the day's
dawn   If he but acquire life's riches   then he wishes to be alone
Ah! the sickness and the healing   when they both do meet.

Ah! the healing and the sickness . . .

*   *   *

MASHAIRI YA TAKIRIRI

Poems in which one or two lines, or the whole or part of a word are repeated *within* each verse are termed *mashairi ya takiriri*. This device takes several forms which may be regarded as a kind of poetic acrobatics indulged in by the poet to show his skill in designing verse. As with the linked verses a *kipande* may be repeated either simply or reversed. Of similar type are songs with a 'turned-over' rhyming word, or rhyming syllables, ending a *kipande* and initiating the succeeding *kipande*.

The following are some examples of the various types of poems with repeated segments, *mashairi ya takiriri*:

Type 1

The first *kipande* is repeated simply or reversed as the final *kipande*. The linked poem, *Nenda na ukiwa wangu*, is an example, and so is the following verse written by Muyaka on behalf of some Mombasans who had failed to get a good price for their maize:

Sili sili wa mtama

Sili sili wa mtama   ungawa na nyingi nazi
Sili msambe ni mwema   sili hauniumizi
Sili kwa uto wa nyama   wala kwa mwingi mtuzi
Sili haunipendezi   sili wa mtama sili.

I do not eat I do not eat millet   even though it has a lot of coco-nut   I do not eat it so do not say it is good   I do not eat it and it does not hurt me   I don't eat it with animal-fat   nor with a lot of gravy   I don't eat it for it doesn't please me   I don't eat millet I don't eat it.

Type 2

The sixth *kipande* is repeated simply as the seventh *kipande*. The following example is from the Taylor Papers:

Kisimbo cha mkunazi

Kisimbo cha mkunazi   nigongea kwacho pembe
Na upatu wa Hejazi   uliyo kama uwambe
Uneteye wapokezi   wambeja wema wapambe
Wambeja wema wapambe   wenye urembo na shani.

With the rod of the zizyphus tree   beat the buffalo-horn for
me   And the cymbal from Hejaz   which is as though it is
covered   Bring me the chorus-maids   the pretty maids in
gay garments (*repeat*)   so well adorned and beautiful.

Type 3

The first, third, and fifth *vipande* are repeated in reverse as the
second, fourth, and sixth *vipande* respectively. This type is termed
mashairi ya takiriri na pindo. The following example is from Sir
Mbarak Ali Hinawy's private collection, and may be compared
with the Persian form known as *tard u 'aks* 'thrust and inversion',
see E. G. Browne, *A Literary History of Persia*, p. 75. It is likely
that Swahili poems derived any Persian influence by way of
southern Arabia, and not directly from Persia.

Lakutenda situuze

Lakutenda situuze   situuze lakutenda
Metufunda wanamize   wanamize metufunda
Kuwa punda tuizize   tuizize kuwa punda
Kwandika tapo tutenda   hilo halipatikani.

What to do don't ask us   don't ask us what to do   He has
crushed us like shore-crabs   like shore-crabs he has crushed
us   To be pack-donkeys we refuse   We refuse to be pack-
donkeys   To be saddled in packs for work   that is what
will not be achieved.

Type 4

Another type of repetitive and 'turned-line' verse is that in
which the first *kipande* is repeated as the last *kipande*, and the sixth
kipande is repeated in the seventh *kipande*. This may be compared
with the Persian pattern known as *raddu 'l-'ajuz 'ala 's-sadr* (see
Browne, op. cit., p. 60), in which the last *'ajuz* is thrown back to
the first *'sadr*. The following example is from the Papers of Sir
Mbarak Ali Hinawy:

Kalizani watapamba

Kalizani watapamba   mukilingana mishindo
Na nziu yungile mwamba   irurume kama nundo
Nina yambo tawafumba   na pasiwe mwenye kondo
Na pasiwe mwenye kondo   watapamba kalizani.

Sing up you gay-robed maidens   and harmonize the sounds   Let
the sound of the gongs reach to the skies   and reverberate like
a hammer   I have things to puzzle you with   without there
being an aggressive person   Without there being an aggressive person   Ye gay-robed maidens sing up.

Type 5

The last two syllables of the second, fourth, and sixth *vipande*
are turned over to become the initial syllables of the third, fifth,
and seventh *vipande* respectively, so to form separate words.
The following example is from the Hichens Papers:

Penda kukwambia neno

Penda kukwambia neno   ambalo la kuwajibu
Jibu basi mundi muno   kwa pole na taratibu
Tibu huipenda muno   harufuye nda ajabu
Jabu si yetu haribu   usambe sikukwambiya.

I want to tell you something   which is in reply to you   Answer
then with due accord   with care and neatness   It likes perfume very much   its smell is wonderful   Is not the lion our
destruction? Don't say I didn't tell you.

This is an exercise in punning, the solution of which lies in
the jingle of *jibu*, *ajabu* and *jabu*. The answer to the riddle is
the perfumed and glamorous person of the lady herself to whom
the riddle is proposed. She is herself the 'destruction' of her
lover's heart (her prey). So he says, 'Don't say I didn't give you
the clue (in the *jabu-jibu*, my riddle)'.

Type 6

This form of turned verse amplifies the last type by turning
over the last two syllables of every *kipande* except the last to
become self-standing words initiating each consecutive *kipande*.
The following example is from the Hichens Papers:

Napenda kusema nawe

Napenda kusema nawe   nawe usiwe khiyana
Jana nalikutaka we   kawe mfano wa nana
Nana nituze nituwe   tuwe wa kusikizana
Zana ya juzi na jana   jana nalikupa wewe.

I like to speak with you   and you, don't be mean   Yesterday
   I wanted you   that you should be as a bride   O bride,
   soothe me that I may be calm   let us be in full accord   As
   to thoughts of yesterday and the day before   I gave you
   yesterday.

★   ★   ★

This jingling of rhymes gave rise to the popular device of making
up a verse to express different meanings of identical syllables, or
to begin or end the odd *vipande* with identical syllables. The
following is an example from Taylor's complete set of aphorisms
in manuscript at Witwatersrand University, Johannesburg:

Nipakiya ni kivuko

Nipakiya ni kivuko	nivuke ng'ambo ya pili
Nipa kiya kifuniko	kifunikiwacho wali
Nipakiya ni kipako	kile kitiwacho kili
Nipa kiya cha muili	cha guu au mkono.

'Put me on board' it is a ferry   that I may cross to the other
   side   Give me something for a lid, a covering   that covers
   rice   'Dye it for me' it is a dye   what is used for plaiting
   matted strips   Give me a joint of the body   of the leg or of
   the hand.

★   ★   ★

Note the repetition of the word *ziwa* in the following example
from the Papers of Sir Mbarak Ali Hinawy:

Kiya wa kule mashamba

Kiya wa kule mashamba	nilikutana na ziwa
Kilinda jua kipumba	kutululu wenye ziwa
Kikutwa niwene komba	wajile katika ziwa
Wenyewe wakamba ziwa	nda kwetu liko mbele.

'Step over' concerning there in the fields   I came across a
   pond   While waiting know ye (I threw) a small clod   to
   disturb the dwellers in the pond   At sunset I saw some komba-
   fish   who had come into the pond   and they said the pond
   belongs to us   our home is there in front.

★   ★   ★

Swahili poets have written verse either upon the central meaning of a word or upon the different meanings of a single word.

Muyaka b. Haji's poem on *Silence* is an example of the former and is found in the Taylor Papers:

Kimya kina mshindo mkuwu

Kimya kina mshindo mkuwu   ndivo wambavo wavyele
Kimya chataka kumbuwu   viunoni mutatile
Kimya msikidharawu   nami sikidharauile
Kimya kina mambo mbele   tahadharini na kimya.

Kimya ni kinga kizushi   kuzukia wale wale
Kimya kitazua moshi   mato musiyafumbule
Kimya kina mashawishi   kwa daima na milele
Kimya kina mambo mbele   tahadharini na kimya.

Kimya vuani maozi   vuani mato muole
Kimya kitangusha mwanzi   mwendako msijikule
Kimya chatunda pumuzi   kiumbizi kiumbile
Kimya kina mambo mbele   tahadharini na kimya.

Silence has a mighty noise   so say the elders   Silence needs girdles   for you to wind round your loins   Despise not silence   nor have I despised it   Silence has a future   so take care of silence.

Silence is a sudden chance   happening to the very ones concerned   Silence will bring forth smoke   so don't open your eyes   Silence may mean deceit   for ever and ever eternally   Silence has a future   so take care of silence.

Silence, lift up your eyes   lift them up and look   Silence brings battles   so wherever you go don't vaunt yourselves   Silence catches the breath   it glides around like a soaring bird   Silence has a future   so take care of silence.

★   ★   ★

The following poem by Muyaka from the same source illustrates the different meanings of the word *Oa*. The complete poem has six verses, but the first two verses will be enough to show that throughout the poem the poet is concerned with commenting on the three different meanings of the word. Poems of the same type by Muyaka are entitled by Hichens *Panda* and *Jinga*.

Oa kwamba u muozi

Oa kwamba u muozi   uzoeleo kuowa
Oa mato maolezi   na mboni ukikodowa
Oa maji maundazi   meupe kama maziwa
Oa sizi ndizi ndowa   aso kuowa ni yupi.

Oa ndiwe muolezi uzoeleo kuowa
Oa sifumbe maozi maninga uchiyavuwa
Oa uzaze uzazi kama ulivyozaliwa
Oa sizi ndizi ndowa aso kuoa ni yupi . . .

Oa, saying that you are a marrying person familiar with marriage *Oa*, the eyes are the lookers and the looking part stares *Oa*, in the waters at high tide as white as milk *Oa*, are not these the meanings of *oa*? Who is he who does not *oa*?

Oa, you are the marrying one familiar with marriage *Oa*, don't close your eyes but throw a glance with them *Oa*, give birth to offspring even as you yourself were born *Oa*, are not these the meanings of *oa*? Who is he who does not *oa*?

This play on words is closely akin to other types of 'catch-words' play in the oral tradition of Bantu peoples, but it is not typical of the much wider reference of Swahili poetry. It represents only a very small percentage of the main content of verse in eight *vipande*. Even the different types of *mashairi ya takiriri* have never been employed with any fluency, not least because their composition strained the inventiveness of the poets far too much. The emphasis was on the pattern of segments within a verse or within a poem rather than on the meaning to be conveyed. But wherever the poet accepted the normal shape of verse with eight *vipande*, without further elaboration of the inward pattern, there has been a ready flow of poems on many different subjects.

Although it is true that most modern poetry in this medium is secular in theme, this is only because most of it is written outside the field of Swahili culture proper. Within the Swahili Islamic community on the East African coast, many religious poems in eight *vipande* are still being written, but they do not find their way to any wider audience through the Swahili press. They remain, as the earlier poems were, the possession only of the local Islamic community. One of the most prolific poets is Sheikh Mohamed Jambein al-Bakri. His poems include a *utendi* of the *Miraj* in 300 verses; *Faradhi*, a poem in eight *vipande* of 185 verses; and his *Maulid* in verse of eight *vipande* with eighty-five verses. There are poems on the keeping of the fast of Ramadhan and on the conclusion of the fast; on the pilgrimage to Mecca, on the giving of alms, and on other religious practices. Although the translation of the Qur'ān into Swahili is frowned upon by orthodox Muslims, there are poetic paraphrases, in verse of eight *vipande*, of chapters from the Qur'ān. Phrase by phrase of a chapter is given, and for each consecutive Arabic phrase there is a verse in Swahili expounding or expanding the meaning. These have been written within the last few years from 1958–60 and meet with the approval of the most orthodox of Swahili Muslims.

But even within the orthodox Islamic community the conventional poetic medium is put to modern purpose, and that, after all, is just what Muyak b. Haji did in applying the medium to his contemporary circumstances. The following poem by Ustadh Ahmad Basheikh b. Husein of Mombasa may illustrate this. He is going for a holiday up-country and is writing a farewell message to his friends. This poem was sent to me in 1960 by my friend Hyder Mohamed al-Kindy.

Shairi twaa baruwa

1. Shairi twaa baruwa   risala mwenye imani
   Utapofika funguwa   usome shairi ndani
   Sauti ya kuongowa   wende nayo kwa makini
   Nalekelea barani   tukaganane kwa heri.

2. Imani wenye fikira   wambeja wenye imani
   Nna safari ya bara   hadi Iringa mjini
   Ndipo haona ubora   kutangaza kwa wandani
   Nalekelea barani   tukaganane kwa heri.

3. Wimbo singaliutunga   ila ni nyinyi wandani
   Na sababuye si changa   hadhi yake wastani
   Ndipo nalipoifunga   safari ikamkini
   Nalekelea barani   tukaganane kwa heri.

4. Moyo umenifumbama   kwa kuepuka wandani
   Lakini nikitezama   sina budi nifanyeni
   Tuombeane salama   nyinyi na mimi soteni
   Nalekelea barani   tukaganane kwa heri.

5. Asili ya kuondoka   hata kwendea barani
   Ni sababu imefika   livu yangu ya kazini
   Na jumatatu kifika   ndipo tapanda garini
   Nalekelea barani   tukaganane kwa heri.

6
    Tuombeane salama   kwa Mola wetu Manani
    Mungu atupe neema   kukeni na kuumeni
    Kwa baraka za hashima   iwe kun fayakuni
    Nalekelea barani   tukaganane kwa heri.

7
    Rabbi tuhifadhi nasi   mitima itamakani
    Twendapo tupa nafasi   kwa shimali na yamini
    Tuwe ni wa taa nasi   ututie sitarani
    Nalekelea barani   takaganane kwa heri.

8
    Ilahi tupe subira   nafusi ziwe makini
    Ututengee na dhara   zilizomo duniani
    Utupe na njema dira   ya kutuongoza nyumbani
    Nalekelea barani   tukaganane kwa heri.

1
Take this poem as a letter   O trusted messenger   and when you arrive open it   and read the poem inside   This voice of direction (the poem)   Take it to a quiet place   I am off up-country   so let us bid one another farewell.

2
O trustful ones and thoughtful   fair maidens of trust   I have a journey up-country   as far as the town of Iringa   and so I thought best   to inform my friends   I am off up-country   (repeat refrain).

3
I would not have composed this song   if it were not that you are my friends   and the reasons (for my going) are nothing special   the circumstances are the usual ones   And so I packed my things   my journey became possible   (refrain).

4
My spirits are low   because of separating from my friends   but if I look into it   I must go or what shall I do?   Let us pray for sound health for us   for you and me all of us   (refrain).

5
The reason for my leaving   and going up-country   is because (my leave) has come   my leave from work   and when Monday comes   I will go by train   (refrain).

6
Let us pray for our common good   to our God the Beneficent   may God give us grace   on the left and on the right   with blessings of respect   and let His will be done (lit. let it be, Be and it is)   (refrain).

7 O Lord protect us   let our hearts be in command   where we
   go give us opportunity   on the right and the left   let us be
   obedient   cover us   (refrain).

8 O God give us patience   that our lives may be dignified   separate
   us from troubles   that abound on the earth   give us a good
   compass   to guide us home   (refrain).

6

MISCELLANEOUS VERSE

THE term 'regular' is applied to verse of eight *vipande* in which the rhyme of the seventh *kipande* responds to that of the sixth *kipande*. In verses with either less or more than eight *vipande* this system of rhyming may be found. They may be referred to as 'regular' verses, using the term 'regular' in a limited and technical sense, namely that the penultimate *kipande* rhymes with the *kipande* immediately preceding it.

REGULAR VERSE OF SIX *VIPANDE*

Poems of this type with the first and third *vipande* rhyming are peculiar to the poets of Manda Island, and are of rare occurrence. They may owe their form to the multiple-poem called by the Persians *musammat* and by the Arabs *muwashshah*. The following example is from the Hichens Papers:

Nali na wajawa kenda

Nali na wajawa kenda	wali taa watiile
Katika siku chenenda	ghafula nijikuile
Nambiwa walikimbile	waka wenye taathimu.

Walikimbile kwa wote	waja wema msharafu
Moyo ndani mtotote	kilia kita asafu
Wapi waja maarufu	wakele ja wana amu.

I had ten slaves   and they were very obedient   One day I went walking   and suddenly things became too much for me   They tell me, They ran away   the honoured ladies (the slaves).

They had all run away   the good women, noble sir   My heart within me stood still   and I cried and called out in despair Where are my lovely slaves   who dwelt like ladies of Lamu?

★   ★   ★

This type of verse is very uncommon with the first and third *vipande* unrhymed. Note the following example from the Taylor Papers:

Howe wapigaje howe

Howe wapigaje howe   nyama usijamfuma
Howe akali mwituni   na maguuye mazima
Howe nda mwenye kufuma   wewe una howe gani.

Howe! How do you cry *Howe*   when you have not yet pierced a beast? *Howe!* while it is yet in the forest   and its legs are whole   *Howe* is the bowman's cry   You—what *Howe* can you claim?

REGULAR VERSE OF TWELVE *VIPANDE*

This type of verse is found in poems that are variants of the *takhmis*, but otherwise only a very few poems of this kind occur in the early poetry. The following example is from the Hamilton Manuscripts in the Library of the SOAS:

Niliketi siku moya

Niliketi siku moya   kweleza katika muji
Mbwene yakanijiliya   mashairi ya kimiji
Yakija yakinambiya   na amali bwana haji
Afuate walikiya   shariati menihuji
Mke akivumiliya   naye ali msubiji
Asi nguo asi uji   bali akajitamali.

One day I sat down   to give advice in the village   and I saw approaching me   the minstrels of the town   Coming, they said to me   and our business concerns Bwana Haji   He used to follow after us well   They have asked me for the law   His wife has put up with a great deal   and she has done so patiently   Without clothes and without food   but she has behaved well.

Deriving from the variant of the *takhmis* verse-form are many modern poems in twelve *vipande* or six lines, and the following poem by Shaaban Robert, written in roman script originally, has a fixed refrain which restricts the rhyming sequence in all second hemistichs. Shaaban's poem is from his collection, *Pambo la Lugha*, and is a love-poem:

Haraka fanya shauri

1
Haraka fanya shauri   sababu nasumbuka
Fanya na tazubiri   nifurahi na kucheka
Moyo wangu si huuri   hauishi kufadhaika
Na fadhaa si nzuri   mwenye nayo hukauka
Japo kimya nasaburi   usambe nafurahika
Mpenzi nasikitika   natafuta njia sina.

2
Litakufa langu jina   kwa hivi nasikitika
Kweli kusema suna   nina wingi wa mashaka
Jambo hili kunena   sina hofu wala shaka
Sababu kila namna   ambayo nakumbuka
Ya furaha sasa sina   ila hasa nateseka
Mpenzi nasikitika   natafuta njia sina.

3
Nilikuwa na tamaa   siku njema itafika
Wewe uwe na wasaa   nipate ninalotaka
Na mimi nimengojea jumaa   miezi na miaka
Kumbe vile ni hadaa   hili halikufanyika
Kusema mengi nazaa   na mjuzi huepuka
Mpenzi nasikitika   natafuta njia sina.

4
Nataka kuhurumiwa   yamenichosha mashaka
Napenda kufasiriwa   nipate kuelimika
Jambo lisiloridhia   ahadi kukamilika
Lipi linalozuia   sema neno thabitika
Baada ya kuelewa   auni nitapeleka
Mpenzi nasikitika   natafuta njia sina.

5
Kama napata dalili   kuwa haitageuka
Mpaka kuwa kamili   ahadi tuliyoweka
Ningenenepa mwili   na moyo kutononoka
Wakutanapo pahali   wapenzi huwa baraka
Kupendana ni halali   machukio yana taka
Mpenzi nasikitika   natafuta njia sina.

6
Haikosi natumai   hurumayo kudondoka
Kurutubisha uhai   wangu unaofujika
Najiuza bila bei   sababu nimetunuka
Katika dunia hii   kwangu uwe mshirika
Na mimi ningekinai   kusikia waridhika
Mpenzi nasikitika   natafuta njia sina.

7 Kaa na kufikiri inama na kuinuka
  Sijachoka kusaburi ila nawe kumbuka
  Kila siku umri hupanda na kushuka
  Japo sina dhamiri kuacha niliposhika
  Bali tunda likisiri kuliwa huharibika
  Mpenzi nasikitika natafuta njia sina.

8 Pahali pa kutua sasa nimekwisha fika
  Jina langu walijua si haja kuliandika
  Wito huu nimetoa napenda ukisha fika
  Kwa mbali kusikia sauti ya labeka
  Hili kama latokea sana ningefurahika
  Mpenzi nasikitika natafuta njia sina.

1 Hurry and do something because I am upset take some action so that I can be happy and laugh My heart is not free it ceases not to be distressed and disquiet is not good who has it dries up Though I am silent I wait patiently Don't say I am happy (refrain) Beloved I am sorry I look for a way but I have none.

2 My name will die and so I am sorry Indeed to say the truth I have great doubts To speak of this I have no fear nor doubt because every way that I think of of being happy now I do not possess it (refrain).

3 I had the desire that the good day would come when you would have the opportunity for me to get what I want And I have waited for it weeks and months and years but lo it is just a deception and this thing was not done To speak much brings contention and the wise person steers clear of that (refrain).

4 I want to be pitied my doubts have wearied me I want an explanation so that I be well-informed The thing which doesn't satisfy me (is) a promise being unfulfilled What prevents it? Say a word in confirmation When I have understood I will send your fare (refrain).

5 If I get a sign that things will not change until it is fulfilled the promise that we made then I would grow fat and my heart would get new strength When lovers

meet at a place   it is a blessing   To love one another is
lawful   and hatred is unclean   (refrain).

I trust it will not fail   for your pity to appear   making my life 6
prosper   which now is so disturbed   I sell myself for nothing   because I long for you   In this world   be thou my
partner   and I would be content   to hear that you are
content   (refrain).

Living and thinking   bending down and getting up   I have 7
not yet exhausted my patience   but you in your turn must
remember   that every day our allotted span   rises and
falls   Even though I have no intention   of letting go where
I have taken hold   If the fruit hides itself   (the joy of) its
being eaten is destroyed   (refrain).

The place for resting   now I have reached it   You know my 8
name   and there is no need to write it   I have sent out
this invitation   and I would like that when it has arrived
    I should hear from afar   the sound of 'Here I am'   If
this came to pass   I would be very happy indeed   (refrain).

REGULAR VERSE IN FOURTEEN *VIPANDE*

This is a very rare form. The following example from the
Hichens Papers has the first three hemistichs rhyming and then
the next three with a different rhyme:

Taire mzyele wangu

Taire mzyele wangu   baba nakwambia heko
Kunitaya kwa matungu   pamoya na sikitiko
Kufariki ulimwengu   hakutafuta uliko
Mwenda kuzimu kauya   wala hana matamko
Visivyokuwa nambiya   kwani mimi sikuwako
Ewe mwana saudiya   watuonyesha vituko
Heko baba yangu heko   kuzimu ulirudiye.

Hail O revered sire   Hail I salute you O father   Men told me
to my sorrow   and bitter grief   that you had left this
earth   and I looked for you   The departed spirit goes
away   and leaves no sound   Things that are not true they
tell me   for I myself was not there   O Prince of Saud   show
us startling things   Hail my father hail   for you have
returned from the place of the spirits.

PLACING THE CAESURAE

In most Swahili poems the divisions made by the caesurae (Sw. *vituo*) give an equal syllabic measure in each *kipande*. There are a few poems, however, in which the *vituo* are placed in a non-medial position as between adjacent *vipande*, i.e. the *vipande* do not have an equal syllabic measure. We have already seen that in Sheikh Muḥyi 'l-Din's poem, *Dua ya Kuombea Mvua*, the *kituo* divides each line into hemistichs of six and nine *mizani* respectively. There are a number of other long poems in this measure, e.g. *Faradhi*, a poem of 185 verses dealing with the laws of inheritance amongst East African Muslims, by Sheikh Mohamed Jambein al-Bakri, and a Maulid by the same author. This device of employing unequal syllabic measures was frequently employed in short poems and especially in popular songs of only one verse. Some of these songs found literary expression in the Swahili-Arabic script. The following examples are from the papers of Sir Mbarak Ali Hinawy:

Kujipinda (4–6 measure)

Kujipinda   na kujitahidi
Kuyatenda   yasiyo muradi
Muchenenda   sisi tumerudi.

For display   ye are ever straining
To array your deeds   that have no meaning
Go your way   we are homeward wending.

Mashauri (4–8 measure)

Mashauri   ya mtu usiyashike
Taghururi   na mwishowe akutuke
Mtu siri   husema na moyo wake.

To man's advice   listen not whoever doth it impart
In avarice   he'll make of thee an ill report
Of artifice   the wise takes commune with his heart.

Wandi wa siri wafiye (8–5 measure)

Wandi wa siri wafiye   wako mavani
Na ambao wasaliye   siwaamini
Sina mwenye kwamba naye   amba na mimi.

Nisikia nikwambiye   mtakalumi
Na ambao wasaliye   wizi wa ndimi
Huna mwenye kwamba naye   amba na mimi.

My bosom friends have passed away   to sleep within the grave
And those who live today   I trust not (each of them a knave)
I have no one to talk with, nay   With whom may I conclave?

Now hearken friend to what I say   O man of words so free
If all the men who live today   would steal thy tongue away
And thou hast none to speak with, nay   Well then, speak thou
    with me.

An interesting example of triple division within each line is in
a poem by Khalfan b. Abdallah b. Rashidi in Sir Mbarak's Papers:

Yujile risala (6–6–4 measure)

Yujile risala   na suwali ngumu   ajabu
Yana masiala   mazuri athimu   taibu
Hayana illa   nimeyafahamu   sahibu.

Your courier has come   with a problem most hard   and
amazing   There are enigmas   most divertingly phrased   and
amusing   Yet few that become   'yond solving by me   and rusing.

The following poem was sent to me by Bwana Mohamed
Hyder Al-Kindy of Mombasa and is a sad little work on dis-
illusion. It is very difficult to translate, because the measure is so
restricted and gaps have to be filled in in the translation in order
to make sense of the Swahili version. This does not mean that the
poem is unintelligible to the Swahili reader. It is a characteristic
of much Swahili poetry that the reader understands what is not
written from what in fact he sees in the script.

Risala wangu wa shani (8–5 measure)

1   Risala wangu wa shani   mwenye ufunzo
    Tukuwa yangu lisani   iwe tangazo
    Mtenda njema ni nani   kalipwa zizo.

2   Zitezamani zamani   zamani sizo
    Kulla umpaye ndani   ana mawazo
    Mtenda njema ni nani   kalipwa zizo.

Hivuwa mato sioni   ya muangazo   3
Na kutowana imani   ndiyo mitezo
Mtenda njema ni nani   kalipwa zizo.

Kiumbe atende nini   mwisho mkazo   4
Angazionya imani   huwambwa hanazo
Mtenda njema ni nani   kalipwa zizo.

Unyonge huwa matoni   kwa zama sizo   5
Hatendi lenyi imani   sitewi tezo
Mtenda njema ni nani   kalipwa zizo.

Nali niketi makini   hivuta wazo   6
Hiepusha nukusani   kumbe si fuzo
Mtenda njema ni nani   kalipwa zizo.

Ili tamati jamani   langu elezo   7
Wema haupatikani   kubakiye matezo
Mtenda njema ni nani   kalipwa zizo.

O my fine messenger   instructed one   carry my message   let 1
it be a proclamation   (refrain) Who is the doer of good   who
was ever thus rewarded?

Look at the days of yore   things were never thus   Each one 2
to whom you give of the spirit (lit. inwardly)   he has his
thoughts   (refrain).

If I look up I do not see   any light   Taking away one another's 3
faith   that is the sport   (refrain).

What is a creature to do?   In the end (he gets) a refusal   Even 4
if he shows faith   he is told he has none   (refrain).

He appears lowly in their eyes   but formerly it was never 5
thus   So one performs no act of faith   I am not fastidious
about fun   (refrain).

I sat in a quiet place   and I was deep in thought   I withdrew 6
from mischievous action   but lo it was no short cut (to
happiness).

This is the end my friends   of my explanation   Goodness is 7
not obtainable   Only harm is left   (refrain).

VERSES WITH A SINGLE RHYME

Poems with a single rhyme are mostly light inconsequential songs. The following examples are from the Hichens Papers:

Bwene dura pende

Bwene dura pende   juu la mtende   nipatiani na winde.

> I beheld a love-bird fair,
> High in the date-palm there,
> Yet how may I that bird ensnare?

Moyo wangu wanambia mema

Moyo wangu wanambia mema   wanambia sala na kusoma   na shetani yunendeme nyuma.

> My heart, speaking of virtue, oft doth say,
> Doth say, Read thou the Holy Book and Pray.
> Yet Satan at my heels e'er treads my way!

Sikubali mpenda kawanda

Sikubali mpenda kawanda   sinwi sili kwa hamu ya nyonda   na
akili siwi nayo kwanda   mambo haya ndiyo nimetunda.

> That a lover grows fat, I can't agree.
> I drink not, I eat not, pining for thee.
> As for sense, I'd none, e'en at first, you see.
> So these are the things love has gained for me!

Masikini . . .

Masikini bibi yangu kasafiri na Waarabu   umbo lake la fedha
shingo lake la dhahabu   ndege wangu mzuri anakwitwa
Tasharabu   akilia machozi huanguka ya dhahabu.

> I am poor, for my wife has gone a journey with the Arabs.
> Her shape is of silver and her neck is of gold.
> My beautiful bird is called Tasharabu,
> If she sheds tears they fall as gold.

Another example is the song of the dying minstrel Mnga recorded by Taylor in *African Aphorisms*, p. 49:

Ndimi Mnga . . .

Ndimi Mnga nimbaye kigoma   alo mbali akamba nafyo-
ma   kwa sauti yangu kuwa njema   nimeshikwa ni ndwele
ya homa   leo nenda na ulele ngoma.

It is, I, Mnga, who sings to the small drum   and the one who is
far off says I am reading (the Qur'ān)   because my voice is so
good   But I am seized with the sickness of fever   Today I
go with the Dead March!

There are many short poems with a single rhyme that have
an odd number of *vipande*, especially three *vipande*. Poems with
alternating rhyme and an odd number of *vipande* to the verse are
extremely rare, but two examples have recently come to our
attention. The first is a religious poem on the praise of the
Prophet, and is by Shariff Abdallah b. Hemed Bunamiy of Takaungu; there are fifty-four verses of which we give the first ten to
illustrate the composition. This was never a popular prosodic
form because in a long poem the short verses give no breathing
space, as it were, to the reader; it is like reading a long synopsis
in one long paragraph. In this example the syllabic measure is
six *mizani*, which, of course, is a further limitation. Short measure
is not suitable for long poems of only three *vipande*.

Naanza nudhuma

Naanza nudhuma   kwa isimu njema   ya Mola karima.
Nihimidi Mola   na kuomba sala   imshukiye Tuma.
Pamoja na aali   na sahaba ali   walio nujuma.
Namuomba Latifu   ili kumsifu   bora wa kauma.
Mwandowe ni nuri   dhati ya Jabbari   kaumbwa Hashima.
Yali ikifura   kwa matumbo bora   hata ikakoma.
Kwa mwana Amina   bibi wa maana   ndake taadhima.
Kamzaa juwa   lenye na sitawa   nuru isokoma.
Alipozaliwa   mato kafunuwa   kangalia sama.
Hiyo ni ishara   ya mweni ubora   kutezama pema . . .

I begin my poem   with the good name   of the Generous God.
I praise God   and ask that prayer   should fall to the Prophet.
Together with the noble ones   with the noble Companions   who
are of good fortune.

I pray the Good God   in order to praise Him   the people's
  Boon.
In the beginning there was light   and by the Will of God   the
  Beloved was created.
It ripened   in the blessed womb   until it matured.
By Blessed Amina   famous lady   the glory is hers.
And she brought forth the sun   the excellent one   the light
  which does not end.
When he was born   he opened his eyes   and he looked hard.
This is the sign   of a noble stranger   when he looks thus
  early . . .

A manuscript from Mombasa in roman script gives nine verses
of what is set out as a single poem. It is more likely that these are
two separate poems, for the first three verses have a refrain and
the other verses have a different measure in the final *kipande*. Both
poems are of fairly early origin, probably mid-nineteenth century,
and the authorship is unknown. The first three verses may be
given here as a separate poem to illustrate verse of seven *vipande*.

Nanena nawe sahibu

Nanena nawe sahibu   pulikiza masikiyo
Duniani si ajabu   limpatalo mwenziyo
Na nyoyo zikikalibu   yoyote hutendwa yayo
  Hii ndiyo hali ya duniya.

Toa chuki na hasira   usigeuze tabiya
Hayano ni mirara   kulla atakapoingiya
Moyoni lingakukera   bora ni kuvumiliya
  Hii ndiyo hali ya duniya.

Hotuba Juu ya Ushairi
Imeandikwa na SHAABAN ROBERT

Ushairi ni sanaa ya vina inayopambanuliwa kama nyimbo,
mashairi, na tenzi. Zaidi ya kuwa sanaa ya vina, ushairi una
ufasaha wa maneno machache au muhtasari. Mwauliza, Wimbo,
shairi na utenzi ni nini? Wimbo ni shairi dogo; shairi ni wimbo
mkubwa; na utenzi ni upeo wa shairi. Mwauliza tena, Kina na
ufasaha huweza kuwa nini? Kina ni mlingano wa sauti za herufi.

Njema za zamani hizi   zishike nta za vyanda
Kwani hazina ukazi   moyoni ungazipenda
Hata akiwa mlezi   ulezi atauvunda
Hii ndiyo hali ya duniya.

I speak with thee my friend   listen to me well   Is not the
world amazing?   (For instance) what happens to your
friend   and hearts turning about   these things happen to
anyone   This is the way of the world.

Get rid of hatred and anger   don't change (your good) character   These things are like the turn of the wheel   everyone
who participates (lit. goes in)   though it vex your heart   the
best thing is to endure all   This is the way of the world.

As for the good things of these times   hold them at your
finger-tips (i.e. keep them at a distance)   for they have
no lasting value   even though you love them in your
heart   Even though a man be a teacher   he may destroy
his own teaching   This is the way of the world.

It may well be that we have not exhausted the varieties of
prosodic forms in the Swahili poetry of the nineteenth century,
though we have certainly illustrated the forms that are best known.
The examples we have given are much more difficult than most
modern Swahili poetry, which is not experimental in its prosody.
Verses either in eight or in four *vipande* have become the popular
medium for compositions in rhyme. Swahili writers are at home
in this medium. We may leave it to a modern Swahili poet,
Shaaban Robert, to tell in his own words what their poetry
means to the Swahili people.

Lecture on Poetry

by SHAABAN ROBERT

Poetry is the art of rhyming which distinguishes songs, poems
(i.e. of the more cultured kind), and heroic verse. Besides being
the art of rhyming, poetry expresses lucidity and preciseness of
style. You may ask, What is a song, a poem or an heroic verse-
narrative? A song is a small poem; a poem is a big song; and
heroic verse is the peak of poesy. You may ask again, What can

Kwa maneno mengine huitwa mizani ya sauti, na ufasaha ni uzuri wa lugha. Mawazo, maono na fikira za ndani zinapoelezwa kwa muhtasari wa ushairi huvuta moyo kwa namna ya ajabu. Muhtasari ni mnofu bora wa ufasaha kuliko nyama nyingine katika usanifu.

Kwa ushairi wake wa maneno machache, Muyaka, stadi wa mashairi mafupi, aliweza kudhihakisha watunga mashairi hivi:

Ushairi wa welevu   jadi ya wenye Malindi
Usambe watoka Jomvu   kwa Ngao na Mwachifundi
Silino jitu pumbavu   nguo livete mapindi
Ujaonapi mnandi   kujenga nyumba kutani.

Ushairi si johari inayopatikana Malindi kulikowapa Waswahili Muyaka. Hupatikana katika nchi zote. Katika simo inenayo, 'Yaliyoko Pemba na Unguja yako', ondoa Pemba na Unguja, useme yaliyoko Ulaya na Afrika yako; ondoa Ulaya, useme yaliyoko Afrika na Asia yako; ondoa Afrika, useme yaliyoko Asia na Amerika yako; ondoa Asia, useme yaliyoko Amerika na Australia yako. Maumbile hujikariri katika mataifa ya wanadamu kuonyesha asili moja na uungano wake mkubwa.

Maumbile ya ushairi hayaonekani kwa wanadamu tu. Huonekana kwa wanyama porini na ndege hewani; hewa na misitu imejaa ushairi; mito hutiririka kwa ushairi na bahari hucheka kwa mawimbi ya mlingano; katika upepo na radi muziki wa ushairi husikilika waziwazi. Wakati wa siku na majira ya mwaka hujigawa kama beti za mashairi katika maisha. Duara yote ya ulimwengu, mambo na matendo yake hutokea kwa sura na namna ya vina mbalimbali. Mgusano na mwendo wa vyombo vyetu vya kila siku huonyesha kadiri fulani ya mlingano ulio sawa na ushairi. Umbo la vitu vyote limejipamba pambo la kimo na kivimbo cha mlingano.

Waswahili hutumia ushairi kwa adili, kinubi, ushujaa na mambo mengine mengi. Madondoo katika Diwani ya Muyaka yatafananisha mashairi ya adili:

rhyme and style be? Rhyme is the harmony of vocal syllables, i.e. their resemblance. These vocal syllables are called *mizani*, and style is beauty of language. When the inward thoughts and emotions are explained with poetic brevity, this attracts in a wonderful way. Conciseness is the pith of good style, more than any other quality of good composition.

In a poem of a few words Muyaka, the expert in short poems, was able to make fun of poets, like this :[1]

Poetry belongs to the wise   to the people of Malindi stock
Don't say it comes from Jomvu   from Ngao or Mwachifundi
Is not this Jitu a fool?   He has got his clothes all coiled up
Have you ever seen the cormorant   building his nest up-country?

Poetry is not something precious obtainable only in Malindi, which gave the Swahilis Muyaka. It is obtainable in every country. In the saying which goes, 'What there is in Pemba is in Zanzibar as well', take away Pemba and Zanzibar, and say, 'What is in Europe is in Africa as well'; take away Europe, and say, 'What is in Africa is in Asia as well'; take away Africa, and say, 'What is in Asia is in America as well'; take away Asia, and say, 'What is in America is in Australia as well'. The created world repeats itself within the nations of human beings in order to show their common origin and their great unity.

The original nature of poetry does not appear only among human beings. It appears among the animals of the bush and the fowls of the air; the air and the forests are full of poetry; rivers glide along with poetry and the sea laughs at the rhythm of the waves; in the wind and the lightning the music of poetry is heard quite plainly. Daytime and the seasons of the year are divided like the verses of a poem in our lifetime. The whole circle of the world, its affairs and its deeds have the appearance and manner of rhymes of various sorts. The contact and rhythm of our everyday objects show in some measure the harmony which is like that of poetry. The shape of all things is adorned with the excellence of measure and with the circlet of resemblance.

The Swahili use poetry for (expressing) proper conduct, lyric utterance, bravery, and many other things. Selections from the Anthology of Muyaka will illustrate the homiletic verse:

[1] For footnote see p. 284.

Dunia mti mkavu   kiumbe siulemele
Ukaufanyia nguvu   kuudhibiti kwa ndole
Mtiwe ni mtakavu   mara ulikwangushile
Usione kwenda mbele   kurudi nyuma si kazi.

Kinubi ni mashairi yaonyeshayo furaha au huzuni. Al-Inkishafi ya Nasir ina mfano maridhawa:

Suu ulimwengu uutakawo   emale ni lipi upendeawo
Hauna dawamu hudumu nawo   umilikishwapo watendaye.

Kumithilisha mashairi ya ushujaa tutadondoa tena kwa Muyaka:

Nalishika ngurumza   kwa mkono wa kushoto
Na mato hayangariza   mfanowe kama moto
Waamu hawafukuza   kama ng'ombe kwa ufito
Hapigwa chombo kizito   haangukia majini.

Na juu ya mambo mengine tuna maombelezo katika Utenzi wa Huseni ya Hemed Abdallah el-Buhuriy, mpenzi mkubwa wa ushairi, alipokuwa akinyemelewa na uzee:

Macho yamesawijika   hayaoni kuandika
kwa kila siku kushika   karatasi na madadi.

Ewe ahi mwanakwetu   macho hayaoni kitu
nalilia kazi yetu   ya tangu jadi na jadi.

Na kuiacha si vema   nitadhuriwa na koma
japokuwa si mzima   afadhali jitahidi.

Tumedondoa mara tatu kwa Muyaka kwa sababu kazi zake zilisifiwa na washairi wa zamani kama Sikujua Abdallah el-Batawiy aliposema:

The world is like a dry tree O created being, do not lean on it
If you press on it testing it with your finger
The wood of it is old and at once you make it fall down
So don't see it as progressing it is easy enough for things to
regress.

A lyric is poetry showing joy or sadness. The *al-Inkishafi* of
Nasir shows this sufficiently:

This world that you want what is its good that you love so
much
It does not last nor you with it were you to govern what would
you do with it?

To illustrate poems on bravery we can choose again from the
poems of Muyaka:[1]

I took hold of the blunderbuss with my left hand
And my eyes shone like as though with fire
And I drove the Lamu people away like cattle with a stick
And I was given a means of escape and I fell into the water.

And concerning other matters we have such poems as the
lamentations in the epic poem of *Huseni* by Hemed Abdallah el-
Buhuriy, a great lover of poetry, when he was being burdened by
old age:

My eyes are stricken they do not see to write
because of the daily holding of paper and of opium pellets
for smoking.

Alas alas O son of ours my eyes see nothing
I grieve for our work (that we have done) for generations.

It is not good to give it up I will be harmed by its ending
even though I am not well it is better for me to make the
effort.

We have selected three passages from Muyaka because his
work was praised by the poets of old like Sikujua Abdallah el-
Batawiy when he said:

[1] For footnote see pp. 285–6.

Alitaka hamuyuza   mashairi ya zamani
Ya waume wapendeza   wana wa Swahili
Wema wa kutumbiza   kwa nyimbo ziso kifani
Nawambia pulikani   yaliyoandikwa mumo.

Nawambia pulikani   hizo zamani za kale
Muyaka ali nishani   kwa mashairi tuwele
Alikingia ngomani   pasiwe mkiya mbele
Akitongoa tongole   yaliyoandikwa mumo.

Akitongoa tongole   mashairi akanena
Ukumbi wa watu tele   penye wavyele na wana
Wote wasimjibule   wakasiri kudangana
Tungo njema za maana   zilizoandikwa mumo.

Tungo njema za maana   mazuri ya uwekefu
Yaliyokufuatana   yasiyokuwa maofu
Yalowashinda kunena   kina mjawiri mbofu
Uwateni ushupavu   yaliyoandikwa mumo.

Mashairi ya fikira   kumbusho za ushuhuda
Yazingayo kwa majira   yapayo watu faida
Alangukiwa ni kura   Muyaka ndiye ziada
Kuwezekana ni shida   yaliyoandikwa mumo.

Katika madondoo yaliyokaririwa juu, wanaume wametajwa kwa sifa. Msiondoke na wazo kuwa hapana wanawake waliotukuka kwa ushairi katika Afrika Mashariki. Mwana Kupona alikuwa mwanamke wa Siu, Kenya. Bibi huyu alikuwa mshairi wa sifa, naye ameacha waridi la manukato katika ufasaha wa Kiswahili.

Kila mshairi ameacha uzuri fulani katika lugha yake uliokaribia ule ulioachwa na Shakespeare katika lugha ya Kiingereza, ingawa Shakespeare alikuwa bahari kuu ya akili ambayo mawimbi yake ya nuru yamefika pwani za kila nchi ulimwenguni. Wameacha vile vile fikara idumishayo uzima wa milele wa kazi zao katika kumbukumbu za wanadamu.

Tutarudi tulikoanza tutaje jambo lionekanalo kuwa halina maana lakini kubwa sana katika mashairi ya Kiswahili ambayo kusudi lake si kusomwa na kukaririwa tu kama mashairi ya Kizungu. Hitilafu hii ingefaa kukumbukwa. Mashairi na tenzi za

He[1] wanted me to tell him   the poems of long ago
About the noble men   sons of Swahili-land
Those good at singing melodies   with matchless songs
I tell you, so listen   to what (poems) are written here.

I tell you, so listen   in those days of old
Muyaka was outstanding   for his noble verses
He used to enter the Fort   nor did he wear his tail in front
Getting right to the point   in what (poems) are written here.

Getting right to the point   he spoke his verse
Before a hall full of people   where there were old and young
With no one answering him   they came to pick up something
Of the good meaningful compositions   which are written down
  here.

Good meaningful compositions   well arranged
Which followed upon one another   not evil verse
But what could not be spoken   by the evil unjust man
Leave off bigotry   (in reading) what is written here.

Thoughtful poems   a memorial to personal testimony
Which follow round with the seasons   giving benefit to people
The lot fell to him   Muyaka is indeed a treasure (lit. bonus)
Such ability is rare   as that in what is written here.

In the selections given above, menfolk are mentioned eulogistic-ally. Do not go away with the idea that there are no women who have been honoured by East African poetry. Mwana Kupona was a woman of Siu, Kenya. This lady was a praiseworthy poet, and she has left a sweet-smelling rose in Swahili style.

Every poet has left at least some beauty in his language which approaches that which was left by Shakespeare in the English language, even though Shakespeare was a great sea of wisdom whose waves of light have reached the shores of every country in the world. They have also left thoughts which make the eternal quality of their work last in the memory of mankind.

We may return to where we began by mentioning a matter which may seem of little import but which is of great meaning in connexion with Swahili poems, the purpose of which is not that they should be read or repeated only, like European verse. This

[1] Sikujua is here referring to Taylor, for whom he worked as informant and copyist.

Kiswahili hutungwa kwa kusudi la kuimbwa kama nyimbo kama
mshairi mmoja alivyotangaza kwamba:

> Ziko siku makusudi   moyo hupata kianga
> Nami nikajitahidi   hakusudia kuringa.

Mfaraka mkubwa waonekana katika nyimbo za mashairi ya
zamani yaliyotungwa kwa utaratibu wa mizani na nyimbo au
mashairi ya sasa yatungwayo kwa tuni. Nyimbo za zamani zili-
kuwa kama mashairi:

> Ulitoka shama   na kaniki chini
> kama si kuimba   ungekula nini.

> Si hoja ya kitu   na sura jamali
> hasara ya mtu   kukosa akili.

Nyimbo za tuni katika lugha yo yote zikosapo vina hupungua
ladha itazamiwayo katika kuimba. Ukiuliza, Mbona hivi? Utaji-
biwa, Hujui kitu, sisi tunaimba kwa tuni.

Hii si hasara ndogo katika tungo za Kiswahili. Kweli twataka
tuni lakini pamoja na vina. Hatutaki tuni isiyo vina. Twakariri
kwamba hii si hasara ndogo kwa sababu imepoteza ufasaha katika
tafsiri ya wimbo wa Suleman katika Biblia wafasiri wake wali-
mojishughulisha kwa uhodari ustahilio sifa na maana na tuni bila
kujali vina. Kwa sababu hii hii tafsiri ya baadhi ya aya za Koran
si nzuri pia. Tafsiri ya lugha kwa lugha kwa sababu ya kusiki-
lizana bila kujali ada za lugha zenyewe si ufasaha ila kuzuzuana.
Haina uzima kama kifo chenyewe.

Vina katika maandiko husaidia kujenga fahamu. Moja ya madarasa kuu ulimwenguni ni El-Hazar katika Cairo. Ni madarasa ya
Kiislamu yenye wanafunzi ishirini na moja elfu. Mtihani wa
kuingilia hutaka kila mwombaji kukariri Koran kwa moyo.
Koran ina juzuu thelathini na sura mia na kumi na nne nayo
kubwa kama Agano Jipya, na siku tatu hutakiwa kuikariri! Siri
iwezeshayo wanafunzi hawa wengi, ambao wengine ni watu wa
akili ya kiasi, kufanya tendo la ajabu kama hili ni utungo wa vina
uliomo katika Koran ya Kiarabu.

Ushairi hutumika sana vile vile katika hadithi na historia. Kwa

distinction deserves to be remembered. Swahili poems and epics are composed to be sung, as one poet proclaimed:

There are days when on purpose   the heart receives a burst of light
And I made the endeavour   and decided to put on airs.

A considerable difference appears between the songs and poems of earlier times which were composed according to their syllabic measure, and modern poems which are composed according to their tune. Early songs were like poems:

You came from the field   with your dress of calico down
    if there were no singing   what would you eat?

It is not the need of a thing   nor a lovely face
    man's real loss   is to lack intelligence.

Tuneful songs in any language, if they lack rhyme, lack the savour expected from singing. If you ask, 'Why sing thus?' You will be answered, 'You know nothing, we sing by tune'.

This is no small loss in Swahili compositions. Of course, we need the tune but together with the rhymes. We do not want a tune that has no rhymes. We repeat that this is no small loss because (for example) it has brought about the loss of style in the translation of the *Song of Solomon*, where the Bible translators skilfully busied themselves in a most praiseworthy way with the meaning and with the rhythm but without attending to the rhymes. For the very same reason the translation of some of the verses from the Qur'ān are just as unsatisfactory. The translation from one language to another by listening without giving attention to the customs of the language is not good style but only fooling around. There is no completeness like death itself.

The rhymes in the writing help to build up understanding. One of the great places of learning in the world is el-Azhar in Cairo. It is a Muslim institution with 1,100 students. For the entrance examination every candidate is expected to repeat the Quran by heart. The Quran has thirty sections and 114 chapters; it is a big work like the New Testament, and three days are needed to recite it all! The secret which enables these many students, of whom some are of moderate intelligence only, to do such a wonderful thing is the arrangement of rhymes in the Quran in Arabic.

Poetry is also used in the writing of stories and of history. For

hadithi fupi hutumiwa mashairi, na kwa hadithi ndefu na historia hutumiwa tenzi. Hapana shaka hili ndilo litukuzalo ushairi juu ya tungo za kawaida.

Lugha itumikayo katika mashairi husemwa kuwa ngumu kufahamika. Hatulaumu wasemao hivi. Kueleza maono na mawazo ya ndani kwa maana na ufasaha hulazimisha washairi kuchagua maneno na matamko mbalimbali yawezayo kuchukua maana na mawazo yao. Waashi hutumia matofali ya kadiri fulani kwa kazi zao. Matofali ya washairi ni maneno fulani na fulani. Nao huweza kuyafupisha, kuyakuza hata kuyabadili katika mpango. Neno lo lote rahisi lisingefaa kusema waliyo nayo mioyoni. Kama maono na mawazo yao yastahili fikira zetu yatupasa kutafuta maana kadha wa kadha. Njia ya kushinda mashaka ya lugha ni kujifunza kwa bidii. Lugha si mali ya mtu asiyetafuta elimu yake. Hawezi kuinunua wala kuikopa. Haiwezi kuwa yenu wala yangu mpaka tuidai kwa taaluma na mazoea.

Baadhi ya watu husema kwamba hawana sikio la kusikiliza muziki wala moyo wa kukariri mashairi. Hilo no moja la madai ya upuuzi ya wanadamu. Mambo yafichwayo na watu katika mioyo yao ndiyo yawafichuayo.

Mtu mmoja alisimulia kwamba alikwenda kwa rafiki aliyekuwa na madai kwamba hakuwa na hamu ya muziki wala ukariri. Walizungumza wakala wakanywa wakalala. Asubuhi yake rafiki yake alipokuwa anaoga alimsikia ametumbuka muziki na ukariri kwa sauti kubwa katika hamamu yake. Labda katika hamamu ndiko mtu yule alikojiona aliweza kuimba bila kudhaniwa na watoto wake kuwa alishikwa na wazimu. Lakini kweli ilikuwa kwamba maumbile yalichukia bumbuazi yakapenda kuchangamka. Ndivyo ilivyokuwa na ndivyo itakavyokuwa milele.

Kadiri za hamu za watu juu ya mambo mbalimbali si moja. Baadhi yao waonekana kuwa na kadiri kubwa hata kubwa kabisa; wengine wanayo kadiri ndogo hata ndogo sana. Lakini kukosekana kabisa haiwezi kuwa hata kidogo. Hamu ingekoma na uanadamu ungekoma mara moja. Asiye na mengi ana machache, hujulikana na kila mtu. Mengi ya wanadamu huweza kupungua kwa uharabu na dharau, na machache yao huweza kusitawi kwa mazoezi na hifadhi.

short stories poems are used (i.e. the quatrain form), and for long stories and histories the epic-form is employed. There is no doubt that this (conscious prosodic form) elevates poetry above the level of ordinary compositions (i.e. like work-songs, &c.).

It is said that the language used in poems is difficult to understand. We do not blame those who say this. To express the emotions and inward thoughts compels the poets to choose words and various phrases that can convey the meaning of their thoughts. Masons use bricks of a certain size for their work. The bricks of the poets are such and such words. And they can shorten them, make them bigger or even change them in the text. What they have to say from the heart may not be expressed by any easy phrase. If their thoughts and emotions deserve our attention we should not mind having to seek out this or that meaning. The way to overcome inability in a language is to learn it with diligence. No language can be the possession of a person who does not go after the science of it. He cannot buy it nor borrow it. It cannot be yours nor mine until we claim it by right of scholarship and use.

Some people say they have no ear for music nor for reciting poetry. This is one of those foolish claims made by human beings. What people hide in their hearts is what usually reveals them as they are.

One man told the story of how he went to a friend who claimed that he had no love for music nor for recitation. They chatted, drank and ate, and then they slept. In the morning when his friend was having a bath he heard him singing and reciting with a loud voice in his bath. It may be it was in his bath that that fellow discovered he could sing without his children thinking he was round the bend. But the truth is that a created soul turned from stupidity and loved being bright and happy. That is how it was, and so it will always be.

People's love for different things varies. Some appear to have a very great love for certain things; others have only a very little. But to be altogether without such love is quite impossible. If such love ceased then the human race would come to an end. The one who may not have much has a little, this is known by everybody. The abundance men have may become less through destruction and indifference, and their penury can become riches by discipline and care.

Katika hotuba hii, ushairi, vina na ufasaha wake katika lugha umeelezwa kinaganaga. Namna na tofauti zake zimetolewa. Mambo mbalimbali yamewekwa wazi pamoja na mifano maridhawa kwa madondoo katika kazi za washairi waliopata kuishi katika Afrika Mashariki. Imetuambia ubora wake juu ya tungo za kawaida na fahari ya uzuri wake usio mpaka vile vile. Hii ni hazina ya majivuno kwa wasemao Kiswahili kama lugha yao ya kuzaliwa na kwa wale wajipatiao elimu yake kwa kujifunza.

Katika kuisikiliza tuna kisa cha mtu aliyekuwa na gari lililopakia mbolea. Njiani alimwona mzee aliyechoka sana akampakia nyuma ya gari lake. Alipofika mbele kidogo alikutana na mtu aliyemjua katika gari jingine wakaamkiana. Mtu katika gari la pili alimwuliza yule wa gari la kwanza alichopakia katika gari lake. Alijibu, Nimepakia mbolea na mzee huyu. Akaenda zake. Baada ya mwendo wa dakika chache alikutana tena na mtu katika gari la tatu aliyeuliza swali lile lile. Alijibu kama kwanza akaendelea katika safari yake. Sasa yule mzee alimpelekea mkono mwenye gari akamgusa begani. Akasema, Bwana, mtu mwingine akikuuliza ulichopakia garini, nitaje mimi kwanza.

Kadhalika mfano ni juu yenu kuweka mbele na kusitawisha ushairi wa Kiswahili.

---

¹ The poems by Muyaka included in this lecture were taken by Shaaban Robert from the *Diwani ya Muyaka*, edited by Hichens, but it is doubtful if even Shaaban Robert understands their topical application. In Taylor's unpublished notes, he writes of this poem: 'Mwenyi Jitu alikwenda kwa Wadi Salim kwenda kutembea wakifundana mashairi akatokea Bwana Muyaka akawaona wamekaa faragha, akajua faragha ile hakuna isipokuwa ya watunga mashairi. Basi ndipo akaimba maneno akamfukuza kwa ushairi huu.' 'Mwenyi Jitu went to Wadi Salim for a walk and to teach one another poems, and Muyaka appeared and found them in secret conclave, and he knew there could be no other reason for their secrecy than that they were composing poems. And so he sang these words and drove him (Jitu) away with this poem.'

Jitu hailed from Jomvu. The point that Shaaban makes about the universality of poetry is in fact quite the reverse of the sentiments expressed by Muyaka's action in making fun of a fellow poet who came from Jomvu. There is a pun on the name, for *jitu* also means a giant, a term used here sarcastically. The first *kipande* in Taylor reads, 'Ushairi mbwa welevu'. *Livete* is given in the margin as an alternative for *lipete*, with the note, 'Neno hili ni la kugoa'; *kugoana* 'to banter, jest together'. *Kutani* in Taylor is *kutwani*, or, in standard *kuchwani*, 'the west, towards sunset'.

In this lecture on poetry rhymes and elegant style have been described with some clearness. We have indicated some distinctions. Various matters have been set out clearly together and examples with selections from the work of poets who have lived in East Africa. We have learnt from this that such (early) verse is better than the usual compositions and we have heard of the excellence of such verses as well. This is a proud treasure for those who speak Swahili as their mother tongue and for those who come to know it by learning the language.

As you listen, we have a story of a man who had a cart loaded with manure. In the roadway he met an old man who was very tired, and so he put him on the back of his cart. When he had gone on a little farther he met someone he knew with another cart and they greeted one another. The man on the second cart asked the first man what he had in his cart. He replied, 'I am carrying some manure and this old man'. And he went on his way. After a few minutes' journey he met a man with a third cart who asked the very same question. He answered as he had done at first and continued his journey. Then the old man stretched out his arm and touched the owner of the cart on the shoulder. And he said, 'Sir, If any one else asks you what you have in the cart, please mention me first'.

Similarly, the moral is that it is up to you to put first and to promote the merits of Swahili poetry.

---

[1] The topical allusions in this verse are explained in Taylor's notes. More intimate knowledge of the events concerned shows that this is not a very suitable choice on the theme of bravery, for Muyaka escapes from his enemies by diving into the sea. Taylor writes: 'Muyaka alitoka Mvita akenda Sawahili kwenda kupakia mtama kusafiri kwenda Shihiri. Basi watu wa Pate na wa Amu walikuwa wamekasirika nae wakamkamia kwa maana ya mashairi yakwe aliyokuwa akiwatukana kwa maneno ya kweli. Basi wakaja wakamzuia wakamshika wakataka kumuua akapisha akili zake, akawahadaa akangia akasafiri, akaandika shairi hili akaona wavuvi akawaambia, Wapelekee Waamu na Wapate, kawaambieni, Inshallahu taala, tawasili kwetu kesho.

'Na taratibu yakwe ilikuwa hivi: alitaka kunyang'anywa chombo na kuuawa akawaambia, Waateni wale wende wakamtolee habari ya jinsi ya kuniua kwangu. Na wale ni watumwa na zile ni mali za watu; itakapokuwa ni kutwaa chombo na mali, ni aibu na fedheha kwenu. Lakini iwapo ni kuniua mimi, kwenu hapana aibu wala fedheha: ndipo mahali penu. Basi wakahadaika wale, wakawaruhusu wale wenyi chombo kwenda zao, ikawa kupamba tanga na kuvuta nanga. Basi, mule mule kuvutani nanga akawambia wale, Niatani nioge nitawadhe nisali, basi kwamba ni kuniua ndipo muniue, wakampa ruhusa. Akangia katika bahari kuoga, akatafakari akasema, Afadhali mimi kuuawa ni maji kama kuuawa ni watu hivi mwenyewe nikiona. Basi akapiga mbizi, hadi ya pumzi zakwe, hata akizuka amezuka karibu na chombo kile, akatupiwa kamba akaigwia akapandia juu ya chombo.'

'Muyaka left Mombasa to go to the Swahili country [i.e. north of Mombasa] to load up with millet for taking to Shihiri. The people of Pate and Lamu were very angry with him and threatened him because of his poems in which he had justly criticized them. And so they came and prevented him (from going farther) and seized him, wanting to kill him, but he used his wits and tricked them, going on with his journey, and he wrote a poem and met some fisherfolk and told them, Take this to the people of Lamu and Pate, and tell them, If God pleases, tomorrow I will arrive home.

'And the circumstances were as follows: He was almost robbed of his boat and killed, and he said to them, Leave them [i.e. the crew] so that they can go and explain about my being killed. For they are slaves and that [the cargo] belongs to other people; by taking the ship and its load you will get shame and disgrace for yourselves. But if it is just a matter of killing me, there is no disgrace nor shame in that for you: that is only expected of you. And so they were deceived, and gave permission for the crew to go home, and so the sails were set and the anchor weighed. Then when they were actually weighing anchor he said to them (the people of Pate and Lamu), Let me go and bathe and wash my feet for prayer, for if you want to kill me, well then kill me; and they allowed him to do this. And he went into the sea to bathe, and he thought to himself, It is better for me to be drowned than to be killed by these people, that is how I see it. And so he dived in, staying down as long as his breath could last, and when he came up he was near the boat (his own), and they threw him a rope and he pounced on it and climbed up into the boat.'

Taylor's notes include: *hapigwa chombo kizito* 'I was given a coup de force, a powerful efficient means of escape'. This is probably in reference to the rope.

TEXTUAL NOTES

THE annotation is restricted to textual and grammatical items which need further explanation, and also to words that are not found in the dictionaries of Sacleux, Krapf, and Johnson.

If a word is different in shape from its equivalents in any one of these dictionaries and yet is derived from the same Arabic word, it will be noted. It is important to observe that in Swahili words derived from Arabic the vowels *a*, *i*, and *u* are often permissible alternatives, e.g. *kutubu* or *katibu*, *mathulubu* or *mathilaba* (also *matilaba*). Usually the forms occurring in the poetry are nearer to the Arabic equivalents, but this is not invariably so. The whole question of vowel alternances in Swahili in relation to corresponding vowels in the Arabic equivalents needs further investigation. As a general guide, it may be sufficient to say that in identifying words related to Arabic, the reader should seek first to identify the consonants while bearing in mind that alternatives occur in Swahili with different vowels.

Grammatical features of frequent occurrence in the texts, for example, the omission of the subjectival concord or of other grammatical elements, will be noted only in their initial occurrences. The following abbreviations are used: Ar. for Arabic; St. for Standard; and Sw. for Swahili.

Ras al-Ghuli

(Pages 7–8)

Verse

4. *ndiani* for St. *njiani*.
8. *tasi*, an instrument for combing out the strands of rope, string, &c.
   hipiga, the prefixes *hi-* and *ha-* in the Amu dialect represent either 1st or 3rd pers. sing. of the participial and the narrative tenses respectively; St. *nikipiga*, *akipiga*.
9. *mbwene* for St. *niliona* or *naliona*, I saw.
10. *zita*, prefix of Cl. 8 occurs as *zi-* or *vi-* in the Amu dialect.
    zali, relative with no infix, for St. *vilivyokuwako*.
12. *halili*, probably for *halali*; cf. *halili*, a beloved person.
19. *kutaharabu* for *kuharibu*; the Arabic sign of conjugation *ta-* is retained in many verbals in Swahili poetry, but with no modification of meaning.
    mathulubu, see in Johnson *matilaba*, desire, intention; Ar. *maṭlūb*.

(Page 29)

Rubricated verses

   tuyabawibu, cf. Ar. *bawabu,* put into chapters, classify, arrange.

   muakafu, end, conclusion; cf. *-akifu* or *-wakafu* or *-wakifu.* The Arabic
   prefixes *mu-* and *ma-* have no grammatical function in Swahili.

(Pages 28–48)

Verse

2. *achenda* for *akienda;* the Arabic symbol for *-ch-* is ‎ چ‎

3. *Bilali,* muezzin to the Prophet.
   keta adhini for *akaita aadhini.*

5. *Ali na Athmana,* in this and the next verse the Four Companions of the
   Prophet are named.

6. *mashiyukh* for the Arabic pl. of *shaikh, mashāyikh;* this term is used of a
   special aristocracy of religious men in Ḥaḍramawt.
   kuhusiri, to lack, be missing, also *-usiri;* Ar. *khusr,* loss.

16. *Abu 'l-Hasani,* an honorific reference to ʿAli as 'the father of his son
    Hasan'.

19. *mtakadamu,* chief of a group, the first to do something, a proposer; Ar.
    mutaqaddum; cf. Ar. *muqaddam,* chief of tribe or of the quarter of a town.

23. *yukheini,* also *yukhini, yukheni, yukhena, ikhena,* probably a Southern
    Arabian borrowing from *yak hīn,* at one time, *yak* being a Persian
    form and *hīn* the Arabic word for time.

26. *ushairi,* story, tale, news, and not meaning poetry or poem here.

29. *siku za zilzilati,* the days of the earthquake, a reference to the Day of
    Judgement.
    bashiri nadhiri, lit. the messenger warner; Ar. *bashr* and *nadhīr.*

34. *madhukuri,* the aforementioned; Ar. *madhkūr.*

42. *kughudhubu,* cf. *-ghadhabika,* be angry.

47. *usudi,* pl. in Ar. *usud,* lions; of Ar. *asad.*

48. *amrati,* women; Ar. *imraʾah.*
    baidhati, probably from Ar. *baida,* white.

49. *pame,* for St. Sw. *pamoja na,* together with.

50. *Tumtiile latifu,* &c. This verse is used frequently in heroic poems as a
    chorus.

51. *Munkari,* one of the interrogating Angels who examine the departed
    after death.

53. *wakitukusa,* inflicting upon us, *-kusa,* cs. of *-kuta.*

64. *Habibu,* the beloved, a frequent title of the Prophet, but in more recent
    times used in Ḥaḍramawt of any Saiyid.

67. *kikendeleza,* this could represent either *akikiendeleza* or *kikiendeleza,* and
    probably the former.

76. *Jibrili,* the Archangel Gabriel.

90. *tahakiki,* without any doubt, certainly; Ar. *taḥqīq,* verification.

92. *ahawana,* an alternative translation here has been suggested, viz., 'I find
    myself rather better', relating the word *ahawana* to Ar. *aḥwan* which, in
    the colloquial Arabic of ʿOman, means 'better'. The word *ahawana*
    may, however, be related to Ar. *hāna yahūn,* become weak (Classical Ar.),

Verse
be abject, contemptible (colloquial), and the translation given in the text corresponds to this second interpretation.

98. *akitaranamu*, Sacleux gives *akitaghanamu, -taranamu*, draw a profit, gain by something; Ar. *ʿḥtanama*.

100. *shibabu*, cf. Johnson, *shabābi*, youth.
kajilabisi thiabu, lit. and he dressed himself clothes. Note the verbal *-labisi*, and compare the related nominal, *libasi*, clothes, noting the transposed vowels.
afkhari, clothes, Taylor gives this meaning, but the word has not been identified.

102. *jadidi*, new; Ar. *jadīd*; *hadidi*, lit. iron; Ar. *ḥadīd*.
durui ya daudi, Daudian chain-mail, also found mentioned in poetry as *deraya ya dodi*.

103. *sawidi*, black; Ar. *aswad*.

108. *hijabu*, curtain; Ar. *hijāb*.

111. *mbayana*, evident, clear; Ar. *mubaiyin/an*; cf. Sw. *-baini*.

117. *asiwe kutama kani*, lit. without finishing strength.

121. *akiamiri na nari*, and he began to light it, lit. he beginning it with a flame.

123. *wakajipiga lahamu*, lit. and they hit themselves meat, i.e. they got down to it, ate heartily.

128. *jiwe la twaani*, in Amu dialect *-twa* or *-twaa* corresponds with St. Sw. *-saga*, grind grain on a stone.

134. *turusi*, shield; Ar. *turs.*, pl. *turūs*.

140. *takibiri* for *-takbira*, repeat the Muslim formula *Allāhu Akbar*, God is Great.

162. *kumdhirisha umri*, lit. to cause him violence to (his) allotted span of life; this is a common phrase in poetry, meaning to kill him off, cut off his life.

The Epic of Lyongo

(Pages 52–70)

Verse
6. *kitakamali*, subjectival concord *a-* omitted; cf. *kamili*, perfect.
kaongeya for *ikaongezeka*, and not related to *-ongea*, converse.

7. *majimbo kawa* for *katika majimbo akawa*, in the districts or provinces he became . . .

8. *jumbe wa Pate*, probably for *ujumbe wa Pate*, the sultanate of Pate; *jumbe* in Cl. 5 usually refers to the Sultan's residence.

13. *una*, note the concord *u-* of Cl. 1, of common occurrence in the poetry instead of St. *a-*.

14. *mkojo hukupoteya*, lit. you lose urine.
tapo, shivering, trembling; cf. *-tapa*, shiver, tremble.
likakuiliya, it makes you shiver, *-iliya*, make to quiver, quake (with cold, pain, &c.).

17. *alikiketi*, he used to dwell; note tense-sign *-liki-*.
i huku yake baiti for *ndiko iliko nyumba yake*.
Mashaha, the old town is still known as Kwa Mwana wa Mashaha; it

Verse

    was on the mainland in the bush country of the Ozi river valley. Note the faulty rhyme on *mashaha*.

23. *akaemeya* for *akalemea*.
24. *panda*, war-horn, made from an antelope horn and blown through an orifice in the side of the base.
30. *asimuhuli*, not delaying; cf. *muhula*, time, period.
31. *wakajujumkana*, in St. Sw. *wakadudumikana*, and they got each other confused.
    wakazengeya mapito, and they searched out places to pass.
49. *zikamngiya* for *zikamwingia*.
51. *huzengeya kuuawa*, lit. they searched for being killed; this is a typical example of cryptic style in Swahili poetry. In full this would be, *huzengeya njia apate kuuawa*, looking for a way that he might be killed.
52. *waSanye . . . na waDahalo*, the Sanye or Boni and the Dahalo tribes of the Tana Valley, see Prins, *The Coastal Tribes of the North-Eastern Bantu*, London, 1952.
58. *makoma*, fruits of the *mkoma*, the hypaene or dwarf-palm, also called in Sw. *mkoche* and *mwaa*.
    hatutokoma, note the tense-sign -*to*- in future tense.
    tukiiterema, from -*terema*, come down from a height, and distinct from -*terema*, be at ease; the objectival concord relates to *miti*, trees, and so literally, we coming down from the trees; they climbed the trees to fetch the fruits of the dum-palm.
60. *uwo*, flight, of arrow, birds, &c.
62. *kuwanguliya* for *kuwaangulia*, to pluck down for you.
67. *ngaa ndima* for *ngaa nzima*, a whole cluster from the top of the tree.
68. *amuwezao* for *amwezaye*, note that the relative infix -*o*- is both of singular and plural meaning in the Amu dialect.
80. *shaha*, Velten wrote: 'Zamani jumbe chini yake alikuwa na mashaha na waziri na mwenyi mkuu na amiri' (*Desturi za Wasuaheli*, p. 225).
    mwao, probably the dance itself at which the *gungu* songs were sung, but there is no explanation of this word in any of the recognized sources.
83. *mumezomwambiya*, note use of the relative concord -*zo*- in a verbal with -*me*- tense-sign.
84. *hawezekani*, lit. he is not possible; in St. Sw. the phrase would read *kuua kumkataza hakuwezekani*.
86. *akapeka* for *akapeleka*.
87. *kwa utungo*, in order, in column; cf. -*tunga*, arrange.
    zembe, arrows; cf. *chembe*, arrow.
89. *tulepuwe* for *tuliepue*, let us avoid it. Note in this verse that *shari* is in Cl. 5.
90. *sana*, lawful, customary or polite act or conduct; Ar. *sunnah*; *nda*, contraction of *ni ya*.
92. *kitouawa* for *akitouawa*, if he be not slain; this negative of the conditional is seldom used in St. Sw.
94. *chanda nikiume*, let me bite my finger; the order of words is transposed here, a common practice in poetry. To gnaw the knuckles is a customary expression of grief or remorse. Note *chanda* for St. *kidole*.

Verse

97. *utapowa*, passive of *-pa*, give, cf. St. *-pewa*.
101. *kuti*, good food; cf. *-kuta*, be satisfied with food; Ar. *qūt*. *wakailiya* for *wakailiya*, and they ate for themselves.

The Song to Saada

Ewe kijakazi . . . In some versions of this poem the first line appears as: *Kijakazi Saada nakutuma* . . ., and this explains why the poem is usually referred to as *The Song of Saada*, cf. Werner, *Fest. Meinhof*, p. 48. The ruse by which Liyongo intends to escape is so patent in these lines that nothing cryptic could be imputed to them. Hichens records a short poem and says of it 'this song is much more likely to have been in the form of the original cryptic message to Saada'. But this is only one of the many short Swahili poems which are extremely difficult to translate. There is nothing to identify it with the present context, but as an example of the more obscure type of Swahili verse, the poem is given as follows:

Ai mama kunituatuwa   ni manana pana gogwe
Sendi machache hapwewa   sendi mangi koweza ngwe
Sendi katoto adawa   na wakumbizi wa kungwe
Ndimi wa kamba na kowa   si lengwe mkokota lengwe
Huoneka siku ya kuwiwa   hiwafunga kwa kamba na nangwe
nisimbone wa kuwafunguwa   hata nao watwa wa kiyongwe.

nikeeze for *nikereze*, let me cut through with a saw or file.
minyoo for *minyororo*, shackles or chains.
nitatage, *-tataga*, get across, cross by holding on to something.
yakiyeyuka, cf. in St. *-ekua dari*, break through a ceiling, and *-ekuka*, be broken, as in *boriti ya dari imeekuka*, a rafter of the ceiling has given way.
ondoni, cf. *ondo*, a kind of high grass used for thatching.
ninyepee, Krapf gives *-nyapia*, creep, stalk in hunting.
mwana nyoka, a fierce snake, not a young snake—so also in *mwana simba*, a fierce lion.
buka, uneasy, grieving, restless.
nimeziye, probably related to *-mazia*, finished up, but could also be for *nimezile*, I have been swallowed up, cf. *-meza*, swallow.
mame for *mamaye*, his mother, his lady.
awasiwe, probably for *awadhiwe*, his disposer, his trustee; Ar. *waṣī*.
104. *nyaka*, pl. of *waka*, a burning object, a fire, *-aka*, burn.
make, contraction of *mamake*, his mother.
wisha for *wishwa*, bran consisting of maize husks, and referred to in another version of Saada's song as *buruburosa*, which, according to a former Sultan of Witu, Umari b. Hamadi, is an old word for the husks of maize after pounding (Werner, *Bulletin of BSOS*, vol. iv, p. 253, note).
105. *kata mbili*, a loaf of 2 *kata* would weigh 7–8 lb.
106. *mpekee haya ngiya* for *mpelekee haya ingia*.

Verse

109. *tasa*, brass gong/s; *pembe*, buffalo-horn used as a trumpet; *siwa*, the royal trumpet or horn used by a Swahili sultan. The renowned *siwa* are two, one of ivory, exquisitely carved, and another of brass, preserved at the D.C.'s office, Lamu. Only accredited persons were (and are) allowed to blow the *siwa*, which are shaped like an elephant's tusks (ivory *siwa* are carved from tusks) with the mouthpiece on one side of the apex.

110. *kusi*, pl. of *ukusi*, hand-clap.

The Gungu Songs

Verse

i. *taikha*, members of the dance-guild; *fuwanye*, the chorus-singers. These names are not found in the dictionaries, but Sir Mbarak vouched for the meanings given here.

Bwana Mwengo, name applied to any minstrel as an honorific meaning Mr. Echo; cf. *mwengo*, echo, answering voice.

ii. *uliliye*, his ceremonial divan; cf. *kilili*, divan.

watenzi, the actors.

ringo, graceful gait; *-ringa*, put on airs, walk with swagger.

zifungo, verses of song with an enigma.

iii. *kumiya shingo* for *kuumia shingo*, to strain the neck.

zitengo, seats of honour.

iv. *pindi sizo* for *pindi hizo*, at that time.

wasiyakaa, cf. St. *hawajakaa*.

v. *mengo* or *mwengo*, a kind of scent, Cl. 3.

yalotuwa, which is rubbed on; St. *-chua*, rub on.

ziungo, ingredients; *-unga*, compound, combine, e.g. *-unga chakula*, season food, *-unga dawa*, compound medicine.

vi. *choche* or *chochi* for St. *moshi*.

vii. *zito*, essential parts, essence.

viii. *mukita* for *mkiita*, as you call, while you call.

ix. *wari* for *waari*; St. *mwali/waali*, young unmarried girls, who at a traditional Swahili wedding were dressed up on the wedding-day to wait on the bridegroom and to fan him.

sabuka, young men, also the general term for the *gungu*-dancers of Pate.

mwango, a united response, a chorus.

x. *lango* for *mlango*, door, the reference here being to the door of Liyongo's cell, for in the oral tradition Liyongo would not sing until the door was opened; cf. in Juma Mbwana's account to Taylor: 'Hata zamani za kuimba yule Liyongo akaambiwa, Imba nawe, akasema, Mimi siwezi kuimba, mnifungulie mlango. Ukafunguliwa.'

zakupa tuzo for *zitu za kuwapa watu kuwatuza*.

tumbi tumbi, very many.

xi. *kwawiya* for *kuwawia*, to irritate; cf. *-wawa*, itch, irritate.

xiv. *akatuza*, either from *-tuza*, make a present, or contracted from *-tuliza*, comfort, and the latter is preferred because *-tuliza moyo us* probably

Verse

    meant to be read here, meaning, comfort the heart. *kimba* for
    wakiimba.

xv. *mgunya*, a native of the coast between Mombasa and Juba.
    tango, perhaps for *mtango*, a wanderer.

xvi. *upijile . . .*, an obscure line; *-pija mfupa* might mean eat off the bone, but
    tanu is not identified.
    bungo, edible fruit of the tree *Landolphis florida*, but the word might be
    read *pungo*, leavings, scrapings.
    mtengotengo, selections, probably of food.

xvii. *pazidiye . . .*, the literal translation here indicates that the poet has added
    fourteen verses to the original poem of forty verses. From verse vi
    onwards it is clear that there is discontinuity of context, and probably
    the verses in our text are a later version of a much longer oral tradition
    of *gungu* songs. It is not possible to make sense of the context here,
    and this is adjusted in the translation.

114. *zitakatapo*, cf. in St. *-chakacha*, pound.

115. *zalipo kikaza* for *zilipokikazwa*, when the handclapping increased.

116. *mbiyo zikawapoteya* for *mbio zikawapoteza*, quickly (their fears) made them
    to be lost.

166. *kamshashiya*, cf. *-shashia*, welcome with joy, distinct from *-chachia*, be
    bad-tempered about something.
    akimnyoa na ziya for *akimnyosha na via*, stretching out his joints.

167 *kimkanda maguuni*, see *Utendi wa Mwana Kupona* for this Swahili custom
    of having the limbs massaged after a journey.
    kumtuya for *kumtua*, to settle him; the ending is changed for the sake of
    the rhyme.

180. *ondo*, knee-joint; *kupiga ondo*, to kneel on one knee.

184. *uko* for *yuko*, the form in *u-* is common in poetry.

186. *mwa*, probably for locative *mwao*, in their (tank).

194. *amedharani* for *amedhuru nini*, lit. what has he injured?

198. *zitono za ndani*, internal wounds.

Mwana Kupona's Poem

(Pages 72–86)

Verse

1. *ngema*, lit. lean on me; note suffix *-a*, a common use in imperatives that
    have 1st pers. sing. objectival concord. The full form would be *nie-*
    gema; cf. St. *niegeme.*
    wasiati, injunction, last will; Ar. *waṣīyat.*
    asaa, perhaps, it may be that; Ar. *ʿasa.*

2. *yametimu*, the agreement is with *maradhi.*

3. *ujilisi*, the verbal stem is *-jilisi*, sit; Ar. *jalasa.*

7. *akepuane* for *akuepuane* elision of vowel in the objectival concord, though
    this does not happen in everyday speech. Other elisions, e.g. in v. 14,
    asoshika for *asioshika* or *asiyeshika*, *sandamane* for *usiandamane*, might well
    occur in speech forms. Note in v. 31, *nasikose* for *na asikose.*

Verse

8. *uifungeto,* the enclitic *-to* in verbals denotes intensity of the verbal action. This intensive was noted by Taylor.
13. *uwa,* imperative of the verb *-wa,* be; cf. St. *uwe.*
27. *dalihini,* right then, at once, for St. *papo hapo;* Ar. *dal-ḥīn.*
33. *kumowa* for St. *kumwosha* or *kumwogesha;* in Amu dialect, *-ówa* or *-oa,* bathe.
34. *bukurata wa ashiya,* lit. early morning and late evening; this is Qur'ānic Arabic.
41. *zandani,* pl. of *chanda* with suffix *-ni.*
44. *ukutiwapo,* when you are met by; passive of applied form of *-kuta,* meet.
51. *umi,* mother; Ar. *umm.*
54. *kashukuru kafawidhi. Shukuru* means primarily 'give thanks', but *-shukuru Mungu* is commonly used to mean, resign oneself to one's fate; *-fawidhi,* entrust a matter to one; Ar. *fawwaḍ.*
57. *mvuli* for *mvulana,* young man, youth.
60. *nla* for *ule,* imperative.
    ushakiri, probably for *ushukuru.*
80. yaumu *li'Arafa,* the day of ʿArafat, i.e. the 9th day of Dhu 'l-Ḥijjah on which pilgrims visit the hill ʿArafah, six hours east of Mecca.
    idi ya udhihiya for ʿĪdu 'l-Aḍḥā, the feast of sacrifice, also called ʿĪdu 'l-Kabīr, is part of the rites of the Muslim Pilgrimage.
81. *kutufu,* the verbal stem is *-tufu,* go round, i.e. circumambulate the Kaaba.
82. *ghayata,* goal, fulfilment; *raghbatahu,* Ar. Thou hast supplicated Him; here used in the sense of He who is supplicated.
83. *bi'asmaika,* Ar. by thy names; *husuna,* Ar. beautiful.
90. *zitunu,* pl. of *kitunu,* pain, distress, probably for *kichunu. Dayanu,* the Recompenser, the Judge, from Ar. *dayan.*
97. *ithimu,* sin; Ar. *ithm.*

The Poem *Inkishafi*

This poem was annotated in Hichens's edition (Sheldon Press, 1939), and words of Arabic derivation are numbered in his vocabulary according to their occurrence in their Arabic form in the Arabic–English dictionary of J. G. Hava (Beirut, 1921). The present annotation excludes reference to most of the material given by Hichens, except where the meaning has to be expanded or is in dispute. Variants from Hichens's transcription will be noted, Hichens being mentioned by the use only of the initial H.

(Pages 90–102)

Verse

2. *illa,* the manuscript gives the double consonant, but the word is properly *ila,* a wrong, a defect, a blemish.
4. *banu Kinana,* the clan or kinsfolk of Qinan b. Khuzaima, of the tribe of Quraish, who was the twelfth great-grandfather of the Prophet.
    maana, in H. *maina,* names.
    ziwaaliye, the verbal is *-alia,* impress upon, leave a mark on.
6. *kwimake* or *kimake, -ima,* stand, halt, stop, and so here, its ending.

Verse
> *kuzikamili*, the objectival concord *-zi-* is in agreement with *himdi na sala* in the next *kipande*.
>
> *makali*, in St. Sw. *makala*.

8. *kinipukiye*, H. has *kiniukiye*.
9. *kitamsi*, subjunctive of the verb *-tamsi*, be effaced, be blotted out.
   > *itadhalali*, a copyist's error for *itadhayali*.
10. *upitwe na*, H. gives *utetwe ni*, but the manuscripts give no indication of this, and alternative readings most frequently do not support H.'s transliteration.
    > *rajimi*, Satan was called *as-Shaitan ar-rajim*, i.e. the Satan stoned, from the tradition that Abraham, tempted not to sacrifice his son, drove Satan away by pelting him with stones; or, in another tradition, Adam, meeting with Satan at the valley of Mina, near Mecca, was adjured by Allah to drive Satan away with stones. A journey to Mina, where the pilgrims throw stones at three pillars representing Rajim, is part of the ritual of the Meccan Pilgrimage.
13. *hunu*, H. has *suu*, this.
14. *mtapaa*, compound form from *-ta*, strike, hit, and *paa*, crown of the head, 'one who butts with the head'.
15. *likichupuza*, H. gives *likitepuza*.
16. *yua lilinganapo*, when the sun is level, i.e. at the meridian.
18. The rhyme is in *-wo*, not, as in H., in *-yo*.
    > *siyo* for St. *hiyo*; H. has *sii*.
20. *Kwami* for *kwangu mimi*, as for me; H. has *kima*.
    > *ni kalifu*, H. has *i kalifu*.
21. *zilala zawo*, H. gives *kwa mizagao*.
24. *akatumbukiu*, H. has *kutubukia*.
    > *nasiwe* for *na asiwe*; H. has *pasiwe*.
26. *zingapi*, H. has *zingapo*.
27. *kuna hadawa mno*, H. has *ya kuliwa bangu*.
28. *sasa mi*, H. has *saa moya*.
35. *iwaokele*, the simple stem of the verbal here is *-oka*, be straight.
42. *juu la zitanda . . .*, this *kipande* in H. reads *iyu la zitanda kwa majodori*. Note the more frequent use of Cl. 5 agreements in poetry, in words which in current St. Sw. are in Cl. 9.
43. *kufunikawa*, the manuscripts give this, but this is probably an error for *kufunikiwa*.
44. *fusi na fusize*, according to the manuscripts, but H. has *mtanga na fusi*; *-fusa*, cs. of *-futa*, wipe away, and Sacleux gives *fusi*, debris, rubbish, and *fusizi*, heap of debris.
45. *mji shubiri*, H. has *moya shubiri*.
    > *dhiki ya kaburi*, H. has *dhiki za ziyara*.
46. *zitukuta zao hutawanyika*, H. has *zitefute zao huwatulika*.
    > *usaha . . . &c.*, H. has *wasakha na damu huwaitika*. The full form of this *kipande* in St. Sw. would probably be *usaha na damu ya watu hawa huitika*.
47. *wote*, H. has *huwa*.
    > *na nyoka na nge*, H. has *majoka na pili*.

Verse

48. *zitamazakiye . . .*, &c., a typical example of transposition in word-order for *juludi zao zilitamazaka*.

49. *ziwele*, in St. *zimekuwa*.

wengeme, in St. *wameangama*, they have clung.

51. *wapende*, for St. *wamepanda*, they have climbed.

54. *mbwongo*, a contraction for *ni uwongo*.

57. *Ali bin Nasiri*, the poet's father. Other ancestors mentioned here are *Abubakr*, probably Abubakr b. Abdallah b. Sheikhan b. Husein b. Sheikh Abubakr b. Salim, the poet's maternal grandfather; *Idarus*, probably Aidarus b. Athman b. Ali b. Sheikh Abubakr b. Salim, the poet's distant great-uncle and author of the Hamziyya; *Muhadhar*, probably the father or paternal kinsman of Saiyid Muhammad Muhadhar, who is remembered as living during the reign of Ali b. Athman (A.D. 1738–53), second Mazrui governor of Mombasa.

wendelepi for St. *walikwenda wapi*.

mbonya for St. *nionyeshe*.

59. *Kiungu . . . Sarambi*, the quarters of Pate where the aristocracy of sharifs and sheikhs lived.

60. *Pate Yunga*, name applied to Pate and popularly said to mean 'Pate the Swaggering', but probably meaning 'Pate the United', i.e. the sultanate as distinct from the city only. The sultanate comprised the city, the island itself, and villages and territory on the mainland coast. Cf. *-unga*, join, unite. Hichens notes: 'The distinction between Pate (the town) and Pate Yunga is not always maintained in Swahili historical and literary records, and this has caused some confusion in certain European translations, especially as some Swahili chroniclers, writing *after* the rise of Pate to power, bestow the name of "Pate" upon sultanates which, though ultimately in the Pate sultanate, were originally dominant sultanates embracing Pate as a part of *their* domain.'

61. *watamiwe na nti za makaburi*, lit. they were gaped open for by the earth of the graves; *-atama*, gape open.

62. *wasiwe*, they were called; *-sa*, say, call.

63. *aimi* for *ai mimi*, ah me!

zidiwa, passive of *-zidi*, increase, excel, and here perhaps used to mean beyond compare, but Stigand reads this as *zindiwa*, little doves.

wasiriye, they are hidden, *-siri*, hide.

mahuwa, the departed.

64. *sawo* for St. *hawo*; *kamawo* for St. *kama wao*.

68. *siku ya kwima kondo*, H. translates this as 'the day of the uprising of the striving multitude', i.e. the Day of Judgement, but his translations throughout the poem are unnecessarily turgid and sometimes depart completely from the text.

69. *amtendeleo* for *aliyomtendea*, what he did to him. This passage on the Judgement, like so many passages in Swahili religious verse, is strongly Qur'ānic, cf. in Sale's translation of the Qur'ān, ch. lxxv, vv. 6 seq.: 'On that Day men shall say, "Where is a place of refuge?" By no means, there shall be no place to fly unto.'—and ch. iii 'for he who

Verse

defraudeth shall bring with him what he hath defrauded anyone on the Day of the Resurrection'.

70. *wadhilimawa* for *waliodhimuliwa*.

72. *akiukimu*, when he proclaims it; the objectival concord *-u-* refers to Jahannam.

73. *na kuta* for *na kucha*, with fearing; cf. Qur'ān, ch. xxvii, v. 87: 'On that Day the trumpet shall be sounded and whoever are in Heaven and on Earth shall be struck with Terror'. The Day of Resurrection will be heralded, in Islamic belief, by three trumpet blasts; first, the blast of consternation; second, the blast of examination; third, the blast of resurrection. Another of the greater signs will be the appearance of the Beast which, among its other unattractive characteristics, will have the voice of an ass, to which the second *kipande* in this verse refers, viz. *sauti ya punda*.

74. *hawiya*, the seventh hell. According to Muslim belief, there are seven degrees of hell, six of which are mentioned in this poem, viz. Jahannam, or hell (v. 72), *laza*, the flaming fire (v. 76, as *ladha*), *sair*, the burning fire (v. 75, as *sairi*), *hutamah*, the crushing disaster (v. 77), *jahim*, the fierce fire (v. 65), *hawiyah*, the abyss (v. 74), and *saqar*, the scorching fire.

77. *limshushiye*, lit. is made to fall from him; note Cl. 5 concord in agreement with *wasakha* or, in St. Sw., *usaha*. This is probably the end of Saiyid Abdallah's composition; the vv. 78 and 79 are, as their context shows, additions in completion.

78. *takhitimu tatia* for *nitakhitimu nitatia*.

79. *namezokhitimu* for *na alizozikhitimu*.

The Maulid of Barzanji

(Pages 104–118)

Verse

2. *nalikhitasiri* for *na amekhitasiri*, and he has abridged; note the change from 1st to 3rd pers. sing.; *-khitasiri*, from the same derivation as the nominal *mukhutasari*, St. *muhtasari*.

3. *tafawuli*, this may be for *tufuli*; Ar. *tafl*, small, minor, and so the proper name for this poem is *mukhutasari*, abridgement.

   ngwa tutimiliza, this verbal tense in *ngwa* is a common form of petition in Swahili poetry, and is discussed in Taylor's *African Aphorisms*, p. 165.

4. *fatiha*, the first chapter of the Qur'ān, used as an introductory prayer either aloud or silently.

6. *sharifu*, a direct descendant of the Prophet through the grandsons Hasan and Husein, and as such they have priority to lead in prayer.

13. *kheri toa tamu* . . . After the chanting of the Maulid, a feast is usually held in its honour. Some coastal Swahilis save money the whole year round for this purpose. In this case the author suggests that if one is unable to provide a feast on a big scale, then a smaller celebration, according to one's means, is equally acceptable to God.

Verse

14. *Sayduna Shata*, a reference to Mansab's teachers in Mecca, Saiyid Ahmad Sahlan and Abu Bakr Shata.
1. *walonakiwa*, who are praised, *-naki*, praise.
2. *iwembe*, everywhere, of what is spread about.
3. *mbeya*, lit. sex.
4. *mwana wa mtindwa*, the last child a woman bears; St. *kitinda mimba.*
   pango ya masitu . . ., the text here is corrupt, and no help can be obtained from the corresponding Arabic verse, for it is indecipherable. There is a clear reference to the Prophet's father, Abdullahi, described in the translation from the Arabic version as 'the one they were going to slaughter' (a descendant of Ishmael), and the word for a cave appears readable in the Arabic version. Our version is frankly a guess at what is meant.
6. *Abdu Manafi*, the great-great grandfather of the Prophet; his son was Abdul Muttalib, Muhammad's grandfather.
11. *siti Mariamu siti Asiya*, the Blessed Virgin Mary is *siti Mariamu*, but the identity of *siti Asiya* is uncertain, possibly 'Ā'isha, عائشة.
14. *kama hashima*, this may refer to the Prophet, like the respected one: *hashim* may also mean an ancestor of the Prophet.
16. *kijuju kikavu na baa mwitu*, the text is corrupt in both Swahili and Arabic versions here, and so the rendering must be accepted with reserve.
18. *Hasani Huseni*, Hasan and Husain were the children of Ali b. Abi Talib, the Prophet's cousin.
20. *kwa kumrehemu akichemuwa*, a reference to the tradition that the Prophet, as he was born, sneezed and began to say, 'Al-ḥamdu lillahi', Praise be to God, and all the angels of Heaven blessed him by saying, 'Tahhamaka Allah, May God bless you'.
21. *yalotupa ada*, there is no reference to an equivalent meaning in the Arabic version, and this may be a copyist's error. The translation of the equivalent Arabic reads: 'By how many miracles on the day of His Birth was the true religion founded'.
25. *alomwamsa*, for *aliyemwamisha*, who suckled him.
27. *mwaka wane wake. . . .* The Swahili version is a misinterpretation of the Arabic one, which in translation reads: 'And in the fourth year near Medina His mother went with him to join his excellent father'. The Swahili version states that the Prophet at the age of four went to Medina, but this would pre-date the Hijra, and Medina has no special significance before the Hijra.
29. *na kanga zake*, with his cloths. This is meaningless in the present context and so the Arabic version has been followed in the translation.
30. *Buraki malaki tini*, a reference to al-Isra, the journey by night on the winged steed under the direction of the Archangel Gabriel.
31. *bayiti li-Makadasi*, Ar. Bait al-Maqdis, Jerusalem. The tradition is that Muhammad led the prayers in the Great Mosque at Jerusalem and that the prophets who had preceded him were present there.
32. *zipindi zitatu*, the reference to the three times of prayer is difficult to understand. The translated Arabic version gives: 'And he shows him

Verse

some of his greatest signs and he achieves his aim in making the five prayers obligatory'.

33. *kaba kawusini*, a reference to the narrow distance that separated Muhammad from God on the night of the flight to Jerusalem. The Arabic measurement of two Arab bows is about 2 yards long. The word *qāb* in Arabic means a measurement, and *qaws* is a bow. *Qāb qaws* in Arabic may also mean the distance between stars. The Arabic version in translation here reads, 'And the beloved one approached very close (*qāb qaws*) until he saw God on high, and he became very happy'. In St. Sw. note *Ametoka kaba kauseni*, He has very narrowly escaped, i.e. from danger, &c.

36. *kangia Madina*, a reference to the Hijra. The mosque founded was the one at Quba near Medina.

48. *saa nda suudi*, Ar. *saʿad*, *suʿud*, happiness and fortune.

50. *twekewe zitaka*, this could be translated, that we may become the sweepings; the text is doubtful here.

2. *kukushiriki*, lit. to associate Thee; referring to shirk, association of Allah with other gods.

5. *tarehe Hijira . . .*, the date of composition of the poem. This is given as A.H. 1309 or A.D. 1891 in the Swahili lunar month *mfunguo saba*. The poem was copied two years later in the month of *mfunguo pili*.

7. *idadi za bayiti . . .* The copyist says that the number of Arabic verses is forty-nine and that he has added six more. This gives the correct number of fifty-five Arabic verses, each with a parallel verse, but it is impossible to say which verses were added by Abdallah himself. It is difficult to understand what is meant by *pakuzaliya*. This may refer to 'birthplace', but the meaning is not clear. In the last verse he claims to have translated from the Arabic word by word. This is not really so, though the gist of the poem is very much the same in both versions.

Strung Pearls

(Pages 118–126)

Verse

1. *wasiilahini*, from *-lahini*, find fault; cf. Ar. *lahn*, grammatical errors.

2. *bijahi*, with honour; Ar. *bi-jāh*.
   bushura, good news; Ar. *bushra*.

3. *tilika*, lit. that; Ar. *tilka*.

4. *thiki*, trust in, adhere to; Ar. *thiq*, diacritics.
   taʾa, obedience; Ar. *taʿah*.

5. *Jannati . . .*, this *kipande* is the Ar. *Jannat na ʿīm fi ʾl-jinān*.

6. *ikikunduwawa*, lit. if they be spread open; in St. *ikikunjuliwa*.

8. *jana*, from Ar. *al-jannah*, Paradise.
   daniya, insignificant, lowly; Ar. *danīyah*.

9. *dhihizini*, in Amu dialect *dhihizi* means 'the mind'; Ar. *dhihn*.
   Dhulikari-nini, Iskander or Alexander the Great, mentioned in the Qurʾān, Surat al-Kahf (xviii), v. 82 seq.; Ar. *Dhu ʾl-Qarnayn*.

Verse

11. *kutufata* for St. *kutufuata*.
12. *baidi*, from Ar. *baʿīd*, far, distant.
    likishitadi, becoming worse; the stem is *-shitadi*; Ar. *ishtadda*, become strong, &c.
13. *yatamshibu*, probably for *yatamshiba*, the final vowel suiting the rhyme; they will be sufficient for them, will make them replete.
    shufaa, intercession; Ar. *shafāʿah*.
14. *sali la jihimu*, burning in hell-fire; Ar. *ṣali īl-jahīm*.
    hari mteu, the derivation here is obscure, neither of these words as they occur in St. Sw. fitting the context.
15. *dhurubu*, strike an example; Ar. *ḍaraba maṯhalan*.
16. *zichaka* for St. *zikiwaka*.
    kokoka, a contraction of *kuokoka*, but in St. *kuokolewa*, to be saved.
17. *dhili ya ʾarishi*, shadow of a throne; Ar. *zill*, a shadow, and Ar. *ʿarsh*. throne.
18. *akirabu*, scorpions; Ar. *ʿaqrab* (sing.); *idhimu*, big ones; Ar. *ʿazim* (sing.).
19. *ghibu nepukia*, the first word is an imperative related to Ar. *ghaʿib*, absent; *nepukia* is an imperative with obj. concord, 1st pers. sing., and the full form would be *niepukia*.
20. *fi li-isirari*, in secret; Ar. *fiʿ l-ʿisrar*.
23. *ludhu billahi*, Ar. *ludh bi-llahi ṯhumma ta-ʿllahi*.
26. *wulati amri*, those having authority from God in this world and the next; Ar. *wulāt al-amr*.
29. *nazo baiti ni thalathini*, the poet gives thirty as the number of his verses, but there are in fact only twenty-nine. The letters ʾaini, mimu, and rei give the poet's name, Umar.

Al-Akida

(Pages 130–142)

Verse

3. *washabihi*, the verbal stem is *-shabihi*, resemble.
   yaum, &c., this *kipande* is Arabic.
4. *mwaka wa ijumaʾa*, a year beginning on a Friday was considered unlucky.
6. *hadha*, that; Ar. *haza*. This *kipande* means literally, that happiness long ago.
12. *ametukiwa*, in St. Sw. *amechukizwa*.
16. *Dauani*, a place name, but unidentified.
19. *tukidhi* for St. Swl. *tukisi*, *-kisi*, estimate, evaluate.
24. *asiya*, lit. a rebel.
28. *shishi . . . anti*, the meaning is obscure here, for no Arabic equivalent has been established, and the words are not Swahili.
32. *chumba cha Wadi Mataka*, Sheikh Mataka of Siu, who had governed Siu, Faza, and Pate, was defeated by the Sultan of Zanzibar and imprisoned in this cell in Fort Jesus.
36. *Ramadhani Kazabeka*, probably a contemporary of the poet.
43. *laala*, it is possible that; Ar. *laʿala*.

Verse

katatanyuwa, subjectival concord *a-* omitted; the stem is *-tatanyuwa*.

45. *nisufahawu*, probably for *nisiufahamu*, without my understanding it.

53. *Rambi Saji*, not identified, but perhaps a Baluchi soldier.

70. *Gaeti*, not identified.

72. *tangu*, of being first; cf. *-tangulia*, be in front.

90. *yenele*, in St. Sw. this *kipande* would read *Baridi ilienea rohoni mwake*.

92. *hu* for *huwi*.

98. *ali* for *ahali*, member of a family; *ahli shari*, of the family of evil.

Love Song

(Page 142–144)

A version of this poem was given without translation by H. E. Lambert in No. 23 of the *Journal of the East African Swahili Committee.*

Verse

1. *mpwasi*, Lambert gives *mbasi*, a friend, but *mpwasi* is an alternative to *mapwaji*, coast, foreshore.

   kwa cha, the word *kijiti* must be understood after *kwa*, and Lambert inserts it in brackets.

2. *uwembe*, Lambert's reading is *uwambe*.

   kwa ya ndovu-kanga, ya relates to unexpressed *pembe*, horn; *ndovukanga* in St. is *tembo mchanga*, baby elephant, and so here the meaning is the tusk of the young elephant.

4. *waye wakele ti*, Lambert gives *waye wa kileti*, let the clever ones come; but *kileti* is not known by any of my informants.

5. This verse is missing in the Lambert version.

8. *ta*, imperative of *-ta*, put forth, strike.

9. *jaizimu*, Lambert is no doubt right in referring this to *jazmah* (*sukūn*), the circle in Arabic writing to denote the absence of a vowel; he gives the corresponding standard version for this, viz. *Tazama jazma jinsi tao lako lizingavyo.*

11. *utengee*, cf. *-tengea*; in St. it is *-tengenea*, be in good order.

    na pasiyaona, and there has not yet been seen. Lambert gives: *napa siyaona*, I swear I have never seen.

    huota miyanga, there spring forth graces; *miyanga*, things that give light, shinings, graces. Lambert gives: *kwakuta mianga*, and in his notes gives *kwakuta* or *kwatoka*, there comes forth.

13. *zizidiye wino*, Lambert has *zaidi ya wino*.

    zitaliye kono, perfect of *-tala*, thrust forth, put forth, and here referring to *nshi*, eyebrows. Lambert gives *zitwalie kono* and gives St. version, viz. *zimetwalia* (*umbo wa*) *mikono*.

    tando, Cl. 10, anything spread out, tapestries, screens.

15. *zifungu huribu* or *zifungu hughibu*. Lambert: *zivungu hurebu*. *-rebu* or *-ribu*, vanish; Ar. *haraba*, flee, disappear, but more probably for *hughebu*, from *-ghaibu*, be unobtainable, be lost. The implication is that the arches of the nose (*zifungu*) are scarcely visible.

    nisita hesabu, I am in doubt as to the number; but Lambert reads this as *ni sita hesabu*, they are six in number, and he notes that though the arches or depressions are scarcely visible, they are six in number. 'The lady would claim to be one of the class known as *waungwana walio na pua nde*, i.e. the highborn who have long noses.'

kuziwanga, to count them, *-wanga*, count.

17. *mkatekate*, simsim oil; prefix *ya* agrees with *mafuta*, oil.

mafuta yakinga for *mafuta ya kukinga*, protective oil. Lambert reads *mafuta ya kwenga* and gives St. as *mafuta yaliyosafishwa sana*.

19. *kamba takwambaye*, in St. *kusema nitakuambiaje*, As for speaking, what shall I tell you?

tatongoa iye, in St. *nitatangaza namna gani*? In Amu dialect *iye* stands for St. *je*?, the interrogative particle.

humo yengayenga, the verb here is *-engaenga*, hesitate, quiver on the brink, i.e. her teeth in her mouth move gently in view. Lambert prefers to relate this verbal to *-lengalenga*, and he gives *humwayengayenga*, in which the vowel *-a-* would then be part of the stem, thus annulling any connexion with *-lengalenga*. In full our text would read : *menoye humo yaenga-enga*, her teeth therein hesitate upon the brink (i.e. of her lips).

20. *akhadharu*, green; Ar. *ad̲kh̲ar*.

shamaru, rose or fennel; Ar. *shamār*.

iwaayo, which shines; *-waa*, shine, glitter.

21. *mkakasi*, a vanity box, of many colours; *ya* refers to *rangi*, colour, which is unexpressed.

ni kufana basi, lit. it is the resemblance therefore, i.e. it is like.

22. *huradidi*, lit. gives back, returns (of her breath); Ar. *radd*.

mkadi, a screw pine with a strongly scented flower, *Pandanus kirkii*; also known in Arabic as *kadhi*.

23. *khassa kidodosi*, lit. especially when she hesitates; *-dodosi*, hesitate in speech, drawl, lisp. Lambert reads *Khasa kidurusi*, and relates *-durusi* to Ar. *darasa*. The meaning might then be 'especially if she proclaims, or speaks out'.

hudengemu, it sounds clearly; Lambert gives *hudighimu*.

yanga, the air.

25. *umbile*, the creature; *karima*, God, the Beneficent.

iyaliye for *ijaliile*, *-jalia*, grant.

The Poem of the Poor Man
(Page 146)

Verse

1. *haisi*, he does not know: *-isi*, know.

hulia, applied form of *-la*, eat.

2. *tule sute* or *tule sote*, but this does not fit the context. Preferable, then, *mtule*, a person of low estate, and *sute*, wasteful.

mwawi, upsetter; cf. *-wawa*, irritate, itch, but this may not be the same verbal here. We follow Taylor's translation.

3. *ha haya* for *hana haya*.

yuwaya, in St. *huwayawaya*, he staggers and sways.

4. *nyota* for St. *kiu*.

The Dream Song
(Pages 146–147)

Verse

1. *ndele*, perfect tense, for St. *nimelala*.
   totomile or *totomele*, subjectival concord *ni-* omitted.
   ndosele, perfect of *-lota*, 1st pers. sing.
2. *ndoseya* for St. *niliotea*; perfect with final vowel *-e* modified perhaps to
   make the rhyme.
   toshee miuya for *nitoshele ni miuja*, I was astounded at the danger.
   nduya for *ndugu yangu*, my kinsman.
3. *nguu kaiyuma*, probably for *nguvu zikajiuma*, lit. (my) strength injured itself.
   ukanima, the verb *-nima* is not known, and this might be a contraction of
   ukaninyima, it refused me, deprived me.
4. *amwawo*, from *amua*, tiptoe; relative with concord omitted of the subject.
   ndonawo for *nilio nao* or *niliokuwa nao*.
5. *ndeteya* for *niletea*, bring to/for me.
   msu chuga chia, probably for *msu nikichuga nikichia*, the sword, I being un-
   prepared and afraid about (not having it). In St. Sw. *-chugachuga*, be in a
   state of uneasiness at not being prepared.
6. *ninoe*, in St. this would be *nanolea*, I sharpen.

The Warrior Song
(Page 147)

mngwa, an alien. Hichens gives this as 'a semi-mythical beast, also referred to
as nunda or nungwa'. Johnson gives *nunda*, a fierce animal or beast of
prey. But this is more likely a nominal with stem *-ngwa*. This stem is
used as an enclitic in Amu dialect, e.g. *shokangwa*, an axe belonging to
other people. Taylor called this the possessive of alienation (*African
Aphorisms*, pp. 166–7).

kaninwa mafuta for *akaninywa mafuta*, lit. and drink me the fat. This construction, though no longer used in Swahili, is typically Bantu, e.g. in *Venda*,
Onndya mapfura, he deprived me of my strength. In the poem it might
mean 'and overcomes me'.

ngwa, probably for *mngwa*.

mwanangwa, a son of other people. This term was used by the indigenous
tribes in reference to the descendants of the Arab immigrants, the nobly
born. Cf. in the *Utendi wa Herkal*, v. 27, '*Na wanginewe ansari wanangwa wa
kuteteya*', and other men, valiant noblemen.

fili, an elephant; Ar. *fīl*.

liuwalo mwangwa, Hichens gives *liowalo mwangwa*, and translates 'death-
charmed by a wizard'. The subject of the relative is *fumo*, a spear, and
the relative verbal is *-uwa* or *-ua*, kill. The word for wizard is *mwanga*,
not *mwangwa*, and both may be read from the script. Taylor (op. cit.,
p. 5) gives *mwamnda* or *katika vitu vya mnda*, i.e. Paradise, Garden of
Eden. The phrase might be translated literally as 'which kills in the
things of others', and is taken to mean here 'in affairs concerning the
alien'.

fiya, the spitting cobra (in other manuscripts and different contexts as *fira, firi, piri, pili*; Ar. *afʿā*, viper. This could also be read as 'rhino', occurring also as *peya*, and in St. as *pera*.

kwa bidiya, *-bidia*, applied form of *-bidi*, compel, put pressure on; in St. *kwa bidia*, by being forced to it.

Utendi wa Hati
(Pages 148–158)

Utendi wa Adili
(Pages 160–170)

These two poems are modern works and although they contain many words that are not in everyday use, these may be found in the dictionaries of Krapf, Sacleux, and Johnson. Since the translation is provided and there are no textual difficulties—for they were written only in roman script—no annotation is considered necessary for these two poems.

Play the buffalo-horn
(Page 175)

pijia for *pigia*, strike on something, beat, play; this injunction to sound the buffalo-horn is a conventional opening for many of the old songs.

kukuteneke, perfect of *-kutanika*, be met together; prefix *ku-* is the locative.

washorongwa, players of drums and cymbals at a dance-tourney.

nyemi, pl. of *ukemi*, shout, cry, joyful noise; cf. *-nyema*, make a joyful noise.

wasikiyewo, this could be for *wasikileo* for St. *waliosikia*, but a more likely reading is to take this as a contraction of *uwasikie leo*, hear them today.

mshika gogo, the one who holds the drum-stick or gong-stick.

towazi, cymbal or large castanet.

azaziyewo for *azazileo* for St. *aliyemzaa*, who bore him.

siku ya yeo, lit. the day of today. Hichens translates this as *sikuja leo*, I did not come today. From this he claims to interpret the poem as a dialogue in which the suitor pleads with a maid to accompany him to a dance, and she refuses.

kawete for *ukawaite*, and call them.

The Song of Shagga
(Page 176)

mmbeja, pl. *wambeja*, a lady of culture.

mwiwa or *muwiwa*, pl. *wawiwa*, a clever, sensible person.

kikaze, probably for *akikaza*.

wasi washinda for St. *wasipokuwapo watu wa kushinda*, where no people dwell.

kasite, from *-sita*, hide; cf. *yufite*, with modified stem and concord *yu-*.

yuu tumuyeni, Hichens translates this as, Let us slay him up aloft. The verbal here is *-uya*, leave, and the full form is *tumuuyeni*.

ngozi kiyungwa, the locality of Kiungwa, now mapped as Kiongwe, to the immediate south of Ras Mtio. For the people of Kiongwe and their migration to Tanga, see 'Habari za Mrima', by Sheikh b. Hemedi, *Mambo Leo*, 1934, p. 134.

tapo, wild fruit like the areca-nut; in St. *popoo*.

kila tiwiye, probably for *tukila chiwi je*, Our eating a bad thing, why?

wa sisi, this is not in concordial agreement with *kikoa*.

yunga or *yu nga*, he is like.

koka for *huokoka*, he escapes.

Pani kiwanda niteze

(Page 177)

pani for St. *nipe*.

kiwanda for St. *kiwanja*; this is another conventional opening.

mweni for St. *mgeni*.

utimbile for St. *aliyechimba*.

muole for St. *mkaone*; *-ola*, see.

kushindwa, the passive here is read as being related to the phrase *maji yashinda kisimani*, water is left in the well, i.e. there is still some left.

Serenade 1

(Page 179)

siliye, concord omitted, for *usilie*.

ukaliza, Hichens translates this as 'listen to, attend to', relating the verb to *-kalia* from *-kaa*, but in other contexts this verb is of fairly frequent occurrence and may be the causative of *-lia*, cry out.

walimbezi, Hichens gives this as 'suitors', but this word has not been traced in any dictionary. It may be *walembezi*, cf. *-lembea*, reach down something from a height.

wenezi, the distributors (of news), cf. *-eneza*; *mwenezi* is also a title for God, the Distributor.

nkutuze, with *nku-* a monosyllable; in St. Sw. *nitukuze*.

kuwakie for *nikuakie*, let me build for you; similarly *kupambie* for *nikupambie*, let me decorate for you.

waowao or *waowawo*, from *-oa*, look at.

wanika, a difficult word here, and only a tentative translation is given.

wa kangange, *wa* before this and the next two words is Arabic for 'and'; Johnson gives *kanganga*, tall reeds or a fern with fronds.

ngoi or *ngui*, possible for *ngozi*, skins.

nana, mint; Ar. *naʿnaʿ*.

wakuteshe for *niwakutishe*, let me involve them in, or, more probably, let me satisfy them, *-kuta*, be satisfied with food.

wamia, imperative, stretch out on the ground, be relaxed lying down.

wali tumbaizi for *walipo watumbaizi*, or more correctly, *watumbuizi*, people who soothe by singing, serenaders.

kitinda, Hichens translates this as 'the young of', but it is more likely for St. *nikichinja*, while I slaughter.

kuwa, strength, energy; Ar. *quwwah*.

yangumi for St. *yangu mimi*.

maozi, eyes; cf. *-oa*, see, look at.

Serenade 2

(Page 180)

mukenge, a fugitive.

yuu la namiri for St. *juu ya chui*; Ar. *namīr*. Note Cl. 5 prefix used in agreements that are in Cl. 9 and 10 in St. Sw.

yuasiye, concord *yu-* of 3rd pers. sing., for St. *aliyemwasi*.

wapozewe, perfect of *-pozewa*, the causative of *-powa*.

wasowene for St. *wasioona*, past or present tense in St.

hawezeki, neuter of *-weza*; in St. *hawezekani*.

huyule, demonstrative of reference, for St. *huyo*.

The Wine Song

(Page 181)

uchi, in Giriama means palm-wine.

mbata, coco-nut in last stage of ripeness, yielding a bitter sap; good wine drawn through the stem of a bitter-sapped nut, when fermented, yields a liquor of thick consistency not unlike kümmel in appearance and like schnapps in taste.

tesheweo for St. *uliotekwa*, perfect of the passive, with relative concord and omission of subjectival concord.

uyayongao kwa zungu for St. *uyayongeshao kwa kizunguzungu*, lit. which makes them (*maguu*, legs) stagger with giddiness.

nyunguni, in the cooking-pots; cf. in the same line, *nyungu*, strength, pungency.

kuwewa for St. *kulewa*, to be drunk.

nilitake, perfect in suffix *-e* of *-taka*, with objectival infix Cl. 5.

embekungu, lit. edged sword; *embe*, sword; cf. *jembe*, a hoe, and cf. *-kunga*, trim, make a border.

mani or *maani*, in St. Sw. *jani*, pl. *majani*.

mba, contraction of *ni wa*.

tungutungu, species of *Euphorbia* known as *mtupa*.

kangika for *likiangika*.

mavungu or *mavugo* or *mavugu*, horns, usually of the African buffalo, sometimes provided with an orifice for blowing, or else played by being beaten with a stick.

magoma ya ezi, the state-drums, beaten only by permission of the ruler or governor; also known as *ngoma kuu* or *vikoma mle*. Wherever it was taken to be beaten it had to remain until a further occasion arose for its use when, upon its removal to another place, it likewise remained there until it was required again. This drum was never put on the ground, and when not in use was hung upon a peg.

mawano mawano, fighting weapons; *-wana*, fight, engage combat; also notched sticks used in divination.
bangu, war.

The Lament

(Page 181)

kuwawato, radical *-wawa*, with intensive suffix *-to*.
shaha shagga, not *shaha shaka*, a title that might have been applied to Liyongo. Hichens notes that the title 'leopard' is meant to apply to Liyongo, but there is no evidence for this.

The Bathing Song

(Page 182)

noa for *naoga*.
chifua for *nikifua*.
nguoza for *nguo zangu*.
mbwenepo for *nionapo* or *nilipoona*.
nisisaze, causative of *-sa*, finish; note the applied form *kasia*. In full this might read *nisisaze hata nikasia nyota*.
nisiize, the stem is *-iza*, refuse.

The Bow Song

(Page 182)

chitanzu for *kitanzu*; note *chi-* for *ki-* in other words, *chiyo, chondoka*, &c.
mtoriyo for *mtorio, Landolphia petersiana*, a wild rubber-vine; the consonant *ya* in the Arabic script is retained throughout in the rhyme-endings because in the last word of the poem it is a functioning consonant. Muhammad Kijuma's manuscript copy of this poem reads either *mbungo* or *mbogo* for *mtoriyo*. The substitution is to provide a more satisfactory rhyme. *Mbungo, Landolphia florida. Mbogo*, a buffalo. Bows of buffalo-horn are still in use by some of the frontier tribes of Kenya.
chiyo for *kioo*, a mirror, a piece of glass.
shikilole kwa mautiyo for St. *sikio lake kwa magutio; -gutia*, shriek.
hepe, verbal interjection; cf. *-hepa*, move aside.
Mwana Mbwasho, Liyongo's mother is referred to in several songs as *Mbwasho*; this could also mean 'Lady Mbwasho', but omission of the possessive element (*mwana wa* . . .) is common in Swahili poetry, and the meaning 'son of . . .' is preferred.
nasha for *na acha*, and leave.
matayo, your weapons; *mata*, pl. of *uta*, bow, with enclitic *-yo* of 3rd pers. sing. of the possessive.

Sifa ya Mnazi

(Page 183)

niwambie for St. *niwaambieni*.
unzapo for St. *uanzapo*.

yanga panga wazi, lit. are like open swords.

huyangua for *huyaangua*, *-angua*, throw down.

hwambua for *huambua*; the combination of a consonant with the vowel *-u-* is often monosyllabic in poetry for the sake of the rhyme.

kifuvuche for *kifuvu chake*.

takize for *chaki zake*.

hamwaya for *wakamwaga*.

katakura yimbi for *akachakura jimbi*.

fusizi for *fusi zakwe* or *fusize*, the final vowel being modified for the sake of the rhyme.

kigogoche for *kigogo chake*.

Sifa ya Ndoa
(Page 184–185)

wandaniwa for *wandani wangu*.

wachanguwa for *wakiangua*.

mnga, a tree, spec. incog., but perhaps for *mninga*.

mtuwa, a shrub or common weed, *Solanum bojeri*.

kongolewa for *wakaongolewa*, and they are granted.

The Aggrieved Wife
(Page 185–186)

unindoziewo, perfect of the radical *-lola*, marry (St. *oa*) in its causative form *-loza*; objectival concord *-ni-* plus *-l-* gives *-nd-*, and relative concord is *-o-* for St. *-ye-*; in St. *uliyenioza*. There is an apparent repetition of the objectival concord, which is difficult to explain. The radical may be *-ndoza*.

mpewo, excess, extreme behaviour, cf. *-pea*.

The Liyongo Takhmis
(Pages 188–192)

M. refers to Meinhof's edition, W. to Werner's, B. to Büttner's, and S. to Steere's texts.

Verse

1. *nabudi* for *nabtadi* or *nabutadi*, I begin; Ar. *nabtadī*.

   kawafi, rhyme; Ar. *qawafi*.

   wajiwaji, S. and M. read this as *wanjiwanji* and translate as 'much, much', but our reading is supported by W., a version taken down from dictation.

   kisiza for *nikisiza*, causative of *-sia*, come to an end.

   kadaliza for *nikaandaliza*, and that I may set out in order.

   kisikiliza for *nikaishiliza* (S.), and that I may bring to completion.

   The metaphor of the lantern-light in this verse is taken from the Qur'ān, Sura 24, An-Nūr, v. 35.

Verse

2. *mwendo* for *mwenzo* or *mwenzio*, your friend.
   ujitile, in St. *ujitie*; the *-l-* in this position may indicate an Amu form *-tila* for *-tia*.
   kani, strength, vigour.
   mbonaye, contraction for *muwonaje*; in St. *mwonaje*.
   mbuzi wako . . ., &c., S. and M. translate this as 'Child, how see you your goat in the pathway, its horns held and a milker milking it?' This translation is effected by reading *mbuzi*, goat, for *mmbuzi*, gossip, companion; *pembe*, horn, for *pembe*, restricted space, corner; *mkami*, milker, for *mkami*, bully; and *-kama*, milk, for *-kama*, threaten, press upon.
3. *mbuya* for *umbu yangu*, my fellow, companion.
   yakujelele, probably perfect of *-jalia*, happen to, grant to, with objectival concord *-ku-*.
   huyi, cf. *-huyi*, urge, put pressure upon.
   kavilekele, S. has this for *havikuelekea*, but both forms are obscure.
   muhakara, shame; Ar. *ḥaqara*, despise.
4. *napa* for *naapa*, I swear.
   mkengeufu, a waverer, *-kengeuka*, be diverted from path or purpose; cf. *mukenge*, a fugitive.
   limbwagazapo, lit. when it hurls me down.
   nalekeza for *naelekeza*.
   katokoza for *nikachokoza*.
   hambiwi for *haambiwi*.
   ninawi, or better *ninawe*, you are mine, lit. I have you; S. translates this as 'wrong and wrong', but this cannot be correct.
   ingatama, even though it come to an end; Ar. *tamma*.
5. *sono*, ease, rest.
   wambo, slanderer; cf. *-amba*, slander, abuse.
   siwenendi for St. *siwaendei*; but S. gives *siwatayi*, I do not mention them.
   muwi, Hichens suggests that this is *muwi*, with radical *-uw-* or *-u-* kill, and so meaning killer, cf. *-wi*, bad, which usually gives *mbi* in Cl. 1.
   kondo, war, conflict.
   mbi kalima, lit. bad voice; the word-order is reversed, and this is very frequent in poetry. Ar. *kalimah*.
6. *msi lango*, lit. wherein there is no door; *msi*, locative *m-* with negative of defective verbal *-li*.
   kapija kifa for *nikapiga kifua*.
   ili, S. gives this as a contraction of *kwa ajili*, and he may be right.
   tule, grievous, hurtful, vexatious; *-tua*, vex, and the order of words is reversed in *tule sifa*.
   tende hakhafa, I make it a small matter; *tende* for *nitende*, perfect, not subjunctive.
   mpeo, a victor, a perfect person; *-pea*, attain the acme of perfection, achieve a record.
7. *harubu*, affray, battle; Ar. *harb*.
   mzafafa, bridal procession on the *lailat al-dukhlah* or night of entrance; Ar. *zafāf*.

Verse

    mtanganya, one who is proud of something.

    khazaya, disgrace; Ar. *khizyān*, pl. *khazāyā*.

    kumbona for *kuniona*. S. translates this 'fearing only disgrace and that my enemy should see me behind people', i.e. in a cowardly position.

8. *sioneki* for St. *sionekani*, I am not visible.

    yama, concourse, throng, in this context of birds.

9. *nithika*, S. gives *nithiika*, M. gives 'von Ar. wathaqa, imp. yathiku'.

    maongope, hasty, proud speech.

    akupe, from *-kupa*, blink, flinch.

    shirikene, S. and M. prefer the meaning 'share' in the sense of the vulture and the beasts of the field sharing life together, but *-shiriki* can have another meaning, e.g. *-shiriki ulevi*, addicted to drink, and here the preferred meaning is of the vulture addicted or devoted to preying upon other animals.

    tope, antelope.

    na mlisha . . ., &c., lit. and the animal browsing on grass on the plain and the mountain-range.

    tani, the same as *yani*, grass.

    zingulima, occurs also as *vyengulima*, mountain-range.

10. *paa*, lit. roof, used here for *utosi*, crown of the head.

    niushile, cf. *-usha*, fly upward, leap upward.

11. *ningatindangile*, I would thrust through; *-tindanga*, push through forest or bush from one side to another.

    sakini, knife; Ar. *sikkin*.

    kiupeka for *nikiupeleka*.

    mwamba, the vault of the sky.

12. *uketeze*, in St. *umekatazwa*.

    wama huwa biqauli, &c., this is from the Qur'ān, Sura 69, v. 41.

    tufutufu, whirling, cf. *-tufa*, go round.

    kamwezi, initial *k-* is probably for *h-*, cf. ditto in *kavilekele* in v. 3.

    Ungama, an ancient town on the shores of what is now Formosa Bay at the southern affluent of the Tana River, which is said to have been overwhelmed by a tidal wave as a punishment for the arrogance and wastefulness of its townspeople, cf. Krapf, p. 405 of his Dictionary.

Wajiwaji

(Pages 192–200)

Verse

2. *kawa kama soyo*, in St. *ningekuwa kama huyo*.

3. *siwe* for *usiwe*; *pite*, the same meaning as *jura* (Johnson).

    tono la mai, in St. *tone la maji*, a drop of water, but here meaning the embryo, a Qur'ānic expression.

    lalokaa, in St. *lililokaa*.

4. *ndiyo yalokuwa*, in St. *ndivyo ilivyokuwa*.

    walimo for *ulikuwamo*.

Verse

thamma, then, while, as well as; Ar. *thumma*.

6. *utunushiyelo*, perfect with extra relative suffix *-lo*; Johnson gives *-tunuka*, set the heart upon.
   hukuwa . . ., &c., in St. *hukuwa ukishukuru kwa vitendo vyake*.
   hungurumza likitetema, the concord *li-* agrees with *fumo*, spear; *hungurumza* may mean either 'it is glittering' or 'he brawls', and the latter meaning is preferred.
7. *huwaliza, -waliza*, consider, contemplate doing.
8. *yawawo* for *yau*, like that; St. *hivyo*.
   ukaziewo, perfect with relative extra suffix; in St. *uliyokalia* or *ulimokaa*.
   gura, in St. *-hama*.
9. *dhati*, purpose, intention; Ar. *dhāt*. An alternative reading is as follows:
   Dhati ya mateto ukitaka wateta naye . . ., A real conflict, if you like, you may wage with him . . .
10. *lati tini*, in St. *ya nchi chini*.
    fi li, in St. *katika*.
11. *kwali*, in St. *kulikuwako*.
13. *nalondikiwa*, the concord is *-lo-*, but this is not in agreement with *umri*.
14. *zundushanye ito*, cf. *-zundukana*, be awake from sleep; in St. *-fumbua macho*, open the eyes.
    ufenyeo, perfect of *-fanya*, in relative construction.
15. *upetecho*, perfect of *-pata*, in relative construction.
    usambe . . ., &c., an alternative reading in the manuscripts is *Usambe kwamba umri huwa yakukata*.
    ushengee, perfect of *-shangaa*.
    uhali mama, state of speechlessness.
16. *aloyokoza*, in St. *aliyejiokoa* or *aliyejiokoza*.
17. *kukokoza* for *kukuokoza*.
    arikani, the five pillars of Islam.
18. *zikupasize*, in St. *zikupasazo*.
    ala, expression of impatience.
    usiziweze, the use of the objectival concord *-zi-* in this subjunctive is typical of the Amu dialect; in St. it would be omitted.
19. *usiyatoka*, this is a fairly frequently employed tense in poetry. In St. the same meaning would be expressed thus: *usitoke kabla ya wakati haujatimia*.
    tumu, the fast of Ramadhan.
21. *ukinuka* for St. *ukiisha*.
    mwati mwa ufukoni, the cavity in which a dead body is placed in a grave was called *ufuko*; *mwati*, inside.
    twawanye for *tugawanye*.
22. *ini huwatinda*, lit. the liver burns them; the liver was believed to be the seat of the affections.
24. *mato ya paani*, Hinawy gives this as 'the eyes on the crown of the head'.
    Paani may mean 'on the forehead'; cf. St. *pajani*, but also 'on the roof/s'.
    The latter is preferred, but a literal translation is not possible.
    yangafumbuwa, in St. *ingawa yamefumbuliwa*.

Verse

25. *enushao*, the concord is left out, and the stem is *-enusha*.

26. *nida* for St. *wito*.

27. *teya* for St. *teleza*; the phrase here would be as follows in St.: *watu ni wengi watakaoteleza*.

29. *uzo uzowezee*, *uzo* is a nominal related to the verbal *-uza*, ask, and *uzowezee* is a relative with perfect ending of the verbal *-zoweza*.

Prayer for Rain

(Pages 202–206)

Verse

1. *nasalia*, I pray for; applied form of *-sali*; in St. *namwombea*.

   tanadi, in Ar. *tunādī*, lit. you call; the day when God calls souls to judgement.

   asi for *waasi*; Ar. *ʿasī*.

2. *alize*, here *ali*, family, race, Prophet's family; *-ze* is the possessive enclitic.

   thama, alike, equally; Ar. *thumma*.

   ajiri, reward; Ar. *ajr*. In St. *-ajiri*, hire, engage for wages.

   siku ya kwima, lit. the day of standing, in this context of standing in battle.

   shururi, evils; Ar. *shurūr*, pl. of *sharr*.

   shima, quality; Ar. *shīmah*. Note that in this *kipande* the nasal of *ndio* (which is not indicated in the script) is not syllabic, though in speech it would be. This is for the sake of the measure. Note also that in v. 5 the nasal *m-* in *mlangoni* and in *mtatuzi* is syllabic, but in v. 3 in *mbwene* it is not, whereas in everyday speech initial nasal would be syllabic in each of these examples.

   dhuli na ari, cf. Ar. *dhull*, humiliation, and *ʿār*, disgrace.

   waokene na J., lit. they have saved one another from Hell; *waokene*, perfect of *-okoana*.

4. *Ai Subuhana*, from Ar. *Allāhu subhānahu*, God, glory be to Him.

   Muwawazi, Disposer of Events, a Bantu title, not Arabic; cf. *-awaza* or *-awadha*, allot, arrange, dispose.

5. *twemele* or *twimile*, perfect of *-ima*, stand.

   mtatuzi, entanglement; in St. *mtatizo*; *-tatua*, disentangle.

   lutufu, charm, kindness; Ar. *lutf*.

6. *utunyesheleze*, a double causative; *-nyesha*, rain, is the causative of *-nya*, of rainfall, be discharged; *-nyesheleza* is the causative of the applied form of *-nyesha*.

7. *mwenye kuwa*, either The Existing One (relating *kuwa* to *-wa*, be) or All-Powerful One, relating *kuwa* to Ar. *quwwah*.

   kuni, the Arabic imperative *kun*, Be!

   wala kutendewa, lit. nor to be done for, to, on behalf of, i.e. God acts and needs no one to act for Him.

   Jala Rabbi, cf. in Ar. *Jalla Rabbi*, my Lord is glorified.

8. *waayisi*, in St. the verbal is *-ajizi*, e.g. *chakula hiki hutia ajizi maungoni*, this food makes the body slack or weak.

   thakili, cf. Ar. *thaqīl*, heavy.

Verse
  tunafisi, in St. *utunafidhi*, save us.
9. *hako*, in St. *hakuna*.
  katu, not at all; Ar. *qaṭʿan*.
  aza, torment; Ar. *adḥā*.
10. *havi*, shaka, for *hakuna shaka*.
  kamurudi, subjectival concord *a-* omitted.
  maani for *maana*; suffix modified for sake of the rhyme.
  ashosilima for St. *asiyesilimu*.
12. *uduuni*, this is obscure, and the translation here is tentative.
17. *usho* for *usio*, in agreement with *shanga*, or better *ushanga*.

Mugogoto wa zamani

(Page 209–210)

Verse
1. *mugogoto wa zamani*, lit. the hammering or knocking of old; *-gogota, knock*, tap.
  ukihimu, in St. *ukihimiza*.
  makao nduni, Taylor's note reads: *wakaao kivita au kwa hadhari*. Cf. Johnson, *nduni*, a novelty, a new thing; *duni*, poverty, wretchedness.
  Mkongowea or *Kongowea*, Mombasa; *weni*, the rock on which Fort Jesus at Mombasa was built.
2. *masombo*, loin-cloths worn by men; cf. *vikobwe*, ditto worn by women.
  sambo, a sailing-vessel of the dhow type; prob. Ar. *sambook*.
  hariwo, the cry, *Hario we*, made on seeing a vessel approaching.
  wayawiapo, from *-yawia*, appear on the field of battle.
3. *waiyewo* for *wajileo*, who have come.
  Mwana Aziza, Taylor writes: There were famous queens on the East Coast in old times of whom the names still remain: Mwana Aziza, of Zanzibar, Mwana Mkisi, of Mombasa, and Mwana Masuru, of Siu.

Kongowea ja mvumo

(Pages 211–212)

Notes on this poem were made by Taylor in his *African Aphorisms*, pp. 81–82.

Verse
1. *Gongwa*, a name for Mombasa.
  mwina . . ., &c., this can be read, 'hole of darkness evil that', but whatever the reading *mbwi* does not have concordial agreement with either *mwina* or *kisa*; *mbwichile* may be a single word and a verb, but it is not identifiable.
3. *Nyalikuwu* for *Nyalikuu*, a synonym here for Mombasa, but actually Nyali on the mainland, a mile or two north-east of the present harbour of Mombasa.
4. *usitupile*, applied form of *-tupa*, leap (*-t-* in the stem is aspirated); cf. *-tupa*, throw; *kutupa ukuta*, leap over a wall.
5. *ilitutile*, *-tutia*, rise high, be lofty.

Watumba mji wa kale

(Pages 214–215)

Verse

1. *watumba*, pl. of *mtumba* (see Johnson); used metaphorically.
   mji wa kale, the old township of Mombasa.
   watasile, cf. *-tasa*, perplex, be perplexed.
   kutinda fundo, the word *fundo* here is probably used in the sense of resentment or contention; *kutinda*, to cut, perhaps here in the same way as *-kata* is used, e.g. *-kata maneno*, end a case, pass judgement.
2. *jisadi*, Ar. *jasad*.
5. *waoleweyo* for *waoleweo*; in St. *walioolewa*.

Risala wa Kongoweya

(Page 217–218)

No annotation.

Nilime mnda Ngozini

(Page 219–220)

Verse

1. *mnda* or *munda*, cultivate plot.
   zipungushewo or *zipungushweo*; in St. *zilizopunguzwa*.
   kikanda, a measure of quantity of grain; 1 *kikanda* = 45 *pishi*.
2. *mbambe*, a plot of cultivated land.
   nlilo, in St. *lililo*.
   kongo, the hole made in the earth for planting seed. The literal translation of this line is either: 'The one who is stooped to the earth is the hoe', or, 'He who is stooped to the earth with hoe, rises with what is in the grain-hole.'
   mrai, imperative; *-rai*, flatter.
   mpembe, imperative; *-pemba*, outwit.
   kiwango, a cowry shell, a form of currency.
3. *siswi*, an obscure word and the meaning here is tentative, though in other contexts this is the independent pronoun 'we'.
4. *panda*, a forked stick for marking the boundary of a plot.
5. *kusenye* for *wakusenye*; in St. *walikusanyika*.
   usiyanambia for *usijaniambia*; in St. *hujaniambia*.
   kusiya or *kusia*, applied form of *-sa*, come to an end.

The Judge and the Sorcerer's Client

(Pages 226–232)

This poem is published in the Appendix to Vol. 2 of *Dictionnaire Swahili–Français*, by Sacleux, pp. 1108–12.

Verse

1. *Ghofira*, forgiveness; Sacleux has *rafughu*.
2. *mizi* for *mizizi*, roots.

Verse
3. *wambwawo* for St. *unaoambiwa*.
   moto, Sacleux has *mutu*.
4. *mwapa* for *mwawapa*, you give them.
5. *chamba*, either for *ukiamba* (St. *ukisema*), or *kwamba*, that.
6. *nikwelezavo*, the rhyme is in symbols *fei* and *wau*, which can be transcribed either as *-vo* or as *-vyo*. In Mvita dialect *-vo* is heard in place of *-vyo*, and the present text may well show Mvita characteristics.
7. Sacleux's text has only seven *vipande* in this verse, and their order differs from that in the present version.
8. *mezi* for *miezi*.
   uzi for St. *udhi*.
10. *yatuambiwe*, Sacleux has *yatuambale*, but this does not rhyme.
11. This verse has only six *vipande* in Sacleux's text.
13. *wajiwapo*, when they are under the influence; *-jiwa*, passive of *-ja*, come.
17. The last *kipande* of this verse is missing in Sacleux's text.
20. *kusuduku*, in St. *kusadiki*.
    udhiya, Sacleux has *shughuli*, which does not rhyme.

The Forge Song
(Pages 234–238)

Verse
1. *eshe simanzi* for *aishe simanzi*, lit. that he should stop (his) tears.
   kwelewo for *kweleo* or *koleo*, tongs, pincers.
2. *tusiufunue mwawo*, lit. without our revealing the scurrilous reports.
3. *yapisiyewo* for St. *yaliyopita*, the concord refers to unexpressed nominal, *mambo*, matters, affairs.
   ikeshawo for St. *Inayokesha*, *-kesha*, watch until morning.
9. *zije za juu*, *zije* may be related to *-ja*, come; this is colloquial for northwest wind.
   demani, mainsail sheet.
   joshini, to windward; also called *upande wa juu*.
10. *ukiifunuwa*, lit. if you discover it, i.e. the land.
    upinduwe for *upindue*, tack about, lit. turn over.
    umande, land wind, also dew.
12. *Shekhe letu*, note use of Cl. 5 prefix.
    kitutu, a little; cf. *katiti*.
16. *uswa*, passive of causative *-usa* from *-uka*.

Risala wangu bashiri
(Page 238)

Verse
1. *huuri*, probably for *huri*, lit. a free-born person, also *huru*; the long vowel here maintains the syllabic measure.
3. *wishapo mkurubia* for St. *ukiisha kumkaribia*.
   mangani or *mwangani*, in the upper air, in the sky.
   upomoke for St. *uporomoke*.

Usinambie papale

(Pages 239–240)

Verse

1. *wajee* or *wajele* for St. *wamejaa.*
   ni pweke tukele, in St. *tumekaa peke yetu.*
3. *si tuwa* for *si kutua,* it is not irritating; *-tua,* vex, irritate.
   mwenye mbeko, this can mean two things; *mbeko,* honour, and so honourable person, and *mbeko,* the calico cloth given as a wedding present to the bride's mother, and so, *mwenye mbeko* could mean, mother of a bride.
   mruwa or *mrua,* pleasing manners; probably related to Arabic *muruwwah.*
4. *usinionye vituko,* lit. do not show me alarums.
   kwako wewe sina suko, lit. towards you I have no disturbance.
   satui, in St. *sichui,* I do not make discord, cause friction.

Alipokwenenda kwawo

(Page 240–241)

Verse

3. *nguo ukazingiliya,* the meaning given follows the interpretation of the verb as *-zingilia,* go round and round, but the verb here may represent *ukaziingilia,* and you made an incursion into them (the clothes), lit. you went into them; *-ingilia,* go in.

Tao la nyanje mwaowa

(Page 243)

Verse

1. *tao la nyanje,* fashionable gait; *-vuta tao la nyanje,* cut a dash with fashionable attire; *mnyanje,* a dandy.
   nali hivuta for St. *ningekuwa nikivuta,* If I were cutting a dash.
2. *silivuti,* I do not cut a dash; objectival infix in agreement with *tao.*
   matengoni for St. *machengoni* or *vyengoni,* in people's houses.
   hatambi, he does not strut.
   kutambiwa for *kutoambiwa,* without being told.
3. *mbwawo,* contraction of *ni wao,* it is theirs.
4. *walishowa,* in St. *walikwisha oa.*
   jangawo, from *janga,* blame, trouble, difficulty.

Mwandani wako mwandani

(Page 245)

Verse

1. *mwendo wa kuwe,* a journey of that place afar; *kuwe* or *kue,* for kule.
   ukawe, cf. *-kawa,* loiter; *-e* suffix of the participial, you loitering, or, as you loiter.
2. *mfeeli* for infinitive *kumfeli,* to do him harm.
   hakuregeza, negative present with suffix *-a,* a feature of Amu dialect.
   ha for *hana.*
3. *ukambwage zani,* lit. and throw him down (by) accident.

Ule dari ukandika

(Page 248)

Verse

1. *ukandika* for St. *uliokandika*, which was plastered (with mud/lime). Note that dari is Cl. 14, not as in St. Cl. 6 or 9.
dongo, in St. *udongo*; note Cl. 5.
linti, probably meaning 'it is beneath or down, i.e. the clay is applied'.
ligendemene, perfect of -*gandamana*.
mbele ywakwe ni mavune, lit. its future is consequences.
bandika, fasten; -*bandua*, take off.
2. *wahaḍaula sharika*, for Ar. *waḥdahu lā sharīka lahu*.
hako, in St. *hayuko*.
ni rama nyoka, this could be read 'it is Rama the snake', but this is unlikely, so it is better to take *rama* as a contraction of *rahama*, the Compassionate One, and *nyoka* for *aliyenyoka*, who is steadfast.
hapazwa for *akapazwa*, and he was/is lifted up.

Baada Dhiki Faraji

(Page 250)

Verse

1. *Ngezi maji*, Taylor gives this as the name of a headland near Pate, and Ngezi is also a place-name in Pemba; the word is used in our interpretation in a metaphorical sense, as if to say 'the eternal deeps'.
2. *uwawo* for *uwao*, the hull of a sea-going vessel.
mwanza mkwawo, also heard in other contexts as *mwanzamkuwa* or *mwanzamkwa*, God, Master, Lord.
3. *swi* for *sisi*, us, we.
si mapevu for *tusio mapevu*, we who are not full-grown.
4. *uemevu* for *ulemevu*, burden, weight.
utuwu for *utulivu*; cf. *utovu* or *utofu*, want, poverty.
5. *uzingatile* for subjunctive *uzingatie*; so also *usingile* for *usiingie*. The -*l*- is inserted for the sake of the rhyme with *milele*.
6. *wata* for St. *uache*.
wvumilile for subjunctive *wvumilie*; also *nisikawile* for *nisikawie*. These endings rhyme with *male* in the first *kipande*.
autani, home; Ar. *awṭān*.

Nenda na ukiwa wangu

(Page 252)

Verse

yakamulikwa, they were shone down upon.
vitungu or *vitungo* for *mitungo*, things arranged together.
pakapekwa, lit. where search was made, from -*pekua*, search diligently, pry hard.

Kisimbo cha mkunazi

(Page 253)

kisimbo for *kifimbo*, a little stick.

mkunazi, the Arabian *sidr*, the tree *Zizyphus Spina-Christi*.

upatu, a gong of considerable significance in Swahili ceremonies, especially weddings, see Velten, op. cit., pp. 113 seq.

uliyo kama uwambe, lit. it is as something covered over; probably referring to the coloured cloths decorating the gong-dish.

uneteye for *uniletee*.

Lakutenda situuze

(Page 254)

situuze for *usituulize*.

wanamize or *wanamizi*, a hermit-crab.

tuizize, reduplicated radical in *-iziza*, absolutely refuse.

tapo, a troop, a number of men or of animals.

Kalizani watapamba

(Page 254)

watapamba, a compound of *wata*, the wearers, and *pamba*, dress up or decorate; cf. *wata-ziyemba*, turban-wearers.

nziu, the sound of the gong or of the horn.

Nipakiya ni kivuko

(Page 256)

nipakiya or *nipakia*, *-pakia*, put on board a vessel, load.

kiya or *kia*, anything used as a lid.

kili, pl. of *ukili*, strips of plaited matting dyed in different colours.

kiya or *kia*, joint of the body.

Nali na wajawa kenda

(Page 262)

wali taa for *wali na taa*, they had obedience; Ar. *ṭāʿah*.

watiile, the same meaning as *wali taa*, they obeyed.

nijikuile, in St. *neno hili limemkulia kubwa*, this thing has grown too much for him; *-kulia*, applied of *-kua*, grow.

waka wenye taathimu, women having respect.

kilia kita for *nikilia nikiita*, I crying and calling.

Niliketi siku moya

(Page 263)

afuate walikiya, lit. let him follow, they used to come, the interpretation here
being, 'they, the minstrels, used to come for advice and Haji used to
come with them'.

msubiji for *msubiri*, suffixal change for the sake of the rhyme.

asi nguo asi uji for *asiye na nguo asiye na uji*.

akajitamali for St. *akajitamalaki*.

INDEX

PRINTED IN GREAT BRITAIN
AT THE UNIVERSITY PRESS, OXFORD
BY VIVIAN RIDLER
PRINTER TO THE UNIVERSITY